Intellectual Property Law in Romania

Intellectual Property Law in Romania

Fifth Edition

Alexandru Cristian Strenc
Gheorghe Gheorghiu
Gheorghe Bucsa

This book was originally published as a monograph in the International Encyclopaedia of Laws/Intellectual Property Law.

Founding Editor: Roger Blanpain
General Editor: Frank Hendrickx
Volume Editor: Hendrik Vanhees

Wolters Kluwer

Published by:
Kluwer Law International B.V.
PO Box 316
2400 AH Alphen aan den Rijn
The Netherlands
E-mail: lrs-sales@wolterskluwer.com
Website: www.wolterskluwer.com/en/solutions/kluwerlawinternational

Sold and distributed by:
Wolters Kluwer Legal & Regulatory U.S.
920 Links Avenue
Landisville, PA 17538
United States of America
E-mail: customer.service@wolterskluwer.com

ISBN 978-94-035-3458-9

e-Book: ISBN 978-94-035-3468-8
web-PDF: ISBN 978-94-035-3478-7

The Authors

Dr Alexandru Cristian Strenc, born on 17 December 1949, graduated from the Polytechnic University of Bucharest, Faculty of Control and Computers, in 1972. He has a PhD in Process Control Systems in 1983.

Since 1988, he has worked with the State Office for Inventions and Trademarks (OSIM) as a patent examiner and between 1990 and 2014 as Deputy and Acting Director General of the same institution. He is the author of numerous articles and papers published in Romania and abroad. In 2000, 2001 and 2003, he effected stages of studies at the Max Planck Institute for Intellectual Property, the European Patent Office, the US Patent and Trademark Office, the WIPO, and the Danish School for Public Administration. In 1997 and 1998, he acted as Vice-President of the General Assembly of WIPO. Between 1996 and 2014, Dr Strenc was a member of the Administrative Council and Patent Law Committee and the European Patent Organization, and between 2012 and 2014, Chair of the Supervisory Board of the European Patent Academy. He also headed the Romanian Delegation in the Administrative Council of the Community Plant Variety Office. He was the head of the Romanian delegation in the Working Party of Intellectual Property-Patents of the EU Council.

Dr Strenc was President of the editorial board of the Romanian Review of Industrial Property and teaches IP matters at Bucharest Polytechnic University.

Actually, he is a European and national patent attorney and is managing the IP Company ‘Strenc Solutions for Innovation’.

Dr Gheorghe Gheorghiu, born on 1 March 1955, was a Judge (1980–1990) and legal expert with the Romanian Government (1990–1994). Since 1992, he has been a professor at various Faculties of Law and, since 1994, an attorney of the Bucharest Bar Association, a claim expert on industrial property. Since 1993, he has been a certified industrial property attorney and member of the AIPPI national group of Romania. He participated in industrial property courses at Strasbourg between 1996 and 1999. He published studies and papers on industrial property law and commercial law.

The Authors

Dr Gheorghe Bucsa (1941–2017) graduated from the University 'Politehnica' of Bucharest (1965), and subsequently (1986), he obtained his doctorate. He also graduated from the Design College of Bucharest (1982).

Between 1969 and 2008, he worked with the State Office for Invention and Trademarks (OSIM). From his duties at OSIM, we mention the Head of the Department of Preliminary Examination within the Patent Section and the Head of the Design Department.

Between 2008 and 2017, he held the position of Scientific Director of Patent and Trademark Agency Inventa, Bucharest.

He also acted as a teacher in 'Politehnica' University of Bucharest, for design and geometry cathedra.

During this entire period of time, he improved his knowledge by performing a series of stages at the main organizations within the field of industrial property, such as the World Intellectual Property Organization (WIPO) in Geneva, Switzerland; Benelux Office for Intellectual Property (BOIP) in the Hague, the Netherlands; National Institute for Intellectual Property (INPI) in Paris, France; United States Patents and Trademarks Office (USPTO) in Washington, US.

He has written over 120 articles and fifteen booklets on industrial property protection. He has written two very important books: *Inventor's Guide* and *Protection of Industrial Design*.

Table of Contents

List of Abbreviations

BOPI	Official Bulletin of Industrial Property (monthly publication with specific sections on patents, trademarks, designs, utility models, European patents with effect in Romania)
CPVO	Community Plant Variety Office
ECJ	European Court of Justice
EPC	European Patent Convention
EPO	European Patent Office
EUIPO	European Union Intellectual Property
GUI	Graphic User Interface
ISTIS	State Institute for Testing and Registration of Varieties (Romania)
NATO	North Atlantic Treaty Organization
ORDA	Romanian Copyright Office
OSIM	State Office for Inventions and Trademarks (Romania)
PCT	Patent Cooperation Treaty
PPH	Patent Prosecution Highway
TRIPS	Trade-Related Aspects of Intellectual Property
UDRP	Uniform Dispute Resolution Policy
UPOV	International Union for the Protection of New Varieties of Plants
USPTO	United States Patent and Trademark Office
WIPO	World Intellectual Property Organization
WTO	World Trade Organization

List of Abbreviations

Preface

The issue of industrial and intellectual property has concerned the Romanian legislator, aiming for harmonization between the national regulations and the international ones. There were several phases of evolution, mostly in connection with the European law system, which is referred to within our work. The most important one is the full compatibilization with the '*acquis communautaire*' made up to the accession of Romania to the EU which took place on 1 January 2007.

However, probably the first major data in the process of European integration of Romania in the IP field and in particular in the field of patents for invention could be considered the 1 March 2003, when Romania became the twenty-seventh contracting state to the European Patent Convention (EPC).

When revising in an important manner, successive editions of the monograph on the Romanian Law of Industrial and Intellectual Property, we took into consideration on one side all significant legislative evolution which took place between the previous reference moment, and on the other side, the enrichment of the national doctrine, where among others all three authors had important contributions and last but not least the national and European jurisprudence. We also feel that we should mention our own increase of experience by acting actively for more than thirty years in the challenging but wonderful field of protection and enforcement of intellectual property.

We may state that this study is the first one written in English to approach the issue of industrial and intellectual property in a comprehensive manner.

We have considered the jurisprudence and the doctrine of western countries and mostly of international bodies in the field.

We would like to thank Prof. Dr R. Blanpain, General Editor and Prof. Dr H. Vanhees, Editor of the International Encyclopaedia of Laws – Intellectual Property, for their suggestions and for encouraging us in writing a substantially improved monograph on the IP landscape in Romania.

General Introduction

§1. General Background

I. Geography

1. Romania is situated in the southeast of Central Europe, north of the Balkan Peninsula, on the Lower Danube and bordering on the Black Sea. Romania lies between 43°37'07″ and 48°15'06″ Latitude North and 20°15'44″ and 29°41'24″ Longitude East. Parallel 45 (midway between the Equator and the North Pole) crosses Romania 70 km north of its capital and meridian 25 Longitude East (midway between the Atlantic coast and the Urals) runs 90 km west of Bucharest..

South Romania has a long natural border made by the lower Danube and, in its southeast part, the Black Sea.

The Carpathian Mountains, which cross the country from the northeast to the southeast, have summits of up to 2,560 metres.

II. Cultural Composition

2. The ethnic genesis of the Romanian people resides in the mixture of the old population of 'Dacia', a strong kingdom at the borders of the Roman Empire, and the Romans which conquered it in 102 AD. Today, the Romanians are the sole descendants of the Eastern Roman world and their language, along with Spanish, French and Italian, is one of the major offspring of Latin.

3. About 85% of the population is of Orthodox religion, 5% Romano-Catholic, 3.5% Reformed, 1% Greek-Catholic, 0.6% Baptists.

III. Political System

4. After the collapse of the communist regime in December 1989, Romania became, in spite of many inherent difficulties, a real democracy with a market-oriented economy.

Romania has a two-chamber Parliament, the Deputies Chamber and the Senate, elected by universal vote for a four-year term and is a semi-presidential Republic. The President has a four-year mandate with the possibility of a single re-election.

The Constitution proclaims Romania as a State of law, democratic and social. Separation of the three public authorities (the Legislative, the Executive and the Judiciary) is stipulated in the Constitution.

Public administration in territorial administrative units is grounded on the principles of local autonomy and decentralization of public services.

IV. Population Statistics

5. The Romanian population comprises about 21 million inhabitants, of whom approximately 85% are Romanians and approximately 15% are ethnic minorities. An important minority in Romania are the Hungarians, of about 1.5 million people, who play an important part in the political and cultural life of the country.

The urban population amounts to approximately 60%.

§2. Historical Background

6. During their history, Romanians have lived in three neighbouring self-dependent principalities: Wallachia, Moldavia and Transylvania. They managed to achieve their national unity for a short period of four months in 1,600, partially (only Wallachia and Moldavia) in 1859 and then during a process completed after the First World War in 1918.

Starting with the last part of the nineteenth century and continuing until the beginning of the Second World War, Romania has developed its economic and cultural life to a decent European level.

After a devastating communist regime which started in 1945 and ended in December 1989, Romania returned to the normality of the market economy and parliamentary democracy.

Two significant historical moments changed the positioning of this country on international and European levels completely and fundamentally. These are the accession of Romania to the North Atlantic Treaty Organization (NATO) which took place in 2004 and accession to the European Union (EU) from 1 January 2007.

Chapter 1. Copyright and Related Rights

§1. Sources: Legislation

7. There have been important changes as regards copyright in the past years, due to the communication and circulation procedures, with consequences not yet clarified. This is especially true with regard to the personality of the author, which is blurred by the increase of collective works, by making the producers or distributors more important and by the necessity of an agent taking the risk of making the work publicly known, etc.

Also, the particularity of the author's right in the law of European States should be noted compared with the copyright, that is, the tendency of the copyright to modify its purpose, becoming an instrument of investors and their investments' protection, rather than an instrument of authors and their works' protection.

All these require the harmonization of the Romanian regulations with the related international tendency. Taking into consideration the purpose of this exposition, we concisely and descriptively approached the issue of intellectual property.[1]

I. National Sources

A. *Historical Development*

8. The Romanian law of intellectual property has developed as follows:

(a) The Press Law of 13 April 1862 is the first Romanian law which regulated the rights of the authors of literary and artistic works and acknowledged the rights of the writers, composers and creators of artistic works to reproduce, sell or transfer their works throughout their lives. The sanction for persons who printed, reproduced or imitated a work without the consent of the author was the seizure of copies of the work, as well as a fine to an amount equivalent to the price of 1,000 copies of the original edition. It was also stipulated that the copyright is transmitted *mortis causa* over a period of ten years. The same rights were acknowledged for foreigners, subject to mutuality.
The International Congress on Literary and Artistic Property that took place in Bucharest in 1906 had important consequences for the synthesis of the domain's rules.

(b) The law of 28 June 1923, deemed a modern law,[2] ensured the protection of authors' rights, independently of any formalities, and acknowledged to foreigners the same rights as for nationals, without any requirement of mutuality.

---

1. Adolf Dietz, *Dreptul de copyright în România şi armonizarea acestuia pe baza normelor europene. EvoluŢie şi situaŢia actual dup aderarea României la Uniunea European* [*The Copyright in Romania and Harmonization Thereof According to the European Norms. Evolution and Current Situation Following Romaniaîs Accession to the European Union*], in RRDPI, No. 4/2009, 13–14.
2. Yolanda Eminescu, *The Copyright-Commentary on Law No. 8/1996* 22 (Lumina Lex 1997); V. Roş, D. Bogdan & O. Spineanu-Matei, *Dreptul de autor şi drepturi conexe. Tratat* [*Copyright and Related Rights. Treaty*] 21–23 (Bucureşti, 2005).

The authors of literary and scientific works, composers, painters, drawers, sculptors, architects, engravers and all creators of intellectual works, regardless of the expressed form of the work, benefited throughout their lives from the exclusive right to publish, represent or perform their works, to authorize their translations, adaptations or reproductions, to exploit, sell, donate or dispose of them by will (Article 2).

The moral right could not form the object of alienation or renunciation. According to this article, the heirs of the copyright benefited from the patrimonial rights over a period of thirty years after the author's death. After the expiry of the period of the exclusive right protection, the right was transferred to the public domain and a permanent control right of the Romanian Academy was established with regard to the moral right of the author (Article 6). For the works unpublished during his lifetime, the author could prohibit by will their publication over a period of thirty years after his or her death.

(c) Decree No. 321 of 21 June 1956 on copyright was influenced by the Berne Convention, to which Romania adhered in 1927,[3] though bearing a socialist stamp on the acts promulgated for the application of the law. It should be noted that the law regulated a different duration of copyright in the case of the transfer by inheritance, depending on the grade of the relationship, as follows: fifty years for descendants, over his or her life for the surviving spouse and fifteen years for the other heirs up to the fourth grade inclusive (Article 6). This regulation led to problems with regard to the preference order and the partition between the heirs. Some reproductions, recordings and transmissions, representing a legal licence, were permitted without the author's consent but with the observance of the other author's rights (Article 13). The remuneration of the author was made through the agency of the unions and associations of the creators.

B. The Present Regulation in Romania

9. Law No. 8 of 14 March 1996 on copyright and related rights was amended several times and the last consolidated version was republished in 2022.

Of particular interest are the revisions from 2015, 2018, 2019 and 2022 respectively.

Thus, the Act on the modification and completion of Law No. 8/1996 on copyright and related rights was promulgated by Romania's President on 24 March 2015 (Act No. 53/2015) and published in the Official Journal of Romania No. 198/2015 Part I was intended to transpose Directive 2011/77/EU of the European Parliament and of the Council of 27 September 2011 amending the Directive 2006/116/EC on the term of protection of copyright and certain related rights.

This act changed the term of protection of economic rights of performers, by extending it from fifty to seventy years. The term of protection for musical compositions with words is correspondingly extended to seventy years from the death of the last surviving lyricists and composers.

3. *Ibid.*, 31.

In terms of the duration of protection, a distinction is made between the publication or the legal communication of a phonogram and the publication or the legal communication other than in a phonogram. The act also regulated issues regarding the interpretation and execution of rights transfer contracts between performers and phonogram producers. To translate the terms of non-recurring and recurring remuneration and to avoid misinterpretation of these terms, the act uses the terms 'single remuneration' and 'compensation paid gradually'.

The law also incorporated the relevant provisions of Law No. 76/2012 on enforcing the amendments to the Code of Civil Procedure and consequently of Law No. 187/2012 on enforcing the amendments to the Criminal Code.

In 2018, Law No. 74/2018 on modification and completion of Law No. 8/1996 was published in the Official Journal of Romania No. 268 on 27 March 2018.

It was intended to transpose into national law Directive No. 2014/26/EU on the collective management of copyright and related rights and the granting of multi-territorial licences for the rights to musical works for online use in the internal market.

The objective of this law was therefore to regulate the aspects related to the organization, functioning and activity of the collective management bodies of copyright and related rights, imposing a series of rules designed to ensure the transparency of their activity, as well as the possibility of the members to control how the sums from the rights are collected and distributed.

Thus, the use of works protected by copyright and related rights requires the licensing of different copyright holders, who have the possibility to choose between the individual or collective management of the rights held.

Also, more precise provisions are introduced regarding the rights of authors and rights holders, as well as the obligation for these rights to be included in the statutes of the collective management bodies.

Further amendments were introduced by Law No. 15/2019, on modification and completion of Law No. 8/1996, as published in the Official Journal of Romania No. 268 of 14 January 2019.

This act transposes into national legislation the provisions of Directive 2017/1564/EU regarding certain permitted uses of certain works and other objects of protection by copyright and related rights for the benefit of the blind, visually impaired or with difficulties in reading printed materials.

Besides these changes, Law No. 15/2019 was meant to overcome findings of the non-conforming transposition in the national legislation of the provisions of the Directive 2001/29/EC, which was the subject of a letter of delay from the European Commission due to the system of compulsory collective management established by previous form of the law, including for the right of public communication of the works.

Accordingly, in line with the authors' right to their works as a fundamental right guaranteed by Article 17 of the Charter of Fundamental Rights of the European Union, the amended law ensures the authors total freedom to use or exercise their rights individually or to choose a collective management body or other entity to make this book on their behalf.

The mentioned law also provides important amendments meant to allow persons with disabilities, without any consent of holder of the author's right or of a related right and without no remuneration, to perform acts which otherwise would constitute violation of the author's right. We will come back to this subject at a later stage. As of 2019, the consolidated law consists of 212 articles classified under four titles. The first title provides for general provisions (subject matter of copyright, object and content of copyright, duration of the copyright protection, limitation of the exercise of copyright, the transfer of the patrimonial copyrights, forms of transfer and the classes of works). The second title regulates the related rights of the interpreting and performing artists, the producers of sound recordings, and television and radio broadcasting bodies. The third title regulates the management and protection of the copyright and of the related rights, and the last title consists of provisions related to the application of the law, transitory and final provisions.

By Law No. 39 of 3 March 2022, for amending the Article 116 paragraph (1) lit. c) from Law No. 8/1996 on copyright and related rights, published in the Official Gazette of Romania, No. 216 of 4 March 2022, has been intended, in application of Directive 2001/29/EC, to ensure a fair, just and legal remuneration of the authors of digital cultural and visual art works, an aspect which was not considered in the previous regulation.

Finally, last amendments were introduced by Law No. 69/2022 for amending and completion of Law No. 8/1996 regarding copyright and related rights ('Law No. 69/2022') as published in the Official Gazette of Romania, Part I No. 321 of 1 April 2022. The normative act entered into force on 4 April 2022, except for some limited provisions that entered into force either thirty days later or respectively six months after publication.

The main aim of these amendments was to transpose into national law two important pieces of acquis comunotaire in the field, namely:

- Directive (EU) 2019/789 of the European Parliament and of the Council of 17 April 2019 establishing rules regarding the exercise of copyright and related rights applicable to certain online transmissions of broadcasting organizations and certain retransmissions of television and radio programmes and amending Council Directive 93/83/EEC, published in the Official Journal of the European Union (OJEU), series L, No. 130 of 17 May 2019 ('EU Directive 2019/789').
- Directive (EU) 2019/790 of the European Parliament and of the Council of 17 April 2019 on copyright and related rights on the digital single market and amending Directives 96/9/EC and 2001/29/EC, published in the Official Journal of the European Union (JOUE), series L, No. 130 of 17 May 2019.

In line with the intended purpose of the two mentioned Directives, the new provisions of the amended law ensure a real updating of the copyright system in Romania by giving due account to the increase in digital and cross-border uses of protected content.

In this respect, there have been regulated exceptions and limitations to the digital and cross-border environment, which include exceptions for text and data mining, use of works in digital and cross-border teaching activities and preservation of cultural heritage.

The amending Law No. 69/2022 provides measures to improve licensing practices and ensure wider access to the content of copyright, facilitating the exploitation of commercialized works, extension of collective licensing agreements by the collective management bodies to holders who have neither authorized nor excluded their works from this mechanism, negotiation of agreements for the provision of works on video-on-demand platforms and the entry into the public domain of the reproduction of works of visual art upon expiry of the initial term of protection.

It also provides concrete measures aimed at ensuring a well-functioning market from a copyright perspective, such as relating to the liability for the use of press publications and protected content by providers of online content-sharing services, as well as providing a contract adjustment mechanism for the remuneration of authors and performers.

It is considered doctrinary[4] that main changes and additions to Law No. 8/1996 made by Law 69/2022 could be included in the following categories:

(a) Terminological changes, new notions introduced or existing notions detailed.
(b) Changes regarding the subject of the copyright.
(c) Changes regarding the content of the copyright.
(d) Changes regarding the limits of the exercise of copyright.
(e) Changes regarding the assignment of copyright patrimonial rights.
(f) New provisions regarding the patrimonial rights of the publishers of press publications.
(g) Other changes regarding copyright-related rights and sui generis rights.
(h) New rules applicable to providers of online content-sharing services (such as platforms like FACEBOOK, INSTAGRAM, etc.).
(i) New rules regarding the rights of broadcasting and television bodies.
(j) Changes and new provisions regarding the management of copyright and related rights.
(k) Transitory provisions.

All relevant provisions will be further presented and discussed throughout this chapter.

10. According to Article 201, the law applies in any of the following situations:

– to works whose authors are Romanian citizens or natural or legal persons whose domicile or seat is in Romania, even if they were not made known to the public, and also to works of architecture built on Romania's territory;
– to performances of interpreting or performing artists which are taking place on Romania's territory, or which are fixed in sound recordings protected under the present law, or were not fixed in sound recordings, but are transmitted by television or radio broadcastings protected under the present law;

4. Ciprin Dragomir – Modificări şi completări privind dreptul de autor şi drepturile conexe; Universul Juridic 20 Apr. 2022; https://www.universuljuridic.ro/modificari-si-completari-privind-dreptul-de-autor-si-drepturile-conexe/.

- to sound recordings whose producers are natural or legal persons having their domicile or seat in Romania or whose first fixing on a material carrier had taken place for the first time in Romania;
- to radio and television programmes broadcast by television and radio broadcasting bodies having their seat in Romania or to those transmitted by transmitting bodies having their seat in Romania.

According to Article 202 of the Law, foreigners, holders of copyright or related rights, shall benefit from the protection provided by international conventions, treaties and agreements to which Romania is party, failing which, they shall benefit by a treatment equal to that for Romanian citizens, under condition of mutuality.

11. The Romanian Copyright Office (ORDA) was established for the record, observation and control of the application of copyright and related rights' legislation. It functions as a specialized body subordinated to the Government and it has the duties and powers set out under Article 181 of the law:

- to organize and administer the record of works and of authors received from the collective administration bodies for author's rights and related rights;
- to grant advisory opinions on the constitutions as legal persons under the terms of the law of collective administration bodies and to follow up the application of the legislation by the bodies whose constitution it had advised;
- to advise, under the terms of the law, the elaboration and negotiation of the tables and methodologies established by the collective administration bodies with the employers' associations of the users;
- to exercise, at the request and expense of the holders of protected rights, functions of observation and control on the activities that might give rise to infringements of the legislation on the author's rights and related rights;
- to conclude finding statements on the infringements of the law, under the terms provided by the Code of Criminal Procedure, and to inform the competent bodies in the case of offences for which the criminal procedure is initiated ex officio;
- to elaborate programmes of instruction and practical and theoretical formation in the domain of the author's rights, copyright and related rights;
- to keep up relations with similarly specialized bodies and with international organizations in the domain in which the Romanian Government takes part;
- to keep the records of the entities authorized to carry out the activities provided for exercising collective management and provides both the European Commission and the access point to information set up by the International Bureau of the World Intellectual Property Organization (WIPO) the name and contact details of the authorized entities, as well as any other data collected following their voluntary communication, by the entities authorized;
- to consult the rights holders, collective management bodies and cultural heritage conservation institutions in each sector before establishing specific requirements and to encourage regular dialogue between representative organizations of users and right holders, including collective management bodies and other relevant

stakeholder organizations, for each sector, with the aim of improving the relevance and use of established licensing mechanisms and to ensure the effectiveness of guarantees for rights holders;
- to inform the European Commission about the scope of non-exclusive licenses granted, the purpose and types of licenses that can be introduced under legal provisions, the contact details of the bodies that issue licences in accordance with that licensing mechanism and the means by which information can be obtained about the granting of licences and the rights of holders provided for in the law;
- to notify the European Commission of the mediators provided in the law, including, if available, the source where the relevant information about the chosen mediators can be found;
- to provide the European Commission, in a timely manner, with relevant and useful information regarding the field managed by ORDA.

Accordingly, we may assert that Copyright Law No. 8/1996 was elaborated under a strict approximation of the *acquis communautaire* presented under next point II and also built up based on a series of domestic laws, as follows:

- Ordinance of the Romanian Government No. 45/2000 with regard to some measures for the control of unauthorized production and trade of phonograms.
- Ordinance of the Romanian Government No. 124/2.09.2000 with a view to rounding up the legal framework of the author's rights copyright and related rights by promulgation of measures for the control of the infringements in the audio, video and computer software fields.
- Law No. 202/2000 on some measures for observance of intellectual property rights within the framework of custom clearance procedures.
- Law No. 285/2004 for amending and completing Law 8/1996 comprises 128 articles intended to harmonize the legislation in compliance with the *acquis communautaire* (Directive 2001/29/EC on the harmonization of certain aspects of copyright and related rights in the information society, Directive 2001/84/EC on the resale right for the benefit of the author of an original work of art and Directive 96/9/EC on the legal protection of databases).
- Law No. 329/2006 for the approval with amendments of the Emergency Ordinance of the Government of Romania No. 123/2005 regarding in particular the rights of management (rights concerning the communication to the public, radio and television broadcasting, satellite transmission, resale), certain limitations on the exercise of copyright (reproduction for personal use), provisions relating to remuneration in respect of carriers and equipment, rights of collective management, bodies, sanctions.
- Law No. 202/2010 on certain measures to accelerate the settlement of trials, to set the competence of law courts in the field of intellectual property.
- Laws No. 53/2015, Nos 210/2015 and 261/2015 on modification and completion of Law No. 8/1996.
- Law No. 74/2018 on modification and completion of Law No. 8/1996.
- Law No. 15/2019 on modification and completion of Law No. 8/1996.
- Law No. 39/2022 for amending the Article 116 paragraph (1) lit. c) from Law No. 8/1996.

– Law No. 69/2022 for amending and completion of Law No. 8/1996.

II. International Sources

12.

(a) By means of Law No. 152/1926, Romania ratified the International Berne Convention of 9 September 1886 for the protection of literary and artistic works, as it was revised at Berlin in 1908. Subsequently, in 1935, Romania ratified the related revision of Rome (1928). The next revised form (Stockholm, 1967) was ratified by Decree 549/1969, exempting the provisions of Article 133 paragraph 1 with regard to the jurisdiction for the claims related to the interpretation and application of the Convention. Law 77/1998 ratified the revised form of the Paris Convention of 1971, as it was modified on 28 September 1979.
(b) By Law No. 76/1998, Romania has ratified the International Rome Convention (26 October 1961) for the protection of performers, audiovisual producers and broadcasting bodies.
(c) By adopting Law No. 78/1998, Romania ratified the Geneva Convention (29 October 1971) for the protection of audiovisual producers against the unauthorized reproductions of their phonograms.

As of 1 January 2007, Romania has become a full Member State of the EU and the Constitution of Romania, as revised, provides that the Romanian State shall guarantee that obligations resulting from the treaties to which it is a party shall be implemented exactly and in good faith.

Under Article 209^2 of the Law No. 8/1996, the Law transposes the following Community enactments:

– Council Directive 91/250/EEC on legal protection of computer programs, published in the Official Journal of European Communities No. L122 of 17 May 1991.
– Council Directive 92/100/EEC on the rental and lending right and other rights related to copyright in the field of intellectual property, published in the Official Journal of European Communities No. L346 of 24 November 1992.
– Council Directive 93/83/EEC on the coordination of certain rules concerning copyright and rights related to copyright applicable to satellite broadcasting and cable retransmission published in the Official Journal of European Communities No. L248 of 6 October 1993.
– Council Directive 93/98/EEC harmonizing the term of protection and copyright and certain related rights published in the Official Journal of European Communities No. L290 of 24 November 1993.
– Directive of the European Parliament and of the Council 96/9/EC on the legal protection of databases published in the Official Journal of European Communities No. L077 of 27 March 1996.

- Directive of the European Parliament and of the Council 2001/29/EC on the harmonization of certain aspects of copyright and related rights in the information society published in the Official Journal of European Communities No. L006 of 10 January 2002.
- Directive of the European Parliament and of the Council 2001/84/EC on the resale right for the benefit of the author of an original work of art published in the Official Journal of European Communities No. L272 of 13 October 2001.
- Directive of the European Parliament and of the Council 2001/84/EC on ensuring the observance of intellectual property rights published in the Official Journal of European Communities No. L157 of 30 April 2004.
- Directive of the European Parliament and of the Council 2011/77/EU of 27 September 2011 amending Directive 2006/116/EC on the duration of protection of copyright and certain related rights, published in the Official Journal of the European Union, the series L, No. 265 of 11 October 2011.
- Directive of the European Parliament and of the Council 2012/28/EU of 25 October 2012 on certain permitted uses of orphan works, published in the Official Journal of the European Union, series L, No. 299 of 27 October 2012.
- Directive of the European Parliament and of the Council 2014/26/EU of 26 February 2014 on the collective management of copyright and related rights and the granting of multi-territorial licences for the rights to musical works for online use on the internal market, published in the Official Journal of the European Union, the L series, No. 84 of 20 March 2014.
- Directive of the European Parliament and of the Council 2017/1,564 of 13 September 2017 on certain permitted uses of certain works and other objects of copyright protection and related rights for the benefit of the blind, visually impaired or with difficulty reading printed materials and amending Directive 2001/29/EC on the harmonization of certain aspects of copyright and related rights in the information society, published in the Official Journal of the European Union, series L, No. 242 from 20 September 2017.
- Directive (EU) 2019/789 of the European Parliament and of the Council of 17 April 2019 establishing rules regarding the exercise of copyright and related rights applicable to certain online transmissions of broadcasting organizations and certain retransmissions of television and radio programs and amending Council Directive 93/83/EEC, published in the Official Journal of the European Union (OJEU), series L, No. 130 of 17 May 2019 ('EU Directive 2019/789').
- Directive (EU) 2019/790 of the European Parliament and of the Council of 17 April 2019 on copyright and related rights on the digital single market and amending Directives 96/9/EC and 2001/29/EC, published in the Official Journal of the European Union (JOUE), series L, No. 130 of 17 May 2019.
- Directive 2006/115/EC of the European Parliament and of the Council of 12 December 2006 on rental and lending rights and certain rights related to copyright in the field of intellectual property, published in the Special Edition of the Official Journal of the European Union (OJEU) number 0 from 1 January 2007.
- Directive 2009/24/EC of the European Parliament and of the Council of 23 April 2009 on the legal protection of computer programs, published in the Official Journal of the European Union (OJEU) number 111L of 5 May 2009.

- Directive (EU) No. 2017/1.564 of the European Parliament and of the Council of 13 September 2017 regarding certain permitted uses of certain works and other objects of copyright protection and related rights for the benefit of blind, visually impaired or print-impaired persons and amending Directive 2001/29/EC on the harmonization of certain aspects of copyright and related rights in the information society, published in the Official Journal of the European Union (OJEU), series L, No. 242 of 20 September 2017.

Moreover, under Article 208, it is stipulated that the European Commission shall be informed regarding the intention for the adoption of certain national provisions for the regulation of certain new related rights, specifying the essential reasons which justify the regulation of such rights, as well as the adequate protection term.

§2. Subject Matter of Protection

I. Different Categories of Protected Works

13. According to Article 7 of Law No. 8/1996, there shall constitute an object of the copyright the original works of intellectual creation in the literary, artistic, or scientific domain, regardless of the manner of creation, the concrete form or mode of expression and independently of their value and destination, such as:

(a) literary and published writings, conferences, sermons, pleadings, lectures and any other written or oral works, as well as computer programs;
(b) scientific works, written or oral, such as communications, studies, university textbooks, school textbooks, scientific projects and documentation;
(c) musical compositions with or without lyrics;
(d) dramatic and dramatic-musical works, choreographic and pantomimic works;
(e) cinematographic works, as well as any other audiovisual works;
(f) photographic works, photogram of cinematographic films as well as any other works expressed by a procedure analogous to photography;
(g) works of plastic art, such as: works of sculpture, painting, graphics, engraving, lithography, monumental art, stenography (scene painting), tapestry, ceramics, gas and metal plastics as well as works of art applied to products designed for practical use;
(h) works of architecture, sketches, scale models and graphic works forming architectural projects;
(i) plastic works, maps and drawings in the field of topography, geography and science in general.

14. Without being prejudicial to the rights of the original work's authors, according to Article 8 of Law No. 8/1996, also constituting objects of copyright shall be:

- derived works which were created by starting from one or more pre-existing works, namely:

- translations, adaptations, annotations, documentary works, musical arrangements, and any other conversions of a literary, artistic or scientific work representing an intellectual, creative work;
- collective literary, artistic, or scientific works, such as encyclopaedias and anthologies, collections and compilations of material or data, protected or not, databases included, which, by the selection or arrangement of the material, constitute intellectual creations.

The scope of protection of the Law is referred to under Article 201 which sets out the categories of work enjoying such protection:

- works whose authors are Romanian citizens, even if they have not yet been disclosed to the public;
- works whose authors are natural or legal persons having a residence or headquarters in Romania, even if they have not yet been disclosed to the public;
- works of architecture built on the territory of Romania;
- performances of performers taking place on the territory of Romania;
- performances of performers that are fixed in recordings protected by this law;
- performances of performers that have not been fixed in recordings but are transmitted by radio or television broadcasts protected by this law;
- sound or audiovisual recordings, the producers of which are natural or legal persons having residence or headquarters in Romania;
- sound or audiovisual recordings, the first fixation of which on a physical medium has taken place for the first time in Romania;
- radio or television broadcasts transmitted by the radio or television broadcasting organizations with the headquarters in Romania;
- radio or television broadcasts transmitted by transmitting organizations with headquarters in Romania.

Foreign natural persons or legal entities, owners of copyright or related rights, shall enjoy the protection provided by international conventions, treaties and agreements to which Romania is a party, failing which they shall enjoy treatment equal to that accorded to Romanian citizens, on condition that the latter, in turn, are granted similar treatment in the concerned countries (Article 202).

II. Works Excluded of Protection

15. According to Article 9 of the Law, the following may not benefit from legal copyright protection:

- ideas, theories, concepts, discoveries and inventions contained in a work, whatever might be the manner of its adoption, writing, explaining or expression;
- official texts of a political, legislative, administrative or judicial nature and their official translations;
- official symbols of the State, public authorities, and organizations, such as the coat of arms, seal, flag, emblem, escutcheon, badge and medal;

- means of payment;
- news and press information;
- simple facts and data;
- photos of letters, documents, documents of any kind, technical drawings and the like;
- materials resulting from an act of reproduction of a work of visual art, whose term of protection has expired, unless the material resulting from the act of reproduction is original, in the sense that it represents the author's own intellectual creation.

A work or other protected subject matter is deemed to be outside the commercial circuit when it can be assumed, in good faith, that the entire work or the entire protected subject matter is not available to the public through ordinary commercial channels after a reasonable effort has been made to determine whether it is publicly available.

III. Special Categories of Works

A. *Computer Programs*

16. Protection of computer programs is regulated by Romanian Copyright Law No. 8/1996 (Chapter 9, Articles 73–82).

As already presented, computer programs are listed within Article 7a of the Copyright Law among specific forms of literary works. This provision is in full accordance with the provisions of Article 1 of the Software Directive 2009/24/EC which provides that 'Member States shall protect computer programs, by copyright, as literary works within the meaning of, the Berne Convention for the Protection of Literary and Artistic Works.'

Consequently, according to Article 73, the protection of computer programs shall include 'any expression of a programme, application programs and operation systems expressed in any kind of language, either in source code or object code, the preparatory conceptive material as well as the handbooks'.

The operating methods, procedures and ideas, the mathematical concepts, and the principles underlying any element in a computer program, including those underlying its interfaces, shall not be protected.

According to the definition stated by the standard law promulgated by WIPO, *software* means a program permitting the performance of an operation by a computer, as well as the adjoining documents.

A *computer program* is defined as a set of instructions to be used in a computer in order to bring about a certain result from an information-processing device. The *adjoining documents* consist of the description of the program and the auxiliary documents, being an accessory of the program.

As a matter of fact, there are three basic types of software:[5]

5. Alexandru Cristian Strenc, *European Software Directives and European Software Patents* 18–19 (Wolters Kluwer 2017).

(1) system programs or operating system, which is a set of programs that manages all the concurrent tasks performed by a computer;
(2) utility programs, which is a collection of programs that perform routine tasks such as copying, compressing data, etc.;
(3) application programs, which perform specialized functions not directly related to the computer itself.

As already indicated, the broad term of computer program includes, besides these, preparatory design material and the conception and development of all three types of computer programs that should be based, in principle, on a large amount of preparatory design material.

The European Court of Justice (ECJ) clearly stated that 'the EU legislature assimilated under the term computer program, both their tangible and intangible copies'.[6]

Computer programs also need to interact and interconnect with two other relevant actors, namely on one side with computer system itself which includes hardware and software, and on the other side, human interrelating with running computer.

A computer program might therefore include confidential or secret information and this fact gives an interference towards trade secrets and know-how protection – *see* Chapter 9.

Provisions of the same Article 7 of the Romanian Copyright Law are also in line with Article 1(3) of the Software Directive 2009/24/EC which provides originality as the unique condition required by copyright protection to determine its eligibility for protection and also refines it, when giving to the program's originality 'the sense that it is the author's own intellectual creation'. The relevant recital[7] brings the important clarification that 'in respect of the criteria to be applied in determining whether or not a computer program is an original work, no tests as to the qualitative or aesthetic merits of the program should be applied'.

The Romanian legislator ruled out the possibility of protection of the programs as such by a patent, in compliance with the European regulations (Convention of Munich on European Patent). This solution stands some criticisms, with regard to the element of the originality of a computer program (the form or the composition) and to the ineffective protection by copyright, taking into consideration the following aspects:

– the exclusive right of the author with regard to the reproduction, and not the use of the work, as it is the case of computer programs;
– while the copyright law authorizes the copies and reproductions for the personal use of copyrighted material, it does not apply to computer programs;
– the author of a computer program can only be protected against identical reproduction, as the protection provided by the copyright is limited to the form of expression.

6. Case C-128/11.
7. Recital 8, Software Directive 2009/24/EC.

17. According to Article 74 of the Romanian Law:

(1) the author of a computer program shall correspondingly benefit from the rights provided under the present law, particularly by the exclusive right to realize and authorize;
(2) the temporary or permanent reproduction of a program, integrally or partially, by any means and under any form, in which case the reproduction should be determined by the charging, displaying, transmission, or stocking of the program on the computer;
(3) the translation, adaptation, arranging and any other transformations operated on a computer program as well as the reproduction of the result of these operations without being detrimental to the rights of the person who transforms the computer program;
(4) the circulation of the original or of copies of a computer program in any form, by rental inclusive.

The first sale of a copy of a computer program on the internal market by the rights holder or the one made with his consent exhausts the exclusive right to authorize the distribution of this copy on the internal market.

Also, according to Article 79:

> The authorization of the copyright's holder shall be mandatory when the reproduction of the code or translation of the form of this code should be indispensable for obtaining information required for the interoperability of a computer program with other computer programs, if the following conditions have been fulfilled:
>
> (a) the translation and reproduction acts are carried out by a person holding the right of use of a copy of the program or by a person carrying out these actions in the name of the previous one, being duly authorized to this end;
> (b) the necessary information for interoperability is not easily and rapidly accessible to persons provided under paragraph (a) of the present Article;
> (c) the acts provided under paragraph (a) of the present article are limited to parts of the program required for the interoperability.

Information obtained by application of Article 79 may not be used for other purposes than 'the realization of the interoperability of the independently created computer program', may not be communicated to other people, except in the case when the communication should prove necessary for the interoperability of the independently created computer program and also may not be used for 'finalizing, production or trading of a computer program whose expression is basically similar or by any other act that might damage the author's rights (Article 78). If a prejudice is caused to the holder of the copyright or to the normal exploitation of the computer program, the provisions under Articles 79 and 80 shall not apply (Article 78).

18. The following deeds shall not be submitted to an authorization of the copyright's holder:

- the deeds provided under Article 74 paragraphs (a) and (b), if these are necessary to permit the user to use the computer program in a way corresponding to its destination, for the correction of errors inclusive, unless otherwise provided by convention (Article 77);
- creating an archive copy or a safety copy to the extent to which this is necessary for ensuring the use of the program (Article 78, paragraph 1);
- observing, studying or testing the operation of this program for the purpose of determining the principles and ideas underlying any of its elements on the occasion of carrying out any operation of loading into the memory, displaying, conversion, transmission or stocking of the program, operations which the authorized user is entitled to carry out (Article 78, paragraph 2).

19. The holder of the copyright of a computer program is the natural person or persons having created it. The patrimonial copyrights on computer programs created by employees engaged 'in the exercise of service powers and duties or carrying out the instructions of the person employing them' belong to the latter (Article 75).

The holder of a copyright may conclude contracts for the use of a computer program with other persons. Failing a convention to the contrary, according to Article 76, it shall be presumed that:

- the user is granted the non-exclusive right of using the computer program;
- the user may not transmit to another person the right to use the computer program.

The Romanian legislator provides expressly that 'the transfer of the right to use a computer program shall not also imply the transfer of the copyright on it' (Article 76, paragraph 2).

Also, Article 82 specifies that the provisions included in Chapter 6 – 'Limitations of the exercise of copyright' – do not apply to computer programs.

B. Databases

20. Under the Romanian Copyright Law and in full compliance with Directive 96/9/EC on the legal protection of databases, two systems of protection for databases are coexisting, namely:

- common-type protection by copyright;
- protection by a sui generis database right.

They are coherent and synergic and have different scope of protection, aspects deriving in fact from their different effects.[8] Protection by copyright is oriented

8. Alexandru Cristian Strenc, *Information Technology. Protection and Enforcement of Intellectual Property Rights. Editura Univers Juridic. Colectia Busines* (2010).

toward rewarding and consequently protecting the creator of database for his originality in arranging the relevant data into the structure of the database. On the other side, protection by sui generis database right is oriented toward rewarding and thus protecting the substantial effort of the database makers, irrespective of the originality of the data arrangement in the structure.

1. Common-Type Protection by Copyright Regarded as Derived Works

21. As indicated in I, Article 8 b of the Law No. 8/1996 republished, mentions within category of derived works 'compilations of protected or unprotected material or data, including *databases,* which, by reason of the selection or arrangement of their subject matter constitute intellectual creations'. For this reason, it seems obvious that all considerations made for derived works should be valid for the protection of databases, which are regarded as original works.

2. Protection of Databases Through a Sui Generis Database Right

22. The sui generis right protects the content of the database, regardless of whether the data in the data layout can be assessed with certain creativity but with the condition of having made a substantial investment in obtaining, verifying or presenting the material.

Unlike the protection by copyright, the protection databases through a sui generis right are owned and exercised by the person who made the database. For the purposes of the law, database means a collection of works, data or other independent elements, protected or not by copyright or neighbouring rights, arranged systematically or methodically and individually accessible by electronic means or in any other way. The sui generis protection does not apply to computer programs used for the making or operation of databases accessible by electronic means.

a. Exclusive Rights of the Databases Makers

23. The maker of a database is the natural or legal person that has made a qualitatively and quantitatively substantial investment for the obtaining, verification or presentation of the contents of a database.

According to Article 141, the maker of a database has the exclusive economic right to authorize and prohibit the extraction and/or re-utilization of the entire or of a substantial part of the database, evaluated qualitatively or quantitatively. Extraction means the permanent or temporary transfer of all or a substantial part, evaluated qualitatively or quantitatively, of the contents of a database to another medium by any means or in any form; re-utilization means any form of making available to the public all or a substantial part of the contents of a quantitative or qualitative apprized database by the distribution of copies, by renting or other forms, including by making available to the public the contents of the database so that anyone may access it in a place and time individually chosen by them. The first sale, on domestic market, of a copy of a database by the right holder of sui generis right or with his consent shall exhaust the right to control resale of that copy. Under the provisions of the law, public sale of a database is not an act of extraction or re-utilization. The exclusive right shall apply irrespective of eligibility for the contents of that database for protection by copyright or other rights. Protection of databases under the provided exclusive economic right of extraction or re-utilization shall be without prejudice to rights existing in respect of their contents. The repeated and systematic extraction or re-utilization of insubstantial parts of the contents of the database implying acts which conflict with normal use of that database or which unreasonably prejudice the legitimate interests of the maker of the database shall not be permitted.

b. Exceptions to Exclusive Rights

24. According to Article 142 paragraph a, 'the maker of a database which is made available to the public through whatever manner may not prevent a lawful user of the database from extracting or re-utilizing insubstantial parts of its contents, for any purposes of the use whatsoever. Where the lawful user is authorized to extract or re-utilize only part of the database, the provisions shall apply to that part'. A lawful user of a database which is made available to the public in whatever manner may:

- not perform acts which conflict with normal use of this database or unreasonably prejudice the legitimate interests of the maker of the database;
- not cause prejudice to the holder of a copyright or neighbouring right in respect of the works or performances contained in this database;
- extract or re-utilize a substantial part of its contents without the authorization of its maker: (a) in the case of extraction for private purposes of the contents of a non-electronic database; (b) in the case of extraction for the purposes of illustration for teaching or scientific research, as long as the source is indicated and to the extent justified by the non-commercial purpose to be achieved; (c) in the case of extraction or re-utilization for the purposes of public order and national safety or an administrative or jurisdictional procedure; (d) if any act of reproduction, distribution, transformation, extraction or reuse is made for the purpose of the provisions of Article 35^1 – *see* §7.

Legitimate user of a database or of a part of a database can carry out, without the consent of its author, any act of reproduction, distribution, communication to the public or transformation necessary for the normal utilization and access to the database or to a part of it.

c. Duration of the Sui Generis Right

25. The rights of the maker of the database shall run from the date of completion of the making of the database. According to Article 143, the term of protection is fifteen years from 1 January of the year following the date of completion of the database. In the case of a database which is made available to the public in whatever manner before expiry of the period previously provided, the term of protection shall be computed from 1 January of the year following the date when the database was first made available to the public. Any substantial change, evaluated qualitatively or quantitatively, to the contents of a database, including any substantial change resulting from the accumulation of successive additions, deletions or alterations, which would result in the database being considered to be a substantial new investment, evaluated qualitatively or quantitatively, shall qualify the database resulting from that investment for its own term of protection.

C. *Others*

1. Cinematographic Works and Other Audiovisual Works

26. The Romanian legislator sets out the audiovisual work in Article 65 as 'a cinematographic work or a work expressed by a procedure similar to cinematography, which makes use of moving pictures or a combination of sound with pictures' and the director or the producer of an audiovisual work in Article 66 as 'the natural person assuming the guidance of the creation and performing of the audiovisual work in his quality as main author', and the producer of an audiovisual work as 'the natural or legal person assuming the responsibility of the production of the work and who in this quality organizes the achievement of the work and provides the necessary technical and financial means'.

The audiovisual work is a joint work by its nature. Therefore, Article 67 sets out as authors: the director or producer, the author of the adaptation, the author of the screenplay, the author of the dialogue, the author of the musical score specially created for the audiovisual work and the author of the graphics for the animated works or animated sequences, when these represent an important part of the work. In the contract between the producer and the director, the parties may agree to include other collaborators who have substantially contributed to its creation as authors of the audiovisual work.

In the event that one of the authors of the joint work shall refuse to finish off his or her contribution to the audiovisual work or shall be in a situation of impossibility to do so, this author may not oppose its use in view of finalizing the audiovisual work; however, he shall have the right to be remunerated for his contribution (Article 68, paragraph 1).

The audiovisual work shall be considered finished when 'the final version shall have been established by common agreement between the main author and the producer'; the final version could be made known to the public and be exploited in any way, with the approval of the main author, without any possibility for the other authors to oppose to it (Article 68, paragraphs 2 and 4). In view of the protection of the audiovisual work, the destruction of the original support of the final version of the work in the form of the standard copy shall be prohibited (Article 68, paragraph 3). The authors of the audiovisual work, other than the main author, cannot oppose public awareness, as well as the specific use of the definitive version of the work, in whole or in part (Article 68, paragraph 4).

2. Works of Plastic Art, Architecture and Photography

27. Chapter 10 of the Law regulates these works and the responsibilities of the persons organizing exhibitions and reproduction of works.

The works of plastic art are regulated by Article 7(g) of the Law. These works may be presented in an art exhibition, and the person organizing it has the obligation to take the necessary measures for the removal of any risk.

The artwork may be reproduced on the basis of a contract, which, according to Article 84, shall contain indications permitting the identification of the work, such as a summary description, a sketch, a drawing, a photograph as well as references to the author's signature.

The reproductions shall be put up for sale only with the copyright holder's approval of the copy that was submitted to his or her examination. All copies of the work must bear the author's name or pseudonym or any other sign permitting his or her identification.

The original models and other elements having served the maker of the reproductions 'should be returned to their holder with any title, if not otherwise agreed. Instruments specially created for the reproduction of the work must be destroyed or rendered useless, if the holder of the copyright on the work should not acquire them, and if not otherwise agreed' (Article 84).

If the architectural studies and projects are exhibited close to the site of the architectural work, it is stipulated that they must bear the name of the author written in a visible place, if not otherwise agreed by contract. The construction of an architectural work totally or partially realized after another project shall be made only with the agreement of the holder of the copyright on that project (Article 85).

The photographic works shall be protected. They include the photograms of cinematographic films, too. 'Photographs of letters, documents and acts of any kind, technical drawing and other similar materials' shall not be included (Article 85).

It is expressly stipulated that the right of the author of a photographic work to exploit his or her own work shall not be prejudicial to the rights of the author of the artwork reproduced in the photographic work. If the photographic work was created in the execution of an individual work contract or on order, the patrimonial rights shall be presumed 'to belong for a period of three years to the employer or the person having ordered it, if not otherwise provided under the contract'. Alienation of the negative of a photographic work shall have as an effect the transmission of the patrimonial rights of the holder of the copyright on it, if not otherwise agreed upon (Article 87).

As a specific element too, it is stipulated that a person's photograph, when made on order, may be published or reproduced by the person photographed or such person's successors without the author's consent, if not otherwise agreed, provided that the name of the author is mentioned on the reproduction, too (Article 88).

3. The Portrait, the Mail Address and the Confidentiality of the Information Source

28. With regard to the circulation of a work containing a portrait, the authorization of the person represented in that portrait is required. Its author, owner or proprietor shall not have 'the right to reproduce it or to communicate it publicly without the represented person's consent or the consent of that person's successors, for a period of twenty years after the respective person's death'; the authorization shall not be required if the person represented in the portrait is a professional model or has received a remuneration for sitting, if not otherwise agreed (Article 89, paragraphs 1 and 2).

The correspondence addressed to a person may be circulated only with the authorization of the addressee and after the addressee's death, for a period of twenty years, of the addressee's successors, if the addressee has not expressed a different wish. The confidentiality of the information sources used in the works shall be observed by the publishers or producers at the author's request; the divulgation of the confidentiality shall be permitted only by the consent of the person who has entrusted it or on the basis of a final and irrevocable judgment (Articles 90, 91 and 92).

4. Folk Protection

29. The issue of folk protection, under domestic or international regulations, is still unsolved. There is a project of a treatise on the protection of folk's expressions, defined as 'productions consisting of elements specific to the traditional artistic heritage, developed and perpetuated by a community or by individuals acknowledged as the representatives of the traditional artistic aspirations of their community'. The protection should be recognized independently of the fixation of the work on a material carrier and the use of the work should be subject to the authorization granted by the State of origin, with a fair remuneration.

Law No. 26/2008 for safeguarding immaterial cultural patrimony has been adopted in Romania. Said law does not define the concept of folklore; nevertheless, under Article 2 letter (b), it is stipulated that 'traditional cultural expressions' represent an element of the cultural patrimony of a nation. Article 1(2) of the same law stipulates that the provisions of the law shall not be used for acquiring protection over folklore or folklore expressions under copyright law.

It is worth mentioning that folklore expressions could benefit from copyright protection under Article 4 of Law No. 8/1996, which stipulates that:

> where the work was disclosed to the public anonymously or under a pseudonym that does not identify the author, the copyright shall be exercised by the person, whether natural person or legal entity, who discloses it to the public.

Said provision is inspired by Article 15(4) of the Berne Convention which relates to 'anonymous unpublished works' but does not contain the word 'folklore'.

As the folklore work is achieved by the members of a community, it could be considered to be a 'work of joint authorship' provided for by Article 5 of Law 8/1996, and, in this context, a national body should be established for the management of rights of the collective author of folklore. The bodies established under Law No. 26/2008 have the role of promotion and coordination of activities that involve preservation and promotion of national folklore works, having no competence to authorize the use thereof.

In Article 95 of Law No. 8/1996, the concept of folklore is used with a view to defining the performers whose related rights in the performance of a work of folklore are recognized. We consider that Law No. 8/1996 should be amended in order to provide recognition of moral and economic rights for the communities as owners of copyright in the folklore works.

5. Advertising Works

30. The advertising works, like posters, drawings, labels, photographs, music, etc., are protected by copyright. The necessity of a regulation that would provide a balance between the exploitation of a work and the remuneration of its author is widely recognized.

6. Titles

31. The titles of writings, essays and magazines are not directly named as object of the copyright law's protection. This is not the case under French law, which provides in Articles L.II 2–4 that the title of an intellectual work is protected, subject to its originality. In the absence of an express provision for the work's titles, it may be inferred that if the work is protected, the title shall be implicitly protected as part of the work. With regard to the titles of magazines, the trend is to protect them as trademarks.

§3. Conditions of Protection

I. Formal Requirements

32. According to Article 1 paragraph 2 of the Law, a work of intellectual creation shall be acknowledged and protected independently of its being made publicly known, simply by virtue of its creation. However, its provisions apply only with strict observance of national law regarding the processing of personal data (paragraph 3).

Romanian law provides that the protection of the intellectual creation may also be granted under other statutory provisions (Article 2). This concerns the provisions related to industrial property, under which it is stipulated that the acknowledgement of author's right is made at the time of its registration by the competent public body, if the legal conditions for granting the protection under a patent, design, industrial model or trademark are fulfilled.

There is no regulation under Romanian law with regard to the legal storage of a work, as it is stipulated under the French law of 20 June 1992 or Article 408 of the Copyright Act.

The amendments made in 2022 to the copyright law have added relevant terms and expressions having important meaning in the content of the law, namely:

(a) auxiliary online service – an online service that consists in the provision to the public, by or under the control and responsibility of a broadcasting or television body, of television programmes or radio, simultaneously with their broadcast by the broadcasting or television body or during a defined period of time after this broadcast, as well as any material that has an auxiliary character in relation to this broadcast;
(b) retransmission – any simultaneous, unaltered retransmission and full, other than cable retransmission, for the reception by the public of an initial transmission from any Member State of television or radio programmes intended for reception by the public, if such initial transmission is carried out by means of wire or wireless, including via satellite, but not online;
(c) managed environment – an environment in which an operator of a relay service provides a secure relay to authorized users;
(d) direct entry – a technical process by which a broadcaster transmits its programme-carrying signals to a body that is not a radio broadcasting or television body so that the programme-carrying signals are not accessible to the public during that transmission;
(e) research organization – a university, including its libraries, a research institute or any other entity whose main purpose is to carry out scientific research or carry out educational activities that also include carrying out scientific research, not for profit or by reinvesting all profits in scientific research or on the basis of a mission of interest public, recognized by law, so that access to the results generated by such scientific research cannot preferentially benefit an entity that exercises a decisive influence on such an organization;
(f) text and data extraction – any automated analytical technique aimed at analysing text and data in digital form to generate information such as but not limited to, patterns, trends and correlations;
(g) cultural heritage conservation institution – a library open to the public or a museum, an archive or an institution for the preservation of cinematographic or sound heritage, as well as any other public cultural institutions that carry out activities in the field of education, organized outside the national formal education system, with the aim of preserving and promoting national culture;
(h) press publication – a collection consisting mainly of literary works of a journalistic nature, but which may also include other works or other protected objects;

(i) publisher of press publications – service provider at the initiative, under the editorial responsibility and under whose supervision it is published, in any form of mass media, written or online, a press publication within the meaning of the provisions of this law;
(j) information society service – a service as defined in Article 4 paragraph (1) point 2 of Government Decision No. 1.016/2004 regarding the measures for organizing and carrying out the exchange of information in the field of technical standards and regulations, as well as the rules relating to information society services between Romania and the Member States of the European Union, as well as the European Commission, with subsequent amendments and additions;
(k) provider of an online content-sharing service – a provider of an information society service, the main purpose or one of the main purposes of which is to store and provide public access to a significant volume of works protected by copyright or by other protected objects uploaded by its users, which it organizes and promotes directly or indirectly, for example, by using means of targeted promotion, for profit.

In the situation provided for in paragraph (1) lit. b) the following conditions must be met:

(a) the retransmission must be carried out by a party other than the broadcasting or television body that carried out the initial transmission or under the control and responsibility of which the initial transmission was carried out, regardless of how the party carrying out the retransmission obtains programme-carrying signals from the broadcasting or television organization for the purpose of retransmission; and
(b) when the retransmission is done through an internet access service, as defined in Article 2 point 2 paragraph 2 of Regulation (EU) 2015/2.120 of the European Parliament and of the Council of 25 November 2015 establishing measures regarding access to the open internet and amending Directive 2002/22/EC on universal service and user rights regarding electronic communications networks and services and Regulation (EU) No. 531/2012 regarding roaming in public mobile communications networks within the Union, this should take place in a managed environment.

To be considered a press publication, it is necessary to fulfil the following criteria:

(a) it constitutes an individual element within a periodical publication or regularly updated publication under a single title, such as a newspaper or a magazine of general or specialized interest;
(b) it aims to offer to the general public information related to news or other topics;

(c) it is published in any form of mass media, written or online, at the initiative, under the editorial responsibility and under the supervision of a service provider organized according to the law. It does not represent publications of press and periodicals that are published for scientific or academic purposes, such as scientific journals.

Non-profit online encyclopaedias, non-profit educational or scientific archives, open source software development and sharing platforms, providers of electronic communications services, online markets, cloud services for businesses or cloud services that allow users to upload content for their own use are not considered providers of online content-sharing services.

II. Substantive Requirements

33. The granting of protection depends on some essential conditions, which are stipulated under the law and synthesized as follows:[9]

- The work must be the result of the author's creative work; that is, it represents some individuality consisting of a personal contribution to the ideas of the work, which bears the stamp of the personality of the author. The work does not necessarily involve either absolute originality or absolute novelty, as is the case of patents. The originality can be found in the subjectivity, the expression and elements of the imagination, in the selection and arrangement of the relevant material.[10]
- The work must be expressed in a specific form, perceivable to the senses, such as: a manuscript, a picture or other concrete form. The form can be either an indispensable material support (e.g., plastic arts) or a presentation of the author (e.g., the choreographic works and pantomime).
- It must be possible for the work to be made publicly known through reproduction, performance, exhibition, presentation or other means.

Under Romanian law, the protection of a work is ensured independently of its value. The doctrine and the jurisprudence pointed out the absurd consequences of this rule and stated the necessity of a value criterion for some classes of works, especially for the derived works, in connection with the author's merit.[11]

The works created by machines are a sensible issue, for which the French doctrine[12] states that the holder of the copyright is the natural or legal person who made the programme. The works that infringe on public order or good morals cannot be protected, as they injure the fundamental values of human society.[13]

9. Yolanda Eminescu, *supra*, 76.
10. André Bertrand, *Le Droit d'auteur et les droits voisines* (Dalloz, 1999), 131.
11. V. Roş, D. Bodgan & O. Spineanu-Matei, *supra*, 101.
12. André Bertrand, *supra*, 123.
13. *Ibid.*, 152.

§4. Ownership

I. The Author (Initial Authorship)

34. Only a natural person may be the author of a work, as it is the result of an intellectual activity and the natural person is exclusively able to carry on such activity.

Romanian law adheres to this concept and establishes under Article 3 the principle of the real author as follows: 'An author shall be the natural person or persons having created the work.' Paragraph 2 of the same article stipulates the exception to the above-mentioned principle: 'in cases expressly provided by law, legal persons and natural persons other than the author may benefit from the protection granted to the author'. The quality of subject of the copyright can be transmitted according to the law, and thus, 'The natural or legal persons, who have acquired this quality by inheritance or assignment, under the law, as well as the publishers of musical works and written works, are recognized and protected as copyright holders for the rights that have been granted to them.' Transferred on the basis of individual agreements and which are entitled to at least part of the income from the rights. In the understanding of the law, user is considered 'any natural or legal person who takes actions conditional on the authorization by the authors or the rightholders, their remuneration or the payment of compensations to them and who does not act as a consumer'.

The doctrine states different foundations of the right of a legal person to be the author of a work, such as the theory of the mandate granted by the authors or the theory of a native right; however, without the rights belonging only to a natural person.[14] As the protection is granted by law, the dispute has no object anymore. It must be noted that the law does not mention a copyright but a protection which is similar to the one granted to the author, except with the moral rights and the status of creator. The issue is difficult, especially for some classes of work, such as audiovisual works. In these cases, the difference between copyright and industrial property is becoming less obvious as the author's specific protection extends towards the auxiliary persons (audiovisual producers, television and radio broadcasting bodies, etc.).[15]

The reverse process was developed with regard to the integrated circuits and computer programs.

35. In the case of derived works, there are two authors: the author of the native work and the derived work, respectively. If the first author cooperates in the creation of the derived work, he or she is the author of the joint work, too. The author of the derived work is obliged to request authorization from the author of the native work for its use and to observe his or her rights.

According to Article 4 of the Law, the author shall be presumed to be, unless otherwise proven, the person under whose name the work was for the first time made publicly known. Thus, the safety of the juristic relationship is ensured; however, it is a simple presumption, *juris tantum*, and it may be removed by counter-proof.

14. Yolanda Eminescu, *supra*, 55.
15. A. Francon, 'L'avenir du droit d'auteur', *Revue de droit intellectuel*, No. 12 (1986): 385.

36. If the author does not wish to disclose his or her status, it is stipulated under Article 4, paragraph 2 that when the work is made publicly known in an anonymous form or under a pen name which does not permit the identification of the author, the copyright shall be exercised by the natural or legal person who makes it publicly known only with the author's consent, so long as the latter does not disclose his or her identity.

II. Joint Work Created by Several Persons

37. The participation of two or more persons in the creation of a work causes different forms of works: cooperative, composite and collective works, respectively. The Romanian legislator has not defined the *composite works*, unlike the French law, which defines them under Article L.1–3 as the works including a previous work, without the cooperation of its author.

According to Article 5 of the Romanian Law, 'a joint work shall be a work created by several co-authors in collaboration' and 'the copyright in a joint work shall belong to its co-authors, among whom one may be the main author, under the terms of the present law'.

The exploitation of the work is made by common agreement, failing a convention to the contrary. A co-author may refuse to give his or her consent, but the denial shall have to be thoroughly justified (Article 5, paragraph 3).

In the event that each co-author's contribution is distinct, such contribution can be exploited separately on conditions that it shall not prejudice the exploitation of the joint work or the rights of the other co-authors. The remuneration shall be due to the co-authors in the proportions they shall have agreed upon. Failing such a convention, the remuneration shall be divided in proportion to the parts of contribution of the authors or equally, if these cannot be established.

38. Article 6 defines the collective work as 'a work in which the personal contributions of the co-authors form a whole, without being possible, given the nature of the work, to ascribe a distinct right to anyone of the co-authors on the work created in its entirety'. Unless otherwise agreed, the copyright in a collective work shall belong to the natural or legal person on whose initiative and under whose responsibility and name the work was created.

The quoted provisions state the difference between the joint works and the derived ones: the first are the result of a joint creative activity, the so-called community of inspiration, producing a unitary work, divisible or not, elaborated in the same period of time, in the case of the latter, there is a subsequent relation between the native work and the derived one, with regard to the inspiration and the time of creation.[16]

16. Yolanda Eminescu, *supra*, 60–61.

§5. TRANSFER

39. Chapter 7 of the law, 'Transfer of the patrimonial copyrights', has four sections: common provisions, publishing contract, theatrical or musical performance contract and rental contract respectively.

I. Transfer of Copyright

A. *Settlement of the Transfer*

40. (a) Forms of transfer: According to Article 40, the author or the holder of the copyright may assign by contract only his patrimonial rights to other people. This transfer may be limited to 'certain rights, for a certain territory and for a certain period of time'.

The assignment of the copyright may be exclusive or non-exclusive. In the event of an exclusive transfer, which must be provided expressly in the contract, not even the holder of the copyright himself shall be able to use the work any longer in the manners, in the territory and for the term agreed with the transferee, nor shall he or she be any longer able to transmit the respective right to another person (Article 40, paragraph 4).

In the event of a non-exclusive assignment, the holder of the copyright may use the work himself and may transmit the non-exclusive right to other people, provided that no prejudice is caused to the transferee. The latter may not transfer his right to another person unless he has the granter's express consent, except when the transferee as a legal person shall be changed by one of the modalities provided under the law (Article 40, paragraph 8).

The transfer of one of the patrimonial rights of the copyright's titular may not have any effect on his other rights, unless differently agreed.

However, it is stipulated that in the event of a transfer of the reproduction right of a work, it shall be presumed that the right to circulation of the copies of such work was also assigned, except for the import right, if not otherwise provided by contract (Article 41).

The chapter also stipulates that 'gaining the ownership on the material support of the work shall not thereby impart a right of exploitation on the work itself' (Article 48, paragraph 6).

Law 69/2022 introduced some relevant provisions 40^1 and 40^2 on non-exclusive licences or assignment of exclusive rights.

When granting non-exclusive licences or assigning their exclusive rights for the exploitation of works or other protected objects, authors and performers have the right to receive adequate and proportional remuneration in relation to the economic value of the authorized or assigned rights, taking into account by the contribution to the whole of the work or other protected objects, or by their effective exploitation, as well as by market practices. Without representing the rule and in the absence of any clauses to the contrary, the payment of a lump sum may constitute an adequate and proportional remuneration.

Upon implementation of the upper provisions, the principle of contractual freedom and that of a fair balance between the rights and interests of the parties are taken into account, and mechanisms such as collective agreements or collective labour contracts are being used, as the case may be.

Application of the principle upper provided with regard to non-exclusive licences does not constitute a prohibition for authors and performers to authorize non-commercial uses, as well as the free uses of works or other protected objects, made through non-exclusive licences.

Authors and performers shall receive from their successors rights or parties to whom they have granted a licence or transferred their rights information regarding the exploitation of the works and their interpretations or performances, depending on the particularities of each sector. This information must:

(a) allow access to recent, complete, relevant and pertinent data regarding the exploitation of works and interpretations or performances;
(b) cover all exploitation modalities and all sources of income, including, if applicable, income generated by promotional products or relevant revenues generated worldwide;
(c) either on the understanding of the author or the performing artist, allow the effective evaluation of the economic value of the rights in question;
(d) or transmitted periodically, at least once a year.

If the rights previously provided have subsequently been the subject of a licence, the authors and performers or their representatives receive, upon request, from subcontractors, additional information if their first contractual partner does not have all the information that would be necessary.

When additional information is requested, the first contractual partner of the authors and performers shall provide information regarding the identity of the subcontractors. Requests can be addressed directly to subcontractors by authors or performers, or they can be addressed through the contractual partner of the author or performer. This obligation is proportionate and effective to ensure a high level of transparency in each sector.

In duly justified cases, in which the administrative burden generated by the obligation as provided, would become disproportionate in relation to the net income generated by the exploitation of the work or the interpretation or execution, the obligation is limited to the types and level of information that can reasonably be expected in such cases.

The obligation as mentioned does not apply if the contribution of the author or performer is not significant considering the work or the interpretation or performance as a whole, unless the author or performer indicates that they need information for the exercise of his rights and requests the information for this purpose.

This obligation established does not apply to contracts concluded by collective management bodies or independent management entities.

41. (b) The clauses of transfer: The Romanian legislator sets out under Article 42 the essential clauses of transfer, providing that the contract shall stipulate 'the patrimonial rights transmitted, the modalities of exploitation, the term and extension of the transfer, as well as the remuneration of the copyright's holder', or otherwise the contract shall be cancelled. If the transfer of patrimonial rights regards the totality of the author's future works, named or unnamed, the sanction is the absolute nullity.

42. (c) The proof of transfer: According to Article 43 of the Law, the existence and content of the transfer contract of the patrimonial rights may be proved only by its written form, except for contracts having as their object works used in press. This means that the written form is an *ad probationem* requirement and the common law applies.

43. (d) The author's remuneration: As a general rule, the remuneration due on the grounds of a transfer contract shall be established by agreement between the parties. The criterion established by law for the calculation of the amount of remuneration is either a percentage of the sums collected from the exploitation of the work or a set sum or any other way. In addition to the remuneration as provided for, the author has the right to collect, through the collective management bodies, the remuneration due from the actual use of the work, if there are no contrary clauses in the assignment contract (Article 44, paragraph 1).

When the remuneration has not been established by contract, the author may request the competent legal bodies to establish the remuneration. This shall be done by taking into account the amount of money usually paid for the same class of work, the destination and term of exploitation, as well as other circumstances specific to the case (Article 44, paragraph 2).

44. (e) The work created by an employee: For works created within the framework of an individual employment contract, the patrimonial rights shall belong to the author of the work created, failing a contract clause to the contrary. If such a clause exists, this shall have to include the term for which the patrimonial copyrights shall have been transferred. In absence of a precise statement of the term, this shall be of three years after the date when the work is handed in (Article 45, paragraph 1). It is provided that the author of a work such created shall preserve to himself the exclusive right of use of the work as part of the whole of his or her creation (Article 45, paragraph 3). In the absence of collective agreements or collective labour contracts, in which a mechanism comparable to the mechanism established in this article is provided for, authors and performers have the right, including through their representatives, to adequate additional remuneration and fair from the party with whom they entered into a contract for the exploitation of their rights or their successors in title when the initially agreed remuneration is clearly found to be disproportionately low in relation to all subsequent relevant net income and significantly higher than the initial estimates, obtained from the exploitation of the works or interpretations or executions. These provisions do not apply in the case of contracts concluded with collective management bodies or independent management entities or in the event that the author or performing artist is remunerated in proportion to the net income generated by the use of his works, interpretations or performances. Conflicts related to the transparency obligation, as well as those relating to the contract adjustment mechanism, may be the subject of mediation. Associations and professional organizations of authors and performers may initiate the mediation procedure as provided at the specific request of one or more authors or performers.

45. (f) The work appearing in a periodical publication: Failing a convention to the contrary, the holder of a copyright on a work appearing in a periodical publication shall preserve the right to use it in any form whatsoever on the condition of causing no prejudice to the publication in which the work was issued. If the work has not been published within a month after its acceptance, in the case of a daily paper, or within six months, in the case of other publications, the holder of the copyright may dispose freely of the work, if not otherwise agreed (Article 46).

46. (g) The future work: Under Article 46, in case of the contract of commissioning future works, unless otherwise provided, the economic rights belong to the author. Said contract should specify both the time limit for the delivery of the work and the time limit for the acceptance of the work. If the work does not meet the conditions set, the person commissioning the work shall have the right to terminate the contract. In such a case, the sums of money collected by the author shall not be refundable, and where preparatory work has been done, the author shall be entitled to repayment of any expenses incurred.

47. (h) The cancellation of the transfer contract: The unilateral cancellation of a transfer contract can be established by agreement, subject to the limitations set by Article 48 of the Law.

As a general rule, the right of the author to request the cancellation of the cession contract of the patrimonial right is provided in the event that the transferee fails to exploit it or exploits it to an insufficient extent, and if thereby the author's justified interests are considerably affected. The author may not renounce beforehand the exercise of his or her right to solicit the cancellation of the transfer contract.

The minimum requested time before the cancellation of the contract is established as two years after the transfer of the patrimonial right on a work. In the case of works ceded for daily publication, this term shall be three months, and in the case of periodical publications, one year.

Only as an exemption, the author may not solicit the cancellation of a cession contract, if the motives of non-exploitation or of insufficient exploitation shall be due to his own fault, to a third party's deed, to a fortuitous case or to a force majeure case.

In the case of the works of plastic or photographic art, there shall not be a reason for cancellation of the deed of the author to exhibit publicly the original of the work, even though it might not have been made known to the public (Article 48, paragraph 4).

Where an author or performer has granted an exclusive licence or exclusively transferred his rights in respect of a work or other protected subject matter, the author or performer has the right to revoke fully or partially the licence or the transfer of rights in case of non-exploitation of the respective work or other protected object. The revocation mechanism as provided for shall be applied taking into account the following:

(a) specific aspects of the musical, audiovisual and publishing sectors and the various categories of works and interpretations or performances;
(b) relative importance of individual contributions and the legitimate rights and interests of all authors and performers or performers, affected by the application of the revocation mechanism by an author or an individual performer or performer, if a work or other protected object contains the contribution of several authors or performers.

The authors or performers may choose to terminate the exclusive nature of the contract instead of revoking the license or transfer of rights. The revocation cannot be requested before the expiry of three years from the date of conclusion of the licence contract or transfer of rights over the works or other protected objects. In the case of works from daily publications and periodicals, this term is one year.

This provision equally applies in the case of audiovisual works.

The author or performing artist should notify the person to whom the licences have been granted or the rights transferred and set an appropriate term, but not less than one year, until which the rights which are the subject of the license are to be exploited or which were transferred. After the expiration of that term, the author or performing artist can choose to terminate the exclusive nature of the contract.

Where an author or performer has granted an exclusive licence or exclusively transferred his rights in respect of a work or other protected subject matter, contractual clauses derogating from the revocation mechanism are allowed only within collective bargaining agreements or contracts and the author or performing artist has no right to fully or partially revoke the licence or the transfer of rights in case of non-exploitation of the respective work or other protected objects, if these works contain the contributions of several authors or artists, performers or performers.

II. Licence

48. The holders of the copyrights may conclude contracts for exploitation of their works, with the observance of the legal provisions.

A. Publishing Contract

49. By this contract, the holder of the copyright transfers to the publisher, in exchange for a remuneration, the right to reproduce and circulate the work. It shall not constitute a publishing contract, the convention by which the titular of a work's copyright empowers a publisher at his or her expense to reproduce and possibly circulate the work. In this situation, the common law provisions referring to the enterprise contract shall apply.

According to Article 50, the holder of the copyright can transfer to the publisher the right of authorizing the translation and adaptation of the work, too, by a distinct contract.

Romanian Law sets out in Article 52 the clauses of the publishing contract with regard to:

- the term of the transfer;
- the exclusive or non-exclusive nature and the territorial extension of the transfer;
- the minimum and maximum number of copies;
- the author's remuneration, established under the terms of the present law;
- the number of copies reserved to the author free of charge;
- the term for the publication and circulation of the copies of each edition or of each printing, as the case may be;
- the term of handing over of the work's original by the author;
- the control procedure of the number of copies produced by the publisher.

Absence of any of the above-mentioned clauses entitles the interested party to request the cancellation of the contract by setting a claim in justice.

Also, under Article 53, the prior publishing right of the work in electronic form is stipulated against other similar offers at an equal price for the publisher who has acquired the copyright of a work in the form of a volume. This right shall be valid for a period of three years after the date of the work's publication and must be exercised within not more than thirty days after the author's written opinion was received.

With regard to the relationship between the publisher and the author of a work, the law stipulates that the first shall be under an obligation to allow the second to make improvements or other modifications of the work in case of a new edition, under condition that these improvements or modifications do not essentially increase the publisher's costs, or change the character of the work, if it is not otherwise stipulated in the contract (Article 54).

The publisher shall have the right to transfer to the publishing contract only with the author's consent (Article 55).

The originals of the artworks, illustrations and any other documents received for publication shall be returned to the author of the original of the work, if not otherwise agreed (Article 56).

With regard to the cessation of the publishing contract, it is stipulated under Article 57 that it occurs after expiry of the term established or after exhaustion of the last edition agreed upon. An edition or printing shall be considered exhausted if the number of unsold copies is smaller than 5% of the total number of copies and at any rate if it is smaller than a hundred copies.

Should the publisher not have published the work within the term agreed upon, the author may request, according to Common Law, the cancellation of the contract and damages for non-execution. In this case, the author shall keep to himself the remuneration received or may ask for the payment of the integral remuneration provided in the contract, as the case may be.

If the term for the publication of the work is not stipulated in the contract, the publisher has the obligation to publish it within a term of not more than one year after the date of its acceptance (Article 57, paragraph 4).

If there are copies left over in stock after a period of two years from the publishing date and the publisher intends to destroy them, he has the obligation to offer them first to the author at a price obtainable by selling them for destruction, if not otherwise agreed.

Finally, the Romanian legislator also regulated the event of the work's destruction owing to force majeure and established the author's right to a remuneration, which shall be paid out to him or her only if the work had been published. If a prepared edition should be totally destroyed prior to its circulation, the editor shall be entitled to prepare a new edition and the author shall have the remuneration right only for one of these editions. If a prepared edition should be partially destroyed before being circulated, the publisher shall be entitled to reproduce without payment of a remuneration to the author only as many copies as were destroyed (Article 58).

B. Theatrical or Musical Performance Contract

50. The object of this contract is the cessation made by the holder of the copyright to a natural or legal person of the right to perform or execute in public a present or future literary, dramatic, musical, dramatic-musical, choreographic work or a pantomime in exchange for a remuneration, and the transferee shall be under an obligation to execute or to perform it under the conditions agreed.

General contracts of theatrical performances may be concluded as well by means of the collective management bodies.

The contract shall be concluded in writing for a determined period of time and for a set number of communications to the public and shall stipulate the term in which the first performance or only communication of the work shall take place, as the case may be, the exclusive or non-exclusive character of the transfer, the area or territory covered and the authors' remuneration.

According to Article 60, paragraph 3, the interruption of the performances for two consecutive years, if not otherwise agreed, shall entitle the author to request cancellation of the contract and damages for non-execution.

The transferee shall be under an obligation to permit the author to control the performance or execution of the work and to sustain adequately the achievement of the technical conditions for the interpretation of the work. Likewise, the transferee must send the author the programme, posters, and other printed materials, as well as reviews published on the performance, if not otherwise provided in the contract (Article 61).

Finally, the transferee shall be under an obligation periodically to communicate to the holder of the copyright the number of performances or musical executions, as well as the situation of the takings, but not less than once a year.

If the transferee fails to perform or execute the work within the set term, the author may solicit cancellation of the contract and damages for non-performance, in which case the author shall keep to himself the remuneration received or may solicit payment of the full remuneration provided in the contract.

C. Rental Contract

51. The rental contract of a work is the contract under which the author conveys the use for a fixed period of time of at least one copy of his or her work, the original or a copy, especially computer programs or works set in sound or audiovisual recordings. The transferee of the rental right shall be obliged to pay a remuneration to the author for the period of use of that copy of the work (Article 63).

The free use of a work by a third party is allowed by law only as an exception; the excepted cases are provided in detail by law and we shall present them under 'The limitation of the exercise of copyright' section.

§6. Scope of Exclusive Rights

I. Moral Rights

52. Romanian law does not define the moral rights of the author, but it identifies them and establishes their legal framework.

Thus, Article 10 names the following moral rights:

(a) the right to decide if, how and when the work will be made known to the public;
(b) the right to claim the acknowledgement of the authorship of the work;
(c) the right to decide under what name the work will be made known to the public;
(d) the right to claim the observance of the work's integrity and to oppose any modification as well as any impairment of the work, if it is prejudicial to his or her honour or reputation;
(e) the right to withdraw the work, indemnifying, if such be the case, the holders of the exploitation rights prejudiced by the exercise of the withdrawal right.

Also, it is provided that moral rights cannot form the object of renunciation or alienation.

After the author's death, the exercise of the rights provided under Article 10, paragraphs (a), (b) and (d) shall be transmitted through inheritance, according to the civil legislation, over an unlimited period of time. Where there are no heirs, the exercise of these rights shall revert to the collective management organization that has managed the author's rights or to the organization having the largest membership in the field of creation concerned, as the case may be (Article 11). The jurisprudence issued several theories on the legal nature of copyright, starting by defining copyright as a property right and ending up by stating that there is a special class of intellectual rights[17] centred on a moral right. The last point of view is endorsed by the Convention of Berne in Article 6*bis*.

It was stated that the moral right transforms the other rights which accompany it, and consequently, the Common Law rules on property can no longer be applied, as the moral right precedes and survives patrimonial rights.

The moral right, due to its features, belongs to the personal rights and it is permanent, non-transferable and has no temporal limitations; only as an exception the moral right can be transferred *mortis causa*, as to the exercise thereof.

Romanian law acknowledges to the author, too, a right of divulging, that is, to decide if, how and when the work will be made known to the public. This right of divulging is absolute, exclusive and non-transferable during his lifetime. After the author's death, the author's wishes shall be considered in order to decide whether the work can be published or not. The intent of the author cannot be presumed. Therefore, in case of the author's silence, the right of divulging shall be passed on to the author's heirs for the benefit of culture.

With regard to the author's right to withdraw or modify the work, this results from the exclusive and absolute character of the moral right and it can be used only after the right of divulging was exercised. These rights can be restricted only in case of the author's breach of law. In case of joint work, if one of the co-authors requests the work's withdrawal, the decision of the other co-authors is conclusive. The courts may be solicited to decide on the equity of the work's withdrawal.[18]

The right of paternity consists of the power of the author to demand that his status as the author of the work be acknowledged and of the right to object to the deeds of rejection of third parties by indicating his name on their works, inclusive. To this end, the right of the author to decide under what name the work will be published – his name, anonymously or under a pseudonym – is acknowledged.

The author's right to maintain the work's integrity and to use the work according to its nature is acknowledged. Therefore, the transferee, owners or users cannot modify the work. The jurisprudence and doctrine tend to appreciate the work's integrity subject to its normal expression. For example, a statue can be moved from one place to another without being destroyed, but it cannot be altered without the author's consent.[19]

Finally, it should be noted that, after the author's death and if there are no heirs, the moral rights may be exercised by the competent public body, namely the ORDA.

II. Exploitation Rights

53. According to Article 12 of Law No. 8/1996, the author of a work shall have the exclusive patrimonial right to decide whether, how, and when his or her work shall be used or exploited, including the consent to the use of the work by others.

17. *Ibid.*, 138.
18. *Ibid.*, 157.
19. The Supreme Tribunal, decision No. 815/1967, in Romanian Law publication No. 10/1967, 116.

For the application of this principle, Article 13 provides that the use or exploitation of a work gives rise to distinct and exclusive rights of the author to authorize:

(a) the full or partial reproduction of his work;
(b) the distribution of the work;
(c) the import with a view to trading on the domestic market of copies from the work, achieved with the author's consent;
(d) the rental of the work;
(e) the lending of the work;
(f) the communication of the work to the public, directly or indirectly, by any means, including by making the work available to the public in such a way that members of the public may access them from a place at a time individually chosen by them;
(g) broadcasting of the work;
(h) cable retransmission of the work;
(i) making of derivative works;
(j) retransmission of the work.

Subsequently, the Romanian legislator defines the reproduction, circulation and all means for the use or exploitation of a work (Articles 14 to 20):

- reproduction means 'the making, in whole or in part, of one or more copies of a work, directly or indirectly, temporarily or permanently, by any means and in any form, including the making of any sound or audiovisual recording of a work, as well as its permanent or temporary storage by electronic means' (Article 14);
- distribution means 'the sale and any other manner of transmittal, for a consideration or free of charge, of the original or of copies of the work, on the domestic market, by the right holder or with his consent'. The distribution right is exhausted once the first sale or the first transfer of ownership of the original or copies of a work, on the domestic market, by the rights holder or with his consent. (Article 15);
- import means 'the introduction on the domestic market, for trading, of the original or of the legally made copies of a work fixed on any kind of physical medium' (Article 16);
- rental means 'making available for use, for a limited period and for a direct or indirect economic or commercial advantage, of a work' (Article 17);
- lending means 'making available for use, for a limited period and without a direct or indirect economic or commercial advantage, of a work through the agency of an institution allowing access of the public for this purpose' (Article 18);
- communication to the public means:

> any communication of the work, directly or by any technical means, made in a place opened for public or in any other place where a number of persons exceeding the normal circle of the members of a family and of its acquaintances assemble, including stage performance, recitation or any other public form of performance or direct presentation of the work, public display of works of

plastic art, of applied art, of photographic art and of architecture, public projection of cinematographic and other audiovisual works, including of works of digital art, presentation in a public place, by means of sound or audiovisual recordings, as well as presentation in a public place, by any means, of a broadcast work. Any communication of a work by wire or wireless means, including by making the works available to the public via Internet or other computer networks, so that any member of the public to have access, from anywhere or at any moment individually chosen, shall also be considered as communication to the public (Article 20).

- broadcasting means 'broadcasting of a work by a radio or television broadcasting organization, by any means servicing for the wireless transmission of the signals, sounds or images, or of digital representation thereof, including the public communication by satellite, for the public reception by the public'; and ' transmission of a work or its representation, by wire, cable, optical fibber or any other similar process, including direct input, with the exception of computer networks, for the purpose of its reception by the public.' (Article 21 letters (a) and (b));
- cable retransmission means 'simultaneous, unaltered and complete retransmission, by cable or through an ultra-short wave broadcasting system for the reception by the public of an initial transmission or of the retransmission that takes place on the national territory or, as the case may be, of an initial transmission from another Member State, by wired or wireless means, including satellite, of television or radio programs intended for reception by the public, regardless of how the operator of a retransmission service via cable obtains the program-carrying signals from the broadcasting or television organization for the purpose of retransmission' (Article 22);
- making of derivative works means 'translation, publication in collections, adaptation as well as any other transformation of a pre-existent work, if it is an intellectual creation' (Article 23).

As regards the exhaustion of the above-mentioned rights, the law stipulates that the distribution right is exhausted upon first sale or first transfer of ownership over the original and copies of a work, on the domestic market, by the owner of the right or with his consent, while the lending right is deemed to be not exhausted upon first sell or first transfer of ownership, nor is the right to authorize or prohibit the communication to the public or the making available to the public upon any act of public communication or of making available to the public.

Lending through the agency of libraries does not require author's authorization and entitles him to an equitable remuneration, except in case of libraries of education institutions and of public libraries with free access.

The author of an original work of graphic or plastic art or of a photographic work benefits, under Article 24, by a resale right representing the right to collect a share from the net selling price obtained at any resale of the work, as well as the right to be informed of the work's whereabouts, where the amount so owed may not exceed EUR 12,500. The following shares are provided for by the law: 5% from EUR 300 to EUR 3,000; 4% from EUR 3,000.01 to EUR 50,000; 3% from EUR 50,000.01 to EUR 200,000; 1% from EUR 200,000.01 to EUR 350,000; 0.5% from EUR 350,000.01 to EUR 500,000; and 0.25% over EUR 500,000.

In the exploitation of the resale right, the seller shall be bound to communicate to the author, within a time limit of two months, any information concerning the resale and shall be responsible for withholding the adequate percentage and for paying the same to the author. The resale right may not be waived or alienated. The same provisions shall be applicable to the copies of original works of art or photography, made in a limited number by the author himself or with his consent, said copies being considered as original works (Article 24(3)).

In the case of the alienated works, the law obliges the owner or possessor of a work, for the purpose of the absolute exercise of the author's right, 'to permit the author's access to it and to put it at his or her disposal, if this fact is necessary for the exercise of his or her copyright, and on condition that the owner or possessor's legitimate interest should not thereby be impaired'. The owner or possessor may claim from the author 'a sufficient guarantee for the security of the work, the insurance of the work for an amount representing the market value of the original as well as an adequate remuneration' (Article 25).

Also, the owner of the original work shall not have the right to destroy it before offering it to the author at the cost price of the material. Should the returning of the original not be possible, the owner shall allow the author to make a copy of the work in an adequate manner. In the case of an architectural structure, the author shall only have the right to make photographs of the work and to request the sending back of reproductions from the projects (Article 26).

A reservation mention on the exploitation is provided for in the law (Article 204, paragraphs 2–5).

Thus, in compliance with the international common regulations, it is provided that the authors and other holders of rights or holders of authors' exclusive rights, to which reference is made in the law, shall have the right to inscribe on the originals or authorized copies of the works the reservation mention of their exploitation, consisting in the symbol C surrounded by a circle, accompanied by their name, the place and year when first published.

Producers of sound recordings, interpreting or performing artists to whom reference is made in the law shall have the right to inscribe on the originals or authorized copies of the sound or audiovisual recordings or on the cover in which they are contained a mention of protection of their rights, consisting of the symbol P surrounded by a circle, accompanied by their name, place and date when first published.

Until otherwise proved, it shall be presumed that the exclusive rights signalled by the symbols C and P exist and belong to the people having used them.

The above-mentioned provisions shall not condition the existence of the rights acknowledged and guaranteed under the law.

§7. Limitations or Exemptions with Respect to Copyright Protection

54. Although copyright is defined as an exclusive and absolute right, there are some limitations with regard to the reproduction and use of a work. They have been established for the purpose of protecting the general welfare under the condition that these limitations are in agreement with good usage and without any prejudice to the author or to the holders of the exploitation rights.

Chapter 6 of the Romanian Law sets out the limitations of the exercise of copyright.

Thus, according to Article 35, the following uses of a work previously made known to the public shall be permitted without the author's consent and without payment of a remuneration, under the condition that the mentioned principles are observed:

(a) the reproduction of a work within the framework of judicial or administrative proceedings, to the extent to which it is justified by their purpose;
(b) the use of brief quotation from a work for the purpose of an examination, commentary, criticism or exemplification, to the extent to which their use justifies the extent of the quotation;
(c) the use of isolated articles or brief excerpts from works in publications, television and radio broadcasts, or in sound or audiovisual recordings exclusively intended for teaching purposes as well as the reproduction for teaching purposes within the framework of public educational or social protection institutions, of isolated articles or of brief extracts from works, to the extent to which it is justified by the purpose pursued;
(d) the reproduction of brief excerpts from works for information or research within the framework of libraries, museums, film archives, sound archives, archives of cultural or scientific non-profit public institutions; the integral reproduction of a work's copy is allowed for its replacement, in case of destruction, severe deterioration or loss of a single copy from the respective archive or library's permanent collection;
(e) specific acts of reproduction made by publicly accessible libraries, educational establishments or museums, or by archives, which are not for direct or indirect economic or commercial advantage;
(f) the reproduction, to the exclusion of any means involving direct contact with the work, distribution or communication to the public of the image of an architectural work, work of plastic art, photographic work or work of applied art permanently located in a public place, except where the image of the work is the main subject of such reproduction, distribution or communication, and if it is used for commercial purposes;
(g) the representation or execution of a work as a part of the activities of educational establishments, exclusively for specific purposes and provided that both the representation or execution of the public's access are free of charge;
(h) use of works during religious celebrations or official celebrations organized by a public authority;

(i) use, for the purpose of advertising, of the images of the works presented within exhibitions with public access or sale, of fairs, public auctions of works of art, to the extent necessary to promote the event, excluding any other commercial use.

Subject to conditions provided for in the paragraph above, the reproduction, distribution, broadcasting or communication to the public, with neither direct nor indirect commercial or economic advantage, are allowed:

(a) of brief excerpts from press articles and radio or televised reportages, for information purposes on current events, except those for which such a use is expressly reserved;
(b) of brief excerpts of lectures, addresses, pleadings and other similar works that have been orally expressed in public, provided that these uses too have the sole purpose of informing on the present;
(c) of brief excerpts of the works, within information on current events, to the extent justified by the informational purpose;
(d) of works, used for the sole purpose of didactic illustration or scientific research;
(e) of works, for the benefit of people with disabilities, which are directly related to that disability and to the extent required by the specific disability.

Temporary acts of reproduction that are transient or incidental form an integral and essential part of a technical process, the sole purpose of which is to enable transfer, in a network between third parties, by an intermediary or the lawful use of another protected object and that should have no separate economic value on their own, are excepted from the reproduction right.

In all cases provided for in paragraph (1), letters (b), (c), (e), (f), (i) and paragraph (2), the source, including the author's name, has to be indicated, unless this turns out to be impossible; in case of works of plastic art, photographic or architecture works the place in which the original is to be found has to be indicated.

Recent amendments brought to the law in 2019 were introduced, in line with the already mentioned European approach, and two new situations where the consent of the copyright holder should not be requested from specific beneficiary persons.

Thus, according to a new Article 35^1:

> without the consent of the holder of any copyright or any related right and without payment of any remuneration, are permitted reproduction, distribution, communication to the public, making available to the public, broadcasting, renting and lending of a work or other protected object, provided that they do not contravene the normal exploitation of the work and do not prejudice the author or rights holders, for the purpose of:
>
> (a) creation, by a beneficiary person or a person acting on its behalf, of a copy in accessible format of a work or other object protected by copyright or related rights, to which the beneficiary has legal access, for the exclusive use of the beneficiary;

(b) creation, by an authorized entity, of a copy in accessible format of a work or other object protected by copyright or related rights, to which the beneficiary has legal access or public communication, making it available, the distribution or the loan, for non-profit purpose, of a copy in accessible format to a beneficiary person or another entity authorized for the purpose of exclusive use by a beneficiary person.

In the understanding of the law:

the expression beneficiary person means, regardless of any other disability, a person who:

(a) is blind;
(b) has visual impairments which cannot be corrected to obtain a visual function equivalent, in essence, to that of a person without such deficiencies and who, as a result, cannot read printed works in essence, to the same extent as a person not affected by such a deficiency;
(c) has a perception disability or reading difficulties and, consequently, he cannot read works printed to the same extent, essentially, as a person who does not suffer from such a disability;
(d) suffers from a physical disability that prevents her from holding or manipulating a book or focusing her eyes or moving her eyes to an extent that would be commonly acceptable for reading.

For the purposes of the law, the specific terms and expressions have the following meanings (Article 35,[1] paragraph 3):

(a) opera or other protected object means a work that is presented in the form of a book, periodical publication, newspaper, magazine or other types of writings, notations, including scores, as well as illustrations related thereto, on any type of media, including format audio, such as audio books, and in digital format, which is protected by copyright or related rights and which is legally published or otherwise made available to the public;
(b) copy in accessible format means a copy of a work or other protected object, which is realized in an alternative way or form and which allows the beneficiary to have access to works or other protected objects, including access under conditions as viable and comfortable as those enjoyed by a person who does not suffer from any of the deficiencies or any of the disabilities provided in the law;
(c) authorized entity means an entity that is authorized or recognized by a Member State for the purpose of providing, for non-profit purposes, beneficiaries, educational services, pedagogical training, adaptive reading or access to information, including public institutions or organizations without for-profit purpose, which offers the same services to the beneficiaries as one of their basic activities or their institutional obligations, or as part of their public interest missions. For the purpose of highlighting, the authorized entities have the obligation to

notify the ORDA, which will communicate the information to the central access point of the European Union and to the access point to information set up by the International Bureau of the WIPO.

The law also defines within this respect several exemptions from the reproduction right allowed for specific situations as necessary to make a copy in an accessible format, namely:

(a) any acts necessary to modify, convert or adapt a work or other object protected by copyright or related rights;
(b) providing the means necessary to go through the information in an accessible format;
(c) changes that may be required when the format of a work or other protected object is already accessible to certain beneficiaries, while it may not be accessible to other beneficiaries due to different deficiencies or handicaps or different degrees of the respective deficiencies or disabilities.

The provided uses must ensure and respect the integrity of the work or objects protected by copyright or related rights, taking due account of the changes necessary to make the work or other object of protection usable in the accessible format.

By the law, 'any contractual provision aimed at removing or limiting in any way the uses permitted is null and void'.

Consequently, to the above exceptions to the consent of the copyright holder for specific beneficiary persons, the new Article 35^2 of the law establishes legal duties for the authorized entities entrusted to carry out the said activities and acts.

Thus:

(1) The authorized entities that carry out the activity provided in Article $35,^1$ paragraph (1) lit. b) have the obligation to establish and follow clear and transparent procedures when fulfilling the following obligations:
   (a) distribute, communicate and make available copies in a format accessible only to the beneficiaries or other authorized entities;
   (b) adopt the appropriate measures to discourage the reproduction, distribution, and communication to the public or making available to the public in an unauthorized way the copies in an accessible format;
   (c) show due care when dealing with works or other protected objects, as well as copies in accessible format and keep records of these operations;
   (d) publish and update, on its own site, if applicable, or through other online or offline channels, information on how it complies with the stipulated obligations;
   (e) comply with the legal provisions regarding the processing of personal data of the beneficiaries.
(2) Any beneficiary person or authorized entity from Romania or from another Member State of the European Union has the right to obtain from an authorized entity that carries out the activity provided in Article 35^1 paragraph (1) lit. b) and which has its headquarters in Romania, a copy in accessible format of a work or other protected object, if it is available.

(3) The authorized entities in Romania have the possibility to request and obtain from an authorized entity from another Member State of the European Union a copy in accessible format of a work or other object protected by copyright or related rights or access to such copy, under the conditions of the national law of the respective state.

(4) At the request of the beneficiaries, other authorized entities or copyright holders, the authorized entity that carries out the activity provided for in Article 35[1] paragraph (1) lit. b) is obliged to make available, in an accessible form, the following information:
   (a) the list of works or other objects protected by copyright or related rights, for which he has copies in accessible format, specifying the available formats;
   (b) the name and contact details of the authorized entities with which it has made copies in accessible format.

(5) The export of copies in accessible format, carried out by an authorized entity established in a Member State to a third country, which is party to the Treaty of Marrakesh, and the import of such copies, from a third country, a member of the Treaty of Marrakesh, carried out by a beneficiary or an entity authorized by a Member State, is carried out in accordance with Regulation (EU) 2017/1,563 of the European Parliament and of the Council of 13 September 2017 on cross-border exchange between the Union and third countries copies in accessible format of certain works and other objects of copyright protection and related rights for the benefit of the blind, visually impaired or having difficulty reading printed materials.

Also, according to Article 36, the reproduction of a work without the author's consent for personal use or that of a normal family circle does not constitute a violation of the copyright under the condition that the work has previously been made known to the public, and the reproduction has not infringed the normal exploitation of the work or been prejudicial to the author or to the owner of the exploitation rights.

However, for the media on which sound or audiovisual recordings can be made or on which reproductions of graphically expressed works can be made, as well as for works apparatuses dedicated for copying, a compensatory remuneration established by negotiation, according to the legal provisions, shall be paid.

The reproduction and extraction of text and data carried out by research organizations and cultural heritage conservation institutions for scientific research purposes from works or other protected objects to which they have access are permitted legally.

The upper provisions also apply to the manufacturer of a database having the exclusive patrimonial right to authorize and prohibit the extraction and/or reuse of all or a substantial part of it, assessed qualitatively or quantitatively.

Copies of works or other protected objects made in accordance with the upper provisions are kept with appropriate security measures and may be kept for scientific research purposes, including to verify research results.

Rights holders are allowed to apply measures aimed at ensuring the security and integrity of networks and the databases in which the works or other protected objects are hosted, without such measures exceeding what is necessary to achieve the respective objective.

Rights holders, research organizations and cultural heritage conservation institutions may elaborate, by common agreement, on practices related to the application of the relevant provisions.

Reproductions and extractions from works and other legally accessible protected objects are allowed for the purpose of text and data extraction. Reproductions and extractions thus carried out can be kept for as long as necessary to extract the text and data.

The exception applies provided that the use of the works and other protected objects has not been expressly reserved by the right holders in an appropriate manner, such as means that can be read automatically in the case of content made public online.

By way of exception from the right of public communication and the right to make it available to the public, as well as from the rights provided for in the law for authors of computer programs and respectively manufacturers of data bases, digital uses of works and other protected objects are allowed, including in the online and cross-border environment, to the extent justified by the non-commercial purpose pursued, by the sole objective of didactic illustration, provided that such use:

(a) take place under the responsibility of an educational institution, in its building or in another place, or in a secure electronic environment to which only pupils or students and teaching staff of the educational institution have access;
(b) to be accompanied by the indication of the source, including the name of the author, except in cases where this proves impossible;
(c) not to pursue a commercial purpose;
(d) not to replace or affect the purchase of materials intended for the educational market.

If the educational institution that uses the works and other protected objects for the sole purpose of didactic illustration through secure electronic media is under the jurisdiction of Romania, it is considered that the use takes place only on the national territory.

It is exempted from the right of reproduction, as well as from the rights provided for the authors of computer programs or manufacturers of data bases, making copies of protected works or objects in the permanent collections of cultural heritage conservation institutions, in any format or on any type of support, for the purpose of conservation and to the extent necessary for such conservation.

The Romanian legislator allows for the modification of a work without the author's consent and without payment of a remuneration, only for the following cases set out by Article 37:

– if the modification is made privately, being neither intended nor made available to the public;

- if the result of the transformation is a caricature, parody or pastiche, provided that the result does not create confusion as to the original work and its author;
- if the modification is called for by the purpose of the use permitted by the author;
- if the result of the modification is a short review of the works for teaching purposes, mentioning the author.

Also, the trading companies engaged in the production or sale of sound or audiovisual recordings, equipment for their reproduction or public communication, as well as the receiving equipment of radio and television broadcasts, are permitted for the purpose of testing the functioning of the products at the manufacturing or selling moment, to reproduce and introduce extracts from works, under the condition that these operations be reduced to the dimensions required for testing. Moreover, in order to supervise the utilization of their own repertoire by third parties, the collective management bodies can monitor, by any means, the activity of the users, without authorization or payment. (Article 38).

As regards the assignment of the broadcasting right of a work to a radio or television broadcasting organization, said organization shall be entitled to record the work for the needs of its own broadcasts with a view to a single authorized broadcast to the public, with no remuneration; however, any new broadcast of the work so recorded shall require the author's authorization and remuneration and, where no such authorization is requested within six months as from the first broadcast, the recording must be destroyed.

§8. Duration of Protection

55. The Romanian legislator establishes the duration of copyright protection in Chapter 5 of the Law, guided by the fundamental principles of the present field: the property of the moral right and the limited duration of the patrimonial rights.[20]

According to Article 27, paragraph 1, the copyright on a literary, artistic or scientific work arises from the moment of the work's creation, regardless of the concrete form or manner of expression and, according to paragraph 2, if the work is created in a period of time, in parts, serials, volumes or in any other form of continuation, the protection term shall be calculated according to paragraph 1 for each one of these components.

The patrimonial rights of the author last for the lifetime of the author, and after his death, they are transmitted by inheritance, according to civil law, for a period of seventy years, whatever the date on which the work was legally brought to public knowledge. If there are no heirs, the exercise of these rights falls to the collective management body mandated during the author's lifetime or, in the absence of a mandate, to the collective management body with the largest number of members in the respective field of creation. The fees collected from the uses are added to the social and cultural fund of the collective management body that exercises these rights. (Article 28(1)).

20. Yolanda Eminescu, *supra*, 207.

The person who, after expiry of the copyright protection, makes legally known to the public for the first time a work unpublished before, shall benefit from a protection equivalent to that of the author's patrimonial rights and the duration of this protection shall be of twenty-five years, beginning after that moment (Article 28, paragraph 2).

Thereafter, the law establishes the terms of patrimonial rights on works as follows:

- For works made known to the public under a pen name or without indication of their author, the term shall be seventy years after the date when they were made publicly known. When the author's identity shall be made known to the public before the expiry of the term provided under paragraph 1 or the pseudonym adopted by the author leaves no doubt about his identity, the provisions under Article 31 paragraph 1 shall apply.
- For works made in collaboration, the term shall be seventy years after the death of the last co-author. In the event that the contributions of the co-authors are distinct, the term of the patrimonial rights for each one of them shall be seventy years after the death of each co-author. The term of protection of a musical composition with text shall expire seventy years after the death of the last survivor of the lyricist and composer, regardless of whether they were or not designated as co-authors, provided that the contribution of those musical compositions with text be created specifically for this purpose (Article 31.3).
- For collective works, the term shall be seventy years after the date when the works were made publicly known. If this is not made for a period of seventy years after the creation of the works, the term of patrimonial rights shall expire seventy years after the creation of the works (Article 28).
- For computer programs, the term shall extend over the whole duration of their author's life, and after his or her death, it shall be transmitted by inheritance according to the civil legislation over a period of seventy years (Article 32).

The established terms shall be calculated 'beginning on 1 January of the year after the author's death or the date when the work was made publicly known, as the case may be' (Article 34). As they are substantial terms, they end on 31 December of the last year of protection.

Finally, it is provided that in the case of non-essential modifications, additions, cuttings or adaptations made with a view to selection or arrangement as well as the correction of a work or collection's content, necessary for the continuation of the collection's activity in the way intended by the work's author, shall not extend the protection term of the said work or collection (Article 33).

§9. Related Rights

56. Title II of the Law concerns the related rights to the copyright and it has five chapters, as follows: common provisions, the rights of performers, the rights of the producers of sound recordings, as well as the rights of producers of audiovisual recordings, common provisions to authors, artists and producers of sound and audiovisual recordings and television and radio broadcasting organizations.

I. The Holders of Related Rights

57. The Romanian legislator defies the holders of the rights related to the copyrights in Article 94, according to which the following categories are recognized and protected as holders of the related rights: artists, performers, for their own interpretations or performances, producers of sound recordings and producers of audiovisual recordings, for their own recordings, broadcasting and television bodies, for their own broadcasts and services of programs, and publishers of press publications, for their own press publications.

58. The publisher of a press publication has the exclusive patrimonial right to authorize or prohibit the online use of his press publications by information society service providers through:

(a) direct or indirect, temporary or permanent reproduction, by any means and in any form, in whole or in part, as well as their permanent or temporary storage on devices of any nature and in any form;
(b) making it available to the public by wired or wireless means, via the Internet, other computer networks or by any other similar process, so that they can be accessed at any place and at any time individually chosen by the public.

59. The upper rights do not apply in the following cases:

(a) the use of press publications for private or non-commercial purposes by individual users;
(b) the introduction of links to internet pages, as well as in the case of reporting simple facts in press publications;
(c) the use of individual words or very short extracts, of a maximum of 120 characters, from a press publication, to the extent that they do not affect the effectiveness of the rights as provided or do not lead to the replacement of the press publication or to the determination of the public to no longer access the press publication.

60. These previously mentioned rights cannot be invoked:

(a) against authors or other rights holders whose works or other protected objects are incorporated in a press publication, their rights remaining intact, so that they can exploit their works and other protected objects independently of the press publication in which they are incorporated, subject to the law and the agreements between the parties;

(b) to prohibit use by other authorized users, when the right to incorporate a work or other protected object in a press publication was granted on the basis of a non-exclusive license;
(c) in the case of the use of works or other protected objects whose protection has expired. The upper provided rights expire after two years from 1 January of the year following the date on which the respective press publication was published. The authors of the works incorporated in a press publication have the right to a corresponding part of the revenues that the publishers of the press publications obtain as a result of the use of their press publications by the service providers of the information society, taking into account the principle of contractual freedom and that of a fair balance between the rights and interests of the parties. The payment of a lump sum may constitute an appropriate remuneration.

61. If where an author has transferred a right or granted a licence to a publisher of press publications, that transfer or licence constitutes the legal basis for the publisher to be entitled to part of the compensation for the use of works made under an exception to the right which is the subject of the transfer or licence or under a limitation of this right.

The related rights shall not impair or limit the copyrights (Article 93).

(a) Interpreting and performing artists.

The interpreting and performing artists are named by Article 95: actors, singers, musicians, dancers and other people presenting, singing, dancing, reciting, uttering with rhetorical effect, acting, interpreting, directing, conducting or executing in any other way a literary or artistic work, a performance of any kind, folklore performances inclusive, variety, circus or puppets.

The following moral rights shall be acknowledged for the above-mentioned artists (Article 96):

- the right to claim the acknowledgement of the paternity of his or her own interpretation, respectively execution;
- the right to claim that his or her name or pseudonym should be shown or communicated at each performance and at each of its recordings;
- the right to claim the observance of the quality of his or her renderings and to oppose any distortion, falsification or other substantial modification of his or her interpretation or execution or any infringement of his or her rights that might gravely impair his or her honour or reputation.

The above-mentioned moral rights may not form the object of some renunciation or alienation, and after the artist's death, their exercise shall be transmitted by inheritance, according to the civil legislation, for an unlimited period of time. After the death of the performing artist, the exercise of the moral rights as provided is transmitted by inheritance, according to civil legislation, for an unlimited period, and the exercise of the patrimonial rights is transmitted under the same conditions during the period of fifty years from the date of performance. If there are no heirs, the exercise of these rights rests with the collective management body that administered the rights of the performing artist or, as the case may be, the body with the largest number of members in the respective field. The fees collected from the uses are added to the social and cultural fund of the collective management body that exercises these rights.

Article 98 sets out the exclusive patrimonial right to authorize or prohibit:

- the fixation of his performance;
- the reproduction of the interpretation of the fixed performance;
- the distribution of the fixed performance;
- the rental of the fixed performance;
- the lending of the fixed performance;
- the import for trading on domestic market of the fixed performance;
- the broadcasting or communication to the public of his interpretation or performance, except in the case when the interpretation or performance has already been fixed or broadcasted;
- under the situations previously provided for in acts of broadcasting or communication to the public is entitled to an equitable remuneration only;
- the making available to the public his fixed performance in such a way that members of the public may access them from a place and at a time individually chosen by them;
- cable retransmission of the fixed performance;
- retransmission of the performance or fixed performance.

Fixing is defined as 'the embodiment of codes, sounds, images, or of sounds and images or of their numerical representations, on any kind of material carrier, even electronic, permitting their perception, reproduction, or communication in any way whatsoever'. The equitable remuneration *in respect of* the broadcasting and public communication of performances shall be established and collected in compliance with the provisions of the law.

According to Article 99, interpreting or executing artists participating actively in the same rendering, such as members of a musical group, a choir, an orchestra, a *corps de ballet* or a theatrical company, shall have to designate a representative from among themselves for granting the authorization provided under Article 98. The designation shall be made in writing, with the agreement of a majority of the group's members. The director, the conductor and the soloists shall be excepted from this designation.

The length of time for the mentioned patrimonial rights is settled by Article 102, and it shall be fifty years, beginning after the date of 1 January of the year following the fixation or performance.

However, the following exceptions are permitted by the law:

- if the fixation of the execution, other than on a phonogram, is the subject of a legal publication or a legal communication to the public during this term, the rights shall cease fifty years after the first publication or the first communication to the public, depending on which of these data is the first;

– in case the fixation of the execution on a phonogram is the subject of a legal publication or a legal communication to the public during this term, the rights shall cease seventy years after the first such.

If the interpreting or executing artist effects renderings within the framework of an individual contract of employment, the patrimonial rights provided under Article 98 may be transmitted to the employer on condition that the transmission of the right is expressly stipulated in the individual contract of employment (Article 100).

Failing a convention to the contrary, the interpreting or executing artist having participated in the realization of an audiovisual work, of an audiovisual recording or of a sound recording shall be presumed to cede to their producer the exclusive right to use the fixed performance by reproduction, distribution, import and lending, against an equitable remuneration.

62. (b) The producers of sound recordings. A sound recording or phonogram, according to Article 104, shall be taken to mean any fixation, exclusively of the sounds originating from the interpretation or the performance of a work or from other sounds or digital representations of such sounds other than under the form of a fixation incorporated in a cinematographic work or in any other audiovisual work.

The producer of sound recordings shall be 'the natural or juristic person assuming the responsibility of organizing and financing the realization of the first fixing of the sounds, whether this constitutes a work in the sense of the present law or not'.

The producers of sound recordings shall have the following rights:

– To inscribe on the material carriers of sound recordings, including on the covers, boxes and other material packing supports, in addition to the information with regard to the author and interpreting or performing artist, the titles of the works, the year of the first publication, the trademark as well as the name and denomination of the producer.

The patrimonial right to authorize or to prohibit:

– the reproduction by any means and in any form of his own sound recordings;
– the distribution of his own sound recordings;
– the rental of his own sound recordings;
– the lending of his own sound recordings;
– the import for trading on the domestic market of legally made copies of the work of his own sound recordings;
– the broadcasting and communication to the public of his own sound recordings, except those published for commercial purposes, in case of which he is entitled to an equitable remuneration;
– the making available to the public his own sound recordings in such a way that members of the public may access them from a place and at a time individually chosen by them;
– the cable retransmission of his own sound recordings;
– retransmission of his own sound recordings.

At the same time, he has the right to prevent copies of his own sound recordings from being imported without his consent.

The duration of the patrimonial rights of the producers of sound recordings shall be fifty years, beginning on 1 January of the year following the date in which the first fixing took place.

The term of protection of economic rights of performers shall be fifty years from the date of interpretation or execution, with the following exceptions:

(a) where a declaration of fixing, other than a phonogram, shall be subject to publication of a legal or lawful communication to the public within this period, the rights shall expire fifty years from the first publication or of the first communication to the public, whichever is the earliest of those dates;
(b) where fixation of the phonogram's execution is the subject of a legal publication or communication to the public for legal during this period, the rights shall expire seventy years after the first such publication or the first such communication to the public, whichever of them took place for the first time (Article 107).

In a special chapter introduced on the occasion of its amendment, the Romanian law provides regulations concerning the rights of the producers of audiovisual recordings.

The videogram or audiovisual recording has previously been defined as any fixation of an audiovisual work or of some sequences of moving images, accompanied or not by sound, irrespective of the method and medium used for said fixation, while the videogram producer has been defined as the natural person or legal entity having the initiative and undertaking the responsibility for the organization and financing of the first fixation of an audiovisual work or of some sequences of moving images, accompanied or not by sound, and in this quality provides the necessary technical and financial means (Article 108). In case of reproduction and distribution of his own videograms, the producer shall be entitled to specify on the physical medium the same data as the producer of sound recordings and shall have an exclusive economic right consisting of the same prerogatives as in case of the producer of sound recordings, for a similar duration. (Article 109).

The producer of an audiovisual recording has the exclusive patrimonial right to authorize or prohibit the following:

(a) reproduction by any means and in any form of his own audiovisual recordings;
(b) distribution of the original or copies of his audiovisual recordings;
(c) renting one's own audiovisual recordings;
(d) lending one's own audiovisual recordings;
(e) importing, with a view to commercialization on the domestic market, one's own audiovisual recordings;
(f) broadcasting and public communication of one's own audiovisual recordings;
(g) making one's own audiovisual recordings available to the public so that they can be accessed in any place and at any time chosen individually by the public;
(h) cable retransmission of own audiovisual recordings;
(i) retransmission of own audiovisual recordings (Article 110).

The duration of the patrimonial rights of producers of audiovisual recordings is fifty years from the date of the first fixation. However, if the registration during this period is the subject of a publication or a lawful public communication, the duration of the rights is fifty years from the date on which any of these took place for the first time.

The duration as provided is calculated starting from 1 January of the year following the event giving rise to rights (Article 111).

II. The Remuneration Owed to the Holders of Related Rights

63. (a) Remuneration in respect of the use of phonograms. The performing artists and producers of phonograms shall be entitled to an equitable remuneration only, in respect of the direct or indirect use of phonograms published for commercial purposes and of reproductions thereof by broadcasting or by other means of communication to the public, the amount of said remuneration being established by the methodology according to the legal procedure provided for under Articles 153 to 165. The beneficiary collective management bodies shall set out the distribution of the remuneration shares between the two categories of beneficiaries through a protocol; in the absence of such a protocol, the remuneration shall be equally distributed thereto.

The right of distribution shall be exhausted upon the first sale or upon the first transfer of ownership over the original or the copies of a sound or audiovisual recording on the domestic market by the right holder or with his consent.

Subsequent amendments to the law have introduced important provisions regarding termination of the contract under which a producer of phonograms licenses the rights to its execution and their remuneration (Article 103).

Where, fifty years after lawful publication of the phonogram or, in the absence of such publication, fifty years after its communication to the public of the phonogram, producer does not provide copies of the phonogram for sale in a sufficient quantity or does not make the phonogram available to the public, by wire or wireless means, in such a way that members of the public have access individually from place and time chosen by them, the performer may terminate the contract under which a producer of phonograms licensed the rights to fix its execution, further called contract of assignment.

The right of termination of the contract of assignment may be exercised provided that the producer, within one year from the date of notification by the artist to the performer of its intention to terminate the contract of assignment, does not carry out the two mentioned exploitation activities.

The right of termination may be the subject of a renunciation on the part of the performer.

Where phonogram performances of several artists performers are recorded, the contracts of assignment will be terminated in accordance with the applicable national legislation. If the contract of assignment shall terminate, the rights of the producer of phonograms shall cease.

Where the contract of assignment provides for the right of the performer to a single remuneration, he shall be entitled to receive from the producer of phonograms a supplementary annual remuneration for each full year immediately following the year of the fiftieth year since the publication of the phonogram or, in the absence of such publication, of the fiftieth year of its legal communication to the public.

The right to obtain an annual supplementary remuneration cannot be surrendered by the side of the performer.

The total amount which the producer of phonograms must allocate additional annual remuneration for payment referred to above corresponds to 20% of the revenue that the producer of phonograms has obtained in the course of the year preceding that for which the remuneration is paid from the reproduction, distribution and making available of phonograms concerned, after the fiftieth year since the publication of the phonogram or, in the absence of such publication, after the fiftieth year after its communication to the public.

Phonogram producers shall provide, upon request, to the performers who are entitled to the payment of additional remuneration on an annual basis, any information necessary to ensure the payment of such remuneration.

The right to obtain an annual supplementary remuneration is managed by collecting societies.

Where a performer has the right to a gradually paid remuneration, no advance payments nor reductions laid down in the contract shall not be deducted from payments made by the artist after the fiftieth year since the publication of the phonogram or, in the absence of such publication, after the fiftieth year after its legal communication to the public.

(b) Remuneration of the authors of sound or audiovisual recordings. According to Article 112, paragraph 1:

> the authors of works susceptible to being reproduced through sound or audiovisual recordings, on any kind of physical medium, as well as the ones of the works susceptible to being reproduced on paper, directly or indirectly, under the conditions provided for under Article 34 paragraph (1) shall be entitled, together with the publishers, producers and with the performers, as the case may be, to compensatory remuneration for the private copy, in accordance with Article 34 paragraph (2). The beneficiaries cannot waive the right to compensatory remuneration for the private copy.

Said remuneration shall be paid by the manufacturers and/or importers of physical media or devices, regardless of whether the process used is analogue or digital. They are bound to register themselves with the ORDA in the National Registry of Private Copy. The list of physical media and devices in respect of which the compensatory remuneration for private copy is due, as well as the amount of said remuneration, shall be negotiated every three years within a committee consisting of representatives of the collective management bodies and of the associative structures mandated by manufacturers and importers of physical media and devices. The so-negotiated remunerations shall be expressed as percentages and shall be calculated at the customs value for imports and at the invoiced value without *VAT* for those distributed by the producers and are due to be paid in the month following import or the invoice date. Under Article 107(8), the law provides for the following percentages: 1% for A4 paper sheets for photocopier, 3% for other physical media and 0.5% for devices. The compensatory remuneration for private copy shall be collected by a sole collector management body for the works reproduced after sound and audiovisual recordings and by another sole collector body for the works reproduced on paper, both of them needing the confirmation of the ORDA.

The compensatory remuneration for private copy shall be distributed to the beneficiaries under the provisions of Article 116(1) as follows:

- in the case of physical media and devices for sound recorded copies, by analogical proceeding, 40% from the remuneration shall be payable, in negotiable shares, to the authors and publishers of the recorded works, 30% shall be payable to performers, and the remaining 30% shall be payable to the producers of sound recordings;
- in the case of physical media and devices for audiovisual recorded copies, by analogical proceeding, the remuneration shall be divided in equal shares between the following categories: authors, performers and producers;
- in the case of copies registered by analogue process, on paper, the remuneration is divided equally between authors, editors and editors of press publications.
- in the case of copies registered by digital means, on any type of support, the remuneration is divided equally between authors and publishers, artists, performers, producers and publishers of press publications.

The compensatory remuneration for private copy shall not be paid in case of unrecorded audio, video or digital media manufactured within the country or imported and commercialized wholesale to the producers of audiovisual or sound recordings or to radio and television broadcasting organizations for their own broadcasts. Moreover, the compensatory remuneration shall not be paid for the import of media and devices made with no commercial purposes in the legally allowed personal luggage.

Where the author or performer has transferred or assigned his rental or lending right to a producer of phonograms or audiovisual recordings, he shall retain the right to an equitable remuneration. Owners who benefit from a compulsory remuneration, by the effect of the law, cannot object to the users who generate it.

III. The Television and Radio Broadcasting Bodies

64. According to the provisions of the law, these bodies have the following rights:

(a) an exclusive patrimonial right to authorize or to prohibit the following (Article 129):

- the fixing of their own broadcasts and services of radio or television programmes;
- the reproduction, in whole or in part, direct or indirect, temporary or permanent, by any means and under any form, of their own broadcasts and services of radio or television programmes fixed on any kind of physical medium, regardless of whether transmitted by wire or wireless, including by cable or satellite;
- the distribution of their own broadcasts and services of radio or television programmes fixed on any kind of physical medium;
- the import for trading on domestic market of their own broadcasts and services of radio or television programmes fixed on any kind of physical medium;
- the retransmission or re-emission of their own broadcasts and services of radio or television programmes by wireless means, by wire, by cable, by satellite or by any other similar proceeding, as well as by any other mode of communication to the public, including retransmission through Internet;
- the communication to the public of their own broadcasts and services of radio or television programmes in places accessible to the public, against payment of an admission charge;
- the rental of their own broadcasts and services of radio or television programmes, fixed on any kind of physical medium;
- the lending of their own broadcasts and services of radio or television programmes, fixed on any kind of physical medium;
- the making available to the public their own broadcasts and services of radio or television programmes, fixed on any kind of physical medium, regardless of whether emitted by wire or wireless, including by cable or satellite, so that members of the public may access them from a place and at a time individually chosen by them;
- retransmission of own broadcasting and television program services.

Re-emission means the simultaneous emission, by a broadcasting organization, of a programme of another broadcasting organization.

Radio and television organizations shall have the exclusive right to prevent copies of their own programmes made without their authorization from being imported (Article 131), except for imports made by a natural person, without commercial purposes, in the legally allowed personal luggage.

According to Article 132, the duration of the rights shall be fifty years, beginning on 1 January of the year and following that in which the first broadcast or transmission of the television or radio broadcasting body's programme had taken place.

The right of distribution of a radio or television broadcasting programme fixed on any kind of physical media is exhausted with the first sale or the first transfer of ownership over the original or copies thereof by the right owner or with his consent (Article 133).

The amendments brought in 2022 to Law 8/1996 introduced new and important provisions on retransmission rights (Articles 133^1 to 133^3). Thus:

> Acts of retransmission of programs carried out by rights holders other than broadcasting or television bodies must be authorized by the holders who hold the exclusive right of communication to the public.

Copyright holders of related rights can exercise their right to grant or refuse authorization for retransmission only through a collective management body.

If a rights holder has not transferred the management of the right to grant or refuse authorization for a retransmission to a collective management body, it is considered that the collective management body that manages rights in the same category for which the retransmission service operator wishes to obtain retransmission rights is entitled to grant or refuse the retransmission authorization for the respective rights holder.

In this situation, in the case of the existence of several collective management bodies that manage rights in that category, it is established, by decision of the director of the ORDA, based on the principle of representativeness, the collective management body that will have the right to grant or to refuse retransmission authorization.

A rights holder has the same rights and obligations arising from an agreement between the operator of a retransmission service and a collective management body as the rights holders who mandated the body or bodies of collective management that will have the right to grant or refuse retransmission authorization. The holder of rights may claim their respective rights within three years from the date of the retransmission that includes their work or other protected object (Article 134^1).

The provisions of Article 134^1 does not apply to the retransmission rights exercised by a broadcasting or television organization over its own transmissions, regardless of whether these rights belong to it or have been transferred to it by other rights holders.

If the broadcasting or television organizations and operators retransmission services begin negotiations regarding retransmission authorization, they have the obligation to conduct them in good faith. (Article 134^2).

Where a broadcasting or television organization transmits by direct input its programme-carrying signals to a signal distributor without the broadcasting or television organization itself simultaneously transmitting those programme-carrying signals directly to the public, and the signal distributor transmits the respective signals carrying programs to the public, it is considered that the broadcasting or television organization and the signal distributor participate in a single act of public communication for which they must obtain an authorization from the rights holders.

For the direct introduction, which constitutes a single act of public communication, authorization must be obtained from the rights holders by the broadcasting or television body for broadcasting and by the signal distributor for retransmission or cable retransmission, as the case may be.

IV. Public Communication by Satellite

65. This is regulated in Articles 135 to 137 of the Law and regards the television and radio broadcasting bodies having as object of activity the public communication of programmes by satellite. This communication shall be defined as 'the introduction, under the control and responsibility of a television and radio broadcasting body within Romanian territory, of programme bearing signals intended to be received by the public in an uninterrupted communication link leading to the satellite and returning to Earth' (Article 135, paragraph 2), and satellite is defined as any satellite operating on the reserved frequency bands, according to the legislation on telecommunications, for the broadcasting of the signal for the purpose of reception by the public or for the private individual communication.

If the signals-bearing programmes are circulated in an encoded form, their introduction into the communication link shall be considered public communication, if the decoding device of the broadcast is put at the public's disposal by the respective body with its consent.

If the body is situated outside Romania's territory or in a State which is not a member of the EU, the responsibility for public communication shall be ensured, according to Article 136, paragraph 2, as follows:

– if the signals are transmitted to the satellite through the agency of an ascensional linking station situated in Romania's territory or in a State which is not a member of the EU, the responsibility devolves upon the person exploiting the station; if no call is made on an ascensional linking station, but the communication to the public has been authorized by a body whose seat is in Romania or in a State which is not a member of the EU, the responsibility devolves upon the body having authorized it.

These bodies must observe the copyright and the related rights protected by law. In order to prevent infringements, it is stipulated that the holders of the copyright or of the related rights may transfer their rights to public communication via satellite only through a contract concluded individually or through the agency of a collective administration body (Article 137, paragraph 1).

The framework contract concluded between a collective administration body and a television or radio broadcasting body for the transmission of a class of works belonging to a certain field shall produce its effects also against the holders of rights who are not represented by the collective administration bodies, with the exception of the audiovisual works, 'if this communication to the public via satellite shall take place simultaneously with the terrestrial circulation effected by the same circulating body. This inference is removed if an individual or collective contract is concluded' (Article 137, paragraphs 2 and 3).

V. Retransmission by Cable

66. Under Article 138(1) of the Law, the holders of the copyright or the related rights may exercise their rights to authorize or prohibit the retransmission by cable on the ground of contracts concluded through the agency of a collective administration body, and if they shall not have entrusted the management of their rights to a collective administration body, the body managing the rights from the same class shall be considered de jure the manager of their rights, too. If there are several collective administration bodies in this field, the holder of rights may exercise an option among them. The claiming of rights by these holders may be made within a term of three years after the date of the retransmission by cable (Article 137, paragraph 4).

As regards the amount of the owed remuneration, the Law stipulates that is shall be established by a methodology negotiated between the copyright collective management bodies and the related rights collective management bodies and the associative structures of cable distributors, under the conditions provided for under Articles 163 and 164, excluding from calculation the programmes for which cable retransmission is legally binding (Article 138(2)).

In case the parties cannot establish methodologies by negotiation before the initiation of the arbitration procedure provided in the law, they may agree to address an optional mediation procedure. This mediation is carried out by one or more mediators chosen by the parties in such a way that their independence and impartiality cannot be called into question. The mediators have the task of assisting the negotiations and can notify a proposal to the parties. Within three months from the submission of the proposal by the mediators, the parties will notify the mediators and the ORDA to reject the proposal or accept it by signing the protocol on the methodologies. Notification of the proposal, as well as its acceptance or rejection, is made in accordance with the rules applicable to the notification of legal acts. Acceptance by all parties is presumed if neither party has notified rejection of the proposal within this time limit.

Provisions of Article 139 do not apply to the rights exercised by radio or television broadcasting organizations in respect of their own broadcasts and services of programmes, irrespective of whether the rights concerned are their own rights or have been assigned to them. For this case, contracts shall be concluded with cable distributors, except in cases in which cable retransmission is legally binding.

VI. Management and Protection of the Copyright and the Related Rights

67. Chapter 1 of Title III of the Law comprises provisions referring to the management of economic rights arising from copyright and related rights. The initial articles of the chapter contain common provisions.

The holders of the copyright and related rights may exercise their legal rights individually or based on a mandate by collective administration bodies. Collective management can be provided only for works that have already been disclosed to the public and for performances that have already been fixed or broadcast, as well as for phonograms and videograms previously disclosed to the public (Article 144(2)) and owners of copyright and related rights cannot assign their economic rights to collective management organizations (Article 144(3)).

The author or the owner of the copyright or related rights has the following rights which are mandatory included in the statute of the collective management bodies:

(a) to choose for which rights, categories of rights or types of works, other protected objects or territories they authorize, on the basis of a written mandate, a

collective management body for their management, regardless of the nationality, residence or place of establishment of the collective management body or the rights holder;
(b) to grant licences for the non-commercial uses of any rights, categories of rights or types of works and other protected objects;
(c) to revoke the management mandate or to withdraw the collective management body, at its choice, any rights, categories of rights, types of works or other protected objects, with a reasonable notice that must not exceed six months;
(d) to collect the remuneration due to him for the acts of exploitation that occurred before the revocation or restriction of the management mandate came into force;
(e) to be informed annually regarding the method of distribution to members of the remuneration collected from users, including the calculation methodology/formula used by the collective management body to calculate the remuneration due to the acts of exploitation that occurred before the entry into force of revocation or restriction of the management mandate (Article 144(4)).

Collective management bodies cannot restrict the exercise of the rights provided for in paragraph (4) by imposing the condition that the management of rights, categories of rights, types of works or other protected objects, which are subject to revocation or withdrawal, be entrusted to another collective management body.

In the event that it authorizes a collective management body, authors or rights holders give their consent, in written form, for each right, category of rights or type of works and other protected objects.

Authors or rights holders who are not members of a collective management body collective management, but which have a direct legal link with it by law, assignment, licence or through another type of contract than the mandate have the following rights:

(a) to communicate, including by electronic means, with the body of collective management in order to exercise the rights from the exploitation of which he is entitled to receive remuneration;
(b) to be informed about the works, types of works or other protected objects, the rights that he manages directly or through representation agreements and the territories covered;
(c) to receive a written, motivated response, within a maximum of thirty days, to the complaints made regarding the rights management authorization and their revocation or withdrawal, the collection, distribution and payment of remuneration, the methodology/formula of calculation used by the collective management body to calculate the remuneration, the deductions applied including in the case of online rights to musical works, according to the procedures established at the level of the collective management body (Article 144(7)).

68. The ORDA centralizes the information received from cultural heritage conservation institutions, collective management bodies or relevant public authorities and communicates them to the single online portal managed by the European Union Office for Intellectual Property, in accordance with the Regulation (EU) No. 386/

2012 of the European Parliament and of the Council of 19 April 2012, in a period that allows publication, at least six months before the works or other protected objects are distributed, publicly communicated or made available to the public in accordance with the license granted or on the basis of the exception or limitation provided in the law, as soon as they are available and when they are relevant, the following:

(a) information received from cultural heritage conservation institutions and collective management bodies for the purpose of identifying works or other protected objects located outside the commercial circuit;
(b) information about the rights of the holders;
(c) the information on the parts of the license contract, on the territories concerned and on the uses of the respective protected works or objects.

69. The collective management bodies take appropriate publicity measures, so that the rights holders are aware of the fact that the respective body has the possibility to grant licenses for works or other objects protected, as well as regarding the uses under the exception provided in the law and the rights of the holders. Those publicity measures must also cover other Member States or third countries if there is evidence that the awareness of right holders could be increased.

70. Parties facing difficulties related to the granting of a licence when seeking to conclude an agreement for the provision of audiovisual works through video-on-demand services may resort to mediation, carried out by one or more mediators chosen by the parties, in such a way that their independence and impartiality cannot be questioned. Mediators provide assistance to the parties in their negotiations and help the parties to reach an agreement, including by presenting proposals in this regard. Collective management is compulsory for the exercising of the following rights:

– right to compensatory remuneration for private copy;
– right to equitable remuneration for public lending;
– resale right;
– right to broadcast musical works;
– right to communication to the public of musical works;
– right to a single equitable remuneration recognized to performers and producers of phonograms for communication to the public and radio broadcasting of phonograms published for commercial purposes or of the reproductions thereof;
– right to retransmission;
– right to a fair compensation for orphan works.

The following rights are subject to extended collective management:

(a) the right of public communication of musical works;
(b) the right of public communication by satellite;
(c) the rights of reproduction, distribution, public communication or making available to the public works or other protected objects located outside the commercial circuit;

(d) the rights to reproduce and make available to the public the works belonging to the publishers of press publications.

The non-exclusive licence authorizations granted by the representative collective management body also apply to rights holders who have not granted a mandate or authorized the respective collective management body, subject to compliance with the following guarantees:

(a) the management body collective, on the basis of its mandates, is representative of the rights holders, the relevant category of works or other protected objects and the rights that are the subject of the licence for the territory of Romania;
(b) authors and rights holders who are members of the representative collective management body, as well as those who are not its members, enjoy equal treatment, especially in terms of licence conditions, access to information on the granting of licences and distribution remunerations;
(c) authors and rights holders who have not authorized the representative collective management body can exclude from authorization all or part of their protected works and objects through a notification sent to the collective management body, both before the license is concluded, as well as during its development;
(d) appropriate publicity measures are taken before the works or other protected objects are used under the licence, according to the provisions of paragraph (4). (Article 145(2)).

Within thirty days of receiving the notification as provided, the collective management body informs the users about the exclusion of the respective protected works and objects from the managed repertoire, issues new licences from which the respective protected works and objects are excluded, and updates the ongoing licences until the end of the thirty-day period. The exclusion does not affect the remuneration due to the authors and right holders for the uses made on the basis of the licences concluded by the collective management bodies prior to receiving the notification.

The publicity measures must be adequate and effective without the collective management bodies being obliged to inform each individual rights holder. Thirty days before the works or other protected objects are used under the licence, the collective management bodies post information on their website regarding the granting of the licence and the possibilities of the rights holders. In cases where the rights holders do not comply with the notification procedure or the collective management bodies do not comply with the publicity measures, the uses are validly made.

The licensing mechanism, as provided in the law, applies only to the rights subject to extended collective management and is used to protect the legitimate interests of rights holders and users. Besides the mandatory collective management, the law also provides, under Article 146, a form of optional collective management concerning the following categories of rights:

- right to reproduction of musical works on phonograms or videograms;
- right to communication to the public of the works, except the musical works and artistic performances in the audiovisual field;

- lending right, except the case provided for in Article 145 paragraph (1) letter (b);
- right to broadcasting of the works and artistic performances in the audiovisual field;
- online rights to musical works;
- right to equitable remuneration resulting from the assignment of the rental right provided for in Article 119 paragraph (1);
- suite right.

For the categories of rights referred to above, collective management organizations represent only the owners of rights who have mandated them and draw up methodologies within the limit of the managed repertoire or negotiate the licence agreements directly with the users. The collective management bodies will allow, at the request of the users, access by electronic means of remote transmission to the repertoire of works managed, among those used by the applicant, as well as to the list of copyright and related rights holders, Romanian and foreign, whom they represent. This collective management activity is under the supervision and control of the ORDA, which acts as guarantor of the application of the law.

The Law stipulates as well that the owners of copyright and related rights have the possibility to negotiate individually or by means of specialized agents (Article 148).

To this end, collective administration bodies are established. These are legal persons established by free association, having as their main object of activity the collection and distribution of the rights whose administration has been entrusted to them by the holders.

These bodies are subject to the regulations regarding non-profit associations and may acquire legal personality under the terms of the law for the management by categories of rights or categories of owners, with the advisory opinion of the ORDA. This Office can grant it, provided that the conditions stipulated under Article 151 are fulfilled, to the bodies having their seat in Romania, which:

- are going to be constituted or operate under legal provisions applicable on the entry into force of the present law;
- file with the ORDA a repertoire of works, performances, phonograms and videograms of their own members, managed by them, as well as the contracts concluded for the management of similar rights with foreign organizations;
- have adopted statutes that fulfil the conditions provided for in the present law;
- have the economic means of collective management and have the human and material means necessary for the management of the repertoire throughout the entire territory of the country;
- allow, as expressly provided in their own statute, access to any owner of copyright or related rights in the field for which they are set up and that want to entrust them a mandate.

The decision of the ORDA on the granting of the favourable advisory opinion to a collective administration body for exercising its rights shall be published in the Official Gazette of Romania (*Monitorul Oficial*).

The collective management bodies are bound to communicate to the public, by means of mass media, the following data, *according to Article 152*:

- categories of owners of rights that they represent;
- economic rights that they manage;
- categories of users and other categories of natural and legal persons that have payment obligations of compensatory remuneration for private copy towards owners of rights;
- normative acts on the grounds of which they operate and collect the remunerations due to owners of rights;
- modalities of collection and persons responsible for this activity on local and central level;
- working hours.

With regard to the statute of the collective management body, the essential elements are provided under Article 150, beginning with the identification elements (name, domain and object of activity), followed by the conditions under which the administration of the rights shall be achieved for their holders, on the basis of the equality of treatment principle, the rights and obligations of their members, the management bodies, the patrimony, the modalities of establishing and the attributions of the general manager, the rules governing the distribution of rights, the modality of establishing the methodologies, the means for verifying the economic and financial management, the means for determining the commission payable to the collective management organization.

The mandate of collective management of the patrimonial copyrights and related rights shall be given either directly by the holders of the copyrights or the related rights by written contracts, and each owner of rights that has entrusted a mandate to the collective management organization is entitled to own vote within the general meeting. Performers are entitled to one by an appointed representative (Article 158).

In the case of an owner which is not associated with any organization, where collective management is mandatory, the competence lies with the organization from the field having the greatest membership, the owner having the possibility to claim the amounts due to them within three years as from the date of notification.

The functioning of collective administration bodies is settled in detail and their obligations are stipulated under Article 162 as follows:

- to act in the interest of the members they represent and not to impose on them obligations that are not objectively necessary for the protection of their rights and interests or for the effective management of their rights;
- to grant to users non-exclusive authorizations, upon their request, made before the use of the protected repertoire, in exchange for a remuneration, by non-exclusive licence, in writing;
- to compile methodologies for their field of activity that include the economic rights payable that have to be negotiated with users for the payment of these rights in the case of works having a manner of exploitation that precludes individual authorization by the owners of the rights;

- to conclude, in the name of the owner of rights that have mandated them or based on conventions established with similar foreign organizations, general contracts with the organizers of shows, television and radio broadcasting organizations and distributors or services of programmes by cable with a view to the authorization of the use of their protected repertoire;
- to protect the interests of their members in relation to the management of their rights due as a result of the utilization of their own repertoire outside the territory of Romania by the conclusion of representation contracts with similar foreign organizations;
- to collect the sums owed by users and to distribute them among the owners of rights according to the provisions of their statutes;
- to ask the users or their intermediaries to provide, in written and electronic format, within 30 days of the request, the information and documents requested to determine the amount of remuneration, as well as information on the works used, stamped and signed by the legal representative;
- to ensure equal treatment to members, authors or rights holders whose rights they manage or of a representation agreement, especially regarding the management commission, the rules regarding the collection, distribution and payment of remunerations, as well as the conditions for granting licenses;
- to constantly update the databases containing the list of members and their repertoires;
- to ensure the access of their own members to the information on any aspect of activity of collecting the amounts owed by users and their repartition;
- to provide specialized assistance to owners of rights and to represent them within the legal procedures, within the limit of their object of activity;
- to ensure the transparency of the collective management activity in relation to public authorities having control duties and, through their mediation, to users;
- to engage in any other activity in accordance with the special mandate received from the owners of copyright or related rights within the limits of their object of activity.
- to present in the computer system they own current, correct and complete data and information in order to organize the records and to simplify the payment of royalties from copyright and related rights by users, as well as the distribution of the collected royalties. The existing information in the computer system of the collective management bodies is determined by the decision of the general director of the Romanian Copyright Office;
- to respond in writing, in the shortest possible time, to complaints, especially in terms of rights management, the revocation of the mandate or the withdrawal of rights, the conditions of membership, the collection of sums owed to authors or rights holders, their withholdings and distribution;
- to keep separately in its accounts the income derived from rights or derived from the investment of these rights, as well as any own assets that it could own them and any income that comes from these assets, from the management commissions or from other activities; to conclude contracts or representation agreements, by which they mandate another collective management body to manage the rights they represent.

- to issue tax invoices to users, which will be sent including through the national electronic invoice system RO e-Invoice to users.

The collective administration may not in any way restrain the patrimonial rights of the holders. Collective management bodies can request in negotiations, from the same category of users, either flat-rate remuneration or percentage remuneration established as a percentage of the income obtained by each user through the activity in which the repertoire is used or, in the absence of income, from the expenses incurred of use. For the broadcasting activity, the collective management bodies can request only percentage remunerations, differentiated by direct proportionality with the share of use by each user – television or radio broadcasting body of the collectively managed repertoire in this activity.

As a consequence of the amendments brought to the Law, the conditions of negotiation for elaborating the methodology by the collective management organizations, as well as rules to ensure the transparency of their activity, have been established.

Thus, the methodologies shall be negotiated by the collective management organizations with the representatives of the users within a time limit of a maximum of thirty days, taking into account the following main criteria:

- the category of owners of rights, members or non-members and the filed for which the negotiation is made;
- the category of users represented at negotiations by associative structures or the other users appointed to negotiate;
- the repertoire, confirmed by the ORDA, managed by the collective management organization, for its own members, as well as for members of other similar foreign organizations, on the basis of the representation contracts;
- the proportion of utilization of the repertoire managed by a collective management organization;
- the proportion of utilizations for which the user has complied with the payment obligations by direct contracts with owners of rights;
- the incomes obtained by users from the activity that uses the repertoire that is the object of negotiation;
- if no incomes exist, there will be used the European practice in the field;
- the European practice regarding the results of negotiations between users and collective management organizations.

The negotiated remunerations may be expressed as lump sums or as percentages, 'taking into account the European practice regarding the results of negotiations between users and collective management organizations' (Article 164(1)) letter g).

The parties' agreement regarding the negotiated methodologies is filed with the ORDA and published in the Official Gazette of Romania, the methodology thus published being opposable to all the users in the field, to importers and producers of physical media and devices in respect of which the compensatory remuneration for private copy is due.

If the parties cannot establish methodologies through negotiation, they may resort to mediation under the conditions set out by Article 165 of the Law.

The understanding of the parties regarding the negotiated methodologies is recorded in a protocol that is submitted to the ORDA. The protocol is published in the Official Gazette of Romania, Part I, at the expense of the entity that initiated the negotiation procedure, by decision of the general director of the ORDA, issued within ten days from the date of submission.

Disputes concerning a collective management body that grants multi-territorial licences for online rights to some musical works such as:

(a) disputes with an existing or potential online music service provider;
(b) disputes with one or more rights holders;
(c) disputes with another collective management body.
could be subject to mediation.

Within thirty days from the completion of the mediation procedure, the parties have the obligation to notify the ORDA of the result obtained in compliance with the rules applicable to the notification of legal documents.

If the parties have not agreed on the methodology through negotiation or mediation, they can apply within fifteen days from the expiration of the terms provided for in the law.

The final decision regarding the methodologies is communicated to the parties, the ORDA and is published in the Official Gazette of Romania, Part I, at the expense of the ORDA, by decision of the general director issued within five days from the date of submission. The methodologies published in this way are objectionable to all users in the area for which it was negotiated and no discounts can be granted for the payment of the remuneration due, other than those provided in the published methodologies.

The methodologies negotiated or established are not opposable to users who, on the date of initiation of the methodology negotiation procedure, are in the process of directly negotiating a licence contract or have already concluded these negotiations with the collective management bodies.

The methodologies established according to the provisions of the law are opposable to all users in the area for which it was negotiated and to all importers and manufacturers of supports and devices for which compensatory remuneration is due for private copying.

With a view to preventing authors from being affected by inflation, remunerations established in a lump sum can be annually modified, based on the inflation index, established at national level. (Article 167).

As far as the transparency of the collective management organizations is concerned, legal provisions have been made regarding the obligation thereof to publish, on their own web page, the statute, the list of the members of the central and local management bodies, the annual statement regarding the balance of the non-distributed amounts, the amounts collected by categories of users or payers, the withheld amounts, the cost of management and the amounts distributed by categories of owners, the annual report and information on general meeting. At the same time, any member is entitled to request information and documents on the amounts distributed to him in the last twelve months, the mode of computation of the rights and the applied withholding, and before the general meeting, any member is entitled to consult the documents to be analysed and subjected to approval, under confidentiality regime (Article 170(2)).

Finally, after the general meeting, the collective management organizations have the obligation to file with the ORDA the annual report, the annual report of the commissions, the modifications to the statute, the updated repertoire and the representation contracts with similar foreign organizations (Article 172).

The following collective management organizations are actually active in Romania:

- In the field of copyright:
  - *AOTO* – managing the rights of authors of works written in the theological, scientific and info-educational field.
  - *ARDAA* – managing the patrimonial rights of author of audiovisual works and videograms.
  - *COPYRO* – managing the rights of authors of written works.
  - *DACIN-SARA* – managing the rights of authors of cinematographic and other audiovisual works.
  - *OPERA SCRISA.RO* – managing the rights of authors of written works.
  - *PERGAM* – managing the rights of authors of scientific works.
  - *UCMR-ADA* – managing the rights of authors of musical works.
  - *VISARTA* – managing the rights of authors in the field of visual arts.
- In the field of related rights:
  - *ADPFR* – managing the rights of phonogram producers.
  - *ARAIEX* – managing the rights of the performers.
  - *CREDIDAM* – managing the rights of performers.
  - *SOPFIA* – managing the copyright and related rights of the producers of cinematographic and other audiovisual works.
  - *UNART* – managing the related rights of the performers.
  - *UPFAR-ARGOA* – managing the rights of producers of cinematographic and other audiovisual works.
  - *UPFR* – managing the rights of phonogram producers.
  - *UPVR* – managing the related patrimonial rights belonging to the producers of videograms.

71. Organization and Operation of the ORDA: The ORDA was established as the sole regulatory authority in the field of intellectual property, the bodies and duties of which are set out under Chapter 2 of Title III.

In compliance with Article 180, the ORDA operates as a 'specialized body under the subordination of the Government, being the sole regulatory authority, registration by national registries, supervision, authorization, arbitration and technical-scientific establishment in the field of the copyright and related rights'.

In the exercise of its competences, the ORDA has the following duties:

- to regulate the activity in this field, by decisions of the general director, according to law;
- to draw up drafts of enactments in its field of activity;
- to keep a record of all the repertoires submitted by the collective management organizations;
- to organize and manage, against payment, the registration with the National Registries and with the other specific national records provided by law;
- to issue against payment holographic sticks usable according to the provisions of the law in the field of the copyright and related rights, at the value of the purchase price to which a 30% administration fee is added;
- endorses the establishment and supervises the operation of the collective management organizations;
- endorses, as a specialized body of the central public administration, according to law, the registration with the Registry existing at the court clerk's office of the court of law, of the associations and foundations established in the copyright and related rights field, including as regards the associations fighting against pirated goods;
- controls the operation of the collective management organizations and establishes the measures of abiding by the law or applies sanctions, as the case may be;
- ensures the secretarial work of the arbitration procedures are carried out according to law;
- performs technical and scientific ascertains with reference to the original character of the products bearing copyright or related rights, at the request of the criminal investigation bodies and at the expense of defendants, if their guilt is proved;
- performs, upon request and against payment, investigations at the expense of the interested parties;
- carries out information activities on the legislation in the field, at its own expense, as well as training activities at the expense of those interested;
- performs representation activities in relation to similar specialized organizations and international organizations in the field to which the Romanian state is a party;
- keeps the records of the entities authorized to carry out the special activities for persons with disabilities – *see* §7 – and provides both the European Commission and the access point to information established by the International Bureau of the WIPO the name and contact details of the authorized entities, as well as any other data collected following their voluntary communication, by the authorized entities;
- consults the rights holders, collective management bodies and cultural heritage conservation institutions in each sector before establishing specific requirements and encourages regular dialogue between representative organizations of users and right holders, including collective management bodies and other relevant stakeholder organizations, for each sector, with the aim of improving the relevance and use of established licensing mechanisms and to ensure the effectiveness of guarantees for rights holders;

- informs the European Commission about the scope of non-exclusive licences granted in conformity with the law, the purpose and types of licences that can be introduced under those provisions, the contact details of the bodies that issue licences in accordance with that licensing mechanism and the means by which information can be obtained about the granting of licences and about the rights of holders';
- notifies the European Commission of the mediators, including, if available, the source where the relevant information about the chosen mediators can be found;
- provides the European Commission, in a timely manner, with relevant and useful information regarding the field managed by it;
- fulfils any other duties provided by law.

§10. Infringement and Remedies

72. Measures of Protection, Proceedings and Sanctions. The Law sets out the right of the author of a work, performer, producer of phonograms or audiovisual recordings, radio or television broadcasting organization or the maker of database to institute technological measures of protection of the rights recognized by the law by using technologies and devices meant to prevent or restrict the acts which are not authorized by the owner of the rights through application of an access control or protection process, such as encryption, coding or scrambling (Article 185). Technical measures, within the meaning of the law, means the use of any technology, device or component that, within its normal functioning, is intended to prevent or limit acts that are not authorized by the holders of the rights recognized by this law.

As an exception, the owners of rights that have instituted technical measures of protection have the obligation to make the necessary means for access available to the beneficiaries of the exceptions legally provided. At the same time, they have the right to limit the number of copies made under the above conditions. These provisions do not apply in the case of protected works, made available to the public, according to the contractual terms agreed between the parties, so that anyone in the public can have access to them at any place and at any time, individually chosen.

The owners of the rights may provide, in electronic format, associated with a work or any subject matter of protection, or in the context of their communication to the public, information on the rights for the identification of the work, of the author or of other owners of rights, as well as the conditions and terms of use of the work.

According to Article 187 of the Romanian Copyright Law, violation of acknowledged and guaranteed rights under the law shall involve civil, contraventional or criminal responsibility, as the case may be. The procedural provisions provided under the present law shall be completed with those of the Common Law.

Holders of violated rights may address the courts or other competent bodies, as the case may be, for the acknowledgement of their rights, the finding of their violation and lay claim to redress of the prejudice. Also, in case of violation of rights acknowledged and protected under the law, their holders may solicit the taking of measures to prevent the production of imminent damages or to ensure their redress.

In Article 188, the Romanian Copyright Law clears up important aspects in this field:

- within a lawsuit, the law court is entitled to demand the supplying of information about the origin and distribution networks of the goods or services prejudicing a right provided for by the law either from the offender or from any other person that was holding or commercialized pirated goods, was using, for commercial purposes, services through which the rights protected by the law were infringed, was supplying, for commercial purposes, goods or services used in activities through which the rights protected by the law were infringed or was indicated as being involved in the production, distribution or rental of the pirate goods or of the pirate access control devices or in the supplying of the products or services through which rights protected by the law were infringed. Such information includes data for the identification of the producers, manufacturers, distributors, suppliers and holders of the goods, devices or services, transporters, wholesalers and retail sellers included, as well as data regarding the quantities produced, delivered, transported or ordered, as well as the price obtained for the respective goods and services;
- lawsuit may be initiated by the management organizations, by the associations fighting against piracy or by the persons authorized to use the rights protected by law, according to the mandate given for this purpose. When the owner has started an action, the persons authorized to use the rights can intervene in the lawsuit, claiming the remedy of the prejudice caused to them;
- the court shall establish the damages while taking into account criteria such as the negative economic consequences, particularly the non-earned benefit, the benefits earned unlawfully by the offender and the moral damages caused to the owner of the right; when such criteria cannot be applied, the court shall grant damages representing the triple of the amounts that would have been lawfully owed for the type of utilization that made the object of the illicit deed;
- when suspicions exist in connection with the infringement of rights protected by the law, the law court may order, upon request by the entitled persons, measures to be taken to prevent the imminent occurrence of damage through the violation of a right, such as forbidding, provisionally, the continuation of the violations brought to the protected right or conditioning their continuation by some guarantees aimed at ensuring the indemnification of the applicant, ensuring measures to be taken on the movable and immovable assets of the person presumed to have infringed the rights, including the blocking of his/her bank accounts and other assets, as well as the taking or handing over to the competent authorities of the goods in connection with which suspicions exist on the violation of a right provided for by the law;
- the right owners or their representatives may request to the law court, even before introducing the action on the merits of the case, to take some measures for ensuring the evidences or finding out the state of fact, where a risk for the infringement of the rights provided by the law exists and if a risk for the destruction of the elements of evidence exists;

- the above-mentioned measures can be ordered by the law courts without summoning the opposite party in the cases in which this shall be necessary, especially when any delay may cause an irreparable prejudice or when there is the provable risk for destruction of the elements of evidence. The opposite party shall be immediately informed, at the latest after the enforcement of the measures;
- the measures for ensuring the evidences or establishing a state of fact ordered by the court shall be fulfilled by an officer of the court, while the owners of the infringed rights shall be entitled to participate in the enforcement of the measures.

I. Special Measures

73. The holders of the violated rights may solicit the court to rule out, according to Article 188, paragraph 10, any of the following special measures:

(a) the remittance of the takings realized by the illicit act;
(b) the destruction of the equipment and means in the property of the offender, whose unique or principal purpose was to produce the illicit act;
(c) the removal from the commercial circuit by confiscation and destruction of the unlawfully affected copies;
(d) the dissemination of information referring to the court's decision, including the posting of the decision as well as the integral or partial publication of it in the mass media at the expense of the offender; under the same conditions, the courts may order additional publicity measures adapted to the particular circumstances of the case, including an extensive publicity.

Such measures shall be enforced at the expense of the offender and the court shall observe the principle of proportionality with the seriousness of the infringement of the protected rights. In order to ensure a licit behaviour, the Government of Romania, through the agency of the ORDA, supports the preparation, by the professional associations and organizations, of the ethics codes at the Community standards.

II. Contraventional Liability

74. Pursuant to Article 190:

> It shall be a contravention and punishable with a fine from RON 3,000 to RON 30,000 the following deeds:
>
> (a) infringement of the provisions of Article 21 (resale right);
> (b) infringement of the provisions of Articles 89 and 90 (protection of the portrait and of the correspondence);
> (c) infringement of the provisions of Article 11407 paragraph (3) (obligation of importers and manufacturers of physical media and devices to obtain the registration certificate);

(d) non-observance by the users of the provisions of Article 149 paragraph (4) or (8) (communication of information to the collective management organizations);
(e) non-observance of the provisions of Article 162 lit. b), e), g), i), k), l), p) and q) (certain rights and obligations of the collective management organizations) and of Article 172 paragraph (1) (papers to be filed with the Romania Copyright Office by the collective management organizations);
(f) fixation, without the authorization or consent of the owner of the right acknowledged by the present law, of the performances or of the radio or television broadcasts;
(g) public communication, without the authorization or consent of the rights holders, of the works or products bearing related rights;
(h) non-observance of the provisions of Article 35^2 paragraph (2) ((right to obtain, from an authorized entity which has its headquarters in Romania, a copy in accessible format of a work or other protected object, if it is available) and, by the users, the provisions of Article 162 lit. f) (information and documents required to determine the amount of remuneration).

It shall also be a contravention and punishable with a fine from RON 10,000 to RON 50,000 and the seizure of the pirated goods or of the pirated devices of control of the access of the deed of the legal or natural persons authorized for permitting the access in the spaces, to the equipment, means of transport, goods or own services, with a view to committing, by another person of a contravention or offence provided for by the law. Where the same deed is committed repeatedly, the complementary sanction of closing the unit shall also be ordered.

Contravention sanctions shall also apply to legal persons. Should the contravener be a legal person carrying out activities that involve communication to the public of works, the limits of the contravention fines are increased twice.

Contraventions are established and are applied by police officers with competence in the field.

III. Criminal Responsibility

75. According to Article 193:

(a) it shall be an offence and punishable with imprisonment for six months to three years or with a fine the following deeds;
(b) making of pirate goods for the purpose of the distribution, without aiming at, directly or indirectly, a material benefit, with any means and in any modality; placing of the pirate goods under a final import or export customs regime, under a suspensive customs regime or in free zones;
(c) any other modality of introducing the pirate goods on the domestic market.

- It shall be an offence and punishable with imprisonment from six months to three years or with a fine for the offering, the distribution, possession, or storage and transportation for the purpose of distribution of pirate goods, as well as the possession of them for the purpose of utilization through the communication to the public at the working locations of the legal persons.
- In the case in which the deeds provided above are committed for commercial purpose, these are sanctioned with imprisonment from two to seven years.
- The rental or offering for rental of pirate goods is sanctioned with same term of imprisonment.
- It shall be an offence and punishable with imprisonment from three months to two years or fine for the promotion of pirate goods through any means and in any modality, including the utilization of public announcements or electronic means of communication or through the exhibiting or presentation to the public of the lists or catalogues of products.
- For the purposes of this Law, pirate goods shall mean: all the copies, regardless of the physical medium, including the sleeves, made without the consent of the owner of rights or of the duly authorized person by him and that are executed directly or indirectly, in whole or in part, from a product involving copyright or related rights or from the packages or their sleeves.
- For the purposes of the present law, commercial purpose means aiming at obtaining, directly or indirectly, an economic or material benefit.
- The commercial purpose is presumed if the pirate merchandise is identified at the premises, at the work points, in their annexes or in the means of transport used by the economic operators whose activity object is the reproduction, distribution, rental, storage or transport of rights-bearing products, copyright or related rights.

In compliance with Article 194, 'it shall be an offence and punishable with imprisonment for one to four years or with a fine, the making available to the public, including through the Internet or other computer networks, without the consent of the owners of rights, of products involving copyrights, related rights or sui generis rights of the makers of databases or copies thereof, regardless the physical medium, so that the public may access them from any place and at any time individually chosen by them'.

Moreover, under Article 195, it is deemed to be an offence and punishable with imprisonment for one to four years or with a fine, the unauthorized reproduction on computer systems of computer programs in any of the following modalities: installation, storing, running or execution, display or transmission in the domestic network.

Article 196 stipulates that:

> It shall be an offence and punishable with imprisonment for one month to 2 years or with a fine, the following deeds committed without the authorization or consent of the owners of rights acknowledged by this law
>
> (a) reproduction of works or products involving related rights;
> (b) distribution, rental or import, on domestic market, of copies of works or products involving related rights, others than the pirate goods;

(c) communication to the public of the works or products involving related rights; broadcasting of works or products involving related rights;
(d) cable retransmission of the works or products involving related rights; making of derivative works;
(e) fixation for commercial purpose of performances or radio or television broadcasts;

For the purposes of the law, by-products bearing related rights are meant for fixed performances, phonograms, videograms or their own broadcasts or services, as well as programmes of radio and television broadcasting organizations.

Article 197 sets out that 'it shall be an offence and punishable with imprisonment for three months to five years or a fine the act of a person who improperly to assume the authorship of a work or to disclose a work to the public under a name other than the one decided upon by the author'.

Under Article 198:

> it shall be an offence and punishable with imprisonment for six months to three years or a fine, the production, import, distribution, possession, installing, maintaining or replacing illicitly the devices for the control of the access, either original or pirate ones, used for the services of programs with conditioned access.

- The deed of a person who unlawfully connects to or unlawfully connects another person to the programs with conditioned access shall be an offence and it is punishable with imprisonment for three months to two years or with a fine.
- Utilization of the public announcements or of electronic communication means for the purpose of promoting the pirate devices for the control of the access to the services of programs with conditioned access, as well as the exhibiting or presentation to the public in any mode, unlawfully of the information needed for making devices of any sort, capable to ensure the unauthorized access to the said services of programs with conditioned access, or intended for the unauthorized access in any mode to such services, shall be offences and punishable with imprisonment for one month to one year or a fine.
- Sale or rental of the pirate devices for the control of the access is punishable with imprisonment for one year to five years.
- For the purposes of the present law, pirate devices for the control of the access means any device of whose making has not been authorized by the owner of rights acknowledged by the present law in relation to a certain service of television programs with conditioned access, made to facilitate the access to that service.

Article 199 stipulates that:

> It shall be an offence and punishable with imprisonment for six months to three years or with a fine the deed of a person that, unlawfully, produces, imports, distributes or rents, offers, in any way, for sale or rent, or possesses for commercial purposes, devices or components that allow the neutralization of the technological measures of protection or performs services which lead to the neutralization of some technological measures for protection, including in the digital environment. It shall be an offence and punishable with imprisonment for six months to three years or with a fine, the deed of a person who unlawfully removes, for commercial purposes, from the works or other protected products or modifies on them, any information under electronic form, on the applicable regime of copyright or of related rights.

The Law provides, as well, for a non-punishment case concerning a person who, before the institution of the criminal proceedings, denounces to the competent authorities its participation in an association or agreement with a view to committing one of the offences legally provided, thus allowing for the identification and criminal accountability of the other participants, while where the denouncement is made during the criminal proceedings, the person shall benefit by the reduction by half of the limits of the punishment.

IV. Civil Responsibility

76. The injured party may require damages within the framework of the criminal trial or may separately bring a civil action for damages. In the case of civil action within the framework of the criminal trial, the criminal investigation bodies and the courts are under the obligation to establish the extent of the damage.

Civil responsibility is provided by the provisions of Articles 1349, 1359 and 999 of the Civil Code, which stipulate that the person who causes damage to another, wilfully or due to negligence, is obliged to indemnify him or her. The plaintiff must prove the infringement, the damages, the causal relation between them and the guilt of the defendant.

§11. Overlap and Relationship with Other Intellectual Property Laws

77. The relationship between intellectual property rights and industrial property rights is examined under the exposition of the second-mentioned rights.

The essential idea is that, according to Article 2 of the Law, the acknowledgement of the rights stipulated under Law No. 8/1996 does not exclude the protection granted by other legal provisions.

Of a particular relevance is relationship with patents, trademarks and designs which is detailed further.

I. Relationship with Patent Protection

78. Most extensive relationship with patent protection refers to computer programs that are protected 'as such' for their expression under copyright law and protected, as the case may be, as a technical solution to a technical problem under patent law. This problem will be largely treated under Chapters 2 and 9 and is not extended here.

Main idea necessary, however, to be underlined here is that under Romanian practice in the field, fully aligned with European one, this relationship is rather treated as a synergic and complementary one than an overlap and/or competition.

II. Relationship with Trademarks

79. This relationship derives directly from the legal provision in Trademark Law No. 84/1998 as republished (*see* Chapter 4), which stipulates among reasons to refuse registration of a sign if 'there is a previous right, … , in particular a right to a name, a right to an image, a copyright, a right of industrial property'.

In practical terms of trademark protection, this provision should be, however, carefully implemented, usually being needed the proof of a certain connection between invoked copyright and nature of the products and/or services involved.

III. Relationship with Designs

80. In a manner very similar to that for trademarks, Designs Law No. 129/92, as republished (*see* Chapter 6), provides that 'The application for registration of a design will be rejected or the registration will be canceled if … incorporates, without the consent of the holder, a work protected by Law No. 8/1996 regarding copyright and related rights, as subsequently amended and supplemented, or any other protected industrial property right.'

Some of the most encountered potential conflictual situations are with reference to works of sculpture, works of architecture, titles of books, and similar.

IV. Remarks

81. From the viewpoint of its structure and substance, the Romanian law on copyright and related rights has been appreciated as a modern law[21] which exhibits, however, some deficiencies identified by the highly reputed author:

- The competence of the ORDA is considered to be excessive because.
- Moral rights are upheld as absolute, although objections should be made as to the diversity and limits of protection.

21. A. Dietz, *supra*, 20 ff.

- Provisions relating to economic rights refer to 'exhaustion on the domestic market' without reference to the European internal market and the provisions concerning exhaustion of rights at the Community level, import rights included.
- Provisions relating to the term of protection should be improved to refer to each category of works.
- In the field of the exercise of rights, Article 5(5) of the Information Society Directive should be wholly transposed.
- The assignment *uno actu* of the economic rights is not expressly regulated.
- Voluntary management of the rights of authors and performers should be provided more clearly by the law.
- The collective management of rights is likely to lead to bureaucratization as a consequence of regulatory excess.
- Articles 6 and 7 of the Information Society Directive have been synthetically transposed, lacking the provisions of Article 34 (private copy in subsequent reprographic forms).

Chapter 2. Patents

§1. Sources: Legislation

I. National Sources

82. Based on an important historical tradition, patent protection in Romania is currently regulated by Law 64/91 on Patents for Inventions, as republished in the Official Gazette of Romania, Part I, No. 541/8 August 2007, and by Government Decision No. 547 concerning the Regulations for Implementing the Patent Law as republished in the Official Gazette of Romania, Part I, No. 456/18 June 2008.

This tradition began on 17 December 1905, when the Chamber of Deputies adopted the first Law on the Patents for Inventions, which was promulgated on 13 January 1906 by Royal Decree No. 102.

This is in fact the birthday of the Romanian Office for Industrial Property, which, in spite of the fact that during the years it had dynamic organizations and affiliations,[22] has been constituted in the actual institutional body.

The Patent Law from 1906 provided the granting of patents for inventions without a substantive examination for a fifteen-year period. The transition to the substantive examination, but only for those inventions which were assigned to the State, has been made on the basis of the Decision of the Council of Ministers No. 943 from 7 September 1950 and by Decree No. 884 from 30 September 1967, a compulsory substantive examination has been instituted for all patent applications.

Finally, Patent Law No. 62/1974 had, for about a quarter of a century and in spite of many elements specific to the communist regime of limitation up to cancellation of exclusive rights conferred by a patent, nevertheless, the merit of a consolidation of the principles specific to substantive examination.

Although present legislation made substantive changes compared with the initial form from 1991, which will be the basis of our presentation, it is obvious that the year 1991 has represented the starting point of modern patent law, adequate to the principles of a market economy and which made possible actual European integration.

Of particular importance to the system of patent protection in Romania, especially with regard to the joining to the EPC, from the 1 March 2003, was Law No. 32/1996 on the Approval of Government Ordinance No. 32/1996 for Ratification of the Agreement between the Government of Romania and the European Patent Organization, signed at Bucharest on 9 September 1994. Generically designated as an 'Extension Agreement', this agreement established the conditions in which the European patent applications and European patents having Romania as 'designated country' could be validated in Romania.

In fact, this law enabled full preparation for the accession to the EPC adopted in Munich on 5 October 1973, as well as to the Act of its revision adopted in Munich on 29 November 2000, to which Romania acceded by the Law No. 611/2002 as published in the Official Gazette of Romania No. 844/22 November 2002.

---

22. Gheorghe Bucsa, 'La protection des inventions en Roumanie', *Revue de droit intellectuel L'ingenieurconseil* (mars-avril, Bruxelles, Belgique, 1991): 176–184.

Accession could not be enacted if the whole patent protection law of Romania was not already, at that time, fully compatible with the EPC and its procedures.

Finally, by acceding to the EU as of 1 January 2007, Romania enforces de jure all the *acquis communautaire* in the field of Intellectual Property and in particular that for patents.

The Patent Law was revised in 2014 as a direct consequence of the new 'Law No. 83/2014 on employee's inventions', which will be discussed later on, and which substantially changed the landscape of employee's inventions, previously regulated under the Patent Law.

The fee regime for the whole procedure of obtaining and maintaining in force of the patents is provided in 'The Government Ordinance No. 41/1998 on Fees in the Field of Industrial Property and their Legal Regime', as republished *in the Official Gazette of Romania, Part I, 959/29 November 2006.*

Finally, it should be noted that legislative measures regarding the enforcement of the patents rights are provided in the Governmental Ordinance No. 100, as published in the Official Gazette of Romania No. 643/20 July 2005, regarding the enforcement of Industrial Property in Romania and which fully implements into national legislation of industrial property the famous Enforcement Directive No. 2004/48/EC.

II. International Sources

83. The main international source was and remains 'The Paris Convention for the Industrial Property Protection' as ratified by Decree No. 1177/1968.

The whole legislation in the patent field was drafted after 1990, aiming at a large harmonization with international treaties and conventions in that field and particularly with the EPC. In this respect, of particular significance is the preamble to the 'Extension Agreement' which specifies that 'the Romanian Patent Law provides for a level of protection similar to that existing in the Member States of the European Patent Organization'.

Although all these aspects will be subsequently analysed again in a more detailed manner, we would like to mention that the international evolution in the field of patent protection, after entering into force of national legislation, made its amendment necessary. The following are particularly taken into account:

- The Trade-Related Aspects of Intellectual Property (TRIPS) Agreement as ratified by Law No. 133/1994.
- The European Directive No. 98/84 in the field of biotechnological inventions.
- The EPC as revised at the Munich Diplomatic Conference of November 2000.
- The European Regulations Nos 1768/92 and 1610/96 on the supplementary protection certificate for pharmaceuticals and plant protection products.
- The Patent Law Treaty-PLT, as ratified by Law No. 537/2004.
- Budapest Treaty on the International Recognition of the Deposit of Microorganisms for the Purposes of Patent Procedure, as ratified by Law No. 75/1999.

It is to be underlined that everywhere within Chapter 2, where it is not otherwise mentioned, the following abbreviations of the terms will be used:

- law – Law No. 64/91 on the Patents for Inventions, as republished in 2014;
- regulations – Regulations for Implementing the Patent Law, given by the Governmental Decision No. 547/2008;
- office – State Office for Inventions and Trademarks (OSIM);
- article – article of the law;
- rule – article of the regulation;
- BOPI – Official Bulletin of Industrial Property – Section Inventions.

§2. Patentable Subject Matter

84. Inventions represent the most evaluated forms, of a technical nature, of human creations and the category of patentable inventions is from both legal and technical and scientific point of view, a subject matter of a particular complexity, having in mind that the category includes those inventions for which the State, according to the national legislation, can grant an exploitation monopoly.

Romanian Law does not explicitly give a concrete definition of the patentable invention, but starting from the general provision of Article 6 that 'a patent shall be granted for any invention having as a subject matter a product or a process, in all technological fields provided that it is new, involves an inventive step and is susceptible of industrial application'. According to international practice, it has a 'negative definition' of the patentable inventions category.

This type of definition presents in a detailed manner a list of subject matter which are either not considered patentable inventions or are excluded from patentability for definite reasons which will be presented later. The whole discussion on patentability should be carried on in conjunction with the definition of the patentability criteria in which the 'potentially patentable' inventions are to satisfy the conditions of novelty, inventive step, and applicability in order that a patent be granted by the Office.

According to Article 7 of the Law 'the following in particular shall not be considered as inventions within the meaning of Article 6 (e.g., patentable): discoveries, scientific theories and mathematical methods, aesthetic creations; schemes, rules and methods for performing mental acts, playing games or doing business, as well as computer programs' fully harmonized with the EPC, the article stipulates further on that 'the provisions of paragraph 1 shall exclude the patentability of the subject matters or activities referred to therein, only to the extent to which the patent application or patent relates to such subject matter or activities as such'.

In fact, the listed subject matters or activities regarded 'as such' have no technical character and contrary to that, those which are not related to solutions 'as such' have a technical character enabling them to be potentially patentable.

According to the Romanian Patent Law and practice, the technical character of an invention may be given if the invention refers to a technical field, or to a technical problem or presents at least essential technical features defining in the claims the subject matter for which protection is requested.

Some examples are relevant. The discovery per se of a substance or of an object existing freely in the nature or the mere discovery of a new feature of a known material, a scientific theory per se, as well as a theory explaining or substantiating practices previously carried out empirically, a mathematical method which is considered to be a particular case of the methods for exercising mental activities, are not patentable. At the same time, apparatuses, devices or processes which can be used in order to put into evidence or to exploit an industrial manner are activities which are technical in nature and thus patentable.

An aesthetic creation refers, by definition, to a product which does not present technical features and the aesthetic effect per se is not patentable either as a product or as a process. However, the technical means, products or processes for obtaining an aesthetic effect are patentable.

Presentation of information per se, characterized only by the content thereof, is not patentable, but the information carrier or the process for transmitting the information may be patentable.

The same applies to computer programs which are considered per se and shall not be considered patentable inventions. However, the inventions whose carrying involve the use of a computer, a computer network, or other programmable apparatus, in which at first sight one or more characteristics of the claimed invention is carried out wholly or in part by means of one or more computer programs, are patentable.

Where a computer program that is the subject matter of the invention runs or is loaded on a computer, it determines or is capable of determining a subsequent technical effect which is more than mere normal physical interaction between the program and the computer on which it is executed; the invention is patentable.

As mentioned, in the 'negative list' should also be mentioned the so-called inventions excluded from patentability; in other words, those inventions which, in spite of the fact that they are patentable inventions and could eventually meet the conditions of patentability, a patent shall not be granted for relevant reasons of ethical and/or moral and/or public order reasons.

Article 8 of the law provides in this respect that:

(a) patents shall not be granted under this Law in respect of: inventions the exploitation of which would be contrary to public order or morality, including inventions harmful to the health or life of persons, animals or plants and which are likely to seriously harm the environment, provided that such exception from patentability shall not depend merely on the fact that exploitation is prohibited by a legal provision;
(b) plant varieties and animal breeds, as well as the essentially biological processes for the production of plants or animals. This provision does not apply to microbiological processes or products obtained thereby; in the application of this provision, the plant varieties and animal breeds shall not be granted patents even if the plant varieties and animal breeds are obtained by means of microbiological processes;
(c) the inventions having as a subject matter the human body in its various stages of formation and development, as well as the mere discovery of one of its elements, including the sequence or partial sequence of a gene;

(d) methods of treatment concerning the human or animal body, by surgery or therapy and methods of diagnosis applied to human or animal body.

The provisions shall not apply to products, particularly substances or compositions to be used in any such method.

For inventions in the field of biotechnology, the extremely important tests of 'morality and public order' are satisfied or, in other words, are patentable if, according to Article 6:

- they relate to: biological material which is isolated from its natural environment or produced by any technical process, even if it previously occurred in nature;
- plants or animals, if the technical feasibility of the invention is not limited to a particular plant variety or animal breed;
- a microbiological process or other technical process or a product, other than a plant variety or animal breed, obtained by means of said process;
- an element isolated from the human body or otherwise produced by a technical process, including the sequence or partial sequence of a gene, even if the structure of that element is identical to that of a natural element.

In the application of Article 8 regarding morality and public order considerations, patents shall not be granted in particular to biotechnological inventions having as a subject matter:

- processes for cloning the human being;
- processes for modifying the genetic identity of a human being germinal line;
- uses of human embryos for industrial or commercial purposes; or
- processes for the modification of the genetic identity of animals, liable to cause suffering without any substantial medical benefit for man or animal, as well as animals resulting from such processes.

Regarding the methods of treatment or diagnosis which as previously mentioned are excluded from patentability, however, a patent may be granted for inventions having as a subject matter:

(a) products, particularly substances or compositions used in any of these methods;
(b) surgical, therapeutic or diagnosis instruments or apparatus used in these methods;
(c) the methods as such but practiced on the human or animal body which is not alive.

The exception to patentability does not relate also to the inventions with therapeutic or diagnosing purposes which are applied to the human embryo, if useful for the same.

As mentioned, according to Article 6, an invention may have as subject matter a product or a process.

It should be mentioned that in the current Romanian practice, under the concept of process, there is a certain differentiation of a formal nature between a method defined as 'an activity having qualitative results' and a process defined as 'activities having quantitative results', namely obtaining or modifying a product.

For example, this would mean that one could have an invention on a certain 'method of measuring temperature' and a 'computer controlled process of paper fabrication'.

85. Product may be an object having determined properties, technically defined by its constructive or component parts, by elements connecting the same, by its constructive shape or the shape of its component parts, by materials used for making it, by the constructive, position and functional relationships between the component parts or by the functional role thereof.

Main categories of inventions having as their object a product are given in rule 12.3 and, without having an exhaustive character, they include:

(a) devices, installations, equipment, machine tools, apparatuses or assemblies of apparatuses operating together or relating to working means for carrying out a manufacturing or working process;
(b) electric, pneumatic or hydraulic circuits;
(c) chemical substances, including intermediates defined by the component elements and their relationship, symbolized by chemical formulae, by the significance of the substituting radicals, molecular structure, steric isomerism, molecular weight or by other features which individualize or identify them;
(d) means or agents, chemical substances indicating the purpose they are used for;
(e) physical or physical-chemical mixtures defined by the component elements, the quantitative ratio between them, structure, physical-chemical properties or other properties individualizing them and making them applicable to solving a technical problem.

For the particular field of computer-implemented inventions, rule 44(12) provides for that 'the product may be a programmed computer, a network of programmed computers or other apparatus, and the process may be achieved by means of such a computer, network of computers or other apparatus by the execution of one or more computer programs'. Furthermore, the same rule provides the extremely important possibility, recently introduced in the law of claiming a computer program as a product claim when stating that 'the product may be in the form of a computer program'.

Romanian legislation and practice explicitly allow the situation where the product cannot be defined by its intrinsic parameters which may be defined by its manufacturing process, so-called product-by-process definition.

The inventions whose subject matter are processes or methods shall be defined by a logical succession of specific operations which lead to the obtaining of a product or a result. Depending on the problem solved by the process or method, it is necessary to define their steps, logical sequence, initial conditions (raw materials or parameters), technical conditions of their evolution, technical or technological means employed, intermediate and final products or results.

A process may consist of a mechanical, physical, chemical, or technological activity with the effect of obtaining or modifying a product, a working method characterized by operating steps, or a new use of a known product or process.

With regard to biological or genetic processes, they have some particularities deriving from the specificity of their technical solutions for the problems to be solved by this type of invention. Thus, the biological processes need to be specified as fundamental procedural elements: individuals who constitute the starting basis, the type and the way of acting upon them, the environmental conditions and others similar to these. In particular, a microbiological process is characterized by starting materials, steps and working conditions, taxon integration, and morphological and biochemical features of the resulting new microbiological material; in case of obtaining a microbiological material, or starting materials, steps and working conditions, taxon integration and morphological and biochemical features of the used microbiological material in case when the biological material helps as a means for carrying out the process or as a starting material.

The genetic processes refer essentially to the separation, sequencing and synthesis of DNA and RNA, these being possibly accompanied by chemical or biological processes.

A special emphasis should be devoted to biotechnological inventions which constitute a very actual and dynamic topic.

As with any other subject matter, biotechnological inventions may have a product or a process as a subject matter, according to Article 7 of the Law.

Products may be biological materials and genetically modified plants or animals. The biological materials comprise:

- microorganisms isolated from their natural environment or obtained by processes which induce mutations or are genetically modified at the genotype level, characterized by the taxon integration as well as by morphological and biochemical features, the term 'microorganism' comprising bacteria and other generally unicellular organisms, having microscopic dimensions, which can be handled and multiplied in the laboratory, viruses and plasmids, unicellular fungi, including yeasts, algae, protozoa, as well as human, animal and vegetal cells;
- genes or vectors, characterized by the succession of nucleotides or with reference to the process for obtaining the same, to a figure such as a restriction map, and to a deposit number of a host cell line comprising them, respectively; or
- proteins or monoclonal antibodies characterized by the succession of amino acids or by a combination of parameters, such as: source, molecular weight and a functional feature.

The inventions that have a biological material as defined as a subject matter are patentable. The biological material may be isolated from the natural environment and used for practical purposes or may be produced by any technical process.

The inventions relating to plants or animals are patentable, if the technical possibility for carrying out the invention is not confined to a certain plant variety or animal breed.

According to Article 6, the inventions relating to a microbiological process as previously defined or another technical process or a product obtained by such a process are patentable, the product being different from the plant variety or animal breed obtained this way.

A patent application may have as subject matter an invention or a group of inventions so linked as to form a single general inventive concept under the condition of the unity of invention, as they will be analysed in §2, II, C.

If a patent application for a single claimed invention, a product or a process or a method invention seems to need no supplementary explanation because this situation is covered by the previous text, some important, possibly big groups of inventions, potentially ascribed to a single general inventive concept, shall be:

- product, process for obtaining the product and mean(s) for achieving the process;
- product, process for obtaining the product and mean(s) for use of the product;
- product, process for obtaining the product and process for use of the product;
- product, process for obtaining the product and mean(s) for achieving the process and mean(s) for use of the product;
- product, process for obtaining the product, mean(s) for achieving the process and process for use of the product.

It is obvious that from the above-mentioned groups of inventions, simpler groups of any two inventions can be derived.

86. Another category of inventions whose patentability is under intense discussion and which has to be thoroughly analysed is that of the so-called software-related inventions, software-implemented inventions or computer-implemented inventions or, as the Law defines, 'the inventions in the field of computer programs' which are to be considered to belong to a technological field.

Though, as already mentioned, the law provides explicitly the restriction to patentability of 'computer programs as such', the Implementing Regulation defines in a well-harmonized European manner the products or processes in the IT field which are in fact patentable, if the patentability conditions are met.

Thus, rule 47 provides for that the computer programs per se shall not be considered inventions within the meaning of the Law. However, the inventions whose carrying involve the use of a computer, a computer network, or other programmable apparatus, in which at first sight one or more characteristics of the claimed invention is carried out wholly or in part by means of one or more computer programs, are patentable.

Further, 'where a computer program that is the subject matter of the invention, runs or is loaded on a computer, it determines or is capable of determining a subsequent technical effect which is more than mere normal physical interaction between the program and the computer on which it is executed, the invention is patentable'.

The inventions in the field of computer programs may have a product or process as a subject matter. The product may be a programmed computer, a network of programmed computers or other apparatus, and the process may be achieved by means of such a computer, network of computers or other apparatus by the execution of one or more computer programs.

Very important from the point of view of patentability of computer-related inventions is the fact that starting with 2007, the provisions of Law recognize that 'the product may be in the form of a computer program'.

The Romanian practice in the field[23] followed carefully and in a compatible manner the very pragmatic international orientations, with a particular reference to the European Patent Office (EPO) practice.[24] Therefore, within actual legislation, a series of patents for the technical solution of technical problems in the field of applied software has been granted. It has to be mentioned that the concept of 'computer program as such', therefore essentially protected under copyright law, is still, in spite of a true explosion of software, a relatively restrained concept and very often, technology needs and uses software in process and machine control, by replacing hardware-based functions with software-based functions.

Based on these assumptions, the practice in Romania has put no major obstacle to the patentability of software-related inventions or computer-related/implemented inventions which can be circumscribed as a technical solution to a technical problem, or in other words, inventions having a technical character.

§3. Patentability Conditions

87. In order to be granted a patent to an invention from the category of patentable inventions, so as to become an object of the industrial property right, the invention has to meet cumulatively the patentability criteria listed in Article 6 of the Law: novelty, inventive step and industrial applicability.

In order to be possible to examine these criteria, from a formal point of view, the invention should be presented in application and subsequently in patent specification as a clear and detailed technical solution to the solved problem and thus, according to Article 17, 'the invention shall be presented in the patent application in a manner sufficiently clear and complete for it to be carried out by a person skilled in the art'. It also is a matter of fact that according to Romanian practice, these criteria are only examined if the invention presented in the application is not excluded or excepted from patentability, in other words, if it is a patentable invention. This is why, although it is rather a question of interpretation than one of substance, the Romanian practice considers the technical character and exclusions from patentability as immanent to the concept of invention and recognizes the existence of the

23. Alexandru Cristian Strenc, Bucura Ionescu & Gheorghe Gheorghiu, *Treaty on Patent Law, Editura Universul Juridic*, vol. I (2005); vol. II (2007).
24. Alexandru Cristian Strenc, *European Patent Convention* 64 (Wolters Kluwer 2018).

three mentioned patentability criteria while both EPO practice as well as some authors include the existence of the patentable invention as the fourth patentability criterion.[25]

I. Novelty

88. The definition of novelty is given in Article 9 of the Law, which provides that 'an invention shall be considered new if it does not form part of the state of the art'.

Article further provides for that 'the state of the art includes all knowledge that has been made available to the public by means of a written or oral description, by use, or in any other way before the date of filing of the patent application'.

The concept of 'made available to the public' has to be understood as 'anywhere in the world' and, according to rule 38(12), 'the date of making it available to the public shall be identifiable'. The knowledge available to the public means the information available to the public, anywhere in the world, by:

(a) presentation of patent documents or other information on various carriers or on different informational channels;
(b) oral description of information that was not subject to any restriction of confidentiality concerning the use or dissemination of this information.

Where the available information contains indications concerning only the month in a certain year or only the year, this information is deemed to have become available to the public on the last day of the month or the last day of the year, respectively.

Available to the public also means that the document comprising the information or the public oral presentation thereof is to be found in a public library with unrestricted access.

The notion of 'public' is to be considered in a broad context, meaning one or more persons not bound by confidentiality and which could disseminate information; the public may be any person and not necessarily a person skilled in the art. The oral disclosure may consist of a presentation at a conference, broadcasting programmes, or recordings on sound reproducing carriers, such as tapes, discs or the like.

The information is deemed to have become available to the public by use if, on the relevant date, any person could take possession of said information by the displaying or use thereof. If a person sells an item to a third party without any limitations, restrictions or obligations regarding confidentiality, the item is deemed to have been rendered available to the public.

The knowledge that becomes available to the public by oral means, by use, or any other means shall be deemed to belong to the state of the art only if it is confirmed

---

25. Frederic Pollaud-Dulian, *La brevetabilité des inventions-Étude comparative de jurisprudance France-OEB* (Imprimerie France-Quercy, Litec, 1997), 44.

by a document containing it and demonstrating the date on which it became available to the public and that represents the relevant document date.

89. The content of the patent applications filed with the Office and international applications that have entered the national phase in Romania or European patent applications designating Romania which have an earlier regular filing date or an earlier priority date and which become public prior to or after the date of the subsequent application for which the novelty is examined, are also part of the state of the art. The content of the patent applications means the disclosure of the invention in the description, claims and drawings, the explicitly presented state of the art, included.

Regarding novelty assessment, a court decision[26] stated that 'in providing the Article 9 of Law No. 64/1991, the novelty requirement in relation to the prior art, the legislator has considered that the prior art should not be reflected in the invention as such, but in a work that reproduces all the essential elements of the invention. Therefore, the comparison between technical solutions should be made in terms of technical characteristics what represents the essence of the invention, respectively of the material from the prior art – to establish the common points, and consequently those of differentiation. In order to meet this goal, the appointed experts have proceeded to the comparison of the claims of the patent, which represents its characteristic part, with technical and figurative elements in the article of the technical magazine. The reference to the claims was made individually for each claim, according to Law, by observing that technical elements considered as new and contained in the patent claims 1 and 2 are identical to those contained in the technical solution presented in the article. Based on these technical findings, correctly, the court first held that the patent does not satisfy the novelty requirement, ordering cancellation of the patent'.

A separate discussion is necessary for analyzing the situation in which the previous applications, which if they were published, would form part of the state of the art, were either not made available because they are kept in a confidential or secret regime, or were not made available because they were withdrawn, rejected or abandoned before publication.

The second situation is expressly solved by rule 38(12), which provides that 'if an application was withdrawn, abandoned or rejected prior to its publication, it did not help as a basis for claiming a right of priority and did not allow the subsistence of rights it is not be deemed to belong to the prior art'.

The first situation has no concrete solution provided in the law, but the Office practice is oriented towards avoiding de facto the unjustified situations of granting double protection for the same claimed invention, so that it assimilates, somehow artificially, only for these particular cases, the unpublished patent applications for previous inventions.

For establishing the novelty of an invention, the state of the art has to be taken into account only individually for each claimed invention in the patent application,

26. Court of Appeal, Division IX of civil and intellectual property cases, decision No. 235 A of 23 Oct. 2008.

with reference to a single document considered as the most pertinent one. In a concise and clear meaning, it is not permitted to use a set of documents considered pertinent in a mosaic system for both a single invention and especially for the case of a group of claimed inventions.

90. An important aspect in examining the novelty is the so-called non-prejudicial disclosure, where the law provides in Article 10 that:

> the disclosure of the invention shall not be taken into consideration if it occurred within the six months preceding the filing of the patent application, and if was due to or in consequence of:
>
> (a) an evident abuse in relation to the applicant or his legal predecessor;
> (b) the fact that the applicant or his legal predecessor has displayed the invention at an official or officially recognized international exhibition falling within the terms of the Convention on International Exhibitions signed in Paris on 22 November 1928 with the subsequent revisions.

The provisions of paragraph 1(b) shall be applicable only if the applicant states, when filing the patent application, that the inventions have been actually displayed and if he files a document supporting his statement within the time limit and under the conditions provided for by the implementing regulations concerning this Law.

II. Inventive Step

91. According to Article 11 of the Law, 'an invention shall be considered as involving an inventive step, if, having regard to the state of the art, it is not obvious to a person skilled in the art'.

The analysis of the inventive step starts from the idea and situation of a person skilled in the art who is able or not to synthesize from a mosaic of solutions which form part of the state of the art, without making any inventive effort, the technical solution which is in fact the subject matter of the patent application.

In the situation when the person skilled in the art, without making any inventive effort, can synthesize that solution, it derives from that that the technical solution 'is obvious' regarding the state of the art and that there is no inventive step. Thus, according to rule 47, ' the inventive step of an invention shall be assessed in connection with the technical problem it solves and with the claimed invention taken as a whole, by comparing the same with the state of the art'. The analysis of the inventive step shall be performed only for the claims fulfilling the novelty condition. The claimed invention taken as a whole is considered to be obvious if, starting from one or more characteristics of the prior art, the use of the general knowledge of the person skilled in the art had allowed that person, on the date of filing or of the application priority, to arrive to the claimed invention.

The definition of the inventive step requires the analysis of at least three concepts, namely:

(1) the person skilled in the art;
(2) the state of the art to be considered when the inventive step is examined;
(3) the obviousness.

As a matter of fact, the first concept – 'person skilled in the art' – and the third – 'obviousness'– are in a well-determined relationship because it seems to be clear that, for instance, not everything that is 'obvious' to a highly specialized scientist, in a particular field, is also and in the same manner 'obvious' for a technician who works in the same field.

By the same rule is accepted the fiction[27] that 'the person skilled in the art represents the person considered to have access to the whole state of the art, having normal abilities and general knowledge in the technical field which the technical problem solved in the invention on the relevant date belongs to'.

Very important is the fact that the area of interest as regards the person skilled in the art is that of producer of the object of the invention and not that of user.

Once the concept of the 'person skilled in the art' has been defined, the fact that for this person, the invention is 'obvious' regarding the knowledge that is part of the state of the art means that for an ordinary practitioner, having average qualities and normal theoretical and practical knowledge, the state of the art considered this time as a mosaic of solutions, indicates or suggests the technical solution to the technical problem, as defined in the patent application for which protection is sought.

When assessing the inventive step, there may be combined in a mosaic system either more documents or parts of more documents, or different parts of the same document belonging to the state of the art and compared with the claimed invention, on condition that this combination is obvious for a person skilled in the art.

For computer/software-implemented inventions, there is a specificity of the concept of inventive step mostly derived from the difficulty of assessing it against the prior art. In that respect, fully in line with European law and practice, the Romanian one has the view that for this category of inventions, the inventive step condition is deemed as being fulfilled, if the invention involves a technical contribution, meaning a contribution to the state of the art in a technical field. As already mentioned, the claimed invention may comprise elements containing non-technical features besides the technical features.

Rule 47(9) makes a synthesis of the conditions for which an invention has a presumed inventive step, of which at least one is necessary to be met:

(a) the non-obvious use of known means for another purpose while producing novel and surprising effects;
(b) a novel use of a known device or material which obviates technical difficulties impossible to surpass in a known manner;
(c) a combination of new or known features carried out in such a manner that they mutually intensify their effects and a new technical result is obtained;

27. Paul Mathely, *Le nouveau droit francais des brévets des inventions* (1991): 96–98 J.N.A.

(d) a selection, within a process, of those technical parameters contained in a known range, which produce unexpected effects on the carrying out of the process or on the properties of the product obtained;
(e) a selection within a very large group of compounds of known chemical combinations of those that have unexpected advantages;
(f) the use of technical means of the claimed invention for solving the technical problem in another way than the one resulting from the documents contained in the state of the art analysed by the person skilled in the art.

A relevant court decision[28] provides for that 'when assessing inventive step, under rule 32B section 2, it was established the state of the art from which has been formed a mosaic of technical solutions which has been compared in its integrality with all claims, and from this analysis of the totality of solutions of prior art resulted that a person skilled in the art could not reach the solution which is the subject matter of the patent, without making a creative effort. The inventive step of the respondents lied in the combination of known elements of the prior art, either separately or in groups, so that resulted in an organic connexion, functional, a mutual influence, an interaction and interconditionality, which led to a global positive effect, a result obtained from a creative effort, conclusion that circumscribe the legal provisions regarding the condition of inventive step'.

Without being necessarily and strictly the reverse of the previous conditions, rule 47(10) provided the following situations when an invention does not imply an inventive step:

(a) the invention represents at least one of the possible solutions that would obviously result in a person skilled in the art for filling a gap existing in the documents in the state of the art;
(b) the invention differs from the known state of the art only by the use of some well-known equivalent mechanical, electric or chemical means;
(c) the invention consists only in a new use employing the known features of a known means;
(d) the invention consists of replacing, within a known device, a material with a recently discovered material whose properties make it suitable for this use, called analogous replacement;
(e) the invention consists only in the use of a known technique in a rigorously similar situation, called analogous use;
(f) the invention consists of juxtaposing or associating known devices or processes, each operating or being carried on in a known manner, without resulting in an interdependence between them;
(g) the invention consists only of selecting a solution from a certain number of suitable possibilities;
(h) the invention consists of selecting certain dimensions; temperature ranges or parameters from a limited range, which could have been obtained by successive attempts or by the use of the known designing methods;

28. Court of Appeal, Division IX of civil and intellectual property cases, civil decision 93A of 24 Apr. 2008.

(i) the invention is obtained only by a simple extrapolation resulting directly from the state of the art.

It results from the previous situations that the inventive step may be situated either at the level of the raised problem or at the level of a new and inventive solution to a problem already raised.

92. For both situations, the examination of the inventive step has some basic elements, which are directly applied by the Office,[29] namely:

- the (non) evidence of the solution and of the problem to be solved by the invention for which protection is sought is analysed from the point of view of the person skilled in the art as it has been defined previously and from the point of view of the examiner, who usually has a level of knowledge above that of the person skilled in the art;
- the (non)evidence is judged with reference to the date the application was filed and not with reference to the examination date, which generally has a gap of one to four years compared with the date of application. Within this interval, even if a lot of things have become 'more obvious' regarding the state of the art, they are completely irrelevant from this point of view.

In relation to the previous idea, the inventive step shall be interpreted in the most objective manner, even if it inevitably maintains an immanent subjectivism. The elimination of the aspects of subjectivism derived from the simplicity or complexity of the invention is taken into account, considering the achievement of minor or major advantages by applying the invention, the achievement of the invention as a result of a systematic or a purely intuitive manner, etc.

With regard to the state of the art taken into account for inventive step and contrary to what has been stated for examination of the novelty, according to Article 12, 'the patent application filed with the Office which became public after the filing date of the application submitted to the examination is not taken into account when assessing the inventive step even if their filing date is earlier'. This provision is justified by the fact that the person skilled in the art cannot be blamed for the 'evidence' of the solution sought for protection with regard to one or more patent applications he knew nothing about and could not know anything about because of the fact that the applications have not been published.

With reference to the national and international practice in the examination of the inventive step, all approaches start from the assertion that the technical problem is essential to determining if the inventive step is or is not present in the solution to that problem and this is contrary to the assessment of the novelty where the technical problem has no relevance. This is expressly stated in rule 47, which has already been mentioned.

29. Alexandru Cristian Strenc, Gheorghe Gheorghiu & Ionescu Bucura, *Treaty on Patent Law*, (Ed. Lumina Lex, vol. I (2005); vol. II (2007)).

93. The EPO has developed and is applying a concrete and practical procedure called 'problem-solution approach', which although cannot eliminate totally the personal interpretation elements if a certain solution has or does not have the necessary inventive step to fulfil the patentability criterion, achieves nevertheless a uniformity of the formal and procedural approach.

The 'problem-solution' approach supposes that the Office carries out three main procedural steps, namely:

- identification of the most pertinent state of the art;
- (re)formulation of the technical problem by taking into account the already found 'most pertinent state of the art';
- final decision on (non)evidence of the solution.

Starting with 2008, based on rule 47, the practice of the Romanian Office may optionally follow this type of approach, meaning that the examiners may examine inventive step based on formal procedure of the EPO but leave it to the examiner's professional and probably intuitive nature the application of the criteria. In this respect, rule 47 defines the closest state of the art, as being 'that combination of features that is disclosed in a single reference of the state of the art and constitutes the best basis for evaluating the obviousness'.

Another important concept which is defined is the objective technical problem to be solved, which represents the objective proposed for modifying or adapting the closest state of the art to obtain the technical effects the invention has in comparison with this state of the art. Of course, it may be and practically in most of the situation is different from the technical problem presented by the applicant in the description of the application. This is due to the fact that having access to larger databases, the state of the art determined by the Office during the examination procedure imposes the modification to the effect of rendering it objective.

III. Industrial Applicability

94. Without changing the basis of the concept in a significant way, we shall mention that, in fact, the law makes reference to the concept of invention 'susceptible of industrial application' and not to that of invention 'industrially applicable'. By this nuance, which can be found in many patent laws, the Romanian legislator gave a greater flexibility to the interpretation of the concept, in the sense of the analysis of the applicability, including a foreseeable future, for instance, as soon as an adequate technology will be operational.

According to Article 12 of the Law, 'an invention shall be considered as susceptible of industrial application if it can be used in any industry activity, including agriculture'.

According to European and international patent practice, the industrial applicability of an invention is presumed, except in situations where the technical use thereof is not obvious and the explicit indication thereof is necessary.

In this respect, in order to cover an important specificity of the biotechnologies where the manner in which the disclosure of the inventions takes place is essential, and following the lines of the biotech Directive No. 98/84, the same article provides that 'the industrial application of a sequence or partial sequence of a gene must be disclosed in the patent application'.

The demand that an invention be susceptible to industrial application in order to be patented is a fundamental one for the definition of a patentable invention in the concrete technical area which passed beyond the phase of an idea, discovery, etc. and allowed or is imminent to allow the solving of a technical problem by a new and inventive technical solution.

The legal definition of industrial applicability needs the analysis of some fundamental elements.

First, the concept of 'industrial' should be regarded in its largest meaning, including agriculture or any other adjacent area in which the technical solution that constitutes the subject matter of the invention whose protection is sought is produced or used.

Second, there is the problem of reproducing the object or its fabrication, repeatedly as the case may be, at any time, whenever necessary, while maintaining its characteristics.

The above-mentioned provision strengthens the role of repeated fabrication of well-developed technology, with the purpose of selecting and eliminating a random result that would not offer the certitude of a real technical solution.

Accordingly, in order to be industrially applicable, an invention 'shall have an industrial character both in its object as well as in its application and result'.[30]

In fact, an invention is susceptible to industrial application if it has technical utility or it can be objectively carried out.

A particular discussion should be oriented towards the so-called perpetuum mobile type inventions, devices or processes whose operation or use is obviously contrary to the laws of physics and which are clearly non-patentable mostly because they lack industrial applicability.

However, in the application of such approach, Romanian law and practice make a distinction between the two situations. Where the claims of the patent application having as a subject matter such a device specify the function pretended to be fulfilled by the invention, as well as the construction thereof, the invention is in fact considered 'not susceptible of industrial application', but in the situation where the device is claimed as a product having a certain construction, objections in respect of the insufficient disclosure may be raised.

§4. Formalities: Procedure for Granting and Obtaining Patent Protection

95. The granting and obtaining patent protection is done by the Office following a complex procedure of examination of the patent application and the necessary documentation.

According to the organizational structure of the Office and to a practice harmonized with the European and international one, the examination has a preliminary

30. Paul Mathely, *supra*, 126.

component. This is when the patent application and the relevant documentation are brought to the prescribed form. Then, the substantive examination takes place, and as a result of verifying whether the patentability criteria are met, the decision to grant the patent or reject the patent application is taken.

I. Formalities

96. In order to constitute the national regular filing, Article 13. provides for that:

> the patent application drawn up in Romanian must contain:
>
> (a) the request for the grant of a patent;
> (b) applicant's identification data;
> (c) a description of the invention;
> (d) one or more claims;
> (e) drawings referred to in the description or the claims.

If the applicant is not the inventor, the patent application shall also contain particulars serving to identify the inventor and shall be accompanied by a document indicating the origin of the right to the grant of the patent. This document must be filed before a decision is taken in respect of the patent application.

According to Article 13, the patent application shall be filed by the person entitled to the granting of a patent, either in person or through an authorized agent whose domicile or registered office is in Romania. The patent application shall be filed with the Office, at the applicant's choice on paper carrier, directly to the General Registry of the Office, by mail, or by electronic means.

In all the proceedings before the Office, the applicant shall be regarded as the person entitled to the grant of the patent.

Patent application may contain one or more priority claims based on one or more prior applications having the status of regular national filings in accordance with international conventions to which Romania is a party. Regular national filing means any filing that is sufficient for establishing the date on which the application was filed, whatever may be the outcome of the application.

The date by which these documents must have been filed is the date of regular national filing, which secures a right of priority starting on that date or on the priority date claimed and recognized in relation to any filing of the same invention effected at a later date or having a later recognized priority date.

According to Article 14 of the Law, the possibility of registering a patent invention application is recognized even in the event of fulfilling only some minimal conditions under the requirement of completion of the patent application in a specified time interval. These minimal conditions, directly derived from the provisions of the Patent Law Treaty-PLT, regard the filing of at least the following documents:

(a) an explicit or implicit indication that the grant of a patent is requested; thus, the existence of an application form is not compulsory, being a sufficient and written indication that what has been registered could be considered a patent application;
(b) indications serving to identify the applicant or to make it possible for OSIM to contact him; establishing the applicant's identity is nevertheless an essential condition necessary for the Office to contact the applicant;
(c) a part which should, at first sight, seem to be a description of the invention; it is sufficient for this first step that the applicant registers a document which at first sight appears to be a description of his invention. Exceptionally, a drawing could also be considered, if it is relevant and at first sight is able to indicate the subject matter of invention.

Where a part of the description is missing, for the purposes of according a filing date, said part can be subsequently filed, the filing date being the date on which said part is filed and on which the fee for the registration of that part is paid. If the missing and subsequently filed part of the description is withdrawn, the filing date shall be the date on which the requirements previously referred are fulfilled.

Where the patent application does not comprise a part which, at first sight, seems to be a description, for the purpose of according a filing date, reference may be made in the patent application, in the Romanian language, to a prior application filed with any office, which replace the description, while observing the provisions of the regulations for implementing this Law. Otherwise, the application shall not be treated as a patent application.

The description according to Article 14 paragraph (1) letter (c) of the Law may also be a reference in the Romanian language to a patent application previously filed with an office and this reference must include:

(a) number of previously filed application;
(b) denomination of the office where the patent application has been filed;
(c) application filing date.

Where the Office can contact the applicant, but the documents provided for in Article 14 have not been filed, the Office shall notify the applicant of the ascertained drawbacks and grant a two-month time period from the date of filing at least one of the documents for submitting the missing documents. In this situation, the patent application filing date is the date on which the documents specified in the notification are filed with the Office.

If, within the time period granted in the notification, the missing documents have not been submitted, the patent application is deemed not to have been filed and this shall be communicated to the person who filed the documents, also indicating the reasons for which the patent application was dealt with in such a way. Consequently, the Office returns the documentation, keeping a copy thereof as a witness copy, that shall not be published and may be consulted at the Office headquarters by the person who submitted the documents following a written request.

Where, upon establishing the filing date, the Office ascertains that a part of the description is missing, it shall notify the applicant who is asked to submit the missing part within two months from the date of sending the notification, but not more than four months from the date on which at least one of the minimal documents provided for in Article 14 paragraph (1) of the Law has been filed with Office. The missing part of the description may also be filed with the Office on the applicant's own initiative within four months from the date on which the Office has received at least one of the minimal documents. Where the applicant files the missing part I, the Romanian, within the legal time limit, the Office will consider that missing part as included in the description. The application filing date will be the date on which the missing part has been filed with the Office and the applicant shall be notified accordingly.

Where a priority of an earlier application is claimed and the missing part is contained in the earlier application whose priority is claimed, the applicant shall, for the purpose of according the filing date, submit the following:

(a) the missing part in the Romanian language, within four months from the date when at least one of the minimal documents provided for in Article 15 paragraph (1) of the Law has been filed with the Office;
(b) a copy of the earlier patent application containing the missing part, with the precise indication thereof, within the time limit referred to under letter (a);
(c) a copy of the earlier application, certified by the office where the application has been filed and the filing date of the application whose priority is claimed, within four months from notification, but not more than sixteen months from the date of the claimed priority;
(d) a translation into Romanian of the earlier application, if this has not been filed in Romanian.

When applying these legal conditions, the following must be observed:

(a) the missing part of the description shall entirely be found in the earlier application;
(b) where the earlier application has already been filed with Office, the applicant shall file only the missing part within the time limit previously referred;
(c) the minimal documents referred to under the provisions of Article 15 paragraph (1) must contain explicit reference to the earlier patent application whose priority was claimed in the patent application.

Where these requirements are complied with, the filing date is the date established according to the provisions of Article 14 paragraph (1) of the Law.

Where the missing part of the description is filed within the time limits provided for, but the Office ascertains that it does not belong to the earlier patent application whose priority was claimed, the filing date of the application will be the date of filing the missing part, and OSIM shall notify the applicant accordingly, indicating the reasons thereof.

If, within one month from the date of the notification concerning the according of filing date, the applicant communicates to the Office the intention of withdrawing the part that initially was deemed to be missing, the patent application filing date will be the date on which the provisions of Article 14 paragraph (1) of the Law are complied with. The copy of the earlier application shall contain: the description, claims and, where appropriate, the drawings; where the earlier patent application does not contain claims and drawings, these shall be submitted within the time limit provided.

The filing date of a patent application resulting from dividing an original application is the same as the filing date of the original application.

Where before the grant of the patent by OSIM, a court decision has established that the right to the patent belongs to a person other than the applicant, the new patent application shall have the same filing date as the original patent application.

By filing this minimal set of documents, the Office registers the application in the National Register of Filed Patent Applications in the sequence of the filing numbers and dates with the General Registry of the Office.

The number received in the National Register is the number of the patent application.

In the event that the applicant does not file at least these three pieces of the dossier of the patent application under the ‘minimal conditions’, the application shall not be registered in the National Register of Filed Patent Applications and the documentation is returned, the Office keeping a copy. This copy is kept for a limited period of time.

If the application is registered under minimal conditions, claims and drawings may be filed within two months from the date of filing the application, provided that the legal fee is paid. In this case, the patent application produces the effects of a regular national filing starting from the filing date. Where the claims are not filed within this time limit, the patent application shall be declared to be withdrawn.

In the case of the international patent application or the European patent application, the filing date shall be the date resulting from the international treaties and conventions to which Romania is party and that date shall be registered in the National Register of Patent Applications.

The failure to complain within this time limit results in the failure to constitute a national regular filing, the application being consequently rejected.

The patent application must be accompanied by an abstract which may not be filed later than two months before the patent application publication date.

97. The filing of drawings follows a similar procedure as the Patent Cooperation Treaty (PCT) one, namely where reference to drawings is made in the description and claims, but the drawings have not been filed with OSIM on the date of filing or within two months from the filing date, the Office shall notify the applicant:

- of the requirement that any reference to drawings in the description and claims should be considered to have been eliminated, with the provision of filing with the Office the description and claims, modified by eliminating the reference to drawings therefrom, within two months from the notification, but not more than four months from the filing date; or

- of the fact that OSIM should carry on the examination procedure only for the parts of the description, not making reference to drawings, in which case the applicant shall file the redrafted description and claims with OSIM within the same time limits.

If the applicant fails to respond to the notification issued by the Office within the granted time limit, the patent application shall be deemed to have been withdrawn.

If the drawings are received within two months from the patent application filing date, the regular filing date will be the date of their receipt. The filing date already established is registered in the National Register of Filed Applications. Within three months from the filing date, the applicant shall file the proof of the payment of the legal filing fee; otherwise, the application will be rejected.

Some elements of the patent application may be noted. The patent application together with all attached documentation shall be drawn up in the Romanian language, which according to the law is the official language. Nevertheless, the law also provides the possibility for foreign applicants to apply the description, claims, drawings and abstracts in a foreign language, under the condition that within two months from the registration of the patent application or from the date of entering the national phase, as the case may be, and the legal fee is paid, the certified translation of these documents is applied in Romanian. The application will be rejected in the case of failure to observe this time limit.

In addition, it can be the case that other documents relevant for the correct defining and granting of the property right may be necessary to be added to the application, allowing for a substantive examination of the patent application.

A. *Description of the Invention*

98. According to rule 16, the description of the invention shall contain successively the following main parts, exposed in the prescribed order:

- the title of the invention, with a concise formulation of the subject matter of the invention, but without disclosing the invention and without containing fanciful denominations;
- specification of the technical field of the invention wherein the invention may be applied;
- presentation of the prior art considered by the applicant to be useful for understanding, performing the documentary search and examining the claimed invention, with the indication of the documents which substantiate it; at least one solution considered to be the closest to the claimed invention shall be presented; where the prior art also contains traditional knowledge, this and its source, if known, shall explicitly be indicated in the description;
- presentation of the technical problem that the applicant proposed to solve by the invention; the technical problem consists of formulating the objective whose solving represents a success in the technical field that the invention relates to;
- disclosure of the invention as claimed, for a person skilled in the art to be able to understand the technical problem, even if it is not explicitly presented, and the

means for solving the same; where the description comprises a group of inventions that meet the unity criterion, each invention in the group will be separately exposed;
- presentation of the advantages of the invention in comparison with the state of the art;
- brief description of the figures in the drawings, if any;
- detailed presentation of at least one embodiment of the claimed invention, by using examples, where appropriate, with reference to drawings, if any; in case of some carrying out versions, at least one embodiment shall be presented for each version;
- explicit indication, if this does not obviously result from the detailed description, of the way in which the invention is capable of industrial applicability.

In the description, there may be presented chemical, physical or mathematical models and formulae, algorithms, programming lines, subroutines or computer programs, and tables, without supporting the presentation of the subject matter of the invention in the embodiment exclusively on them. The description shall be presented in the manner and with the succession of the chapters referred to under paragraph (1), except where, by the nature of the invention, a different presentation would lead to a better understanding of the invention.

The description in the field of computer-implemented inventions has some particularities which have to be underlined.[31] Thus, for a better understanding of the invention, the description according to the provisions may be attended by diagrams presenting the data processing operational stages or steps such as program organization diagrams, graphs or the like. More than that, in the description, short fragments of a program for the data processing units are accepted in a usual programming language, if they better explain the manner of carrying out the invention.

B. Claims

99. Claims have two major functions given by the law, namely:

(1) the content of the claims determines the extent of the protection conferred by the patent or the patent application – Article 31;
(2) the content of the claims defines the matter for which protection is sought – Article 17.

Being in fact the most important part of the patent application, they shall be drafted clearly and concisely, both individually and wholly, and they shall be supported by the description.

According to Romanian law – rule 18(3) – and practice, the claims shall be exposed in the so-called two parts manner, namely:

31. Alexandru Cristian Strenc, *Information Technology. Protection and Enforcement of Intellectual Property Rights. Editura Universul Juridic, Colectia Busines* (2010).

(1) A preamble indicating the title of the invention and the technical elements thereof which are necessary for defining the subject matter of the invention and which are part of the prior art.
(2) A characterizing part stating concisely the new technical features necessary for the definition of the subject matter of the invention, in combination with the technical features stated in the preamble.

The two parts shall be connected by the expression 'characterized in that'. The new features are presented in the characterizing part of the claims, stating their interdependence connections.

However, the claims may also be drawn up in a single portion which contains the presentation of a technical feature or a combination of more technical features which define the subject matter for which protection is claimed.

Depending on the complexity of the invention, there may be several claims, independent and/or dependent, so that if the patent application refers to two or more inventions and the unity of the invention is observed, an individual claim for each individual invention can be drawn up.

At the same time, any independent claim may be followed by a reasonable number of dependent claims which should refer thereto and should develop or explain the technical feature already stated in the independent claim or in the embodiment of the subject matter of the invention.

The independent claim should clearly state all the essential technical features necessary for the definition of the subject matter of the invention.

The dependent claim should implicitly contain all the features of the independent claim to which it is subordinated and it shall develop or explain the essential technical features of the invention already enunciated in the independent claim or relate to particular embodiments of the invention or contain other technical features than the ones in the independent claim, but which do not represent essential features for defining the subject matter of the claimed protection.

The dependent claim normally contains a reference to the claim it is subordinated to, without any reference to the state of the art being made at the beginning of the claim. They may be followed by one or several dependent claims subordinated thereto and they may represent multiple dependent claims. In this case, the dependent claims subordinated to one or more previous claims shall be grouped and located in the most suitable possible manner.

A patent application relating to a group of inventions forming a single general inventive concept shall contain at least one independent claim for each invention. However, a patent application may contain more than one independent claim of the same category (product, process, installation, use), only if the subject matter of the patent application relates to more interdependent products or various uses of a product or of an installation, or alternative solutions for a certain problem when these cannot be contained in a single claim.

In particular case of computer/software-implemented inventions, the claims shall be drawn up in a manner to present how the new features of the product may be achieved by means of a computer program in a system which comprises means adapted to achieve an equivalent process, or how the process may be achieved in a system if the program determining the carrying out of the process can be run within a system.

C. *Drawings of the Invention*

100. The drawings are often key elements in understanding the invention and the elements of novelty thereof.

They shall contain reference signs, which should indicate the component elements corresponding to their presentation in the embodiment of the invention. The flow sheets and diagrams, except for the tables, shall be considered drawings. Drawings shall not contain texts, except for a word or some isolated words strictly necessary, such as: 'water', 'steam', 'open', 'closed', and for the flow sheets and diagrams illustrating the process steps, keywords absolutely necessary for understanding them.

D. *Priority Documents*

1. Conventional Priority

101. The applicant for a patent application may take advantage of the priority of a previous application for the same invention if he files with the patent application a declaration claiming the priority of the earlier application justified by priority documents.

Priority documents mean either priority certificates issued by national or regional offices where the previous applications having as object the same inventions have been filed or exhibition certificates granted as a result of the exposure of the products which constitute the subject matter of the inventions at international or internationally recognized exhibitions organized in Romania or in the Member States at international conventions to which Romania is a party.

With a view to recognizing the claimed priorities, the applicant transmits to the Office, upon request, a conformed translation of the priority certificate in Romanian.

According to rule 10, the declaration shall indicate the date of filing the earlier application, the number of the earlier application, the denomination of the State in which the earlier application has been filed, if the earlier application is a national application, the denomination of the authority that granted the regional patent, pursuant to the provisions of the regional patent treaty, where the earlier application is a regional application or the denomination of the receiving Office where the application has been filed, where the earlier application is an international application.

102. If an exhibition priority is claimed, this has to be reasoned in order to be recognized by an exhibition certificate, which according to rule 28 shall be filled by the applicant within four months from the patent application filing date and shall contain:

- name and registered office of the administration responsible for the industrial property protection in the exhibition in which the invention was displayed and that issued the certificate;
- name of the official or officially recognized exhibition, address and opening date;
- identification data, address or the premises of the natural or legal person who deposited the object in the exhibition;
- ascertainment that the invention was in fact displayed in the exhibition;
- the date of the first disclosure of the invention;
- number and date of the exhibition certificate;
- a copy of the description of the exhibited object, certified by the administration of the exhibition, indicating that the object displayed is identical to the one described, and a translation of this description in Romanian.

When the first disclosure of the invention is subsequent to the date of opening the exhibition, the certificate shall mention the date of the first disclosure. The certificate may be accompanied by a document for the identification of the inventor, authenticated by the mentioned administration concerning the identification of the inventor.

103. A patent application may contain one or more priority claims based on one or more previous applications having the status of regular national filings and whose subject matter has eventually been displayed at official or officially recognized exhibitions in different countries.

In this situation, the basic conditions are:

(a) observation of the invention's unity;
(b) priorities may be recognized only for those elements contained in the applications taken as a priority basis, contained in the application where the priorities are claimed or which obviously result from these.

It is not allowed to claim several priorities in cascade; that is, one cannot claim the priority of an application which was already claimed for a previous application. Also, if, for a patent application, several priorities are claimed, the time limits from which the priority date starts are calculated, taking into account the earliest date of priority.

The priority-claiming fee shall be paid for each priority within four months from the application filing date, if the priority claiming was made on that date or at the time of opening the national phase. It is to be understood that failure to pay the priority-claiming fee in the legal amount and time limit provided for leads to the non-recognition of priority.

In a patent application claiming one or more priorities of earlier applications, the claiming of any of these priorities is also recognized in the conditions in which the application contains one or more features not contained in the application or applications whose priority is claimed, provided that, in both cases, there exists a unity of the invention. Where one or more priorities are claimed in a patent application, only that part of the subsequent application filing contained in the first application or first applications filing shall be recognized; for the parts not contained in the application or applications whose priority is claimed, the subsequent application filing generates a priority right in the conditions of the Law.

Where some features of the invention from a subsequent application wherein a priority was claimed cannot be found in any claim drafted in the earlier application, the priority may still be recognized, if these features obviously result from the assembly of the earlier application.

The applicant may avail himself of the right of priority derived from the first filing of a non-unitary patent application, no matter if the patent application was divided or not in the country of origin.

Where a patent application results from dividing a patent application, the applicant benefits from the right of priority claimed in the divided application.

In the last amending of the law, in line with Patent law, treaty provisions have been introduced to two main facilities regarding the priority right, namely correction of the data contained in the declaration and reinstatement of priority right for certain clear reasons and conditions to be defined.

Thus, according to rule 10(15):

- the data contained in the declaration may be corrected if a request signed by the applicant or by the professional representative thereof, explicitly requesting the correction of the data, is filed within two months from the expiry of the twelve-month time limit from the date of priority;
- the fee for publishing the correction of the data relating to claiming priority is paid within four months from the date of filing the patent application or of opening the national phase.

Reinstatement of priority right is provided for in rule 10(16) which stipulates that 'in a patent application having the filing date within the twelve-month time limit from the date on which the priority of an earlier application could have been claimed, the priority may be claimed within two months from the expiry of the twelve-month time limit calculated from the filing date of the earliest application whose priority was claimed'.

In this situation, the priority claimed may be recognized only if a request signed by the applicant or by the professional representative thereof, explicitly requesting the addition of priority claiming, is filed at the latest within two months from the expiry of the twelve-month time limit and the fee for claiming the priority after the date of filing the patent application is paid at the time of claiming the priority.

Further on, priority may be recognized only where:

(a) there exists a request signed by the applicant or his professional representative which explicitly requests the reinstatement; when on the date of filing there was not claimed the priority of the earlier application, the request shall be attended by the priority claiming;
(b) the request referred to under letter (a) is filed within the two-month time limit from the expiry of the priority period;
(c) the request referred to under letter (a) presents the reasons for failure to file the patent application within the priority period and a statement or other proof can

be attached to sustain the reasons; the legal fee for claiming a priority is paid at the time of filing the request under letter (a).

These provisions shall be applied if the request for all situations is filed before the applicant requests the publication of the applicatio, or before OSIM complies with a request for withdrawal or takes a decision of rejection.

If these provisions are not fulfilled, the Office shall decide the non-recognition of the priority.

2. Internal Priority

104. Amendments brought in the patent legislation a prolongation of the conventional priority granted within similar conditions to nationals. Thus, according to Article 20, if a subsequent patent application is filed by the applicant of the earlier application or by his successor in title within a time limit of twelve months from the filing date of a patent application accorded by OSIM, a priority right named internal priority right may be claimed in the subsequent application for the same invention.

Where an internal priority right is claimed in a subsequent application, the earlier application whose priority is claimed shall be deemed to be withdrawn, if a decision has not been made thereon.

Internal priority may be claimed on the date of filing the subsequent application or within two months of that date.

The internal priority of an earlier application claimed in a subsequent application shall not be recognized if:

(a) at least one of the patent applications enjoyed a priority right under Article 16 above;
(b) internal priorities were claimed in the earlier application, the date of one such priority being earlier than the twelve-month time limit calculated from the filing date of the subsequent application;
(c) the internal priority document was not filed within the time limit prescribed by the regulations for implementing this Law.

Internal priority gives an important possibility to national applicants to apply as soon as they arrive at a certain degree of solution for their invention and then, during twelve months, to file subsequent application(s) where they may claim internal priority for certain improvements based on previously applied solution(s).

E. Authorization of Transferring the Priority Rights

105. Where the applicant of a patent application claims a priority right belonging to another person, in order to have the priority recognized, it is necessary to file with the Office an authorization from the assignor of the priority right proving that the applicant was assigned by him the right to claim priority of the earliest filing. Thus, according to rule 24, the authorization shall be filed to the Office by the assignor of the priority right and shall mention the right thereof of claiming the priority of the first filing. The time period for filing the authorization is a maximum of seventeen months from the priority date; otherwise, the Office decides the non-recognition of the claimed priority. If, within the priority period, successive assignments of the priority right took place, these shall be registered with the Office within the time period already mentioned. In the case of international applications, the authorization shall be filed with the Office within three months from the date of opening the national phase; otherwise, within six months from the date of opening the national phase, the Office decides the non-recognition of the claimed priority.

F. Abstract of the Invention

106. According to Article 13, the abstract shall be filed, at the latest, until two months before the patent application publication date.

It shall indicate, in a concise manner, the title of the invention and the technical field the invention or the group of inventions belongs to and also a brief presentation of the invention disclosed in the application, which should allow the understanding of the technical problem, the essence of the solution for solving the technical problem and the main use of the invention and, where appropriate, the chemical formula selected from the formulae contained in the patent application, which best characterizes the invention. As a rule, it shall not contain more than one hundred and fifty words.

As unanimously accepted, the goal of the abstract is to be an informative source for both the examiner as well as for other specialists, without being taken into consideration when assessing the scope of the protection. Thus, the abstract is useful both as a means for selecting the technical information for specialists and for making a decision concerning the need to consult the patent application.

The abstract is accompanied by an indication of the figure, or exceptionally, the figures in the drawings proposed to be published. However, the Office may decide the publication of another (other) figure(s) together with the abstract if it considers that this or these better characterize(s) the invention; each of the main features mentioned in the abstract and illustrated in the drawing shall be followed by a reference sign placed between brackets.

G. Power of Attorney

107. Rule 22 provides for that 'appointment of the professional representative which stands for the applicant, owner, assignor or any other person shall be made by a special power of attorney filed with Office at the time of filing the patent application and it shall contain the name and signature of the represented person'.

Where the power of attorney is not filed on the filing date of the patent application or on the date of opening the national phase, it can still be filed within two months from the date on which the applicant is notified by the Office with reference to filing the missing document, or within four months from the filing date, or from the date of opening the national phase, whichever expires later.

A special case often encountered in the patent practice is that concerning the power of attorney referring to procedures corresponding to more patent applications or patents of the same represented person, named general power of attorney. This will be entered in the register for general powers of attorney held by the Office, provided that all the patent applications or patents are identifiable within the power of attorney, or the ones for which the representation is not made are specified, as the case may be, and also that for each patent application and patent, a copy of the power of attorney certified by the Office with the number in the register for general powers of attorney and the signature of the professional representative is filed with the Office.

A legal fee for certification and issuance of the power of attorney copy should also be paid.

As far as foreign applicants are concerned, representation by a patent attorney is compulsory; otherwise, the patent application shall be rejected. Where the power of attorney is not drawn up in the Romanian language, this shall be accompanied by a translation certified to be in compliance with the original.

H. Document Certifying the Deposit of the Biological Material with an International Depository Authority

108. If the patent application relates to biological material or to use of biological material which is not available to the public and which cannot be described in the patent application in such a manner as to enable the invention to be carried out by a person skilled in the art, it is obligatory to complete the application with a document certifying the deposit of the biological material with an officially recognized national depositary institution designated by the Government or with an international depository authority. According to rule 25, the document shall be filed with the Office and shall contain:

- denomination of the biological material;
- denomination and address of the depository institution where the biological material has been deposited;
- order number assigned to the deposit;
- date of the deposit of the biological material with the depository institution.

The document must prove that the biological material was deposited with the international depository institution on an earlier date than the date of the deposit or than the date of the recognized priority of the patent application.

Where the invention in the patent application relates to a microorganism, in default of the certification document, the application shall be refused.

The information in the patent application regarding the deposit of the biological material should be communicated to the Office:

- within sixteen months from the filing date or, if a priority is claimed, from the priority date, the time limit being considered to be observed if the information is communicated until the end of the technical procedures with the view of publishing the patent application; or
- up to the date of presenting the request for publication of the patent application; being applicable to the time limit to expire first.

After the communication of this information, the applicant shall be considered to consent unreservedly and irrevocably to render the deposited biological material available to the public.

I. Declaration of the Inventor

109. Where the applicant is not the same as the inventor or is not the only inventor, the designation of the inventor shall be made in a separate document annexed to the patent application. The designation document states the surname, first name and complete address of the inventor, these data being identical to the ones contained in the document proving that the applicant acquired the right to be granted the patent.

The declaration of the inventor is done under the applicant's responsibility and it has as final date within eighteen months from the date on which substantive examination was requested. Nevertheless, for applications subject to a confidential regime, the final date is that of the publication or when the Office took the decision.

The inventor(s) as declared by the applicant may ask by a written document, according to Article 34, that they should not be mentioned in the published patent application or in the patent. In this case, the inventor shall file a statement with OSIM, at the latest, one month before the date of publication of the patent application.

The modification of the group of inventors may be asked by the applicant or by the patent owner at any time but no later than the date when the decision to grant a patent is taken; otherwise, the Office does not take into account the applicant's request for the modification of the collective of inventors. This supposes the filing with the Office of a legalized declaration stating that the person(s) initially mentioned agree either with the exclusion of one or more of them or with the inclusion of other persons, mentioning the order in which they will be written in the patent. In this last situation, the declaration shall include their agreement on the assignment of the rights to the applicant.

J. Document for Transfer of the Right to Be Granted a Patent

110. This document may be filed with the Office either at the initiative of the applicant when the inventor(s) assigned the right to be granted a patent to a natural or legal person prior to filing the patent application or at the Office's request if, from the documentation of the patent application, it does not result that the applicant is entitled to be granted a patent for invention.

The document shall be filed in its original or legalized copy until a decision is made in respect of the patent application. If the applicant fails to file the document up to the date a decision is made in respect of the patent application, the Office grants him another six-month time limit to file it; failure to file the document shall lead to the refusal of the patent application.

If the right to grant a patent for invention was transferred after the regular filing, the time limit to file the document shall extend to the taking of a decision by the Office. The failure to file the document within the aforementioned time limit will mean that the patent will be granted in the patent applicant's name.

II. Formalities for the International PCT Applications

A. *OSIM: Receiving Office*

111. According to the PCT provisions and its regulations, OSIM acts as a receiving office for those patent applications which, for the purpose of international patenting, are filed in Romania and the filing date of the Office is recognized as being the filing date for all countries designated in the application and which are PCT members.

When protection in Romania following the national procedure has been requested first, the applicant may obviously claim the conventional priority of the first filed application.

Both Romanian nationals as well as nationals of other States having their permanent domicile in Romania or Romanian and foreign legal persons having their registered office in Romania may file with OSIM as receiving office. If an international application is submitted by more applicants, it shall suffice for one of them to fulfil this condition. The Office as a receiving office shall receive, check and transmit the international applications to the International Bureau, according to the PCT and the Implementing Regulations under the PCT.

The international application is drawn up by the applicant in three copies, in Romanian, English, French or Russian, at the applicant's option and typed on the standard forms elaborated by WIPO. Where the description, claims and drawings have been filed in another language than one of the languages accepted by the international search authority elected by the applicant, this shall file, within one month from the date of filing the application, a translation of the documents into the accepted language where the mentioned conditions have not been fulfilled, the international application shall be deemed to be received by Office on behalf of the International Bureau, as a receiving office, and the whole documentation shall be transmitted to the International Bureau, subject to the payment, by the applicant, to the benefit of Office, of a fee in an amount equal to the transmittal fee. Where the translation has not been submitted within the mentioned time limit, this may be submitted within one month from the notification but not later than two months from filing the international application, subject to the payment of the fee for subsequently filing the translation of the international application.

In the international application, the applicant shall declare the inventor(s), indicating the designated States. The application shall include the signature of the applicant or that of the authorized representative and the identification data of the representative, if the applicant will be represented by him.

When in the international application, the priority of one or more filings is claimed, the priority documents shall be filed with the Office at the same time as the application or subsequently sent by the applicant to the International Bureau of WIPO within sixteen months from the priority date of the patent application.

As receiving office, OSIM checks if the international application is in compliance with the provisions of the PCT and its regulations and, if not, notifies the applicant to remedy the deficiencies. The failure to comply within the prescribed time limit with the requested corrections leads to the consideration of the application as abandoned and its rejection.

If an international application claims the priority of an application having a filing date earlier than the priority date, the applicant may file an application according to rule 26*bis* 3 of the Implementing Regulations under the PCT, subject to payment of a fee in an amount equal to the amount of the fee of an application for reinstatement. The Office shall take the decision to accept that application where it has been ascertained that the applicant made all efforts to file the international application within the priority time limit or that the priority term was not exceeded by intention.

If the application meets all the provisions of the PCT and its regulations, in order to proceed to international protection, the applicant together with the Office decides on which international authority will be in charge of either international search or international preliminary examination to carry out the procedures involved.

The payment of the relevant fee is a necessary condition for that. If the Office does not receive the proof of payment of the relevant fee, it will consider the international application as abandoned and in its quality of receiving office will suspend the consideration of the application as an international application.

OSIM, as receiving office, transmits the international application to the International Bureau of WIPO and to the International Search Authority at the latest in the twelfth month since the international application or the thirteenth if a priority is claimed.

B. OSIM: Designated Office

112. OSIM is considered a designated office if, in the international application of a foreign applicant, Romania is identified as the designated State where the protection of the applicant's invention is claimed.

An international application that was accorded an international filing date with a receiving office shall have the same effect as a patent application filed in Romania on the same date. If the applicant desires to continue the international application in Romania within thirty months from the international filing date, or if a priority has been claimed from the date of priority, he shall open the national phase in Romania. These provisions shall also apply if, for justified reasons, the applicant opens the national phase within two months from the date of the expiry of the thirty-month time limit, subject to payment of a fee in an amount equal to the amount of the fee for filing an application for reinstatement.

Opening of the national phase is performed by filing with the Office the form requested to open the national phase, accompanied by a copy of the international application and a translation into Romanian of the description, claims, drawings, and abstract of the invention at which shall be annexed the document stating the payment of the national fees.

The patent application filing date will be the date of the international application and this date will be recorded in the National Register of Filed Patent Applications.

By opening the national phase, the international application is completely subject to the provisions provided in the national law, including the transmittal of the conformed translations in the Romanian language, of the claims and eventually of the title, as modified by the applicant, after the search report has been made by the competent authority.

The Office may accept, upon request by the applicant, the continuation in Romania of only a part of the international application, and in this case, he shall file the translation of that part only and shall make a statement showing the parts of the international application not included in the translation and the reason for giving them up.

When the applicant requested the opening of the national phase, subsequently, within the mentioned time limits, the Office decided to reject the patent application.

If the International Search Authority is subjected to the international search only a part of the international application which relates to two or more inventions forming a single general inventive concept, the applicant may continue the international application in Romania for all the inventions contained therein.

For the international application entered in the national phase, the applicant may transmit to OSIM any of the certified translations of the description or claims as amended during the procedures the application undergoes in the international phase; the amendments shall not go beyond the limits of the disclosure of the invention in the international application, as filed with the receiving office. Where the applicant fails to send the translation of the claims as originally filed, the Office shall notify the same to submit the translation within ninety days; in case the missing translation is not submitted within the time limit specified in the notification, the Office shall carry on the procedures based on the filed translated claims.

The description, claims and drawings of the international application for which the national phase was opened in Romania, translated into Romanian, shall be published immediately after the expiry of a six-month time limit from the date of opening the national phase, according to the provisions of Article 22 of the Law. However, the application cannot be published earlier than twenty months from the date of filing or from the date of the claimed priority without the applicant's consent. Where a search report is requested according to the provisions of Article 23 of the Law, this shall be drawn up based on the translation of the description, claims and drawings indicated by the applicant.

The examination procedure of the international application which entered the national phase shall start after the expiry of the time limit of thirty months and only upon express request by the applicant, drawn up before this time limit. Within four months from opening the national phase, the applicant may correct, subject to payment of the legal fee, the deficiencies in the priority indicated during the international phase procedure.

The Office shall recognize the priority claimed in an international application having a filing date subsequent to the priority time limit, provided that the applicant requests within two months from the opening of the national phase, subject to payment of the legal fee, the reinstatement of priority right.

If a receiving office refuses to accord a filing date to an international application or decides that the application or the designation of Romania is deemed to be withdrawn, the Office shall, upon request by the applicant, analyse the decision in order to establish whether it is justified, with a view to carrying out the procedures by the national route, and shall review it, where appropriate.

A request for review shall be presented by the applicant to the International Bureau prior to the expiry of the time limit provided for by rule 51.1 of the Implementing Regulations under the PCT in order that a copy of all the documents annexed to the international application should be transmitted by the International Bureau to Office; the Office shall comply with the request for review prior to the expiry of the time limit, provided that the applicant files a translation of the application with Office and pays a fee in an equal amount to the fee for lodging an appeal.

If the Office states that the decision of the receiving office or of the International Bureau was not justified, the application shall be subjected to the procedures provided for by the Law.

If an international filing date has not been accorded by the receiving office, the filing date of the application shall be the date on which the Office considers that the filing date should have been accorded. If the international application fulfils the requirements concerning the form and substance provided for by the PCT, the application shall have the effect of a national application in Romania from the date of filing.

C. OSIM: Elected Office

113. When the applicant avails himself in the international application of an international preliminary examination report, he shall then file to the Office, which is thus considered as elected Office, the translation in Romanian of the international application, along with a copy of the international application and the national fees within thirty months from the international application priority date.

If, as a result of the international search report, the claims are amended and these amendments are attached to the report, a translation of these amendments shall also be filed.

The withdrawal of the demand for the international preliminary examination or of the election of the office can be made under conditions stipulated by the PCT, but this does not mean that the international application has been withdrawn if Romania still remains a designated State.

III. Granting Procedure

A. *Preliminary Examination*

114. After constituting the regular national filing, the patent application is subject to a preliminary examination. This will state, on one hand, the check of all data referring to the defining of the legal status of the patent application, the person entitled to be granted the patent, the authorized representative, the declaration of the inventor(s), the correctness of the priority claim by relevant documents, the payment of fees and, on the other hand, the fulfilment of the prescribed conditions referring to all components of the patent application: description, claims, drawings, other documents which are annexed to the application.

At this stage, the unity of the invention 'at first sight' is also examined as a very important aspect, if the subject matter of the invention is within the category of patentable inventions or within legal categories of inventions excepted or excluded from patentability.

This is the moment and the place when the possible non-observation of public morality of the invention and the inclusion in the category of scientific theories or discoveries are analysed.

If the preliminary examination department notices some irregularities, it notifies the applicant or his authorized representative by indicating time limits for answers and correction of the irregularities.

At the same time, the application is preclassified, based on the claims and the subject matter of the invention, in order to be distributed according to the subject matter of the invention, to the specialized substantive examiner. The initial classification could be confirmed, completed or modified during the patent application search and examination procedures, or may also undergo modifications as a consequence of limitation of the granted patent, to be exposed latter on.

According to rule 33, the Office checks also the fulfilment of other relevant preliminary conditions and, at the same time, indicates, together with the time limit for remedying, the possible drawbacks that have been ascertained, such as:

- failure to file the prescribed form;
- lack of applicant's or professional representative's signature on the form or identification data;
- lack of the title of the invention on the form;
- lack of translation into Romanian of the description, claims and drawings contained in the patent application;
- lack of proof of payment of the legal fees concerning the subsequent translation into Romanian of the description, claims and drawings or of the claims and/or drawings, as the case may be;
- lack of the professional representative's power of attorney, where the applicant mentioned his representation in the application;
- failure to indicate the legal provisions based on which the applicant is entitled to be granted the patent, including the lack of the document proving this;
- lack of claims and/or drawings and/or abstract;

- the applicant's entitlement to the patent for invention, when he is not the inventor;
- the professional representative's right to represent the applicant before OSIM;
- whether the inventors have been declared;
- whether the conventional priority has correctly been claimed and sustained by the priority documents filed with the Office;
- whether the application results by dividing an earlier application, when this fact is mentioned in the application;
- the fulfilment of the conditions in respect of the document certifying the deposition of the biological material with an international depository institution.

One of the most important conditions checked within the preliminary phase, which in fact is crucial for the possibility of continuing with examination, is the fulfilment of the conditions concerning the drawing up of the description, claims and drawings, so that at first sight, the invention is clearly and completely disclosed within the patent application.

The preliminary examination board may make decisions within the preliminary examination procedure in compliance for the area of its competence.

B. Publication of the Patent Application

115. According to the Law, the standard procedure provides for the publication of the patent applications filled by national route immediately after a time limit of eighteen months from the regular filing date or, in the case of one or more priority claim(s), from the date of the earliest recognized priority. Patent applications filed under the PCT shall be published as soon as possible after the expiry of a period of six months from the opening of the national phase.

At the request of an entitled natural or legal person, publication may be effected within a shorter time than the prescribed one. Where the decision to grant the patent has been made before the expiry of the time limit of eighteen months, the patent application shall be published simultaneously with the publication of the notice mentioning the decision to grant the patent.

The publication of the application may be requested only by the applicant or professional representative who also owes the publication fee. Where the legal conditions for the publication of the patent application are fulfilled, the applicant is notified about the date of publication of the application.

In case of failure to observe the deadlines for payment and the amount of the fee for publication, the Office shall declare the application as deemed to be withdrawn.

According to Article 23(7) of the Law, the patent application publication is made by rendering available to the public, at the Office headquarters, the description, claims and, where appropriate, drawings of the patent application as filed and the date of publication shall be the date of the issuance of BOPI containing the mention of application publication.

The patent application publication may be accompanied by a search report, which, if it is not made available together with the application, will be published separately at a later stage.

According to the Law, there are some distinct situations when the patent application will not be published after eighteen months from the regular filing date.

The first one is where before the expiry of the eighteen-month period a decision to reject has been made or the patent application has been withdrawn or declared as deemed to be withdrawn and thus, missing the object of the request, the patent application shall not be published.

Second, the patent applications for which the specialized institutions established a 'secret regime', which ends by the decisions of the same institutions, shall be published within three months from the date on which the classified status of the information comprised therein has been lifted.

Finally, if another person than the applicant or the professional representative thereof has requested the publication and/or paid the publication fee, the Office shall not comply with the publication procedure; however, if the applicant or the professional representative, as the case may be, agrees with the payment of the publication fee by another person, this shall communicate his agreement to the Office which shall comply with the publication of the application. In the absence of the agreement, the amount paid shall be considered to be undue and shall be refunded to the person that has paid it.

If, during preliminary examination, it has been stated that the patent application is obviously non-unitary, the applicant will be notified accordingly and will be given a two-month time limit to divide the application. If the applicant does not perform the division of the application, the patent application will be published in the non-unitary form. Where the applicant, after having been notified or by his own initiative, has divided the patent application within the time limit referred to, the Office publishes the description, claims and, where appropriate, the original drawings as well as the claims of the invention or group of inventions remained by dividing this application. The application resulting from dividing an initial patent application shall be published within three months from the date of filing with OSIM but not earlier than eighteen months from the filing date of the basic application or, if a priority has been claimed, from the date of priority thereof. In the situation already mentioned, in the part edited by OSIM, there will be published the number and date of filing the basic application from which the new application resulted by division.

The publication will include all admissible amendments or completions to descriptions, claims or drawings sent to the Office until the sixteenth month from the filing date.

As already specified, the publishing of the application ensures the setting up of the provisional protection, its scope being determined by the content of the claims, as they have been published in the patent application. The effect of the provisional protection is retroactive, beginning with the filing date and ensures, until the granting of the patent of invention, the same rights as those conferred by the patent.

According to rule 36, the patent application rendered available to the public shall not contain:

– texts and/or drawings contrary to public order or morality;
– allegations disparaging products, processes or assessment of the value of the patent applications or patents of third parties;

– elements obviously irrelevant or useless in connection with the disclosure of the invention.

Where the patent application contains such elements which cannot be published, the Office shall omit them from publication, indicating their place within the submitted documentation and the number of words and/or drawings that have not been published. The applicant or the professional representative, as the case may be, will be notified in respect of the elements omitted from publication and shall send him a copy of the application rendered available to the public.

C. Search Report

116. The search report is an important part of the procedure because it supplies, after its publication, information relating to the relevant state of the art in respect of the invention contained in the patent application claims to the applicant and third parties, which may be used by the applicant in order to decide on the continuation or not of the patenting procedure. In order to have a clearer image of its chances of being granted a patent, the applicant may ask that the search report be accompanied by a written opinion. The Office proceeds to draw up and publish the search report where the applicant submits a request and the proof of payment of the legal fee.

The patent application may be subjected to the procedure of drawing up and publication of the search report with or without written opinion, if the date of the written request is until the twentieth month from the filing date of the application or from the opening of the national phase.

The publication of the search report shall be made at the time of publication of the application, immediately after the expiration of an eighteen-month time period of the filing date of the application or subsequently to the publication of the application. The applicant may request the search report to be drawn up based on the description, claims and, where appropriate, drawings modified on his own initiative or as a consequence of an OSIM notification.

The search report cannot be made and the applicant/representative will accordingly be informed under the following conditions:

– the request for drawing up the search report has been filed after the time limit;
– the legal fee has not been paid in the legal amount and time limits;
– the invention that is the subject matter of the patent application is not sufficiently clear and completely disclosed or excluded or excepted from patentability;
– the office has made a decision to refuse the patent application, has taken note of the withdrawal of the application or has declared the application as being deemed to be withdrawn before the date of requesting the search report;
– the patent application contains classified information;
– the publication of the application is made together with the mention of the decision to grant a patent;
– the patent application filing does not have the effects of a regular national filing.

In the situation of insufficient disclosure, the Office shall publish the mention of the fact that the search report could not be drawn up. If, during the procedure of drawing up the search report, it has been ascertained that the patent application contains two or more inventions failing to comply with the condition of unity of invention, the applicant shall be notified about the lack of unity of invention and asked to indicate the invention or group of inventions in the filing for which the search report can be drawn up based on the paid fee. If the applicant fails to transmit the indication, the search report shall be drawn up for the first claimed invention or unitary group of inventions.

The search report shall be transmitted to the applicant together with the copies of the relevant parts of the cited documents.

If the search report is accompanied by a written opinion, the applicant shall be notified, and the Office does not render the written opinion available to the public.

The publication of the search report shall be made by rendering it available to the public at the Office headquarters on the date of publication of the mention of drawing up the report in BOPI.

In the situation when, after the date of the search report, the applicant transmits the amended claims to the Office, during the substantive examination procedure, a supplement of the search report shall be drawn up for the new elements introduced into the claims.

In the search report, there shall be cited documents contained in the state of the art, available on the date of drawing up the same, that can be considered for assessing the novelty and the inventive step, there being indicated, for each citation, the claim in the patent application referred to; there shall be indicated the degree of relevance thereof, by using the internationally assigned symbols as well as the relevant parts of the cited documents, where appropriate.

The search report does not contain any appreciation relating to the fulfilment or non-fulfilment of the patentability conditions.

The search report distinguishes between the cited documents published before the date of the priority claimed, between the priority date and the date of filing and on or after the date of filing.

If, after the analysis of the patent application, OSIM considers that it does not meet the provisions for carrying out a meaningful search in the state of the art on the basis of all or only some claims, it shall either declare that the search is not possible, situation in which the fee shall not be refunded, or shall, in so far as applicable, draw up a partial search report; the declaration and the partial report shall be considered for the purposes of the subsequent proceedings that the patent application undergoes. The search report shall be communicated to the applicant within a time limit allowing him to respond up to ending the preparations for publication.

The written opinion contains observations relating to the fulfilment of the provisions of the sufficient disclosure of the invention and contains a concise appreciation with regard to novelty, inventive step and industrial applicability of each claim in the patent application, as well as explanations in respect of the relevance of documents cited in the report relative to the corresponding claims. Until the completion of the preparations for publication, the applicant may transmit his viewpoint to the written opinion, accompanied, where appropriate, by the modification of the application.

D. Substantive Examination

117. The substantive examination is done within the departments specialized in substantive examination and it has as its main goal the verification of the meeting of patentability conditions.

The substantive examination may be asked at the filing date or within thirty months from that date. If this time limit is not met, then the patent application is considered to be withdrawn and is rejected.

The specific procedure will examine the meeting of the following conditions:

- the documentation meets the conditions for the substantive examination to be started;
- the invention is disclosed clearly and completely for it to be carried out by a person skilled in the art;
- the invention is not included in the categories of inventions excepted or excluded from patentability;
- the invention is not contrary to morality or public order;
- the claimed priority;
- the unity of invention;
- the patentability conditions.

During the examination procedure, the Office may request the applicant or his successor in title to provide explanations or documents deemed necessary in connection with the regular filing made or in order to meet the conditions of patentability.

During the substantive examination, the applicant may modify the claims, the description or the drawings either at the Office's request or upon his/her own initiative, but with the observation of the fundamental condition that such modifications do not extend beyond the limits of disclosure of the invention on the filing date of the patent application.

The absence of notifications shall not absolve the applicant, patent owner or interested person from the obligation to meet the requirements of the Law. The applicant shall file with OSIM all public documents connected to his invention, including copies of patents granted in other States.

118. Referring to the unity of invention, in the application of the law, the condition that the patent application should relate only to a single invention is fulfilled if the technical problem that the invention proposes to solve is unitary and all its essential technical features are necessary or at least adequate for solving this problem.

Where a group of inventions is claimed in the patent application, the condition on the unity of invention shall be fulfilled only when there is a technical relationship among these inventions involving one or more identical or corresponding special technical features; the expression 'special technical features' means those technical features which define a contribution which each of the claimed inventions, considered a whole, makes over the state of the art.

The determination of the existence of a single general inventive concept in case of a group of inventions should be made without regard to whether each invention is claimed in separate claims or as alternatives within a single claim.

General inventive concept may consist of:

- solutions to more technical problems, if based on the technical interdependence thereof, they are subsumed to a single general unitary problem;
- independent technical solutions, if the solved technical problem is new, or though it is not new, it is solved for the first time;
- related technological solutions to a single technical problem;
- unitary effect obtained by more inventions; or
- claims of various categories, if they present a technical interdependence relationship.

Any of the following combinations of independent claims of different categories are in fact allowed in the same patent application:

- in addition to an independent claim for a given product, an independent claim for a process specially adapted for manufacturing the product and an independent claim for the use of said product;
- in addition to an independent claim for a given process, an independent claim for a device or a means specially conceived for the application of the said process; or
- in addition to an independent claim for a given product, an independent claim for a process specially adapted for the fabrication of the product and an independent claim for a device or means specially conceived for the application of the process.

It should be noted that the list of combinations of independent claims given is not exhaustive with other combinations being possible.

A process is considered to be specially adapted for the fabrication of the product, if said process leads directly to obtaining the claimed product; also, a device or a means is specially conceived for carrying out the process, if the device or means is suitable for carrying out the process, there existing a technical relationship between the device or means and the claimed process.

If, in the course of the substantive examination, the Office states that the patent application refers in fact to a group of inventions which are not linked so as to form a single general inventive concept, then the Office notifies this to the applicant or to his successor in title.

The applicant or the professional representative, as the case may be, has the opportunity to divide the application by filing a divisional patent application for each invention or group of inventions fulfilling the condition of unity of the invention. Where multiple priorities have been claimed in the original patent application, the applicant must indicate the corresponding priority in each divisional application. If, until a decision is made for the original application, the applicant fails to file patent applications for the inventions not complying with the condition of unity of the invention, these will remain in the description but without being the subject matter of the claims.

Where the applicant or the professional representative, as the case may be, has failed to file divisional patent applications and OSIM has examined the patent application whose subject matter is the first invention or the first group of inventions fulfilling the condition of unity of the invention, the protection by patent shall be considered not to have been claimed for the other inventions contained in the original application.

The applicant may divide the application and file with the Office a divisional patent application for each application or group of inventions, which meet the requirement of unity of invention and is obliged within a maximum of six months from the date when the examination is demanded to file a written option and a description, claims and drawings for the invention which shall be examined in the original filing.

The other divisional applications may be filed up to the moment of taking a decision concerning the original filing.

The filing date of the original application will be automatically extended on the filing date for every divisional application, provided that the applicant observes the limits of the disclosure of the original filing for each divisional application.

In a similar manner, the priority right for divisional applications applies to the original application and if multiple priorities have been claimed in the original application, then in every divisional application, the priority to which it relates should be indicated by the applicant.

If, up to the taking of a decision on the first filing, the applicant has not filed divisional patent applications, then the procedure continues by taking into account the description of the invention which does not respect the principle of unity, but without making reference to the relevant claims of that part.

The lack of unity of the invention may not be set forth within the actions for revocation or cancellation of a patent of invention.

119. Within eighteen months from the request of examination, the specialist examiner draws up the examination report on the basis of which an Examination Board of the Office decides to grant a patent of invention or to refuse the patent application, as the case may be, by taking into account the existence of a patentable invention, which is not contrary to morality or public order and which meets the patentability criteria. The examination board also takes note of the patent application withdrawal where the applicant requests the withdrawal in writing or shall declare the applications that are in one of the legal situations as deemed to be withdrawn. The specialized examination boards within the Office are constituted according to technical fields or to the examination procedure and consist of a chairman appointed by the Director General of the Office, the state examiner in the industrial property field who has performed the patent application examination and has drawn up the examination report and a second examiner appointed by the chairman. For the inventions of special complexity, the board may be extended by two more examiners upon the chairman's proposal.

The patent application examination report according to the provisions of Article 28 of the Law is the document by which the procedure of examination of a patent application is completed and drawn up and signed by the examiner who has instrumented the patent application file.

The examination report contains all considerations made by the examiner of the file regarding technical and legal basis enabling it to take a decision and includes also the examiner's proposal addressed to the Examination Board concerning the grant or the refusal of the patent application, there being invoked the legal grounds thereof. After completing the patent application substantive examination procedure, the Office notifies the applicant or the professional representative, as the case may be, about the intention to grant the patent and to communicate the corresponding decisions, subject to payment of the fee for publication, printing and issuance of the patent. The notification is accompanied by the documentation containing the description, claims and drawings based on which the board will make the decision to grant the patent where judicial procedures have commenced regarding the right to the patent or the right to the grant of the patent, in order to suspend the patenting procedure until the court decision becomes final and irrevocable, the applicant's successor in title or the professional representative, as the case may be, shall:

- file a request with OSIM to expressly request the suspension of the proceedings that the patent application undergoes;
- pay a fee for extension of the time limit for the proceedings; and
- file with Officer certified copies of all documents justifying the request for suspension.

The procedure may be resumed at the express request of the successor in title or of the professional representative, as the case may be filed with the Office, to which the documents attesting the status of successor in title shall be appended. In this situation, the Office notifies the interested parties of the date of resuming the proceedings.

In case of suspension caused by the death of the professional representative and appointment of a new professional representative, the Office shall resume the proceedings only after the submission of the power of attorney for the representation of the applicant; otherwise, the patent application shall be rejected, or the proceedings shall be resumed considering that the applicant is not represented by the professional representative, as the case may be.

Based on the provisions of the law, the Office refuses the patent application in the following cases:

- the patent application does not meet the requirements regarding representation in the case of foreign applicants;
- the invention to which the application relates is not patentable, is excluded from patentability, or does not meet the patentability conditions;
- the invention to which the application relates does not meet the requirements of clear and complete disclosure;
- the time limit for opening the international phase for internationally registered applications has expired;
- the twelve-month time limit from the date on which applications were deemed to be withdrawn has elapsed;
- has been requested a refusal of the patent application by the person entitled to the grant of the patent established by a court;

- the applicant, other than the inventor, has not proved, within the legally prescribed time limit, that he is entitled to the grant of the patent;
- examination of the patent application in view of the grant of a patent has not been requested within the time limits prescribed.

The office shall take note of the withdrawal of the patent application provided that the applicant expressly requests the withdrawal in writing.

Patent applications shall be declared as deemed to be withdrawn in the following cases:

- the inventors were not declared within eighteen months from the date on which substantive examination was requested;
- the applicant did not respond, within the established time limit, to the notifications of OSIM to make the form of the description and drawings correspond to the content of admitted claims;
- the application lay at the basis of the priority claim in a subsequent application filed either by national route or by international route and which has been entered in the national phase in Romania;
- the person entitled to the grant of the patent by a decision of the court files a new application and the initial patent application is in the circumstance to be deemed as withdrawn;
- the applicant did not submit the claims within the time limit of two months;
- non-payment of at least one of the legal fees.

All decisions issued by the Office in respect of patent applications shall be substantiated and registered in the National Register of Patent Applications and shall be communicated to the applicant within one month from the date on which a decision was taken. In the same register, mentions concerning withdrawn patent applications or the declarations pursuant to which the patent applications are deemed to be withdrawn shall also be registered, which shall also be communicated.

For all the patent applications for which the publication fee, printing and issuance of the patent have been paid, the mention of the decision to grant the patent shall be published in the first BOPI issue following after the expiration of the legal fee for lodging an appeal. The mentions concerning the decisions to refuse the patent application shall be published in the first BOPI issue following the expiration of the legal fee for lodging an appeal.

In case of lodging an appeal, the publication of the mention of the decision shall be made within one month from the date when the appeal was settled.

OSIM shall publish the mention of the decision to grant the patent and, simultaneously with the publication, it shall make the patent description and drawings available to the public, provided that publication fee, printing fee and patent issuance fee are paid. If publication fee, printing fee and patent issuance fee are not paid within the time limits laid down by the law, the patent application shall be deemed to be withdrawn and the patent shall not be deemed to have been granted.

The decision to grant the patent shall only take effect from the date on which the mention thereof is published in the Official Industrial Property Bulletin.

A particular situation occurs when the Office, in spite of the fact that generally it acts of the basis on own applicant responsibility, finds out that it must not grant the patent to the applicant. In this respect, rule 29 provides that:

> where the Office, on the basis of solid proofs, finds that the applicant, other than the inventor, is not entitled to the grant of the patent, it may proceed to postpone the notification of the decision made, not exceeding a six-month period since its date; if, within that period of time, the applicant cannot prove that he is entitled to the grant of the patent, the decision to grant the patent shall be revoked and the patent application shall be refused.

In case of death of the applicant – natural person or dissolving the legal person, the examination procedure shall be discontinued until OSIM is notified of the successor in title.

Where judicial procedures have commenced regarding the right to the patent or the right to the grant of the patent, the patenting procedure shall be suspended until the court decision becomes final and irrevocable. The interested party shall communicate the mentioned decision to the Office.

The decisions to grant a patent are published in the BOPI within thirty days of its granting and the patent specification is made available to the public within three months.

The decision to reject the application is taken by the Office in one of the following situations:

- the substantive examination has not been requested within the legal limit of thirty months;
- the legal registration, examination, or publication fees have not been paid;
- the substantive examination patentability criteria have not been met;
- the application has been abandoned;
- the application has been withdrawn with an explicit request.

The decisions of the Office are motivated and the decisions together with the motivations shall be communicated to the applicant or his successor in title within thirty days after the date of the taking thereof and they shall be registered in the National Register of Patent Applications.

Up to the communication of the decisions, the Office may revoke its decisions ex officio, under the conditions that when according to some circumstances it reached the conclusion that the legal conditions for the aforementioned decisions have not been met. This situation occurs sometimes if, within the revocation period, the Office has identified documents liable to change these decisions. The ex officio revocation according to Article 28 of the Law shall be made by the Examination Board that has made the decision.

If it has been ascertained that the decisions of the Board contain material errors or omissions, particularly with regard to the inventor's, the applicant's or patent owner's identification data, the Examination Board shall decide the remedying thereof, without the revocation of the decision. The mention of ex officio revocation shall be entered in the Register of the examination boards within the division where the decision has been made.

Romanian law is also flexible in another particular procedural situation which occurs many times and which refers to the so-called reinstatement of rights. Thus, rule 53 provides that when the applicant or patent owner fails to comply with a time limit for an action within a procedure before Office, having the effect of loss of rights in respect of the patent application or the patent, the Office, upon request thereof, may reinstate the same in the previous situation, within two months from the cessation of the cause, but not more than one year from the expiration of the time limit, provided that the following requirements are fulfilled cumulatively:

- the applicant, patent owner or professional representative, as the case may be, expressly request the reinstatement;
- the request is formulated within due time;
- the application is justified; and
- the legal fee paid at the time of filing the application.

The submitted request cannot be refused wholly or in part before the office has notified the applicant, the patent owner or the professional representative, as the case may be, about the reasons for refusal and has granted a two-month time limit for submitting the observations. OSIM decides the rejection of the request for reinstatement, if this refers to one of the situations expressly excluded by law.

The decision to accept or reject the request for reinstatement shall be communicated to the applicant, patent owner or professional representative, as the case may be.

E. Appeal and Revocation

120. For a six-month period from the publication date of the mentioning of the decision to grant a patent in the BOPI, the patent specification is made available to the public at the Office; within this time limit, any interested person may formulate requests for revocation of all or some of the decisions of the Office provided that:

- the subject matter of the patent is not patentable;
- the subject matter of the patent does not disclose the invention in a manner sufficiently clear and complete for it to be carried out by a person skilled in the art;
- the subject matter of the patent exceeds the content of the patent application as filed.

Where the grounds for revocation only relate to a part of the patent, the patent shall be revoked in part.

After the revocation time limit and under the conditions that either the revoking action has not been initiated or the revocation action has been rejected, the patent is issued by the Director General of the Office on the basis of the granting decision. Patents are registered in the National Register of the Patents of Inventions.

The decisions of the Office may be appealed against by the applicant within three months of the communication. The object of the appeal may also be a limitation of the patent.

Both appeals and requests for revocation are solved within the Department Board of Appeal by a Board of Re-examination consisting of a chairman and two to four members, after hearings and examination of the written interventions made by parties.

According to rule 59, regarding the appeals, the Board of Appeal may decide:

(a) to accept the appeal wholly or in part by changing the decision to refuse, by cancelling the same and returning the case to the substantive examination for the continuation of the examination procedure within the competence limits specified in the decision of the Board of Appeal;
(b) to accept the appeal, to cancel the decision to grant and to send the case back to the examination for the continuation of the examination procedure within the competence limits specified in the decision of the Board of Appeal;
(c) to accept the appeal and the modifications requested by the appellant in the appeal procedure, to change the decision to grant and to send the patent for publication with the modifications brought by the Board of Appeal;
(d) to reject the appeal and to maintain the decision appealed against.

In case of the appeal having the object of patent limitation, the Board of Appeal may decide:

(a) to accept the appeal based on the claims amended by the applicant, to modify the decision to grant made by the Examination Board and to transmit the patent with the modifications accepted by the Board of Appeal for publication;
(b) to reject the appeal and transmit the patent as granted by the Examination Board for publication.

In case of the requests for revocation, the board of appeal may decide:

(a) to accept the request wholly and to revoke the patent;
(b) to accept the request for revocation in part and the claims amended by the patent owner within the revocation procedure, to maintain the patent as modified by the owner within the revocation procedure and to transmit the patent to be republished;
(c) to accept in part the request, by maintaining the patent as modified after the decision made by the Board of Appeal and to transmit the patent for publication;
(d) to reject the request for revocation and to maintain the patent as modified by the owner within the revocation procedure and to transmit the patent to be republished;
(e) to reject the request for revocation and to maintain the patent as granted by the Examination Board.

The decisions of the Board of Re-examination shall be communicated within fifteen days and may be appealed before the Court of Bucharest within three months of their communication.

IV. European Patents with Effects to Romania

121. On the basis of Law No. 611/2002 on the accession of Romania to the EPC already mentioned in §2, any person may request and may obtain, under the condition of observing the patentability criteria, a patent granted by the EPO and designating Romania. Article 2 provides for that 'in the case of a conflict between the provision of the EPC and that of the Law of Accession or of the Patent Law, the provisions of the EPC shall prevail'.

This supposes that the applicant of the European patent application, who wants a protection on a territory which includes Romania, indicates in the patent application Romania as 'designating country'.

According to the Law, 'a European patent application and a European patent extending to Romania shall, subject to the provision of this law, have the effect and be subject to the same conditions as a national patent application, or a national patent under the law'.

The European patent application means either an application for a European patent filed under the EPC or an international application filed under the PCT for which the EPO acts as designated or elected office and in which Romania is designated. According to Article 4 of Law No. 611/2004 and in line with Article 14 of the EPC, European patent applications, excepting the divisional ones, may be applied in any admissible language. Any European patent applications which refer to an invention containing information classified as secret of State shall be applied with the Office.

The European patent application which has been granted a filing date and in which Romania is designated is perfectly equivalent to a national patent application and has the benefit, as the case may be, of the claimed priority for this European patent application, whatever its subsequent outcome may be.

The equivalence with a national patent application extends to the setting up of the provisional protection for the published European application, beginning from the date at which a translation in Romanian of the claims of the European application has been published by OSIM, after the payment of the fee provided in Romanian law.

The European patent application is processed and examined and the patent is granted by the EPO according to the EPC and its regulations.

As from the date of publication of the mention of its grant by the EPO, the European patent shall confer the same rights as would be conferred by a national patent granted under Romanian law.

The Law provides the condition that the owner shall furnish to the OSIM a translation in Romanian of the European patent, together with the publication fee, within three months from the date on which the mention of the grant of the European patent has been published, as a condition of the validity of the European patent to Romania. If the translation of the European patent is not applied within this term, the owner of the European patent may apply with the office within the next term of three months, subject to the payment of a supplementary legal fee. The failure to file within the mentioned time limit of the translation of the patent specification or of the publication fee has the effect of considering the extended European patent void *ab initio*. However, the provisions of the law referring to the reinstatement of the rights shall be applied *mutatis mutandis*.

The Office has the legal obligation to publish any translation filed according to the previous specifications.

If, as a result of an opposition filed with the EPO, the European patent is revoked, then the European patent and the European patent application which has been the basis for granting of the patent shall be considered not to have had *ab initio* the specified effects.

If, as a result of the opposition procedure filed with EPO, the European patent is maintained with amended claims, the owner shall, within three months from the date on which the decision to maintain the European patent as amended was published, furnish to the office a translation of the amended claims in Romanian and pay the publication fee.

As has already been mentioned, sending a translation of the European patent specification in Romania is the legal condition for the patent validity in Romania.

An important problem under these conditions is taking into consideration the translation in the administrative or legal procedures in Romania. The agreement provides that the authentic text in any proceeding in Romania shall be the text of the European patent application or a European patent in the language of the proceedings before the EPO. However, it is recognized that the translation in Romanian also has the quality of an authentic text, except in cancellation proceedings, where the application or patent in the Romanian language confers protection which is narrower than that conferred by it in the language of the proceedings.

Where the applicant or the owner of the patent wishes to correct the text translated in Romanian, he can do that by transmitting the corrected version to the Office, given that the legal effect of the translation begins after its publication by the Office.

It is possible for a person who in good faith uses or who has made effective and serious preparations for using the invention, the use of which would not constitute infringement of the application or patent in the original translation, and by the filing of a corrected version which extends the initial scope of protection, to infringe the right conferred by the application or by the patent.

Taking into consideration good faith is a fundamental element and the lLaw correctly assimilates this situation with an exception of the exclusive right conferred by the patent, as presented in §6.

Consequently, after the corrected translation has produced its effects, that person may continue to use the invention without payment of compensation or other civil or criminal consequences.

Finally, another substantive question provided in the agreement is the situation of avoiding simultaneous protection.

Thus, where an extended European patent and a national patent having the same filing date or where priority has been claimed, the same priority date, have been granted to the same person or his successor in title, the national patent shall have no effect to the extent that it covers the same invention as the European patent from the date on which the time limit for filing an opposition to the European patent has expired, without an opposition having been filed or from the date on which the opposition procedure has resulted in a final decision maintaining the European patent.

122. In Article 8, the accession law also has important provisions referring to the renewal fees. First, it is provided that renewal fees shall be paid to the Office for the years following the year in which the mention of the grant of the European patent was published by the EPO in the amounts provided for in Romanian Law. Renewal fees shall be paid with the Office before the anniversary date of the patent application. After the expiry of the three-month term, the renewal fee may be paid up to a new six-month period from the anniversary date of the application filing, with an increase of 50% of the standard fee. The Office shall deliver in the account of the EPO the share of 50% of the paid renewal fees.

123. In line with the impact on national law provided for in the EPC, a European patent application which designates Romania may be converted into a national patent application where the European patent application is deemed to be withdrawn under Article 77 paragraph 3 of the EPC or where the translation of the application was not filed in due time under Article 90 paragraph 3 of the EPC. If the request for conversion has been filed with the Office under Article 135 paragraph 1 of the EPC, the Office shall invite the applicant to apply, within two months from the registration with the Office of the conversion request, translation into Romanian of the European patent application and, if the case may be, the text as amended during the procedures before the EPO, and to pay the legal procedural fees. If the conversion request, accompanied by a copy of the European patent application deemed as withdrawn, has not been transmitted to the Office, or if such a European patent application has been filed with the Office, the previous provisions shall apply *mutatis mutandis.*

The transmission of rights registered with the European Patent Register produces effect in Romania only after the publication of the European patent specification.

As it is known, the Unitary Patent system (UPS) was successfully launched on 1 June 2023, meaning that seventeen Member States, including three Member States in which the highest number of European patents had effect in 2012, Germany, France and Italy, ratified this agreement.

By Decree No. 1,643 of 8 December 2023, signed by the President of Romania and published in the Official Monitor No. 1107 of 8 December 2023, has been submitted to the Parliament for ratification, the Agreement on the Single Patent Court signed by Romania in Brussels on 19 February 2013.

Thus, it could be indeed considered that Romania has made a significant step in joining the Unitary Patent System, while there are foreseen no major obstacles to its approval in the Parliament in 2024.

V. Patent Prosecution Highway for Romanian and US Patents

A. Background

124. Patent Prosecution Highway (PPH) is a Pilot Programme started in 2006 by the United States Patent and Trademark Office (USPTO) in partnership with a similar office in Japan (JPTO). According to this programme, an applicant who receives a positive ruling on patent claims from one participating office may request accelerated prosecution of corresponding claims in the other participating office. The applicant is thereby allowed to obtain a patentability decision in the second office based on the examination results from the first office and thus the patenting procedure should be accelerated in respect of applications filed with the two offices. In January 2014, the Global PPH Pilot Programme was launched, grouping now seventeen national offices, with the view of consolidating and replacing earlier bilateral PPH programmes.

On 15 April 2015, the Romanian OSIM and the USPTO started the bilateral PPH Pilot Programme based on a Memorandum of understanding signed between the two offices. Its main provisions are presented in the next part of the chapter.

It will run for a period of four years, ending on 14 April 2019, but the trial period may be extended if necessary and useful; this period gives both offices the possibility to evaluate if the programme needs to be modified for more effective operation or a flexible implementation of the Global PPH pilot programme.

According to provisions of the Memorandum, the offices may terminate the pilot programme earlier and replace the bilateral framework while adopting the multilateral one in the Global PPH project.

B. Procedure Within USPTO

125. In spite of the fact that OSIM is not currently a Global PPH participating office and accordingly its partnership with USPTO is exclusively carried on a bilateral basis, a PPH request submitted with the USPTO based on OSIM examination results shall be treated under the Global PPH standards.

C. Procedure at OSIM for an Accelerated Examination

126. The PPH Pilot Programme enables applicants of a patent application whose claims have been determined to be patentable by the USPTO, considered *Office of First Filing OFF, to undergo an accelerated examination in the OSIM*, considered Office of Second Filing OSF, with a simple procedure according to a request from the applicant/applicants.

(1) Request to the OSIM.
The applicant has to file with the OSIM a request for an accelerated examination under PPH by submitting a bilingual Romanian/English form requesting

entering into the accelerated examination under the PPH Pilot Programme, accompanied by the relevant supporting documents. The form is accessible on the OSIM website www.osim.ro.

(2) Requirements for Requesting Accelerated Examination under the PPH Pilot Programme at the OSIM are:
   (a) The RO (Romanian) patent application is:
      – an application in which priority under the Paris Convention is recognized to one or more applications filed in US;
      – a PCT national phase application in Romania, representing a first filing and with a national phase application also in the US;
      – an application in which priority under the Paris Convention is recognized to one or more PCT applications with a national phase in the US; or
      – an RO patent application being a divisional application of the application filed under (i)–(iii).
   (b) At least one corresponding US application has one or more claims that have been determined to be patentable by the USPTO.
   (c) All the claims in the RO application for the accelerated examination under the PPH must sufficiently correspond to one or more of those claims indicated as patentable in the USPTO.

(3) Claims are considered to 'sufficiently correspond', where, accounting for differences due to translations and claim format, the claims in the RO application are of the same or similar scope as the claims indicated as patentable/allowable in the corresponding US application.

(4) A claim in the RO application that is narrower in scope than the claims indicated as allowable/patentable in the US application will 'sufficiently correspond' if presented as a claim dependent upon a claim that is of the same or similar scope as a claim indicated as allowable/patentable in the US application. In this regard, a claim that is narrower in scope occurs when a US claim is amended to be further limited by an additional feature that is supported by the written description of the RO application (description and/or claims).

(5) A claim in the RO application which introduces a new/different category of claims to those claims determined to be patentable/allowable in the US application is not considered to sufficiently correspond. For example, if the USPTO claims only contain claims to a process of manufacturing a product, then the claims in the RO application are not considered to sufficiently correspond if the RO application claims introduce product claims that are dependent on the corresponding process claims.

The OSIM has not yet started the (substantive) examination procedure of the patent application.

(1) Required Documents for Accelerated Examination under the PPH Pilot Programme at the OSIM:
   (a) a copy of all office actions relevant to the substantive examination for patentability on the corresponding US application(s);

(b) copies of USPTO office actions in the English language are accepted and need not, as a rule, be translated into Romanian. No copy of the office actions needs to be supplied if the office actions are available via the website of the USPTO. Should the office action in English language not be comprehensible to the OSIM examiner, he may request an additional translation into Romanian from the applicant;

(c) a copy of the claims examined and found to be allowable/patentable by the USPTO;
No paper copy of the claims needs to be supplied if the claims are available via the website of the USPTO. Should the claims in English language not be comprehensible to the OSIM examiner, he may request an additional translation into Romanian from the applicant.

(d) a completed claim correspondence table in Romanian or English language showing the correspondence between the claims of the RO application for accelerated examination under the PPH and the claims of the corresponding US application considered allowable/patentable by the USPTO;

(e) sufficient correspondence of claims occurs where the claims satisfy the requirements under 2c). When the claims are just literal translation, the applicant can just write down that 'they are the same' in the table. When claims are not just literal translation, it is necessary to explain the sufficient correspondence of each claim based on the criteria 2c);

(f) a copy of the document(s) cited by the USPTO examiner;
If the cited document is a patent document, it does not have to be submitted, as it is generally available to the OSIM via EPOQUE. Only if the RO examiner has difficulty in obtaining a patent document will he ask the applicant to submit it.
As a rule, cited documents need not be translated.

(g) procedure for Accelerated Examination under the PPH Pilot Programme at the OSIM;
The applicant has to provide the relevant information by filling in a form to request an accelerated examination under the PPH Pilot Programme which is available for download from the OSIM website. The form should be sent to the OSIM along with the relevant supporting documentation.

If the requirements under point 1 are met, the OSIM will conduct the accelerated examination.

127. Thus, after registering the request for the accelerated procedure, according to the PPH, OSIM decides within two months whether the request is admitted. If the application does not qualify for participation in the PPH Pilot Programme, the applicant will be informed accordingly and the applicant will be given the opportunity to correct the request. If the defects are not corrected within the time limit indicated, the applicant will be notified and the application will be further processed under the standard Romanian procedure without acceleration.

If the application is admitted, the OSIM examiner will examine, within two to three months of receipt, the fulfilment of the patentability conditions according to Patent Law No. 64/1991 as republished, and OSIM will take a decision.

The documents accompanying the request for the accelerated examination are paper documents that are transmitted by post.

Applications for utility models, plant varieties or design cannot be subjected to the accelerated examination procedure according to the PPH Programme.

§5. Ownership and Transfer

128. Article 45 of the Romanian Patent Law defines three fundamental rights under patent protection, namely: the right to the patent, the right to the grant of the patent and the rights conferred by the patent. However, the newly issued Law No. 83/2014 on employees' inventions provides for, according to the international and European doctrine and practice, 'the right in the invention' namely a more general legal concept which covers both moral author's right on his invention and the patrimonial right to the patent.

This presentation shall follow this line by including all other important rights that are derived from the mentioned classification.

I. Right to the Patent

A. *Rights of the Inventor*

129. Article 3 of the Romanian Patent Law states the fundamental principle according to which 'the right to the patent shall belong to the inventor or to his successor in title'. This provision shall be completed with the provision of Article 4, which stipulates that 'where an invention has been made jointly by two or more inventors, each shall have the status of joint inventor and the rights shall belong to them jointly'.

This is a fundamental principle because, first, it recognizes the ownership of the spiritual creation representing the invention and belonging to its author, who is the inventor in a generic sense.

Second, by mentioning the possibility that the patent should belong, as an alternative, 'to his successor in title', the law consecrates the inventor's freedom to assign his invention to a possible successor when it has not been patented or divulgated.

The patent, as a title of protection for invention, as it is recognized in Article 2 of the Law, has to be requested by the inventor, the principle being that the right to the patent shall belong to the inventor as a first applicant.

The first filing thus has a right constitutive character. As it may happen rather often, in technological competitions in which the results of the research can be extremely narrow, that is, solving some known problems with new solutions, there is the possibility that more inventors have made the same invention but independently of each other. In this situation, Article 4 of the Law provides that 'where the invention has been created jointly by several inventors, each of them shall have the status of joint inventor and the right shall belong to them jointly. Where two or more persons have made the same invention independently of each other, the right to the patent shall belong to the person who filed the patent application having the earliest filing date'.

The legal provision considers the general concept of person. The applicant can be both a natural and a legal person or a combination of both.

The procedure by which a legal person acquires the right to the patent will be analysed in §5, I, B.

Inventors who have their domicile or registered office outside the Romanian territory shall, on the basis of the law as well as on the basis of the Paris Convention and TRIPS Agreement to which Romania is a party, enjoy the same rights as the Romanian inventors.

Along with the right to the patent, the inventor enjoys an important moral right to his invention, namely to be recognized as such 'author of the invention'.

Thus, in Article 34 of the Law, it is provided that 'the inventor shall have the right to the mentioning of his full name and status in the patent granted, in his employment record and in any other documents or publications concerning his invention'.

Where the patent owner is not the same person as the inventor, a duplicate patent shall be issued to the latter. Upon his express request and subject to payment of a prescribed fee, the inventor's full name will not be published.

As previously mentioned, the applicant has to mention expressly in the patent application the inventors; if they are not the same as the applicant, the sanction for not mentioning the inventors in the time limit provided by law being the rejection of the patent application.

The inventors have the moral right to oppose their names being mentioned in the publication of the patent application or in the granted patent.

Finally, the category of inventors' rights also includes the right of the employee-inventors to be correspondingly remunerated, as it will be presented in §5, I, B.

B. Employees' Inventions

130. As mentioned before, the matter of employees' invention is regulated since 2014 by Law No. 83/2014 on employees' inventions applicable to inventions created by an individual inventor or by a group of inventors, where the individual inventor or at least one member of the group of inventors is an employee of a private law legal entity or a public law legal entity and also applicable to the inventions referred to which can be protected by patents or registered utility models.

Within the meaning of that law, *employee* may be any natural person who carries out a paid activity, based on an individual employment contract, for and under the authority of a person referred to above.

Article 3 of the Law on employees' inventions stipulates the employees' inventions shall meet the following conditions:

(a) resulted from the carrying out of inventor's duties, either specifically assigned to him within the employment contract and the job description or set out by other legally binding documents providing for an inventive mission;

(b) were made during the individual employment contract, or during a period of two years, at the most, following the termination of this contract, as the case may be, having knowledge of and using the employer's expertise, using the employer's means, as a consequence of the professional training acquired by the employee-inventor due to the employer's care and on the employer's expenses or using information resulting from the employer's activity or made available by him.

All other inventions shall be 'free inventions' which shall belong entirely and in any condition to the employee.

In the following consideration, we will call 'mission inventions' inventions done under the conditions from Article 3 let. a and 'inventions related to the employer' those made under conditions from Article 3 let. b.

The competent person to decide whether an invention made by an employee falls or not in the category of employee's inventions and also upon the type of employee's invention shall be the employer.

In any condition, the employee who creates an invention has the obligation to communicate to his employer, without delay, a presentation describing the solution to the problem solved by the invention in a sufficiently clear manner for it to define the invention and the conditions of its creation.

In the absence of a longer time limit stipulated in the employer's internal regulations, within a time limit of four months of the receipt of the communication referred to under paragraph (2), the employer shall inform the employee-inventor about the invention's falling in the category of employees' inventions and about his claiming the right in the said invention.

The above-mentioned classification of an invention by the employer may be appealed against by the employee before the competent law court, under civil law, within a time limit of four months.

The employees' inventions may be subject to a trade secret.

The employee-inventor is bound not to disclose or publish the invention without the employer's written agreement. The same interdiction of disclosure or publishing applies to the employer, as well as to the persons other than the inventor, who, by the nature of their service duties, have knowledge of the existence of the invention.

In case of disclosure of the employee's invention, the persons in cause can be liable for it by virtue of the individual employment contract concluded between the employee and the employer, where a confidentiality clause is provided therein.

Where the individual employment contract does not contain a confidentiality clause and a prejudice results from the disclosure of the employee's invention by those persons, it may entail civil liability, as provided by Article 1349(1) and (2) corroborated with Article 1357 of the Civil Law Code.

131. As a general rule, the Law provides for in Article 5 that the right in the inventions where the employee received an inventive mission from his employer shall belong to the employer. This is entirely true for a private law legal entity and a public law legal entity with no research & development activity.

However, where said employer is a public law legal entity having research & development among its objects of activity, the right in the inventions shall belong to the employer in the absence of an otherwise stipulating contractual provision.

The inventive mission referred to above must set out the technology field of the technical problem(s) for the solving of which the employee-inventor is bound, under the contract or other legally binding documents, to bring a creative contribution according to his employment duties.

132. The right in the inventions 'related to the employer' shall belong to the employee-inventor if the private-law or public-law employer does not claim the invention under the conditions already mentioned.

Three remarks are of particular importance here.

The first one refers to the clear precondition set to the employer to claim the employees' invention, if it intends to get the right to the invention and thus to the patent.

The second one touches on the necessity for the employer to clarify within its internal regulations all necessary details and clarifications meant to give a clear understanding of what is in fact an invention 'related to the employer'. This would prevent possible difficulties and even conflicts on the classification of an 'employees' invention' made by employer and not considered as such by its inventor.

133. In order to summarize the factual situation, the right in the invention belongs to:

(a) *the employer*, in the following situations:
   - the invention is a mission invention and the employer is a private law legal entity;
   - the invention is a mission invention and the employer is a public law legal entity without having research development among objects of activities;
   - the invention is a mission invention, the employer is a public law legal entity with activities in research and development and there is no contrary contractual provision;
   - the invention is related to the employer and the employer has not claimed the invention in legal terms.

(b) *the employee-inventors*, in the following circumstances:
   - the invention is a mission invention, the employer is a public law legal entity, having research and development among its object of activity and there is a contractual provision which grants the right on invention to the inventor;
   - the invention is related to the employer and the employer has not claimed the invention in legal terms;
   - Invention is not a mission invention and is not related to the employer.

C. Employee and Employer Rights and Obligations

134. Employee Rights and Obligations under Law No. 83/2014:

- informs the employer of carrying out the invention;
- may request assistance from the employer's patent attorney for a detailed presentation of the invention;
- receives from the employer within four months (in the absence of a longer term provided in the internal regulations of the employer) the decision on the admission of the invention in the category of employees' inventions and if the employer claims the right to it;
- may challenge within four months, the way the employer has classified his invention at the law court, according to the civil law;
- be informed in writing by the employer regarding a patent application or a utility model registration;
- at the employer's request, he shall provide assistance for protection and exploitation of the invention;
- the employee has the obligation not to disclose or publish the invention (considered an employee's invention) without the employer's written consent;
- may apply for protection right, if the employer assigns the ownership of the invention, not wanting to proceed with the filing of the patent application;
- the employee is entitled to a remuneration determined by the employer where was made an employee's invention referred as 'invention related to the employer'.

If the employee's inventions do not fall within the situations provided by Law No. 83/2014, and the right to the inventions created by employees belongs to the employee-inventor, the latter is entitled to seek protection in Romania and/or in other countries, by claiming the priority right in Romania.

Employer Rights and Obligations under Law No. 83/2014:

- is informed by the employee-inventor of the existing invention and receives its detailed description;
- assists the employee through the industrial property attorney with the detailed presentation of the invention;
- analyses the invention and classifies it in the category of employee's inventions, and if it claims ownership, he will respect the deadlines;
- notifies the employee regarding the decision to classify the invention and its ownership;
- may request employee's assistance for obtaining protection and capitalizing the invention;
- may apply for a patent or for the registration of a utility model;
- informs the employee of the filing of the patent application or registration of a utility model;
- ensures the necessary costs for obtaining a patent or the registration of a utility model for a claimed employee's invention;
- remunerates the employee-inventor in accordance with the law;

- assigned to the employee-inventor, at his request, the right to protection in case he no longer wishes to continue with the procedures subsequent to the patent application or he's not interested in protecting the invention in some countries.

If the right to the employee's invention belongs to the employer, he is entitled to apply for a patent or for the registration of a utility model in Romania and/or in other countries by claiming the right of priority in our country. The application for a patent or the registration of a utility model is accompanied by documents attesting to the right of the invention. The right to obtain a patent or a utility model and the rights deriving from these acts can be transmitted to third parties in whole or in part. The transfer can be made by exclusive or non-exclusive assignment or licence or by legal or testamentary succession. Transmission takes effect against third parties only from the publication date of the mention regarding the transfer registered with OSIM (Article 45 of Patent Law No. 64/1991) in the BOPI.

In case the employer does not want to continue the proceedings subsequent to the filing of the application for the protection of the employee's invention or in case he is not interested in the protection of the invention in certain States other than Romania, the employer shall assign the right to protection to the employee, subject to a non-exclusive licence to be granted by the employee to the employer, in respect of the patented invention. The conditions for granting the above-mentioned non-exclusive licence shall be specially stipulated in the employer's internal regulations concerning this matter. In the absence of such special provisions, the conditions for granting the licence shall be agreed upon by the parties. The employer shall also transmit in due time the documents needed for resuming the procedure.

Upon request by the employee, in respect of the States for which the employer declared his lack of interest in acquiring industrial property rights, the employer shall assign the right to apply for the protection of the employee's invention to the employee within a time limit sufficient for him to enjoy the priority periods provided for by the international industrial property conventions and treaties to which Romania is a party.

According to Article 12 of the Law, for the inventions resulting from research & development or didactic activities carried out in a university-level institution which owns the protection right, this institution shall grant to the inventor, upon request and free of charge, a right to exploit the invention in the respective field of didactic and research activity, based on a non-exclusive licence contract, even if the inventor is not an employee.

The term of the contract shall be equal to the period of time during which the inventor carries out the said didactic and research activities.

After obtaining the patent/utility model, the holder is entitled to:

(1) ownership of the invention by patent/utility model entitles the holder to prohibit third parties from performing the following acts without his authorization:
   - for products: manufacturing, using, offering for sale, selling or importing for the purpose of using, offering for sale or selling;
   - for processes or methods: their use.

(2) exclusive right to exploit the invention;

(3) the right to publish the invention;
(4) entitlement to the payment of damages in case of infringing the protection conferred to the invention according to Article 59, paragraph 4 of Patent Law No. 64/1991.

The rights of the inventor who is not the holder of the patent/registered utility model are:

- entitlement to the mentioning of the name, first name and his capacity in claiming the employee's invention in employment records and other documents and publications relating to said invention (at the specific request of the inventor, his full name shall not be published);
- entitlement to the duplication of the invention description;
- the right to be informed by the applicant of the examining stage of the patent/utility model application and the stage of the patent application.

In the case of employees' inventions, the patent owner shall notify the inventor of his intention to renounce the patent. At the inventor's request, the holder is obliged to give the inventor the patent rights and the related patent documents, provided that the employer grants the employee a non-exclusive licence for the patented invention. The conditions for granting exclusive licences shall be determined by specific provisions of the internal regulation of the employer, and in the absence of such specific provisions, the conditions for granting are established by agreement; renunciation is possible only with the consent of the licensee (Article 38, Patent Law No. 64/1991).

The patent holder should take care of:

- Paying the patent maintenance fees. Failure to pay such fees shall cause the forfeiture of patent rights and its inclusion into the public domain, with the possibility of revalidation.
- Invention exploitation.

135. Law has specific provisions regarding remuneration and compensation due to inventors where right to inventions belongs to employers.

In respect of the employees' inventions 'related to the employer' which have been claimed by the employer, the employee-inventor is entitled to a remuneration to be established by the employer under the conditions set out under Article 7 of the Law.

It provides that the employer shall specially provide the criteria for establishing the said remuneration within its internal regulations. In the absence of such special provisions, the employer shall take into account, depending on each case, one or several of the following criteria:

(a) the economic, commercial and/or social effects arising from the exploitation of the invention by the employer or by third parties, with the employer's consent;
(b) the extent to which the employer is involved in carrying out the employee's invention, the employer's resources made available therefor included;

(c) the creative contribution of the employee-inventor, where the invention is created by a plurality of inventors.

In respect of the employees' inventions made by employees whose employers are public law legal entities having research & development among their objects of activity and claimed by the employer, according to the provisions of the Law or according to a contract concluded between the parties, and exploited by the employer, the employee-inventor is entitled to a percentage of the income made by the employer based on the said inventions.

The percentage referred to under paragraph (1) cannot be lower than 30%. The understanding of the notion of 'income' used by the Law should be obviously considered 'net income' obtained by the employer from that invention after deducting all expenses caused by its implementation.

II. Right to the Grant of the Patent

136. In Article 13, it is provided that 'in all the procedures before the Office, the applicant shall be regarded as the person entitled to the grant of the patent'.

According to law, the right to the grant of the patent shall be transferable, either wholly or in part, more or less in the same manner as the rights conferred by the patent, a problem which will be presented in §5, IV.

For this reason, an important part of the protection that may be enforced up to the grant of the patent, namely the provisional protection, will be presented here.

A. Provisional Protection

137. The rights conferred by the patent on the invention are effectively opposable to third parties only from the date of the publication of the decision to grant a patent and if they have remained definitive, which happens after a significant period of time from the filing date.

Romanian Law has, like the legislation of many other European countries, an important provision regarding the setting up of the so-called provisional protection, which becomes relevant much earlier than the date of the grant of the patent, namely beginning with the publication date.

Thus, according to Article 32 of the Law, 'starting from the date of its publication ... the patent application shall provisionally confer on the applicant the protection laid down in Article 31'.

The legal provision results with clarity that provisional protection is set up from the publication of the application and has a retroactive effect beginning with the national regular filing of the patent application and lasts until the granting of the patent.

Infringement of the rights by third parties after the publication of the patent application shall make the infringers liable for damages under civil law, and the entitlement to the payment of damages shall be enforceable after the grant of the patent.

Nevertheless, the acts provided by the law which normally are considered infringing the rights, performed by third parties before the date of publication of the patent application or before the date of the summons made by the applicant and accompanied by a certified copy of the patent application shall not be deemed to infringe the rights conferred by the patent.

Also, it results with clarity that it is provisional to the extent that it is transformed into an effective protection conferred by the patent of invention because in the case when the application has been rejected, the applicant does not benefit from this provisional protection.

The scope of the provisional protection is given by the content of the claims as they have been published.

Although, generally, the published claims have an imperfect form both from the point of view of drawing up as well as, mostly, from the point of view of the scope of protection as it has been indicated by the applicant and which has not been made objective by the search and substantive examination activity, the provisional protection has a major role in discouraging infringement of the patent rights.

Consequently, the scope of the protection as it results from the published claims may incur important modifications during the specific substantive examination proceedings or, later on, in the appeal procedures in the office or, as the case may be, in the court.

The effect is retroactive, so that once it remains definitive, this form of claim gives retroactively the scope of protection from the filing date and until the ceasing of the protection conferred by the patent.

III. Rights Conferred by the Patent

138. According to Article 31 of the Law, 'the patent shall confer to its owner an exclusive right of exploitation throughout its entire duration'.

This provision referring to the exclusive right of exploitation should be judged in connection with the owner's right to prohibit third parties from performing the following acts without his consent:

(a) manufacturing, using, offering for sale, selling or importing for the purpose of using, offering for sale or selling, where the subject matter of the patent is a product;
(b) using the process and offering for sale, selling or importing for those purposes the product directly obtained by the patented process, where the subject matter of the patent is a process.

The exploitation of the invention represents a concept with multiple characteristics, which in its essence refers to its industrial use on a chain. This starts with fabrication and continues with its marketing, including taking all necessary measures to achieve this goal, and it has as its final step the use of the subject matter of the patented invention.

139. Fabrication of the product means the effective achievement of the subject matter of the patented invention.

Marketing of the product refers to any means of making the product available to the public, such as selling, renting, franchising, etc.

The legal provision shall be interpreted in the sense that not only is effective marketing an exclusive exploitation act, but even offering for sale or importing or storing for the purposes of selling or offering for sale has the same effect.

The use of the product, as an act of exploitation of the invention, refers to the use of the product on an industrial scale.

The import of the product is an act of exploitation, while it is irrelevant from this point of view whether the product has been licitly achieved in the country of origin.

With regard to the patented process, the law deals not only with its use but also covers the extension of the protection conferred by the process patent on the product that is directly obtained through that process. In this context, the significance of the word 'directly' must be unambiguous, namely covering only the product resulting without any other influence from the use of the process.

140. The rights conferred by the patent have as strict subject matter the claimed invention, meaning that part of the technical solution which satisfies the patentability criteria. This is legally expressed by the provision contained in Article 31, which specifies that 'the extent of protection conferred by a patent or by the patent application shall be determined by the content of the claims. They shall be interpreted by the description and drawings of the invention'.

Throughout the period of time up to grant, the extent of the protection conferred by the patent application shall be determined by the published claims.

The patent, as granted or as amended during the revocation or cancellation in part, shall retroactively determine the protection conferred by the patent application in so far as such protection is not thereby extended.

As previously mentioned, where the subject matter of the patent is a process, the protection conferred by the patent extends to the product obtained directly by the patented process.

A special extension of the protection provided for in Romanian law refers to biotech inventions, and in this respect, according to Article 31, 'the protection conferred by a patent relating to a biological material having specific characteristics shall be extended to any material derived by reproduction or multiplication from the patented material, in an identical form or differentiated, and having the same characteristics'.

Following the same approach, the protection conferred by a patent to a product containing genetic information or consisting of genetic information shall be extended to any other material incorporating the product and wherein the genetic information is contained and exercises its function, except for the human body in the various stages of its formation or development.

These extensions of protection do not extend to the biological material derived by reproduction or multiplication from a biological material sold or offered for sale on the territory of Romania by the patent owner or with his consent, where the reproduction or multiplication necessarily results from the utilization for which the biological material was put on the market, provided that the obtained material has not been used subsequently for other reproductions and multiplications.

The exact interpretation of the extent of protection conferred by the patent of invention is essential in assessing the counterfeiting cases of the subject matter of invention. Consequently, the legal provision needs a series of explanations based on Romanian practice.

The first one is that, besides the function to establish the extent of protection, the claims must also define, as it has been presented in §4, I, B, in technical terms, the subject matter for which protection is being sought and to indicate the technical feature of the invention. Although in some papers, some speak even of a 'conflict' between the two functions of the claims, the widely accepted interpretation given to the two functions is that of complementarity.

141. As far as the scope of protection is concerned, one can say that once the subject matter of the claimed invention is defined, it is established directly and complementarily to the first function, that is, the scope of protection by analysing 'the content of the claims'.

Fully in line with the EPC, 'the content of the claims' is analysed under two distinct but complementary meanings. Thus, according to rule 64:

- provisions of law shall not be considered to mean that the extent of protection conferred by the patent is determined in a strict and literal sense of the text of the claims, the description and drawings helping only for the elimination of ambiguities concerning the claims;
- the claims help only as guidelines; and the protection is also extended to what, in the opinion of a person skilled in the art that analysed the description and claims, the patent owner wanted to protect.

The provisions of the Law shall be interpreted as defining a position between these extremes, which should ensure at the same time an equitable protection to the patent owner and a reasonable degree of certainty to third parties.

First, it is about the 'literary content' of the claims. Here, it is essential to find again as such the elements of the claimed invention in the elements of the state of the art or, in the event of counterfeiting, in the elements of the object presumed to counterfeit the subject matter of the patented invention.

Second, 'the technical content' of the claims is analysed in order to establish whether the inventive concept and the technical solution to the problem in question can be circumscribed to the scope of the protection conferred by the patent.

The Romanian practice, following the practice of continental Europe, adopted a balanced attitude with regard to the two interpretations. Therefore, though it is recognized as important, the literary interpretation of the claims is not given the weight which the doctrine gives in the USA. As a matter of fact, the technical content is interpreted in connection with the description and drawings.

Paul Mathely[32] has synthesized in a very suggestive manner that 'the patent does not protect but what is claimed and it is not allowed to claim but what is described'.

32. Paul Mathely, *supra*, 270–274.

Referring to the interpretation of the claims, although Romanian law and practice do not recognize the explicit application of a 'doctrine of equivalents' however, Article 32 provides that 'to determine the extent of the protection conferred by the patent, due account shall be taken of any element equivalent to an element specified in the claims'. According to Romanian Patent Law and practice, an element is deemed being equivalent to an element specified in the claims, if, for a person skilled in the art, it is obvious that by the use thereof there is essentially obtained the same result as the one obtained by the element specified in the claims.

Therefore, an analysis of the use of some existing equivalent means has the necessary legal basis. This is true with the state of the art, when compliance with the patentability criteria by the patent application is examined, as well as in the case of extrapolation to a product supposedly counterfeiting the subject matter of a patented invention.

IV. Co-ownership

142. In its revision in 2007, the Romanian patent introduced a necessary clarification and extension of the legal status of ownership, namely co-ownership. This mainly refers to the exploitation and transfer of rights arising from the common invention, possibility of initiating actions in the court and division of the incomes.

Thus, rule 84 provides that 'where a patent jointly belongs to more owners, each of them is a co-owner and in this situation the exploitation of the invention may be performed according to a written agreement of the co-owners concerning the manner of exploitation. In default of a written agreement of the co-owners concerning the manner of exploitation of the invention, each of the co-owners may exploit the invention to his own benefit, with the obligation to pay equitable indemnification to the other co-owners who do not exploit the invention personally, or who have not granted exploitation licences; in default of an agreement, the indemnification shall be established in the law court according to the civil law'.

Each of the co-owners may bring an infringement action to his own benefit; the co-owner bringing an infringement action shall notify this action to the other co-owners.

Each of the co-owners may, to his own benefit, grant a non-exclusive exploitation licence to a third party, on condition that an equitable indemnification should be paid to the other co-owners who do not exploit the invention personally or who have not granted an exploitation licence; in default of an agreement, this indemnification shall be established by the law court according to the civil law. An exclusive exploitation licence can be granted only with the agreement of all co-owners or according to a final and irrevocable decision of the law court.

Each co-owner may, at any moment, assign his share of ownership to the patent. The co-owners dispose of a preference right which shall be exercised within three months, starting from the notification of the intention to assign the patent; in the absence of an agreement concerning the price of the assigned quota, the price shall be established by the law court, according to the civil law. The co-owner of a patent may notify the other co-owners that he renounces his quota to the benefit of the others; starting from the date of entering the renunciation in the National Register of

Patents for Invention, said co-owner has no other obligation to the other co-owners; after the renunciation, the other co-owners shall redistribute the renounced quota, except where it has otherwise been provided for.

The previous consideration normally applies *mutatis mutandis* in case of co-ownership of a patent application.

V. Transfer of Rights

143. Once the owner has acquired the right to the patent, he can fully exercise all the rights conferred by the title of property.

Besides the exploitation of the invention by using its own technological capacities, the owner may use his right as any other owner; he may transmit this right or eventually may even give up his right.

The transfer of rights regarding the patents of invention, that is, the selling or the acquisition of the exclusive rights on a patented invention or the obtaining of the right to use the patented invention, takes place by establishing a legal relationship between the owner of the patent and the person or legal entity who acquires these rights.

This legal relationship is of a contractual nature, meaning that the owner agrees with the transfer and the beneficiary agrees to acquire those rights.

Article 42 provides that:

- the right to the patent, the right to the grant of a patent and the rights deriving from a patent shall be transferable, either wholly or in part. Transfers may be effected by assignment, by the grant of exclusive or non-exclusive licenses, or
- by legal or testamentary succession. Transfers shall produce effects in respect of third parties only as from the date of publication in the Official Industrial Property Bulletin of the mention of the transfer registered with the Office.

As it can be noted from the formulation of the legal provision, the mentioned transfers refer not only to a patent of inventions but also to a patent application. Therefore, the aspects that will be presented infra can be extended *mutatis mutandis* from the level of a patent to the level of a patent application.

All the transfers shall be binding on third parties from the date on which they are registered at the Office.

A. Assignment

144. The assignment may be total or partial. The total assignment, which is the most frequent case, assumes the transfer of the patent entirely, without any further maintenance of a right by the owner of the patent.

The concept of partial assignment covers a wide area and may refer to:

- the assignment of a part of the exploitation rights conferred by the patent;
- the assignment of a part of the invention protected by a patent;
- the assignment of a part of the application domain of the subject matter of the patented invention.

All these aspects should be rigorously specified in the assignment contracts, which should clearly and unambiguously state that the delimitations of the assigned parts from the general property on the patent.

The total or partial assignment may also set up a regime of co-property of the patent, both in the situation when the patentee assigns a part of his property of the patent, as well as if he assigns his property wholly to more persons.

Article 42 states that the assignment shall be binding on third parties as from the date on which they are registered at the Office and consequently once this official registration has been made. The new owner holds the right to prosecute the facts of counterfeiting intervened after that date.

The law does not provide whether the assignment, total or partial, of a principal invention may have any repercussion on the inventions for improvement. The last mentioned have their own property regime.

Also, the law contains no special provisions regarding the total or partial cessation of the production or trade fund in connection with the total or partial assignment of the right to the patent. This means that the contractual basis is determined.

The priority right may be transferred by assignment only with the agreement of the parties.

The assignment may be limited in time.

B. Licence

145. Similar to assignment, the licence may refer to both a granted patent and a patent application.

However, the patent application regarding the granting of a patent as a title of property after it gained provisional protection, eventually by publication, is characterized by a relative incertitude. This explains why, to date, the licensing of the rights deriving from the registration of a patent application has only been rarely practised in industrial property law.

The licence supposes the maintenance of the property right by the owner of the patent of invention, including the right to enforce the rights conferred by the patent.

According to the above-mentioned Article 42, the licences may be total or partial, respectively exclusive or non-exclusive.

Depending on the character of the licence, total or partial, the owner may transfer:

- all or part of the acts which constitute the exclusive right of exploitation;
- all or part of the patented invention;
- all or part of the domain of application of the subject matter of the patented invention;

– all or part of the duration of the patent; all or part of the territory of Romania, where the patent of invention is valid.

Thus, the licence is total if it relates to all rights of exploitation, to the whole patented invention and to the whole territory; the licence may be limited to a shorter period of time than the duration of protection period of the patent.

If the licence is exclusive, the owner will transfer the right to the exploitation, having the obligation not to transfer to other persons another licence for the same subject matter. In the case of an exclusive licence, if not otherwise provided for, the licensor maintains the right to exploit the invention.

The licence is non-exclusive if the licensor reserves the possibility of granting the right to exploit the invention to other persons.

Using the will of the owner as a criterion, we can distinguish two distinct categories of licences specific to the patent of invention. They are voluntary or normal licences that the owner grants under the conditions and at the moment chosen by him and, respectively, compulsory licences, granted under specific conditions and independently of the owner's will. The latter ones will be presented distinctly at §6, noting that they essentially constitute important limitations to the exclusive right of the owner to freely exploit his invention.

The litigations resulting from licence agreements are under the jurisdiction of the courts and shall not be subject to stamp duty (Article 64).

The licensee may grant sub-licences only with the licensor's consent. The licensee cannot start an infringement action in the court without the patent owner's consent, unless otherwise provided by the licence agreement. By exception, the beneficiary of an exclusive licence may start an infringement action in the court if, after having notified the infringement acts, he took knowledge of to the patent owner this did not act within the time limit requested by the licensee.

If the patent owner does not exploit the invention or if the exploitation is not sufficient on the territory of Romania, the importation of the subject matter of the patent by the patent owner shall be considered to be an exploitation of the patent in Romania.

In case of the transfers of rights registered by a foreign applicant or patent owner, the Office may, where appropriate, request a translation into the Romanian language of the original document of the certified copy of the right transfer contract.

§6. Limitations and Exceptions to the Scope of Patent Protection: Compulsory Licences

146. Limitations of the exclusive rights conferred by the patent of invention are contained in the Paris Convention and TRIPS Agreement, as well as other international treaties and agreements. In the meaning of Romanian law, these limitations of the exclusive rights conferred by the patent of invention are situations with a special character, where it can be considered that the exploitation of the patented invention by third parties, without the consent of the owner, is not actually an infringement of the owner's rights.

147. A first limitation is mentioned in Article 33a of the Law, which provides that what does not constitute an infringement is:

> the exploitation of the invention in the construction and operation of land vehicles or aircraft and aboard vessels or in devices used in the operation thereof that belong to the states party to international conventions concerning inventions to which Romania is also party, when the vehicles, craft or vessels enter the territory of Romania either temporary or accidentally, provided that such exploitation is exclusively for the needs of the vehicles, craft or vessels.

148. Another limitation is in the situation of 'previous use' by a person who has applied the invention or has taken real and effective steps towards exploiting it, in good faith, within the territory of Romania and independently of the owner of the patent, and before a regular national filing concerning the invention has been effected or before the recognized priority date. In this situation, the former may continue exploitation of the invention up to the date of the regular national filing or recognized priority. However, the right to use may only be transferred along with the assets of that person or the part of the assets assigned to the exploitation of the invention.

149. The third limitation of the exclusive right is the use of the subject matter of the patented invention exclusively for experimental purposes. This is obviously connected with the necessity that the monopoly created by the patent of invention shall not constitute an obstacle towards research, scientific experiments or performance education. A broader limitation provided for in Article 34 1c of the Law refers to performing any of the acts which constitute exclusive rights exclusively privately and for non-commercial purposes; production or, as the case may be, the use of the invention exclusively privately and for non-commercial purposes;

150. Another limitation is concerned with the so-called exhaustion of rights, which, because of EU membership in Romania, applies at the EU territory level. This represents the marketing or offering for sale, within the territory of the EU Member States, of specimens of the product constituting the subject matter of the invention that have previously been sold by the patent owner or with his express consent.

151. Finally, the situation in which a third party exploited or took real and effective steps to exploit the invention during the time between the forfeiture of the patent owner's rights and the reinstatement of the patent shall not constitute an infringement of the exclusive right.

It is obvious that within this time period, there was not an exclusive right de jure, and even more, the third party could not anticipate the reinstatement of the patent. From this point of view, there is a similar situation to the 'previous use'. In this context, the legal provision that the invention can be used further to the same extent by such third parties as those before the reinstatement appears therefore justified. However, the invention may not be transferred without the assets or a part of the assets of the person using the invention.

A limitation, in fact, a self-limitation of the exclusive right, is that the invention or the part of the invention in respect of which protection has been renounced may be freely exploited by third parties. This interpretation follows the legal provision according to which the owner may renounce the patent, wholly or partly, by filing a written statement with the Office.

A special type of limitation comes from the provisions of the EPC and refers to the situation where a European patent application intervenes in a modification of the claims translation which might reduce the scope of protection as compared to the previous one. Thus, based on Article 33.2, any person who, in good faith, exploits the invention or has taken real and effective steps to exploit the invention in so far as the rights conferred by a patent application or a European patent in its original translation are not thereby infringed upon, may continue to exploit the invention, after the correct translation becomes effective, within his enterprise or for its necessities, without payment and not exceeding the extent existing on the date on which the original translation became effective.

I. Compulsory Licences

152. Contrary to voluntary licences, the beneficiaries of the compulsory licences receive the right to perform the acts covered by the exclusive right on the basis of authorizations given by governmental authorities, independently of the will of the owners.

There are two important distinct cases where compulsory licences can be granted:

- abuses which might result from the exercise of the exclusive right conferred by the patent of inventions;
- public interest, which imposes the solving of situations of an exceptional nature and of a national interest, such as public health, national defence and security and economic development.

The Patent Law contains specific provisions in this sense.

153. According to Article 43 of the Law:

> at the request of any interested party, the Court of Bucharest may grant a compulsory license, after four years have elapsed from the patent application filing date or after three years have elapsed from the grant of the patent, whichever period expires later. The provisions shall only apply where the invention has not been exploited or has been insufficiently exploited on the territory of Romania, and the patent owner cannot justify his inaction and where no agreement has been reached with him regarding the conditions and commercial methods for applying the invention. The Court of Bucharest shall authorize the compulsory license, provided that it considers, based on given circumstances, that, in spite of all efforts made by the interested person, no agreement could be reached within a reasonable time period.

The premise is that the solicitor of the compulsory licence could not reach an agreement with the patent owner regarding the transfer of rights.

The compulsory licence shall be non-exclusive and shall be granted under well-determined conditions regarding duration, royalty amounts and economic rights accruing to the inventor.

The patent owner has the right to ask the Court to revoke the compulsory licence if the licensee does not comply with its obligation to exploit the invention under the agreed conditions. The compulsory licence shall be effective as from the date of the registration with the Office.

154. Besides the cases already mentioned, a compulsory licence may be authorized by the Court of Bucharest:

– in national emergency cases;
– in other cases of extreme emergency;
– in cases of public use for non-commercial purposes.

The grant of the compulsory licence, for one of the reasons indicated above, does not require the fulfilment of the conditions mentioned as 'unjustified insufficient exploitation'. Nevertheless, the licensee must inform the applicant or patent owner about the authorization given by the Court within the shortest delay. In national emergency situations or in other extremely urgent situations, a compulsory licence may be granted by the Law Court of Bucharest without being necessary that the interested person requesting the compulsory licence prove the attempt to obtain a contractual licence.

In cases of public use for non-commercial purposes, the Government or third parties authorized by the Government, if they know or have demonstrable reasons to know that a valid patent is or will be used by the Government or the third parties, shall inform the patent owner accordingly, within a reasonable time.

An interested person may request the grant of a compulsory licence only if on the date of the request there exists a published patent application for which the Office has not made a decision to reject or that was not withdrawn or deemed to be withdrawn or there exists a patent in force on the territory of Romania. The beneficiary of the compulsory licence has no right to start an infringement action. The Law Court of Bucharest shall decide with regard to the withdrawal, extent, and duration of a compulsory licence as well as with regard to the remuneration due to the patent owner. The object of a compulsory licence is only the information contained in the patent application or in the patent.

Another relatively distinct case of compulsory licence is the so-called dependency licence granted for the cases where a patent cannot be exploited without infringing the rights conferred by other patent based on an application having a prior regular national filing date.

In this case, compulsory licence for exploiting the second patent may only be authorized if the following additional conditions are cumulatively fulfilled:

- the invention claimed in the second patent involves an important technical advance of considerable economic significance as compared with the invention in the first patent;
- the owner of the first patent is entitled to a cross-licence on reasonable terms for using the invention claimed in the second patent;
- the use authorized in respect of the first patent shall be non-transferable, except for the transfer of the second patent.

In case of a compulsory licence authorized in these conditions, the owner of the earlier patent is entitled to a licence for the exploitation of the patent granted on the basis of the subsequent application.

Where a patent cannot be exploited without prejudicing the rights conferred by another patent granted for a patent application whose filing date is earlier, the reference to use authorized in respect of the first patent will be non-transferable, except for the transfer of the second patent, relates to the fact that the authorized use in respect of the earlier patent is uninterrupted, except when the right in the subsequent patent has been assigned. A compulsory licence for a patent may be exploited without prejudicing the rights conferred by another patent granted for an application whose filing date is earlier than the date of the application for which there was granted the patent which is the object of the licence; a compulsory licence may be requested while observing the conditions of insufficient exploitation already mentioned.

Beneficiaries of the compulsory licence can also be the Government or third parties authorized by the Government. Compulsory licences shall be authorized mainly to supply the market. The extent and duration of compulsory licences shall be limited to the purposes for which they have been authorized.

In case of the inventions in the semiconductor technology field, the licence shall be granted only for public non-commercial purposes or to remedy a practice declared as anti-competitive as a result of a judiciary or administrative procedure.

When the owner of a plant variety patent cannot exploit the patent without infringing a prior patent, he may request a compulsory licence for the invention protected by said patent. When the owner of a patent relating to a biotechnological invention cannot exploit the patent without infringing a prior plant variety patent, he may request a compulsory licence for the exploitation of the plant variety protected by said patent.

The compulsory licence shall not be transferred other than to the part of the enterprise or the stock of goods benefitting from said use.

Upon the justified request presented by the interested person, the Court of Bucharest may withdraw the compulsory licence, when the circumstances leading to the grant of the licence ceased to exist, provided that the legitimate interests of the licensee should be protected adequately. The licence shall not be withdrawn if the circumstances which determined the grant of the licence are likely to occur again. The decisions of the Court of Bucharest concerning the authorization for using a compulsory licence, as well as those concerning the remuneration prescribed against the use of the licence, may be appealed against with the Court of Appeal of Bucharest within fifteen days from communication. The final and irrevocable Court decisions concerning the grant or the withdrawal of the compulsory licence, as the case may be, shall be communicated by the interested person to the Office which registers said decisions in the National Register of Patent Applications or in the National Register of Patents, as the case may be, and publishes the mention of such decisions in the Official Industrial Property Bulletin within one month from communication. For the purpose of entering the compulsory licence in the National Register of Patents and of publication in BOPI, the interested person has to communicate the decision of the Law Court of Bucharest relating thereto.

§7. Duration of Protection: Maintaining and Termination of Patent Protection

155. The patent duration shall be twenty years as from the date of filing the application (Article 30). For European patents, the duration runs from the date on which the regular national filing of the patent application was effected, pursuant to the EPC.

For patented medicaments or plant protection products, a supplementary protection certificate may be granted under the Council Regulation (EEC) No. 1768/92 of 18 June 1992 concerning the creation of a supplementary protection certificate for medicaments and the Regulation (EC) No. 1610/96 of the European Parliament and of the Council of 23 July 1996 concerning the creation of a supplementary protection certificate for plant protection products.

For each of the protection years, the patent owner has to pay a legal annual fee, which is the condition for maintaining into force the patent. Maintenance fees may also be paid in advance for a period not exceeding four years.

Fees due to be paid by foreign natural or legal persons shall be paid in convertible currency and entered into the account of the Office.

According to rule 43, for the patent maintenance in force, the fee for one year of protection shall be due on the first day of the respective year of protection, with the following exceptions:

- for the first two years of protection, for which the owner does not owe these fees;
- for the period comprising the protection years following the first two years, including the year following the year when the mention of the grant of the patent was published, when the fee is to be paid within twelve months from the date of publication in BOPI of the mention regarding the grant of the patent.

As soon as the legal conditions for the patent maintenance in force are fulfilled, the Office shall notify the patent owner or the professional representative thereof, as well as the fact that the fee for the patent maintenance in force shall not be refunded irrespective of the subsequent modifications with reference to the legal status of the patent. The fee for maintenance in force of the patent for one year of protection that was not paid according to the conditions provided for in paragraph (1) may be paid with a 50% increase up to the end of the six-month period from the due date. Failure to pay the legal fee for patent maintenance in force for one year of protection after the expiry of the time limit shall cause the patent owner's loss of rights conferred by the patent.

Fully in line with Patent Law Treaty-PLT provisions, the payment may be made by any person, provided that the data for the identification thereof and of the patent owner, the number of the patent, the title of the invention which is the object of protection by patent, the year or the period for which the fee is paid are indicated and provided that a copy of the payment document and of the documents proving, where necessary, that the patent owner has fulfilled the conditions for the reduction of the amount, are filed with Office. In case the patent owner or the professional representative failed to pay the fee for the maintenance in force up to the end of the time limit mentioned, and the payment was made by another person, then the legal conditions for the patent maintenance in force are fulfilled and the Office shall notify this.

In case when the patent owner that has lost the rights conferred by the patent requests the revalidation thereof, and the legal conditions are fulfilled and there is paid the fee for maintenance in force for the period for which the payment was not made, Office shall decide, through a board within the Patent Directorate, on the request for revalidation. The revalidation decision shall be entered in the National Register of Patents, communicated to the patent owner and published in BOPI within the legal time limit. The patent owner may, according to rule 51, lodge an appeal against the decision concerning the request for patent revalidation.

Generally speaking, the rights conferred by the patent of invention cease in the following distinct cases:

- revocation of the decision to grant a patent;
- cancellation of the patent;
- termination of the legal period of protection of twenty years;
- renunciation in whole or in part of the patent by the patent owner;
- forfeiture of the rights as a result of failing to pay the annual fees, according to what has been previously stated.

Below, we will analyse each of these situations.

I. Revocation of the Granting Decision

156. Within six months of the publication of the mention of granting a patent, any interested party shall be entitled to apply in writing, on valid grounds, to the Office for the revocation, either full or in part, of the decision to grant a patent (Article 49). Revocation may be asked if at the date of regular national filing at least one of the following conditions was not met:

- the subject matter of the patent is not patentable;
- the subject matter of the patent does not disclose the invention in a manner sufficiently clear and complete for it to be carried out by a person skilled in the art;
- the subject matter of the patent exceeds the content of the patent application as filed.

Where the grounds for revocation only relate to a part of the patent, the patent shall be revoked in part.

The contestation, or the request for revocation, shall be considered within three months of registration thereof by the Board of Appeal of the Office. The decision taken in connection with the revocation request shall be notified to the parties within fifteen days of pronouncement and may be appealed against before the Court of Bucharest within three months of such notification.

All final decisions regarding the revocation request shall be published by the Office within thirty days.

II. Cancellation of the Patent

157. Patents granted by the office, as well as European patents with effects in Romania, may be cancelled upon request. Request for total or partial cancellation may be addressed throughout the term of validity of the patent and shall be ruled upon by the Court of Bucharest, if, at the date of registration of the patent application, the following conditions were not met:

- the subject matter of the patent is not patentable;
- the subject matter of the patent does not disclose the invention in a manner sufficiently clear and complete for it to be carried out by a person skilled in the art;
- the subject matter of the patent exceeds the content of the patent application, as filed;
- the protection conferred by the patent has been extended;
- the patent owner is not the person entitled to the grant of the patent.

It is to be noticed that completely harmonized with the EPC, the first four of the conditions for cancellation of the patent are the same as the conditions of revocation, to which is added a new one regarding the person entitled to the grant of the patent. In the situation of an action for the patent cancellation based on this condition, the Office shall grant the patent to the entitled person based on the fact that the entitled person shall communicate the final and irrevocable decision to be published in BOPI and the interested person shall pay the legal fee for the modification of the patent legal status, the fees for printing, publication and issuance thereof as well as the fee for patent maintenance in force. The Office shall publish in BOPI the final and irrevocable court decision the mention of patent issuance and shall enter all these data in the National Register of Patents.

The cancellation decision shall be registered at the Office and published within thirty days of the communication.

According to Article 51, 'the cancellation of the patent may be requested after the time limit for the application for revocation have elapsed and throughout the entire duration of the patent'.

The decisions of the Court of Bucharest may be appealed against before the Court of Appeal of Bucharest within thirty days from communication. The final and irrevocable decisions to cancel the patent shall be registered with the Office by the interested person. Mention of the decision to cancel the patent shall be published in the Official Industrial Property Bulletin within sixty days of the registration of the decision with the Office.

The law provides that the failure to meet one or more of the formal requirements concerning the patent application shall only constitute grounds for revocation or cancellation of the patent, either wholly or in part, where said failure resulted from fraudulent intentions. A patent shall not be revoked or cancelled, either wholly or in part, without giving the owner the possibility to present observations concerning the revocation or cancellation and to make, in a reasonable period of time, amendments or corrections allowed by the Law.

In the situation of revocation or partial cancellation, only the rights born in the cancelled claimed invention to the owner will be cancelled or revoked. This is materialized either by cancellation of one or more claims, or by narrowing the respective part(s) of the claim(s).

In the case of revocation or cancellation as a whole, the rights born by the patent stop *ab initio*.

III. Termination of the Legal Period of Protection

158. This problem has been analysed in the first part of this chapter.

IV. Renunciation of the Patent by the Owner

159. The owner may renounce the patent either wholly or partly, by virtue of a written statement filed with the Office, at any moment during the validity period of the patent.

In the case of employees' inventions, the patent owner shall notify the inventor of his intention to renounce the patent; the patent owner shall transfer the patent rights to the inventor, at the latter's request, as well as any records relating the patent, provided that the employee grants the employer a non-exclusive licence in respect of the patented invention. The conditions for the grant of the non-exclusive licence shall be set by specific provisions in the employer's internal regulations. In the absence of these specific provisions, the conditions for the grant of the licence shall be set through the consent of the parties.

Where the patent is the subject of a licence agreement, renunciation shall be possible only with the agreement of the licensee.

The invention or part of the invention in respect of which protection has been renounced may be freely exploited by third parties.

The patent owner may renounce a patent granted for inventions containing classified information only after such secrecy has been lifted and the mention of the decision to grant the patent and the description, claims and drawings of the patented invention have been published.

According to rule 65, the Office takes act of the patent owner's renunciation if:

- the request is express, indicates whether the renunciation is made wholly or in part and indicates the claims referred to;
- the request is filed after the date the mention of the decision to grant the patent has been published in BOPI;
- the request is signed by the patent owner or, where the patent has several co-owners, the request will be signed by each of them separately;
- the owner proves that the provisions of Article 36 relating to obligations coming from previous contractual relationships are fulfilled.

Thus, depending on the case and the situation in which the owner finds himself in a contractual relationship with an interested person, the law provides some obligations of the patent owner with regard to the person who comes from the relationship established prior to the moment of declaration of the intention to renounce. Therefore:

- if a licence agreement which is under development has been concluded, the renunciation of the patent owner of the patent shall be possible only with the agreement of the licensee;
- if the invention under discussion has been given a secret character, the renunciation to the patent shall be done only with the agreement of the institution which gave this character;
- if the invention, owned by the employer, belongs to the category of service invention, he has to inform the inventor(s) of his intention to renounce and, if they so request, the owner is obliged to transfer the right on the patent to the inventor(s). In this situation, at the inventor's request, the patent owner shall transfer wholly or in part the right in the patent to the inventor, wholly or in part, and the inventor or inventors shall file with the Office a signed request for taking over the right in the patent, the original or authenticated copy of the document of renunciation and transfer of the right wholly or in part as well as of the proof of payment of the fee for the modification of the legal status of the patent;
- finally, if there are more owners of the patent of invention, the renunciation does not produce any effects but is done with the mutual agreement of all co-owners.

The mention of renunciation to the patent shall be entered in the National Register of Patents and shall be published in BOPI within sixty days from the date of its registration with Office and they shall come into effect on the date of its publication in the Official Industrial Property Bulletin.

V. Failure to Pay Annual Fees

160. We shall add to what has been previously stated that in the event of forfeiture of the rights, the patent owner may apply to the Office, stating legitimate grounds for reinstatement of the patent. The patent owner who, for legitimate grounds, was unable to observe a time limit in proceedings before the Office, shall have his rights re-established, provided that he submits a substantiated request within two months from the removal of the cause that prevented him from acting, but no later than one year since the expiry of the non-observed time limit.

Reinstatement shall be published by the Office.

§8. Infringement and Remedies

161. Infringement of the exclusive right of the patent owner supposes an unauthorized exploitation of the subject matter of the patented invention by a third party.

In the general approach of the defence of exclusive rights, a multitude of facts and circumstances in which the infringement of the patent owners has been committed by third parties are taken into consideration.

The most important elements the patent owner has to prove for the establishment of the infringement are:

- the unauthorized performing of one of the specific acts of the exclusive rights, as established by law;
- the moment of performing the unauthorized act, namely before or after the enforcement of provisional protection, following the publication of the patent specification;
- performing of one or more unauthorized act(s) on the national territory;
- existence of one or more cases considered not to be an infringement of an exclusive right, as mentioned in §6.

Where the infringement of the exclusive right conferred by the patent has been established, the law provides two kinds of remedies, namely civil sanctions and criminal sanctions.

162. As a rule, civil sanctions are applied in general cases where there are no elements of intentionality, while criminal sanctions include as a rule the intentional component.

Civil sanctions include the granting of compensations, the seizure of counterfeited products and eventually their destruction, decisions of interdictions of the unauthorized exploitation of the patented invention, etc. For prejudice caused to him, the patent owner or licensee shall be entitled to damages, as provided for by civil law, and may request to the competent law court to order the infringing products to be confiscated or destroyed, as the case may be. The same provisions shall be applied to materials and equipment that directly served to the perpetration of the infringement offence.

The law defines the offence of infringement as the unauthorized manufacture, use or putting into circulation of the subject matter of a patent or any other infringement of the rights under a patent during the term of validity thereof.

Thus, according to Article 56 of the Law, violation of article of law providing exclusive rights shall constitute infringement and shall be punished with imprisonment from three months to two years or a fine. Reconciliation of parties shall remove criminal liability.

For prejudice caused to him, the patent owner or licensee shall be entitled to damages, as provided for by civil law, and may request to the competent law court to order the infringing products to be confiscated or destroyed, as the case may be. The same provisions shall be applied to materials and equipment that directly served to the perpetration of the infringement offence.

Infringement of the rights by third parties after the publication of the patent application shall make the infringers liable for damages under civil law, and the entitlement to the payment of damages shall be enforceable after the grant of the patent.

However, the exclusive acts referred to, performed by third parties before the date of publication of the patent application or before the date of the summons made by the applicant and accompanied by a certified copy of the patent application, shall not be deemed to infringe the rights conferred by the patent.

163. Criminal proceedings shall be initiated ex officio and may have as result a punishment of imprisonment for six months to two years or a corresponding fine.

The patent owner shall be entitled, for prejudice caused to him, to damages as provided under Civil Law, and the infringing products may be confiscated as provided for in Criminal Law.

Any infringement by third parties of rights derived from provisional protection after the publication of the patent specification shall make the infringers liable for damages under Civil Law, and the entitlement to the payment of damages shall be enforceable after the grant of the patent. Notwithstanding this provision, the acts referred to in the Law regarding prohibition to perform the acts of exploiting the invention without the owner's consent performed by third parties before the date of publication of the patent application or before the date of the summons made by the applicant and accompanied by a certified copy of the patent application shall not be deemed to infringe the rights conferred by the patent. Where the acts referred to continue to be done after summoning, the law court may, upon request, order such acts to be discontinued until the Office makes a decision on the patent application. Said measure may be ordered subject to payment by the applicant for a security fixed by the law court.

If a decision to prohibit the infringement act is given, the Court issues an ordinance that expressly prohibits the person who infringes the right from continuing with the infringement.

As previously stated, the basic premise is that the infringement action starts with the preliminary filing of a complaint by the aggrieved party, which has to prove before the Court the infringement of his/her rights.

164. Regarding the extension of the protection conferred by the process patent on the product directly obtained by that process, in Article 58, the 'reversal of the burden of proof' has been provided. This supposes that, for the purpose of a civil proceeding in respect of the infringement of the right of a process patent, the burden of proof shall lie with the defendant that the process used to obtain an identical product is different from the patented process.

In applying such a provision, any identical product when produced without the consent of the patent owner shall, in the absence of proof to the contrary, be deemed to have been obtained by the patented process in at least one of the following circumstances:

- if the product obtained by the patented process is new;
- if there is a substantial likelihood that the identical product was made by that process and the owner of the patent has been unable through reasonable efforts to determine the process actually used.

Upon presentation of the proof to the contrary by the patent owner, the legitimate interests related to the manufacturing and trade secrets of the alleged infringer shall be taken into account.

Another offence provided for in Article 56 of the law is the unlawful claim, in any way, of the status of inventor and the punishment is imprisonment for six months to two years or a corresponding fine. Reconciliation of parties shall remove criminal liability.

Finally, the Law states the competence of the courts regarding any litigation concerning the status of inventor or patent owner, other rights arising from the patent, including the inventor's patrimonial rights under assignment or licensing contracts, or the failure to comply with the obligation of mutual information between employer and inventor.

§9. Overlap and Relationship with Other Intellectual Property Laws

165. The law and practice of patent protection in Romania present important relationships and connections with other intellectual property laws. This aspect is the direct result of international trends and is influenced to a large extent by the extraordinary technological development of the last decade.

Professor Cornish[33] speaks of a true 'expansion of the intellectual property rights', including elements of 'convergence'.

A first interference with copyright law has already been pointed out and it refers to software-related/implemented inventions or computer-related/implemented inventions.

According to Law No. 8/1996, as republished, relating to copyright and neighbouring rights, protected creations also include computer programs. The legal protection of computer programs includes:

- any expression of a program;
- application programs and operating systems expressed in any kind of language, either in source code or object code;
- preparatory conception material;
- manuals.

---

33. William Cornish, *Expansion von Schutzrechten, Symposium in Max Planck Institute* (12–13 Oct. 1999).

166. Taking into consideration the provision of Patent Law according to which 'computer programs as such' are not considered 'patentable inventions', one can make the general assertion that 'computer programs as such' are protected in Romania by copyright. However, technical solutions which imply or contain computer programs are potentially patentable if, besides the condition of existence of a technical solution, the patentability conditions – novelty, inventive step and industrial applicability – are also met.

If, for instance, a computer program for matrix inversing is based on a reversal algorithm that is entirely a mathematical method, an image compression-decompression software has at its basis a specific technical method and leads to the obtaining of a technical effect. The software 'as such' will not be protected by a patent, but the method, exposed in a manner specific to the patent specification and to the claims, is potentially patentable. A detailed description of the steps of the method, based on a technical concrete solution given by the used hardware, provides to the process patent the certainty of strong protection for the achieved software conferred by the patent.

It is very clear that, in this case, by virtue of an exclusive right conferred by the process patent, any third party could not counterfeit the technical solution of the mentioned software. Even more is permitted and eventually recommended. The description of the process patent shall include flowcharts and subroutines that illustrate the process steps. This brings new obstacles to unauthorized copying and these are important probation elements in the courts, supplementary to the general conception and the steps of the patented process.

Even if, according to the Patent Law, it is forbidden to introduce program lines, subroutines or programs in the claims, this comes from the legal requirement not to grant protection for programs as such. This does not constitute a limitation by any means because the claims are judged and interpreted in connection with the description, where, as mentioned, illustration with these components is allowed.

Practically, a 'software product' may be seen as a computer program as such, so that without any doubt it is an assembly of instructions in source code or object code. Moreover, having a perfect technical function could be achieved by software techniques, which can be achieved similarly by hardware modules.

All these aspects lead to the conclusion that between copyright protection and patent protection for computer programs, there is a remarkable synergy and complementation which enables them to complete IP protection.[34]

Another clear relation refers to database protection, which can be considered protected from the point of view of creator of derived work or from the point of view of maker, thus being protected in a sui generis manner, as provided for in the copyright law. If no overlapping could be imagined as regards pure databases, the software programs having as subject matter database management systems might have in principle a technical character which qualifies them as patentable. This would mean that a complex creation including creation or making of a database which includes within its technical solution, *inter alia*, a system able to automatically manage the data introduced and/or extracted in/from database would imply a complex

34. Alexandru Cristian Strenc, *Information Technology. Protection and Enforcement of Intellectual Property Rights* (Ed. Universul Juridic 2010).

protection ensured from both copyright as well as from patent side interlinked in a synergic manner of ensuring and enforcing its protection.

167. Another type of interference is with the sui generis protection ensured by Law No. 255/1998, as republished on the protection of new plant varieties.

The Patent Law, fully harmonized with European Directive 98/84 regarding the protection of biotechnologies and the EPC, provide for that inventions having as subject matter plant varieties and animal breeds, as well as the essential biological processes for obtaining plants and animals, are excluded from patentability.

At the same time, it is stipulated that inventions having plants or animals as subject matter are patentable if the possibility of technical achievement of the invention is not limited to a certain plant variety or animal breed.

However, Law No. 255/1998, as republished, ensures exactly a complementary protection for plant varieties, which lead in fact to overlapping and interested relationships.

It is a fact that in scientific circles, there are still important discussions with regard to the border between the plant protection conferred by the patent relating to that conferred by the plant variety patent, which is not the subject matter of this presentation.

Anyway, a clear problem of interference is the cross-licensing between a patent owner and a plant variety proprietor, deriving exactly from the interlinks and connections between these two areas.

This is solved by Article 44 of the Patent Law which provides that 'when the owner of a plant variety patent cannot exploit the patent without infringing a prior patent, he may request a compulsory licence for the invention protected by said patent'.

Reciprocally, 'when the owner of a patent relating to a biotechnological invention cannot exploit the patent without infringing a prior plant variety patent, he may request a compulsory licence for the exploitation of the plant variety protected by said patent'.

168. An extended area of overlapping and relationship is derived in a direct and immanent manner according to Law No. 350/2007 on the protection of utility models. This problem has been dealt with largely and extensively in Chapter 4.

169. Another possible zone of interference concerns the protection by the industrial design certificate, notably for a product whose aspect is under discussion: whether it is dictated or not dictated by a technical function.

This problem will be dealt with in Chapter 6.

170. Finally, in the case of semiconductor products, either in the situation where they are presented as technical solutions derived directly from their electronic function or in the case of technical solutions for the achievement of such circuits, they are obviously potentially patentable if the patentability criteria are met.

It is very possible that, in the framework of a presentation of an example of realization, the three-dimensional disposal of the semiconductor product elements and of interconnections or of a part of the interconnections may be a part of a technical solution, while the illustration of the example of realization may be exactly the original topography.

It is obvious that the protection conferred by a patent shall refer to the semiconductor product as a technical solution and the protection conferred by the topography certificate to the disposal of the said elements. There is an interesting functional interdependence between the scope of the patent protection and the scope of the certificate.

Chapter 3. Utility Models

§1. Sources: Legislation

I. National Sources

171. Up to 2007, Romania had no special legislation on the protection of utility models. Nevertheless, in its various historical developments, the Patent Law approached the problem of protection of 'smaller inventions' or the equivalent of 'small patents', but it was not expressed as (registered) utility models.

172. Thus, Law No. 62/1974 on Inventions and Innovations regarded innovation as a smaller invention by defining it as 'technical realization which presents novelty on national scale, progress and technical or social advantages, solve a problem in industry or in any other field of economy, science, health protection and defence of the country ... and was not applied on the territory of Romania'.

Starting with Law No. 64/1991 on patents (republished in 2002 and finally in 2014), the Romanian legislator renounced the protection of innovations under the mentioned definition and introduced the concept of 'technical realizations which is new at the level of an enterprise and useful to it'.

Filing the necessity of Romanian SMS's to have an adequate, affordable, easier and cheaper protection, the national IP legislation enriched in 2007 with a package dedicated to utility models protection, comprising:

- *Law No. 350/2007* on utility models, as republished in 2014.
- Governmental Decision No. 1457/2008 on the Implementing Regulations to the Law on Utility Models.

The Law also provides the fee regime for the protection procedure and maintenance.

Once the utility model protection is enforced and proven to work adequately, the intention of Romanian legislator is to renounce in the near future the protection of 'technical achievements' by considering it obsolete.

II. International Sources

173. On international and even European levels, harmonization in the field of utility model protection was unfortunately impossible.

Under these circumstances, the Romanian legislator followed an original approach based mainly on the best practices from some European countries with important history in utility model protection, mainly Germany and Austria.

Another important international source was the 'Amended Proposal for a European Parliament and Council directive approximating the legal arrangements for the protection of inventions by utility model' from 1999, in spite of the fact that the proposal met a certain resistance and was not finally adopted.

This proposal was considered nevertheless an important step toward a harmonized position in Europe and due consideration has been awarded to many concepts and procedures as provided in it.

It is to be underlined that everywhere within Chapter 2 where it is not otherwise mentioned, the following abbreviations of the terms will be used:

- Law – Law No. 350/2007 on Utility Models as republished in 2014.
- Regulations – Regulations for Implementing the Law on Utility Models, given by the Governmental Decision No. 1457/2008.
- Office – OSIM.
- Article – article of the law.
- Rule – article of the regulation.
- BOPI – Official Bulletin of Industrial Property – Utility Models section.

§2. Subject Matter Protected by Registered Utility Models

174. Under the law, a registered utility model protects any technical invention, provided that it is new, it exceeds the framework of mere professional skill and it is susceptible to industrial application.

The law gives a similar 'negative definition' of the categories of protected inventions as presented in the previous chapter dedicated to the Patent Law.

Thus, according to Article 1 of the Law, 'the following, in particular, shall not be deemed to be protectable inventions: discoveries, scientific theories and mathematical methods, aesthetic creations, schemes, rules and methods for performing mental activities, playing games or doing business, as well as computer programs, presentations of information'.

These exclusions from protection are in fact due to the lack of technical character of the above-mentioned inventions considered 'as such'.

This means that by contrary, the mentioned provisions do not exclude the protection by registration of the above-mentioned activities or subject matters if the utility model application or utility model relates to activities or subject matters *not regarded* 'as such'; in other words, if for these activities or subject matters can be put into evidence a certain 'technicality'.

The law provides some important exclusions from protection based on moral or public order considerations, namely for inventions the commercial exploitation of which would be contrary to public order or morality, including inventions harmful to the health or life of persons, animals or plants or which are likely to seriously harm the environment, provided that said exception shall not depend merely on the fact that exploitation thereof is prohibited by a legal provision.

They are also excluded from protection by registered utility model, plant varieties and animal breeds, as well as inventions having as a subject matter biological material.

Besides, the exclusions based on 'moral norms' have also been considered by the Romanian legislator 'conceptual exclusions' of the inventions having as a subject matter a product consisting of a chemical or pharmaceutical substance and those having as a subject matter a process or a method, in fact of those inventions which are deviating from the traditional concept of 'utility model'.

By excluding processes from protection, a clear consequence is that in fact they could be protected by registration of those inventions whose subject matter are products not expressly excepted or excluded from protection by law rule 4 that defines product as the subject matter of an invention, in so far as it constitutes the technical solution of a problem.

In Romania, two distinct types of products could be considered subject matter of a utility model registration, namely:

- objects having determined properties, technically defined by its constructive and/or component parts, by elements connecting the same, by its constructive shape and/or the shape of its component parts, by materials used for making it, by the constructive position and functional relationship between the component parts or by the functional role thereof;
- software products, which means products in the field of computer programs.

Products within the meaning of objects may be, for example:

(a) devices, installations, equipment, machine tools, apparatuses or subassemblies thereof employed for carrying out a manufacturing or working process;
(b) electric, pneumatic or hydraulic circuits;
(c) physical mixtures defined by the component elements, the quantitative ratio between them, or other properties individualizing them and making them applicable to solve a technical problem.

Products in the field of computer programs as a subject matter of a utility model application can be programmable apparatuses, in which at first sight the technical characteristic of the invention is carried out by means of a computer program, as well as the computer program products for data processing systems expressed by the logical running thereof.

§3. Conditions of Protection

175. As presented in §2, in order to be protected by registration, the inventions as subject matter of a utility model application should have a technical character as an intrinsic condition and should be new, exceed a common level of professional skill and industrially applicable.

I. Technical Character

176. Similar to inventions protected by patents, technical character means that at least an essential technical characteristic is involved in the solution given to the solved problem posed by invention.

The mixture between technical and non-technical characteristics does not put into discussion the technical character of the inventions, once the above-mentioned condition is met.

The technical character of an invention may be given by the fact that the invention belongs to a technical field, solves a technical problem or presents at least one essential technical feature to define within the claims the subject matter for which protection is sought.

According to the law, in the field of computer programs, the technical character of the invention derives from the fact that, when run or uploaded in a computer, the program determines or is capable of determining a subsequent technical effect exceeding the mere normal interaction between the program and the computer.

II. Novelty

177. Completely similar to the provision of the Patent Law, Article 3 of the law provides that 'an invention shall be considered to be new if it does not form part of the state of the art'.

The state of the art shall be held to comprise all knowledge that has been made available to the public by means of an oral or written description, by use or in any other way, prior to the date of filing of the utility model application.

The state of the art shall also be held to comprise the content of the utility model and patent applications filed with the OSIM (hereinafter referred to as 'OSIM'), as well as the content of the applications with effects in Romania, as filed, provided that they have the filing date prior to the filing date of the utility model application, and they were duly published on or after that date.

Law defines the so-called non-prejudicial disclosure by providing that 'the disclosure of the invention shall not be taken into consideration if it occurred within the six months preceding the filing date of the utility model application and if it was made, directly or indirectly by the applicant or his predecessor in title, or as a consequence of an obvious abuse in relation to the applicant or his predecessor in title'.

This means that on one side, the utility model application should be filed with OSIM within a maximal time limit of six months from the date on which the invention was made available to the public and on the other side, the disclosure should appear as an obvious abuse.

Rule 11 defines as an obvious abuse in relation to the applicant or his predecessor in title, the disclosure of the invention by a third party who has purloined the invention from any of these persons, or one of these persons communicated the invention to, on condition of not being rendered available to the public.

Under these circumstances, the obvious abuse, within the before said meaning, is supposed to be intentional and may be invoked by the applicant, even if the abuse has not been made relative thereto but relative to his predecessor in title.

III. Exceeding the Framework of Mere Professional Skill

178. According to rule 12, an invention is deemed to exceed the framework of the mere professional skill if, as compared with the state of the art, it presents an advantage as a result of solving the technical problem.

The advantage may be of a technical nature or a practical one in carrying out or using a product, or an advantage for the user, such as an advantage obtained in the field of education or leisure.

In a similar manner to the condition of inventive step from patent protection, the utility model applications and patent applications, although forming part of the state of the art, shall not be taken into consideration when assessing the condition of exceeding the framework of mere professional skill.

IV. Industrial Applicability

179. Article 4 provides that 'an invention shall be considered as susceptible of industrial application if it can be made or used in any kind of industry, including agriculture'.

The industrial applicability of an invention is rather supposed, when the applicant makes a sufficient disclosure of the invention.

Nevertheless, industrial applicability is seriously questioned when physical laws of nature are presumably not respected within the proposed solution to the problem (e.g., a perpetuum mobile type solution), nor when the solution cannot be reproduced with a sufficient degree of repetition of the inherent products or of the results obtained therefore.

§4. Formalities: Registration Procedure

I. Formalities

180. Formalities are performed in the specialized department of the Patents Directorate of the Office called 'Preliminary Examination'.

The utility model application shall be drawn up in Romanian and shall be filed with the Office on paper or, at the applicant's choice, in other form and by electronic means of transmittal.

The complete application which is to be understood under the concept of 'national regular filing' should contain the following data and/or documents:

(a) the applicant's identification data;
(b) the request for protection through utility model, accompanied by the title of the invention;
(c) a description of the invention;
(d) one or several claims;
(e) drawings to which reference is made within the description or claims.

The utility model application shall contain indications meant to allow the applicant's identity to be established.

Where the applicant is not the same person as the inventor, he must declare the inventor and prove, by a document filed with OSIM before a decision is made, that he is the person entitled to the registration of the utility model. Nevertheless, the filing date of the utility model application is still granted at the date when the so-called minimal requirements have been received by the Office:

(a) an express or implicit indication to the effect that a utility model is requested;
(b) indications allowing the identity of the applicant to be established or allowing the applicant to be contacted by OSIM;
(c) a part which, at first sight, appears to be a description of the invention.

Claims and drawings relating to the invention may also be filed within a time limit of two months from the filing date.

Where the requirements referred to in (a) and/or (c) are not complied with, OSIM shall notify the applicant indicating the deficiencies ascertained and requiring the correction thereof within a time limit of two months from the date on which at least the condition referred to in (b) was complied with.

The filing date of the utility model application is the date on which the documents remedying the deficiencies ascertained in the mentioned notification are filed with OSIM.

If the deficiencies have not been remedied within the granted time limit or if they relate to the condition referred to in paragraph 1(b), the filing date shall not be granted and the utility model application shall be deemed to not have been filed.

The filing of the utility model application shall have the value of a regular national filing as from the filing date, granted if the legal conditions have been directly met or the requirements exposed in the notifications have been complied with in due time.

The Romanian law does not allow the protection by registered utility model for complex inventions bound by a unitary concept, as the case is for patented inventions, with a direct implication that for each invention shall be filed a utility model application.

The claims shall clearly define the matter for which protection is sought; they shall be concise and completely supported by the description of the invention.

The application shall be accompanied by an abstract of the invention. The abstract shall contain a brief presentation of the invention which is intended exclusively for technical information and cannot be taken into consideration for other purposes, in particular for determining the scope of protection.

The invention shall be presented in the utility model application in a manner sufficiently clear and complete for it to be carried out by a person skilled in the art.

The clarity and completeness of the application are met if the utility model application contains sufficient technical information to allow a person skilled in the art to carry out the invention as claimed, without any inventive activity, and to solve the proposed technical problem, and if it allows third parties to understand the contribution the claimed invention brings to the state of the art.

The condition is to be understood in the sense that the clear and complete disclosure of the invention refers to the utility model application as a whole, including description, claims and, where appropriate, drawings.

The disclosure of the invention must be already made on the filing date of the utility model application.

Especially for the field of computer programs, description in the utility model application may be accompanied by graphical representations presenting the data processing operational stages or steps such as organization charts, graphs or the like.

Once the filing date of the application is granted with the meaning of national regular filing, the application is classified according to the IPC and enters into the registration procedure, as presented in III.

II. International Applications for Protection by Utility Model

181. According to Article 9 of the PCT and Article 25 of the law, an international application which has been granted an international filing date in a receiving Office and which has Romania as a designated State shall have the same effects as a utility model application filed with OSIM on the same date.

Directly derived from the principles of that treaty, an international application shall not have effect in Romania in the cases referred to in Article 24, paragraphs (1) (I) and (ii) in the PCT. Where the applicant intends to continue his international application in Romania, he shall open the national phase for a utility model in Romania within a time limit of thirty months as from the international filing date or, if a priority has been recognized, from the priority date.

For justified grounds, the applicant may still open the national phase within two months from the expiry of the thirty-month time limit, subject to the payment of the fee for late opening of the national phase.

For entering the national phase in Romania, the applicant shall file an application containing an explicit or implicit request for the opening of the national phase for a utility model, the certified translation into Romanian of the description, claims and drawings of the international application and he shall pay the filing fee.

After entering the national phase, the international application shall be subject to the procedures provided for by Romanian law.

Where the applicant failed to comply with the requirements previously exposed, as the case may be, the international application shall be deemed to have never had the effects of a utility model application in Romania.

An applicant who is a Romanian natural person or legal entity or a natural person or legal entity having residence in Romania or having a real and effective industrial or commercial establishment in Romania, within the meaning of Article 3 of the Paris Convention, may file an international application with OSIM, as a receiving office. The priority may be claimed either on the basis of a utility model application or on the basis of a patent application.

III. Registration Procedure

A. *Examination*

182. Under the procedure of Romanian law, the utility model registration is a more affordable, simplified and cheaper process than that of patenting procedure, mainly due to the fact that the Office does not examine substantive conditions of registration.

First of all, the Office examines formal conditions linked with the granting of the filing date and if they are met, it examines sufficient disclosure of the inventions, technical character of the inventions and exclusions from protection.

If the conditions are met, the Office drafts a search report. The search report is intended normally to stay on the basis of the decision of the applicant to continue the procedure and, if this is the case, at the decision to exploit the invention protected by the registered utility model.

Consequently, according to Article 17 of the law, the Office shall examine whether the utility model application contains sufficient information regarding:

(a) inventor's identity;
(b) person having the right to the registration of the utility model;
(c) the contents of the utility model application;
(d) the conditions concerning the filing;
(e) conditions concerning the recognition of priority;
(f) conditions that the application contains a single invention.

The Office shall examine whether the invention which is the subject matter of the application:

(a) is not excluded from protection by utility model;
(b) is sufficiently disclosed.

As previously mentioned, it shall not examine the subject matter of the utility model application to assess if the conditions of being new, exceeding the framework of mere professional skill or being industrially applicable are met.

Amendments to the application shall be allowed prior to the date on which a decision to register the utility model is taken, provided that they do not extend beyond the subject matter of the application. No rights can arise from amendments extending beyond the subject matter of the application.

B. *Drawing up the Search Report*

183. For all the utility model applications complying with the requirements concerning the utility model registration, the Office shall draw up, within a time limit of six months from the filing date, a search report mentioning the documents taken into consideration as regards the known conditions of registration: novelty, exceeding the framework of mere professional skill and industrial applicability.

The Office shall draw up the search report based on the regular national filing constituted under the provisions of the law. For the search report, the applicant shall file with the Office the proof of payment of the legal fee within a time limit of two months from the date on which the application was filed or from the filing date, as the case may be.

No search report shall be drawn up for the applications resulting from the conversion of a patent application for which a search report has already been drawn up and published by the Office.

The search report together with copies of the cited documents shall be sent to the applicant, accompanied by the Office notification requesting the applicant to file the proof of payment of the publication fee, the fee for issuing the certificate and the maintenance fee for the first six years of protection, within a time limit of two months. At the substantiated request of the applicant, said time limit may be extended only once by another two months.

The applicant may amend the claims within two months with a possible extension by request of another two months, by filing a new set of claims. In such cases, the Office shall not conduct an additional search and shall not modify the search report.

Where, within the time limit previously referred, the proof of payment of the legal fee has not been filed with the Office, the application shall be declared as deemed to be withdrawn.

Where the search report has not been made available to the public on the date of publishing the description, claims or, where appropriate, amended claims and drawings, it shall subsequently be published.

Any person may apply to the Office for the drawing up of a search report based on amended claims.

The search report, under the provisions of Article 18 of the law, shall provide the applicant with information relating to the relevant state of the art with regard to the invention contained in the application claims, in respect of which he can exercise his exclusive rights, as provided by law.

After its publication, the search report shall provide third parties with information relating to the relevant state of the art with regard to the invention contained in the application claims.

The search report cannot be made in at least one of the following cases:

(a) the invention which is the subject matter of the utility model application lacks technical character;
(b) the invention is excluded or excepted from protection under the provisions of the law;
(c) the invention is not sufficiently and completely disclosed;
(d) the fees for drawing up the search report have not been paid.

As has been mentioned, a registered utility model shall not have as subject matter complex inventions, even in the eventuality that they could be considered as having a unitary character. In this respect, for the application where the Office ascertains that the application contains two or three inventions, the applicant shall be notified accordingly and asked to file the claims corresponding to the invention for which the search report shall be drawn up. Under the provisions of Article 18 of the law, the search report shall be sent to the applicant, who, within the granted time limit, can communicate to the office if he desires the publication thereof, together with the publication of the mention of the registration decision. Where the search report has not been published together with the publication of the mention of the registration decision, it shall be published subsequently upon request by the owner or third parties.

The request for publication shall be filed with the Office in writing, not later than four months before the end of the time limit of six years from the filing date:

(a) the search report may be requested, in writing, by a third party not later than six months before the end of the first six years of protection;
(b) where a third party has requested that the Office draw up a search report based on amended claims, the Office shall publish the original search report drawn up for the applicant, while the second search report shall be published immediately after its having been drawn up and transmitted to the owner and the third party.

C. Amending the Claims

184. The utility model registration procedure shall be based on the regular national filing of the application, the amending of claims by the applicant, being admitted only as a consequence of receiving the search report drawn up by the Office.

Where the amended claims provided are filed subsequently to the end of the time limit, they shall not be published and shall be returned to the applicant.

The Office shall not publish amendments made after the filing date if they extend beyond the subject matter of the application and in this situation.

The Board shall not examine the amended claims filed in due time. It is to be understood that the amended claims shall confer on the owner the exclusive right of exploitation referred to in §5 paragraph III and shall determine the scope of protection conferred by the registered utility model.

However, the amended claims shall not extend beyond the subject matter of the utility model application on the filing date. The amended claims shall be assessed within the cancellation procedure according to paragraph G.

D. Registration

185. The examiner who has instrumented the application file drafts an examination report signed by him, on which a decision of the Examination Board will be based.

The examination report shall contain:

(a) bibliographic data of the utility model application;
(b) a brief presentation of the subject matter of the invention for which the utility model registration is requested;
(c) mention of the procedures the application has undergone subject to the payment of the fees, as well as of the analysed documents;
(d) explanations concerning the fulfilment of the conditions of registration as mentioned in III;
(e) the examiner's proposal to register the utility model or refuse the application while specifying the legal grounds thereof.

According to Article 19 of the law, decisions concerning the utility model application shall be made by a specialized examination board within the Patent Directorate of the Office based on the examination report.

According to rule 16, the competence of the Examination Board shall be the following:

(a) to make the decisions to register the utility model or to refuse the application;
(b) to declare the utility model applications as deemed to be withdrawn;
(c) to take note of the utility model application withdrawal upon the express request of the applicant.

The Examination Board consists of:

(a) chairman appointed by the Director General of the Office;
(b) state examiner in the industrial property field who has drawn up the examination report;
(c) a second examiner appointed by the chairman.

Decisions made by the Examination Board shall be justified and a mention thereof shall be entered in the National Register of utility model applications, where the mentions concerning the withdrawn utility model applications and the mentions concerning the applications declared as deemed to be withdrawn shall also be entered.

Mentions of the decisions to register the utility model application shall also be entered in the National Register of registered utility models.

The decisions made by the examination boards, the document concerning the withdrawal of the utility model application or the declaration that the application is deemed to be withdrawn shall be communicated to the applicant or the professional representative, as the case may be, within one month from the date of making the decision, or from the date on which the document concerning the withdrawal was issued.

Upon request by the applicant, the decision concerning the registration of the utility model may be deferred without exceeding a time limit of eighteen months from the filing date or from the date on which the application was filed.

In this situation, the Office shall defer the decision on the utility model registration if the applicant files a grounded request and pays the fee for extension of the time limit for proceeding starting from the seventh month from the filing date; otherwise, the registration procedure shall be continued by the Office.

Where an appeal is lodged, the mention of the decision shall be published within a time limit of one month from the date on which the appeal has been settled.

If the legal conditions of registration are complied with and the publication fee, the fee for issuing the certificate and the fee for maintaining the utility model in force for the first six years of protection are paid, the Office shall decide the registration of the utility model.

Decisions shall be either the registration of the utility model if the legal conditions are met or the refusal of the registration.

The Office shall decide to refuse registration of the utility model in the following cases:

(a) the invention which is the subject matter of the application is excluded from utility model protection;
(b) the utility model application does not comply with the provisions of Article 10, paragraphs (1) and/or (2) or paragraph (7), or the provisions of Articles 11 or 12;
(c) the applicant has opened the national phase after the expiry of the time limit of thirty months as from the international filing date or from the priority date, or if the applicant has not found justified grounds to open the national phase within two months from the expiry of the thirty-month time limit, as the case may be;
(d) the applicant, who is not the same person as the inventor, has not proved, within the prescribed time limit, that he is entitled to the registration of the utility model.

The utility model application shall be declared as deemed to be withdrawn in the following cases:

(a) the inventors were not declared according to the law;
(b) the application represented the basis of the priority claim in a subsequent application filed by the national route or for which the national phase has been opened in Romania;
(c) the applicant failed to file the claims and/or drawings within a time limit of two months from the filing date of the utility model application;
(d) the utility model application resulting from the conversion of a patent application in respect of which a decision to grant the patent was made after the conversion;
(e) one of the legal fees has not been paid in the amount and within the time limits specified in the Laws;
(f) the applicant fails to divide the non-unitary utility model application before a decision of the Office on the original application has been taken.

The mention of the decision to register the utility model or to refuse registration shall be published in BOPI within one month from the expiry of the time limit provided for by the law for lodging an appeal.

At the time of publishing the mention of the decision to register the utility model, the description, claims or, where appropriate, amended claims and drawings shall be made public, as well as the search report, unless this shall be published later.

E. *Publication of the Utility Model Registration*

186. The utility model registration is published by making the description, claims and drawings included in the regular national filing and, where appropriate, the amended claims available to the public at the Office premises, starting from the date when the mention of the registration decision has been published in BOPI. The search report is also published by being made available to the public at the Office premises.

Publication, as previously mentioned, includes a first page which comprises at least the following:

(a) filing number and date of the utility model application;
(b) index of the international classification;
(c) standard code for the identification of various types of utility model documents;
(d) title of the invention;
(e) owner's identification data;
(f) identification data of the professional representative appointed by the applicant;
(g) inventor's identification data;
(h) claimed priorities;
(i) application abstract agreed and figure indicated by the applicant to be published;
(j) number of the claims and figures of the utility model application;
(k) mention of publication of the search report, where appropriate.

Decisions on utility models produce effects for third parties as from the date of the publication in BOPI of their mention.

At the time of the publication, the changes in the legal status filed with OSIM up to the date on which the preparations for the publication of the utility model are finalized shall also be published.

F. *Granting the Certificate of Registration*

187. The Office issues the utility model certificate together with the description, the claims and, where appropriate, the drawings of the utility model to its owner, according to the decision of registration made by the specialized examination board.

The date of issuance of the certificate will be the date on which the mention of the registration decision is published.

The utility model certificate is a protection title granted without examining the substantive conditions as mentioned in §3.

Direct consequence of this approach is the fact that the exclusive rights will be exercised on the owner's entire responsibility, taking into account the search report drawn up by the Office.

The owner has to look very carefully at the results of the search report and interpret them in a professional manner. On one side, they should lead him to fully exercise his legal rights obtained through registration of the utility model, and on the other side, to avoid possible infringements of third parties' rights previously obtained through patents, registered utility models or even designs or copyrights.

G. Appeal and Cancellation

188. According to Article 22 of the Law, decisions of refusal of registration or that of registration may be appealed against the Office, in writing and on valid grounds, by the applicant or the owner of the utility model within two months of communication.

The appeal is settled by a re-examination board within the Board of Appeal of the Office.

The re-examination board decides upon the acceptance or rejection of the appeal and communicates the decision to the appellant.

The law provides in Article 23 that in the case when the registration has been made without respect to at least one condition of registration, a utility model registered with the Office may be cancelled in full or in part upon request throughout its duration.

Contrary to the situation for patenting procedure where after a six-month period of revocation within the Office, the patent can be cancelled only through a judicial procedure before a court, cancellation of a registered utility model is settled by the same Board of Appeal with the Office.

Cancellation may take place if it is ascertained that:

(a) the subject matter of the utility model does not meet the substantive conditions as exposed in §3 or belongs to the categories exposed in §2, not recognized as inventions or excepted from registration, as the case may be;
(b) the subject matter of the utility model does not present the invention in a manner sufficiently clear and complete for a person skilled in the art to be able to make it;
(c) the subject matter of the utility model extends beyond the content of the application, as filed;
(d) the owner is not the person entitled to the registration of the utility model;
(e) the scope of protection granted to the utility model has been extended.

Where the grounds for cancellation only relate to a part of the utility model, it shall be cancelled in part.

Cancellation is settled by a re-examination board within the Appeals Department of the Office.

The substantiated decision of the re-examination board shall be communicated to the parties within a time limit of fifteen days since pronouncement and may be appealed against by an appeal lodged with the Law Court of Bucharest within thirty days of communication.

Decisions of the Law Court of Bucharest may be appealed against by recourse lodged to the Court of Appeal of Bucharest within fifteen days of communication.

Cancellation shall be effective as from the filing date of the utility model application.

Where a utility model registration is cancelled for the legal reason that the owner is not the person entitled to the registration of the utility model, the Office issues the certificate to the entitled person, subject to payment of a fee corresponding to the legal fee for filing modifications in the legal status of the utility model.

This new legal status needs to be brought to the public and for the purpose of publication in BOPI, the person entitled to the issuance of the certificate must submit the proof of payment of the fee previously referred and the final and irrevocable decision establishing the new owner, as the case may be.

In Article 24, the law provides that 'at the request of the law court, OSIM shall submit the papers, documents and information necessary for judging the cause entrusted to the law court, those documents being finally retrieved, Summoning to the court shall be made only for this purpose'.

As in all cases dedicated to industrial property, petitions to the law court are exempted from judicial fees.

§5. Ownership and Transfer of Rights

I. Right to the Utility Model

189. Article 2 of the law statutes the fundamental right of inventor to its invention by providing that 'the right to the utility model shall belong to the inventor or his successor in title'.

The concept of inventor is to be understood within a large meaning which includes team of inventors, and in this respect, law provides that 'where the invention has been created jointly by several inventors, each of them shall have the status of joint inventor and the right shall belong to them jointly'.

A distinct situation is when more inventors create same invention independently and without any possible connection between them, and in this situation, the right to the utility model shall belong to the person who filed the utility model application having the earliest filing date.

The 'service inventions' or 'employees' inventions' have the same status as in Article 5 of the Patent Law – *see* Chapter 2.

Nevertheless, as can be easily understood, employees' inventions filed as utility model applications should be less encountered situations, as compared with those filed under the Patent Law.

Utility model is by excellence an invention made without special resources offered under an employment or research contract, or even less, under the duties of an inventive mission granted by the employer.

Where the inventor is an employee, in the absence of a contractual provision more favourable to him, the right to the invention shall belong:

(a) to the employer, in the case of inventions made by the employee under a contract of employment that explicitly provides for an inventive mission corresponding to his duties; the inventor shall be paid additional remuneration specified by contract;
(b) to the employee, in the case of inventions made by him, either in the course of his duties or in the field of activity of the employer, through knowledge or use of technology or means specific to the employer, or information available on the premises of the employer, or again with material assistance from the employer, except where otherwise provided by the contract.

Where the invention is the result of a research contract, unless otherwise provided, the right to the patent shall belong to the employer who commissioned the research, the inventor being entitled to additional remuneration specified in an additional clause of the contract.

In all cases, the inventor and the employer shall have the obligation to inform each other in writing of the creation and the stage of development of the invention and to refrain from disclosing it. Failure to observe the obligation to inform shall result in the liability of the person responsible.

If, in the cases of inventive mission or a research contract, the utility model application has not been filed with OSIM within sixty days of the employees having informed the employer in writing on the drawing up of the description of the invention, the right to the registered utility model shall belong to the employee, unless otherwise agreed between the parties.

In the case of an invention made by him, either in the course of his duties or in the field of activity of the employer, through knowledge or use of technology or means specific to the employer, or information available on the premises of the employer, or again with material assistance from the employer, the employer shall have a preferential right to conclude a contract in respect of the invention of his employee.

This right should be exercised within three months from the employee's offer with the specification that in the absence of an agreement on the contract price, it shall be fixed by judicial decision.

II. Right to the Registration of the Utility Model

190. In all the procedures before OSIM, the applicant shall be deemed to be the person entitled to the registration of the utility model.

The right to the registration of a utility model shall be transferable, either wholly or in part.

If, during the registration procedure, the applicant, which is not the same person as the inventor, has not proved, within a time limit of four months, that he is entitled to the registration of the utility model, the application shall be rejected.

III. Rights Conferred by Registered Utility Model

191. Law provides for *mutatis mutandis* similar rights as those conferred by the Patent Law.

Consequently, the registered utility model shall confer on its owner an exclusive right of exploitation throughout its entire duration.

It is prohibited to perform, without the owner's consent, manufacturing, using, offering for sale, selling or importing for the purpose of using, offering for sale or selling the product which is the subject matter of the registered utility model.

The extent of the protection conferred by the registered utility model shall be determined by the content of the claims, which shall be interpreted based on the description of the invention and drawings.

The utility model, as registered or as amended during the revocation in part, shall retroactively determine the protection conferred by the utility model application in so far as such protection is not thereby extended.

To determine the extent of the protection conferred by the registered utility model, due account shall be taken of any element equivalent to an element specified in the claims.

The following acts shall not constitute infringements of the mentioned rights:

(a) exploitation of inventions in the construction and the operation of land vehicles or aircraft and aboard vessels or in devices used in the operation thereof that belong to States party to international treaties and conventions concerning inventions to which Romania is also a party, when the vehicles, crafts or vessels enter the territory of Romania, either temporarily or accidentally, provided that such exploitation is exclusively for the needs of the vehicles, crafts or vessels;
(b) performing any of the acts previously referred to by a person who has applied the subject matter of the registered utility model as published or has taken real and effective steps towards producing or exploiting said subject matter in good faith on the territory of Romania, independently of the owner of the utility model and before the regular national filing concerning the invention has been effected or before the recognized priority date; in that case, the invention may continue to be exploited by that person to the same extent as on the date of the regular national filing or recognized priority, but the right of use may not be transferred otherwise than with the assets of that person or the part of the said assets assigned to the exploitation of the invention;
(c) performing any of the acts previously referred to, exclusively privately and for non-commercial purposes; production or, as the case may be, use the invention exclusively privately and for non-commercial purposes;
(d) marketing or offering for sale within the territory of the EU of specimens of the product constituting the subject matter of the invention that have been previously sold by the owner of the registered utility model or with his express consent;
(e) use of the subject matter of the registered invention for exclusively non-commercial experimental purposes;

(f) exploitation in good faith or taking real and effective steps towards exploiting the invention by third parties in the interval between the registered utility model owner's loss of rights and the reinstatement of the utility model; in that case, the invention may continue to be exploited by that person to the same extent as on the date of publication of the mention of re-establishment of rights, but the right of use may not be transferred otherwise than with the assets of the person exploiting the invention or the part of said assets assigned to the exploitation of the invention;
(g) exploitation by third parties of the invention or part of the invention in respect of which protection has been renounced.

The right of the inventor to the mentioning of his name is another important right, and in this respect, the law provides that 'the inventor shall have the right to the mention of his full name and status in the patent granted, in his employment record and in any other documents or publications concerning his invention.

Where the owner of the registered utility model is not the same person as the inventor, a duplicate of the certificate shall be issued to the latter'.

Upon his express request, the inventor's full name shall not be published; such request shall be subject to payment of the prescribed fee.

For employees' inventions created under an inventive mission with a contrary clause and those created during a research contract, respectively, the inventor shall enjoy economic rights determined by contract concluded with the applicant or the owner of the registered utility model, as the case may be.

The economic rights shall be determined according to the economic and/or social effects resulting from the utility model exploitation or the economic contribution of the invention.

Any person who affixes on his products or the packaging thereof a sign capable of creating the impression that those products are protected as utility models under this Law or any person who uses such a sign as a heading for his official correspondence, his firm, his business cards or announcements shall be bound to give, upon request by any interested person, information relating to the utility model on which the use of that sign is based.

In the event of loss of rights, the owner of the registered utility model may apply, for justified grounds, with the Office for reinstatement of the rights within six months of the date of publication of said loss. Within sixty days from the registration, the Office decides upon the request for reinstatement, subject to payment of the prescribed fee. Mention of the reinstatement of the registered utility model shall be published in the BOPI within thirty days from the date on which the decision becomes final and irrevocable.

IV. Transfer of Rights

192. Article 3 of the law provides that all three fundamental rights, 'the right in the utility model, the right to the registration of the utility model and the rights arising from said registration are transferable, either wholly or in part'.

Transfers may be effected by assignment, by the grant of exclusive or non-exclusive licences or by legal or testamentary succession.

In order to produce effects in respect of third parties, the mention of the transfer registered with the Office is published in BOPI and these transfers are opposable to third parties as of the date of this publication.

The assignment is total, if it relates to the whole invention registered as a utility model and to all of the exploitation rights conferred by the registered utility model. The assignment is partial, if it is limited only to particular rights conferred by the registered utility model or only to a certain part of the invention protected by the registered utility model.

The priority right may be transferred by assignment only with the agreement of the parties.

The assignment may be limited in time for a period which cannot exceed the duration of protection.

A partial assignment normally leads to the co-ownership of the registered utility model.

The licence is exclusive when the licensor has committed himself not to transfer the rights of exploitation of the invention to other persons.

In the case of an exclusive licence, if not otherwise provided for, the licensor maintains the right to exploit the invention.

The licence is non-exclusive if the licensor reserves the possibility of granting the right to exploit the invention to other persons.

In its turn, a licence is total if it relates to all rights of exploitation, to the whole invention registered as a utility model and to the whole territory of protection; the licence may be limited to a shorter period of time than the duration of protection period of the registered utility model.

The licensee may grant sub-licences only with the licensor's consent. The licensee cannot start an infringement action in the court without the patent owner's consent, unless otherwise provided by the licence agreement.

Nevertheless, by exception to the before-mentioned provisions, the beneficiary of an exclusive licence may start an infringement action in the court if, after having notified the infringement acts he took knowledge of to the owner of the registered utility model, this did not act within the time limit requested by the licensee.

If the owner of the registered utility model does not exploit the invention or if the exploitation is not sufficient on the territory of Romania, the importation of the subject matter of the utility model by the owner shall be considered to be an exploitation of the utility model in Romania.

In case of the transfers of rights registered by a foreign applicant or owner of the utility model, the Office may, where appropriate, request a translation into the Romanian language of the original document of the certified copy of the right transfer contract.

It has to be mentioned that all assertions made on transfers of rights deriving from registered utility models apply *mutatis mutandis* to the rights deriving from utility model applications.

§6. Duration of Protection: Maintaining and Termination of Utility Model Protection

193. According to Article 7 of the law, the duration of a utility model is six years from the filing date.

The owner of the right may obtain, based on a written request filed with the Office, the renewal of the utility model protection for a further two-year period, but not earlier than one year and not later than six months before the expiry of the first mentioned duration.

Finally, the owner of the right may obtain, based on a written request filed with the Office, the renewal of the utility model protection for a second and last two-year period, but not earlier than one year and not later than six months before the expiry of the second period of duration.

This means that the overall duration of the utility model cannot exceed a time limit of ten years from the filing date.

The renewal fee may be paid up to the date of expiry of the duration previously referred, as the case may be, or in a time limit of six months from any of said dates, with a surcharge of 50% of the amount of the due fee.

As a facility offered to the applicant/owner, they may cumulatively pay the maintaining fees and the renewal fees for the entire period of protection.

In the case of renewal of protection, the Office enters in the National Register of registered utility models and publishes in BOPI the notice of protection renewal immediately after the expiry of the first or second protection duration, as the case may be, if:

(a) the owner has requested the renewal of protection in writing within the legal time limits as previously mentioned;
(b) proof of payment of the renewal fee is made according to the time limits and conditions just exposed.

The Office does not enter the notice of protection renewal where, before the expiry of the protection duration, a final and irrevocable decision to cancel the registration certificate has been made, or the owner has waived his rights conferred by the utility model registration.

Nevertheless, as soon as the legal conditions for the renewal of utility model protection are fulfilled, the Office issues the renewal certificate to the owner and publishes the notice of protection renewal in BOPI.

Another facility in paying the fees offered by law is that where the owner has not renounced the utility model, the renewal fee can be paid by any person, provided that the identification data thereof and the owner's data, the utility model certificate number, the title of the invention which is the object of utility model protection and the period for which the fee is paid are indicated and a copy of the payment document is registered with the Office.

Where the owner or the professional representative has not paid the renewal fee before the end of the mentioned legal time limits, but the payment has been effected by another person, the legal conditions for the renewal of utility model protection shall be deemed to be fulfilled and the Office notifies the owner or professional representative, as the case may be, accordingly.

Where protection lapses for failure to pay the renewal fees under the legal conditions of time limits, the owner may apply with the Office for revalidation of registration, for justified grounds, within two months, at the most, from the expiry of the time limits.

The Office decides on the application for revalidation under the condition of the payment of the legal fee.

The notice of utility model registration revalidation shall be published in BOPI within thirty days of the communication of the decision. The notice of renewal of protection for the first and second periods, with time limit of two years, is published in BOPI.

As a general rule, the rights conferred by the registered utility model cease for one of the following reasons:

(a) cancellation of the registered utility model;
(b) termination of its legal period of protection;
(c) by renunciation by the owner of the registered utility model.

Below, we shall analyse each of these situations. The utility model shall be deemed not to have a retroactive effect from the filing date, if a patent is granted for an application:

(a) claiming the priority of the utility model application; or
(b) which has been converted into a utility model application, and the applicant has not expressly requested the withdrawal of the patent application.

I. Cancellation of the Registration

194. The cancellation procedure and the reasons thereof have been exposed in §4 section III.G.

In the case of the cancellation of the registration, the termination of protection shall become effective on the day following the date of expiry of the utility model duration.

Nevertheless, where a utility model registration is cancelled for the reason that the owner is not the person entitled to the registration of the utility model, the Office shall issue the certificate to the entitled person, subject to payment of a fee corresponding to the legal fee for filing modifications in the legal status of a patent.

For the purpose of publication in BOPI, the person entitled to the issuance of the certificate shall submit the proof of payment of the legal fee and the final and irrevocable decision establishing the new owner, as the case may be.

II. Termination of the Legal Term of Protection

195. As previously exposed, the utility model registration may last up to ten years from the filing date, following a first duration of six years and the possibility offered by the law of two supplementary renewals based on a written request, each of a two-year period.

The termination of protection becomes effective on the day following the date of expiry of the utility model duration, namely six, eight or ten years, calculated as from the filing date and depending on the request and fulfilment of the conditions of renewal.

III. Renunciation of the Utility Model by the Owner

196. The patent owner may renounce the registered utility model, either wholly or in part, by virtue of a written statement filed with the Office.

In the case of employees' inventions where by the effect of the law the employer is entitled to the invention, the owner of the registered utility model shall notify the inventor of his intention to renounce the utility model and shall transfer the rights deriving from the registered utility model to the inventor, at the latter's request.

Where the registered utility model is the subject of a licence agreement, renunciation shall be possible only with the agreement of the licensee.

The invention or part of the invention in respect of which protection has been renounced may be freely exploited by third parties.

Renunciation by the owner to the rights conferred by a registered utility model within the validity period shall be made by filing a request with the Office, which takes note of the registered utility model owner's renunciation, if:

(a) the request is express, indicates whether the renunciation is made wholly or in part and indicates the claims referred to;
(b) the request is filed after the date the mention of the decision to register the utility model has been published in BOPI;
(c) the request is signed by the utility model owner or, where the utility model has several co-owners, the request will be signed by each of them separately;
(d) the owner proves that he fulfilled the conditions of either notification of the inventor – if he is the employer – either with the agreement of the licensee or if the utility model is subject to a licence agreement.

The mention of renunciation to the utility model shall be entered in the National Register of Utility Models and shall be published in BOPI within sixty days from the date of its registration with the Office.

At the inventor's request, the owner of the utility model shall transfer wholly or in part the right in the patent to the inventor, wholly or in part, and the inventor or inventors shall file with OSIM a signed request for taking over the right in the utility model, the original or authenticated copy of the document of renunciation and transfer of the right wholly or in part as well as of the proof of payment of the fee for the modification of the legal status of the utility model.

The termination of protection shall become effective on the day following the date of communication of renunciation by the owner.

Where the renunciation only relates to certain parts of the utility model, it shall remain in force for the other parts. The Office shall take note of the renunciation without examining whether the remaining parts of the utility model still comply with the requirements of the law and whether the limitation is acceptable.

§7. Infringement and Remedies

197. The acts performed as a violation of exclusive rights of the owner, namely manufacturing, using, offering for sale, selling or importing for the purpose of using, offering for sale or selling of the inventions protected under a registered utility model, shall constitute infringement and shall be punished with imprisonment from six months to two years or with fine.

Criminal proceedings shall be initiated ex officio. For prejudice caused to him, the owner of the registered utility model or licensee shall be entitled to damages, as provided for by civil law, and may request to the competent law court to order the infringing products to be confiscated or destroyed, as the case may be. The same provisions shall be applied to materials and equipment that directly served to the perpetration of the infringement offence.

Litigations concerning the status of inventor, utility model owner or other rights arising from the registered utility model, including the economic rights of the inventor under assignment or licence contracts, or concerning failure to comply with the provisions of the law regarding employees' inventions shall be within the jurisdiction of the law courts.

The interested person shall communicate the court decision to OSIM within thirty days from the date on which the decision became final and irrevocable in order to be entered in the National Register of Utility Model Applications or in the National Register of Registered Utility Models and published in the Official Industrial Property Bulletin. In the absence of the publication in the Official Industrial Property Bulletin, the decision shall not be opposable to third parties.

The owner of the registered utility model, as well as the licensee authorized to use the rights arising from the utility model, may request the law court:

(a) to order withholding measures when there exists the risk of infringing on the rights arising from a registered utility model and if said infringement risks cause irreparable prejudice or if there exists the risk of destroying the probative elements;
(b) to order, after the grant of the customs clearance, certain measures for stopping the acts of infringement on the rights arising from a registered utility model performed by a third party on the occasion of putting certain imported goods into the commercial circuit, causing thus damages to such rights.

The law court may decide that the infringer of the rights arising from the registered utility model should inform the owner of the identity of the third parties who took part in producing and distributing the goods concerned, as well as on the distribution circuits.

The withholding measures may be ordered subject to payment by the plaintiff of a security established by the law court. The provisions of civil law are applicable to order the withholding measures.

The law court may demand the plaintiff to provide any probative elements available to him in order to prove himself to be the owner of the infringed registered model or of a registered utility model, the infringement of which is unavoidable.

Customs authority may order, either ex officio or upon request by the owner of the registered utility model, that customs clearance operations be suspended for the import or export of goods or to place such goods under a suspended customs status.

Customs competence concerning the enforcement of patent rights at the borders belongs to the National Customs Authority, according to Law No. 344/2005, concerning certain measures for ensuring the enforcement of intellectual property rights within customs operations.

According to the law, there are some important exceptions concerning the infringement of rights, practically all deriving from situations where the inventions protected under registered utility model are used for internal, scientific, and non-commercial purposes.

In particular, the following acts do not constitute an infringement of the rights provided for in the law:

(a) the carrying out of the tests and studies necessary for obtaining the authorization for placing a medication on the market, as well as the practical requirements resulting therefrom;
(b) use for education purposes of the information contained in the registered utility model;
(c) the acts concerning the research and development of information contained in the registered utility model, on condition that they are destined exclusively to experiments or studies which intend to evaluate the technical data from the registered utility models.

Another offence provided by the law is the unlawful assumption, in any way, of the status of inventor which shall be punished with imprisonment from six months to two years or with a fine.

In any case, upon request by the law court, the Office submits the acts, documents and information necessary for judging the cause entrusted to the law court and those documents being finally retrieved. Summoning to the court shall only be made for this purpose. Petitions to the law court in the industrial property field shall be exempt from judicial fees.

§8. Overlap and Relationship with Other Intellectual Property Laws

198. The most direct overlap and relation of the utility model law is with Patent Law and this situation derives clearly from the similar subject matter of protection, namely inventions.

Excepting inventions having as a subject matter a product consisting of a chemical or pharmaceutical substance and inventions having as a subject matter a process or a method, all other inventions could be in principle protected either as utility models or as patents; the question of 'level of inventive step' remaining 'the trigger' of the protection.

Depending on the different stages of the process of examination in which the applications are located, the law provides for the possibility to convert/transform a utility model application into a patent application and vice versa.

This derives mostly from the fact that the applicant may decide on a more adequate way of protection than which he/she applied at the very beginning of the process.

I. Conversion of a Utility Model Application into a Patent Application

199. The request for conversion filed under the provisions of Article 15, paragraphs (1) or (3) of the Law shall contain:

(a) the express request for conversion for the invention which is the subject matter of the utility model application;
(b) filing number and date of the utility model application having the value of regular national filing whose conversion is requested;
(c) applicant's identification data.

If the requirements provided for are complied with, the Office shall make copies of the description, claims and, where appropriate, drawings constituting the regular national filing of the utility model application, enter the patent application into the National Register of filed patent applications and notify the applicant on the number of the patent application resulting from the conversion.

In respect of the patent application resulting from the utility model application, the legal conversion fee shall be paid. Where the legal conversion fee was not paid at the moment of filing the request, it can still be paid within a time limit of two months from the filing date.

Where, in the utility model application, the priority of a prior application was claimed and recognized, then the patent application resulting from the conversion of the utility model application shall also benefit from the claiming of said priority.

A utility model application having the value of a first regular national filing, from which a patent application has resulted by conversion, shall generate a convention priority right if, within twelve months from the filing date, it has not been refused, withdrawn or deemed to be withdrawn.

If the utility model application has been refused, withdrawn or deemed to be withdrawn within the time limit previously referred, the patent application resulting from the conversion of the utility model application shall generate a conventional priority right.

The registration procedure shall be continued in respect of the utility model application from which a patent application resulted by conversion, according to the law, in the absence of an express request to withdraw the utility model application made by the applicant.

A patent application can result in conversion from a utility model application only once.

A patent application can no longer result from an international application which has entered the national phase with a view to obtaining utility model protection.

The patent application resulting from conversion shall be subject to the procedures provided for by Patent Law No. 64/1991 as republished.

Where, in respect of the utility model application, the applicant has declared the inventors and/or proved that he is the person entitled to the registration of the utility model, the same requirements shall be deemed to be met in respect of the patent application.

In case the legal provisions of conversion are not complied with, the Office shall notify the applicant that no patent application resulted from conversion from the utility model application.

II. Transformation of a Patent Application into a Utility Model Application

200. According to Article 14(1) of the Law, a utility model application can also result from a patent application having as a subject matter the same invention, provided that the applicant files a request for transformation:

(a) during the patent application examination procedure, prior to the finalization of technical preparation for publishing the mention of the decision to grant the patent or to reject the patent application;
(b) within a time limit of three months from the date on which the Office publishes the mention of a final and irrevocable decision to cancel the patent as a consequence of lack of inventive step.

If the mentioned requirements are met, the utility model application resulting from the transformation shall benefit by the same filing date, as well as by the priority right arising from the patent application.

The transformation shall have no effect after the expiry of a ten-year period counting from the filing date of the patent application.

For a patent application transformed into a utility model application, the examination procedure shall be continued if the applicant does not expressly request the withdrawal of the patent application.

European patent applications under Article 135 of the Convention for the grant of European patents (EPC adopted in Munich on 5 October 1973, to which Romania accessed by Law No. 611/2002 with the subsequent revisions) can also be converted into utility model applications, under the conditions provided for by the law.

The request for conversion filed under the conditions provided for in Article 14, paragraphs (1) and (3) of the law shall contain:

(a) the express request for transformation in view of registration of the utility model for the invention which is the subject matter of the patent application;
(b) filing number and date of the patent application having the value of regular national filing whose transformation is requested;
(c) applicant's identification data.

Applications resulting from the division of a patent application having a product and a process as a subject matter can also be transformed into utility model applications. In that case, the applicant shall request the transformation into a utility model application for the divisional patent applications having the product as a subject matter.

If the requirements previously provided are complied with, the Office makes copies of the description, claims and, where appropriate, drawings constituting the regular national filing of the patent application on which the conversion is based, enter the utility model application into the National Register of filed utility model applications and notify the applicant on the number of the utility model application resulting from transformation.

Where the legal transformation fee was not paid at the moment of filing the request, it can still be paid within a time limit of two months from the filing date. Where the legal conversion fee has not been paid as mentioned, the utility model application shall be declared as deemed to be withdrawn.

As provided for in Article 14, paragraph (1), letter (b) of the Law, within a time limit of three months from the date on which the Office publishes the mention of a final and irrevocable decision to cancel the patent as a consequence of lack of inventive step, the owner of the cancelled patent may file, together with the request for transformation, a copy of the final and irrevocable decision of cancellation, accompanied by the copy of the claims cancelled for lack of inventive step.

A patent application can be transformed into a utility model application only once.

An international application which has entered the national phase in view of the grant of a patent can no longer be transformed into a utility model application.

For the purposes of registration as a utility model, the application resulting from the transformation of a patent application shall be subjected to the procedures provided for by the law.

After the utility model application resulting from a patent application has been filed, the Office shall publish the search report drawn up for the patent application, if it has not been made public up to the date of the conversion request.

Claims amended as a consequence of the search report drawn up for a patent application can be filed together with the conversion request.

The filing date is in this case the filing date of the patent application for the case claiming the priority of the utility model application and respectively the filing date of the utility model application for the case in which it has been transformed into a utility model application, and the applicant has not expressly requested the withdrawal of the patent application.

The utility model shall be deemed not to have retroactive effects from the filing date, in so far as, on the date of publishing the mention of the grant of the patent, it protects the same invention and has the same owner as the patent.

Where a transfer by licence occurs for the utility model application, and a patent is granted based on the patent application, the transfer effects shall cease from the filing date of the patent application.

The applicant for a patent may, before a decision for the grant of the patent is made, either:

(a) request the withdrawal of the patent application; or
(b) renounce the right conferred by the registered utility model, if he is the owner of such a right.

Where, in the patent application converted into a utility model application, a priority has been claimed and recognized, it shall also be deemed to be claimed and recognized in the utility model application.

A patent application having the value of a first regular national filing, from which a utility model application has resulted by conversion, shall generate a convention priority right if, within twelve months from the filing date, it was not refused, withdrawn or deemed to be withdrawn.

If the patent application was refused, withdrawn or deemed to be withdrawn within the legal time limit, the utility model application resulting from the transformation of the patent application shall generate a conventional priority right.

The Office notifies the applicant that the patent application cannot be transformed into a utility model application or that the provisions of the law are not complied with.

The national patent application resulting from the conversion of a European patent application can be transformed into a utility model application if:

(a) documentation of the converted European patent application has been received by the Office within a time limit of twenty months from the European patent application filing date or, where a priority is claimed, from the priority date, provided that it contains the request for conversion into a national application in Romania;
(b) within a time limit of two months from the receiving by OSIM of the documentation referred to under letter (a), the applicant files with OSIM the translation of the description, claims and, where appropriate, drawings contained in the documentation, for which he wants procedures to be carried on with a view to obtaining utility model protection, accompanied by the express request for transformation into a utility model application.

In case the conditions are not complied with, the Office notifies the applicant that the national patent application resulting from the conversion of the European patent application cannot be transformed into a utility model application.

III. Relation with Designs Law

201. Based on Article 4 E(1) of the Paris Convention, design protection can be applied by virtue of a priority right based on the filing of a utility model application, and the priority term will be six months.

Based on this provision, the Office may receive design applications where aesthetic aspects specific to this type of protection could be derived from description and claims of the utility model applications which clearly are oriented towards presenting technical character of the invention.

This approach could lead to a complex protection where technical part of the invention will be protected by the utility model and the aesthetic part, by registered designs, and by invoking a priority right based on the utility model application.

IV. Overlap and Connection with Copyright Law

202. All considerations made in Chapter 4 on Patents are equally valid for utility models having as subject matter computer- or software-implemented inventions.

While a software 'as such' is undoubtedly a copyright matter, a technical invention may be obviously protected by a registered utility model under the conditions already exposed.

These specific forms of protection are non-contradictory, mutually beneficial and even more synergic.

Chapter 4. Trademarks and Geographical Indications

§1. Sources: Legislation

I. National Sources

203. Trademarks' protection began in Romania with the promulgation of the first Law on Trademarks on 14 April 1879. This is a rather remarkable fact, given that it was the seventh modern law in the world after those of France (1857), the Austro-Hungarian Empire (1858), the United Kingdom (1862), Italy (1868), Germany (1874), and Belgium (1879).

Although the use of the mark was voluntary, for medicinal products as well as for those for hygiene and public health, 'the Government could declare its use as compulsory and even significant'. In the legal system of 1879, the filing of the mark was declarative and not attributive.

The trademark set up an individual, absolute and exclusive exploitation right and the duration of protection was fifteen years, with the possibility of a prolongation for a new term of fifteen years, subject to the condition of making a new filing.

It is remarkable that the law has had a very long existence, of about eighty-eight years. It was replaced by Law No. 28 of 29 December 1967 on Trademarks, as it was modified by the Decree No. 485 of 27 December 1977. Although it had some restrictions specific to the political regime of that time, the mentioned law established the passing of a substantive examination of the trademarks for the first time. Moreover, the law also extended the scope of protection to both services and to collective marks. It is to be remarked that there was no specific protection for appellations of origin or geographical indications, but they could be protected as collective marks.

204. Today, the protection of the trademarks and geographical indications in Romania is achieved in complete harmonization with the system of European and EU trademark law and in full compliance with the TRIPS Agreement and Trademark Law Treaty-TLT. A major step in this respect was due to the adoption of Law No. 84 on Trademarks and Geographical Indications, which entered into force on 23 July 1998 and of the Governmental Decision No. 833 of 19 November 1998 on Regulations for Implementing the Law. In order to update the trademark law with the last developments on EU level and with Singapore Treaty, the Law has undergone substantial amendments when has been republished in 2010 as Law No. 84/1998 on trademarks and geographical indications republished in the Official Gazette of Romania, part I, No. 350 of 27 May 2010, and respectively *Governmental Decision* No. *1.134/10 November 2010 on Implementing Regulation – published in Official Gazette* No. *809/3 December 2010.*

205. In 2022, the Government issued Decision No. 1197/2022 on the amendment and completion of the Governmental Decision No. 1.134/10 November 2010 for the approval of the Implementing Regulation of the application of Law No. 84.1998 as republished. The declared intention of this act was to transpose Article 23 paragraph (2), Article 24 paragraph (2), Article 25 paragraph (5), Article 27 lit.

a), Article 30 paragraph (2), Article 43 paragraph (2) and Article 49 paragraph (1) and (3) of Directive (EU) 2015/2.436 of the European Parliament and of the Council of 16 December 2015 on the approximation of the laws of the Member States regarding trademarks.

206. Some years later, the law has been amended and republished in the Official Gazette of Romania, Part I, No. 337 of 8 May 2014, by incorporating the relevant provisions of Law No. 76/2012 on enforcing the amendments to the Code of Civil Procedure and consequently of Law No. 187/2012 on enforcing the amendments to Criminal Code.

207. In 2020, the law was substantially revised and republished, according to Article IV of the Law No. 112/2020 for amending and completing the Law No. 84/1998 on Trademarks and Geographical Indications, published in the Official Gazette of Romania, Part I, No. 603/9 July 2020, corrected in the Official Gazette of Romania, Part I, No. 675/30 July 2020.

208. By-Law No. 112/2020, it is transposing the Directive (EU) 2015/2436 of the European Parliament and of the Council of 16 December 2015 on the approximation of the laws of the Member States relating to trade marks, published in the Official Journal of the European Union (OJEU), L series, No. 336 of 23 December 2015 (EU Directive 2015/2436).

209. Briefly, main legislative changes bought by this law, which will be further extensively presented, are:

- elimination of the requirement for graphic representation of marks among the conditions for registration;
- absolute/ relative reasons for refusal of the trademark registration/ cancellation have been modified/ completed;
- additions have been made regarding the indication of the products and services for which trademark protection is requested;
- deadlines for the registration of the application have been reduced;
- additions have been made to the possibility of formulating observations on the trade mark application;
- possibility of division of a trademark registration has been introduced;
- the opposition procedure was modified from '*ante-registration*' to '*post-registration*' procedure;
- clarifications have been provided regarding the date of completion of the trademark registration procedure and the deadline for payment of the fee for its registration in the Trademark Register;
- the rights of trademark holders have been enhanced, excepting a certain limitation derived from the principle of legal certainty;
- amendments/ clarifications regarding the transfer of trademark rights;
- clarifications have been introduced regarding the real rights of trademarks;

– introduction of an administrative procedure for cancellation or revocation of trademark rights and removal of the five-year time limit for bringing an action for trademark cancellation;
– the subjects of law regarding the holders of collective marks or certification marks, as well as the conditions regarding registration, cancellation and revocation of those marks, have been regulated in a timely manner.

A special chapter and annex of the Governmental Ordinance No. 41/1998 as republished in 2006 on fees in the field of industrial property deals with the fees and their terms of payment specific to the domain of trademarks and geographical indications.

Of significant importance is Law No. 304/2005 on 'Measures to Ensure Compliance with Intellectual Property Rights within Customs Operations' which although refers to all titles of intellectual property, is of particular importance for trademark border enforcement. It is an important law on border enforcement that normally stops in great measure the entrance of counterfeited and pirated products into Romania and contributes to reducing substantially piracy and counterfeiting on the Romanian market.

II. International Sources

210. Romania became a member of the Madrid Agreement Concerning the International Registration of Marks on 6 October 1920, but in fact, it applies the revised form adopted at Stockholm in 1967 and modified in 1979.

Also, Romania is a member of the Protocol to the Madrid Agreement Concerning the International Registration of Marks. Though Romania signed the convention at the date of its conclusion, in 1989, the document was ratified only in 1998, by Law No. 5/1998, published in the *Monitorul Oficial No. 11* of 15 January 1998. As mentioned, Romania adhered to the Trademark Law Treaty concluded in Geneva in 1994 by adopting Law No. 4/1998, published in the *Monitorul Oficial No. 10* of 14 January 1998.

This list of sources for trademark protection also includes Law No. 3/1998 from 8 January 1998, published in the *Monitorul Oficial No. 10* of 14 January 1998, by which Romania adhered to the Nice Agreement Concerning the International Classification of Goods and Services for the Purposes of the Registration of Marks (1957) and the Vienna Agreement Establishing an International Classification of the Figurative Elements of Marks (1973).

More recently, Romania ratified by Law No. 360/2007, published in the *Monitorul Oficial, part I No. 49* din 22/01/2008, the Singapore Treaty on the Trademark Rights whose main provisions have been incorporated in the revised trademark law from 2010.

As an EU Member State, it is obvious that for Romania, the main international source is the so-called *acquis communautaire* in the trademark field and particularly the Regulation (EU) 2017/1001 of the European Parliament and of the Council of 14 June 2017 on the European Union trade mark and the Directive (EU) No. 2015/

2436 of the European Parliament and of the Council of 16 December 2015 to approximate the laws of the Member States relating to trade marks.

Multiple Cooperation Agreements were signed during the last few years between the OSIM and the Office for Harmonization of the Internal Market in order to participate and build a common approach in administration, implementation and cooperation between the national trademark protection and enforcing system and that of EU trademark system.

Everywhere in this chapter, if not otherwise specified, the following abbreviations will be used:

- Law – Law No. 84/1998 as the last version amended.
- Regulation – the Regulations for Implementing the Trademark Law adopted by Governmental Decision No. 1134/2010.
- Office – The OSIM.
- BOPI – Official Bulletin of Industrial Property – TM section.

§2. Subject Matter of Protection

211. As already mentioned in the previous subchapter, the law defines the conditions for obtaining, maintaining and enforcing the rights regarding two objects of industrial property, namely *marks* and *geographical indications*.

The differentiation of the goods or services offered by a natural or legal entity, as well as the facile recognition by the consumers of the goods or services, including by associating them with a certain level of quality, has imposed the *mark* as a very concrete form of industrial property. Its importance is probably most perceived in the industrial and commercial environment.

In an internationally harmonized manner, the definition of *trademark protection* is subject to the conditions of worldwide trade with goods or services, which are more and more achieved on transnational bases and are seen as an objective necessity.

Especially after the entering into force of the TRIPS Agreement, the definition of the marks gained a major importance. The fact that the Romanian law regulates it together with the provisions regarding geographical indications has not only a legal and technical justification regarding the similitude of their function and general manner of protection. It is also explained by a series of laws in which geographical indication or eventual appellations to origin are effectively treated as marks. Consequently, the presentation will make a parallel reference to both mark and geographical indication, as it is regulated in Romania.

I. Signs Which May Serve as Trademarks

212. According to Article 2 of the Law, ‘trademarks may consist of any sign, such as: words, personal names included, or designs, letters, numerals, colours, figurative elements, the shape of goods or of packaging thereof or sounds, provided that such signs are capable of: a) distinguishing the goods or services of one enterprise from those of other enterprises and b) being so represented in the Trademark Register as to enable the competent authorities and the public to determine the clear and precise subject matter of protection granted to their owner'. Some important remarks can be made regarding the signs, which, according to Romanian Law, may constitute marks.

One can note the *facto* identity with the definition of the EU trademark[35] brought by the amended Law which excluded two previous provisions in the definition of a trademark which were not in line with this harmonized approach. The first one refers to the exclusion from the trademark definition of 'combination of colours, holograms, sonor signals'. The second one refers to the replacement of condition of 'graphical representation of the trademark' with a more complete condition 'to be represented in the Trademark Register as to enable the competent authorities and the public to determine the clear and precise subject matter of protection granted to their owner'.

To be noticed that the sound marks, which, according to Romanian Law, are listed between signs which can be protected, should be understood as subject to the condition of being capable of representation in the Trademark Register as to determine a clear and precise subject matter of granted protection, in other words, if they can be represented on an ordinary musical staff, attached to the TM Register.

This provision is harmonized with the provision of Article 15 TRIPS, which, along with others, gives Member States the freedom to require 'as a condition of registration, that the signs be visually perceptible'.

As it can be noted, the list of signs which may constitute a mark is not exhaustive, and there are at least two other considerations which the case law associates with the definition of the mark.[36]

213. First, it is about the 'individuality of the sign', which needs to be regarded as synonymous with relative autonomy and not in its possessive sense.

Viewed as an abstract concept, this individuality could indicate the fact that any sign capable of graphical representation might be considered a mark.

However, there are two elements that demand a concrete approach to the 'individuality of the sign'. On the one hand, there is a multitude of signs used in combination with other signs, and on the other, there is the fact that, unavoidably, the combined signs associate themselves with some goods or services.

The concreteness of the concept of individuality of the sign leads to the conclusion that, among all possible signs given by the individualization in an abstract sense, only those signs which 'although used in combination with a multitude of other signs, are presenting a sufficient individuality to perceive them as autonomous signs, shall be in fact capable to be considered as marks'. In other words, except for the collective marks that will be presented in §2, II, the individuality of the sign for

35. Article 3– Directive (EU) 2015/2436 of the European Parliament and of the Council of 16 Dec. 2015 to approximate the laws of the Member States relating to trademarks.
36. Thierry Van Innis, *Les signes distinctifs* (De Boeck & Larcier, 1997), 100–108.

an individual mark means that it refers to the goods or services which belong exclusively to the owner. By no means does it refer to similar products of a group of manufacturers, which are possibly in competition.

214. The second consideration refers to the distinctiveness of the sign, a concept that, although in a determined relationship with its individuality, is still completely different from it. The relationship between the two concepts is that a sign which has no individuality cannot have distinctiveness either, but a sign which presents distinctiveness also has individuality. With regard to the distinctiveness of signs that may be considered marks, the case law accepts the following principles of appreciation:[37]

- the sign that constitutes the mark shall be analysed in its entirety;
- the sign should be able to distinguish the origin of a specified undertaking;
- the distinctiveness of the sign shall be appreciated with respect to the goods or the service to which it shall apply;
- the perception of the public is determined;
- it is sufficient that the sign is capable of distinguishing itself;
- the exclusive decorative sign is not distinctive;
- the distinctiveness is not constant in time and space;
- the existence of 'weak' and 'strong' marks should be accepted;
- a mark may be (very) descriptive but not exclusively descriptive.

In practice, three distinct situations in connection with distinctiveness are accepted as a condition for protection of signs as trademarks.

The first situation is concerned with the so-called inherent distinctiveness, which can be characterized by the fact that the sign chosen as a mark is 'distinct' as such or, more exactly, that there is no direct relationship with the goods or the service in connection with which the mark is used.

The mark for which an 'inherent distinctiveness' can be defined is sometimes called 'arbitrary' or 'fanciful'.

Although this problem will be analysed in §3, for the moment, we shall note that, in order to determine the inherent distinctiveness, a negative test will be applied as a rule. This is needed in order to appreciate the sign's independence from other considerations than its own verbal or figurative form.

One fact is taken into account, and this is if the sign which constitutes the mark is exclusively chosen due to technical considerations, such as the nature of the products or services for which it is protected, generic or usual indications regarding quality, quantity, value, scope, place of origin, time of production as well as any other similar considerations, then it is obvious that this sign cannot ensure the distinctiveness of the mark. Furthermore, the sign might even lead to severe distortions of the notion of the exclusive right of exploitation, specific to industrial property.

If at least one situation exists, the mark lacks an inherent distinctiveness. However, this does not mean a priori that the sign is not distinctive in the sense of the principles of appreciation previously listed.

37. *Ibid.*, 108.

The second situation refers to the fact that a mark without inherent distinctiveness may acquire, in some special cases, a distinctiveness by use. These situations are in practice imposed by the consumers, who, following a frequent use of the sign, give it the basic function of the mark to distinguish the goods or the services of a person from those of another person.

Finally, the third situation is practically the reverse of the previous one and it has in view the loss of the inherent distinctiveness through use. It is probably a 'tribute' paid by the owner of such marks due to some exceptional qualities of the goods or services offered under those marks. These qualities made the mark well known and famous and then the public associated the mark definitively with some category of goods or (sometimes) services. In other words, the mark became 'generic' for them. In Romania, such generic marks are relatively numerous: fax, Xerox, aspirin, cellophane, etc. But we believe that marks having Romanian owners cannot be enumerated among them.

II. Categories of Marks

215. The law defines and has in view the protection of some important categories of marks.

First, we shall note that, on the one hand, the criteria for their classification are complex, and on the other, these criteria are sometimes controversial.

The framing of the mark in a certain category has important consequences for the determination of its legal status. Even this complexity makes this appreciation of eventual infringements with regard to the right to the mark to be at least equally complex.

Traditionally, from the point of view of their destination, marks are categorized as trademarks and factory marks, but from the point of view of their objects, goods marks and service marks. It should be underlined from the very beginning that, formally, the law does not distinguish between the legal status of these marks. The element of differentiation results from the classes of goods or services to which they apply and the type of the applicant and of the owner.

From the point of view of the owner of the right to the mark, the law defines precisely three types of marks, namely:

(a) the individual mark, in other words, the mark whose owner is a determined natural or legal person;
(b) the collective mark, which according to Article 3(e) of the Law, is 'a mark which is described as such when it is applied for and which is capable to distinguish the goods or services of the members of an association which owns the rights in the mark from goods or services belonging to other persons';
(c) the certification mark, defined in Article 3(f) as being 'a mark indicating that the goods or services for which it is used are certified by the owner as to the material, method of manufacturing goods or mode of providing services, quality, accuracy or other characteristics and which is capable to distinguish said goods or services from the goods or services which are not so certified'.

216. The applicants of a collective mark may be associations of manufacturers, producers, suppliers or traders which draw up a regulation governing the use of the collective mark, in which the applicant shall specify the persons authorized to use the mark, the conditions of membership of the association, the conditions for using the mark, the grounds on which a member of the association may be prohibited from using the mark and the sanctions that may be applied by the association. As a rule, the regulation governing the use of the collective mark may require that the collective mark may be transmitted by its owner only with the consent of all the members of the association.

For the collective mark, the quality function is essential and this is directly expressed by the regulation of use, while for the individual mark, the quality function has an expression that derives from the quality of the goods or services protected in connection with the trademark.

Although, eventually, it is also an individual mark, the certification mark is essentially different from the latter because the applicant and the owner of these marks respectively cannot be but a natural or legal person, including institutions, authorities and bodies governed by public law, entitled to certify the goods and the services in connection with which it is protected. Therefore, persons that manufacture, import or sell goods or services other than those for quality control cannot apply and receive protection by marks.

In a relatively similar manner to the collective mark, the applicant or the owner of the protection has to file a regulation governing the use of the certification mark. The regulation shall indicate the persons authorized to use the mark, the elements and characteristics that are to be guaranteed by the mark, the manner in which the competent certification authority shall verify these characteristics and supervise the use of the mark, the fees payable for use of the mark and the procedures for settling disputes. One can state that, as is the case with the certification mark, the quality function is directly imposed even by its own regulation of use.

Y. Eminescu indicates[38] other criteria of differentiation, namely the number of the used signs and classifies the marks according to this, in simple and combined, and after the nature of these signs, classifies them in verbal, figurative and sound. Finally, in the same paper, another criterion is identified, this is the effect of the mark, and the corresponding classification differentiates them as audio, figurative and intellectual.

Therefore, as we have already stated, trademark classification is a complex one, and depending on the imposed criterion, it may leave out classes of marks considered characteristic from other points of view.

For instance, according to a practical criterion, having an administrative nature and used by the Bureau Benelux of Marks, the marks are categorized as verbal, figurative, three-dimensional and complex when they accumulate at least two of the mentioned categories.

217. A 'French' classification is proposed,[39] namely in categories of audio, figurative and combined audio and figurative marks. This classification is criticized for

38. Yolanda Eminescu, *The Legal Status of the Trademarks* 86–87 (Lumina Lex 1996).

39. A. Chavanne & I.J. Burst, *Droit de la proprieté industrielle* (Daloz, 1990), 532.

not taking into account the concept that might carry an audio or figurative mark. Thierry van Innis[40] starts from this classification and proposes a variant to the French classification, as follows:

- non-conceptual audio marks;
- conceptual audio marks;
- non-conceptual visual marks;
- conceptual visual marks;
- complex marks.

The conceptualization which Innis has in view takes into account the degree to which the audio or visual sign can carry a significance of a certain nature, as, for instance, gamma – a letter of the Greek alphabet, a word having a significance, a slogan, a patronymic name which is reported to a known person, a noble title, an emblematic mark, all figurative forms, etc.

Generally, when a mark carries a certain concept, or, as in the previous perception, is 'conceptual', it is possible that this concept is a potentially absolute reason for refusal. In any case, the situation shall be treated very carefully because, besides the sign's appearance, it also carries an a priori significance, which may conflict with the grant of the exclusive right given by the registration of that sign.

III. Geographical Indication

218. According to Article 3(g) of the Law, geographical indication means 'the name serving to identify a product that originates in a country, region, or locality of a State, in those cases where a certain quality, reputation or other specific characteristic may be essentially attributed to that geographical origin'.

A geographical origin supposes a major imprint of the place on the product originating from that place. The simple fact that a product originates from that place has no relevance to the protection of the geographical indication that makes reference to that good.

§3. Conditions of Protection

I. Marks

219. The definition of the mark must be obligatory and considered together with a category of 'signs excluded from protection'. This category of signs constitutes what in the practice of mark protection leads to the definition of 'absolute grounds of refusal of protection'.

These questions will be analysed later on in this study. For the moment, we will limit ourselves to providing an exhaustive list of the signs that cannot be registered

---

40. Thierry Van Innis, *supra*, 209.

as marks due to the absolute grounds of refusal. It is worth mentioning that they are practically identical in Romanian Law to those listed in the EU trademark regulations.

Therefore, according to Article 5(1) of the Law:

> Registration shall be refused or, if registered, shall be liable to be declared invalid, for the following absolute grounds:
>
> (a) signs that cannot constitute a trademark;
> (b) trademarks which are devoid of any distinctive character;
> (c) trademarks which consist exclusively of signs or indications which have become customary in the current language or in the bona fide and established practices of the trade; (d) trademarks which consist exclusively of signs or indications which may serve, in trade, to designate the kind, quality, quantity, intended purpose, value, geographical origin or the time of production of the goods or of rendering of the service, or other characteristics of the goods or services;
> (d) trademarks which consist exclusively of the shape of the good or of other feature which results from the nature of the goods themselves or which is necessary to obtain a technical result or which gives substantial value to the goods;
> (e) trademarks which are liable to mislead the public as to the geographical origin, the quality or nature of the goods or services;
> (f) trademarks which are excluded from registration pursuant to the European Union legislation, to the national legislation or to the international agreements to which the European Union or Romania are party, providing for protection of designations of origin and geographical indications;
> (g) trademarks which are excluded from registration pursuant to the European Union legislation or to the international agreements to which the European Union is party, providing for protection of traditional terms for wine;
> (h) trademarks which are excluded from registration pursuant to the European Union legislation or to the international agreements to which the European Union is party, providing for protection of traditional specialities guaranteed;
> (i) trademarks which consist of, or reproduce in their essential elements, an earlier plant variety denomination registered in accordance with the European Union legislation, the national legislation or the international agreements to which the European Union or Romania are party, providing protection for plant variety rights and referring to plant varieties of the same species or of closely related species.
> (j) trademarks which contain, without the consent of the owner, the likeness or surname of a person of repute in Romania;
> (k) trademarks which contain signs of high symbolic value, in particular religious symbols;
> (l) trademarks contrary to public policy or to accepted principles of morality;

(m) trademarks which contain, without the permission of the competent authorities, reproductions or imitations of armorial bearings, flags, State emblems, signs, official hallmarks of control and warranty, coats of arms belonging to countries of the European Union and which are governed by Article 6ter of the Paris Convention;

(n) trademarks which contain, without the permission of the competent authorities, reproductions or imitations of armorial bearings, flags, other emblems, abbreviations, initials or denominations which are governed by Article 6ter of the Paris Convention and which belong to international intergovernmental organizations to which one or more countries of the European Union are party.

(o) trademarks which contain, without the permission of competent authorities, badges, emblems, coats of arms, escutcheons, heraldry of public interest, other than those covered by Article 6ter of the Paris Convention.

Registration shall not be refused or, if registered, shall not be liable to be declared invalid under the provisions of previous paragraph, letters (b), (c) or (d) if, prior to the date of the application for registration or before the date of the application for declaration of invalidity, as the case may be, the mark has acquired a distinctive character following the use which has been made of it.

Provisions of previous paragraph shall also apply where the distinctive character was acquired after the date of application for registration but before the date of registration of the mark concerned.

Hereinafter, we will present some Romanian practices concerned with the mentioned category of signs that cannot be registered as marks.

220. The *distinctiveness of the sign* is considered to be the fundamental criterion for protection, being the defining element in judging the so-called risk of confusion with marks previously registered. When it creates this risk, it is appreciated that the mark does not meet its basic function, as given in its definition, namely to distinguish the goods or services of a person from those of another person.

As has been stated in §3, Part I, the distinctiveness can be achieved also by use. Consequently, the legal provisions referring to the non-registrability of the mark for reasons of lack of distinctiveness as such or of inherent distinctiveness will not apply.

Marks such as 'consuming late', 'table wine', 'apple vinegar', etc., which refer to the exclusive composition of the marks or signs, giving usual indications or designating usual characteristics, may not be subject to protection.

The marks in connection with the shape of the good, its nature or the imprint of its shape, either of a technical nature or of a substantial value to the product, shall be carefully examined. They have been subject to discussions and even case law both in Romania and abroad.

One can remark that the law refers to the obvious cases where the signs cannot be registered, namely those where the shape is either an 'exclusive' element or is required by other considerations (technical or those giving a substantial value to the good). However, it shall be noted that, in accordance with what has been specified in §2, Part I, the definition of the mark also includes the shape of the product among the protectable elements, as well as other three-dimensional shapes.

Often, it is difficult to admit that, in the case of the marks of industrial goods, the shape of the products is completely separated from at least one technical consideration. The mark registration of the famous company that symbolizes the bottle 'COCA COLA' is an interesting example where it has been appreciated that there is no predominance of technical considerations, though we can admit that its limit is uncertain.

The non-registrability of the marks which are likely to mislead the public as to the geographical origin, including spirits or wines, or of services, as well as of their quality or their nature, constitutes an obvious measure aimed at respecting the basic function of the mark.

Already in the 1990s, Romanian production followed international practices. For instance, the production of drinks under the mark 'COGNAC' or 'CHAMPAGNE' was stopped, though Romania had a significant tradition in this type of spirit and these famous marks have been replaced with domestic denominations like 'VINARS' or 'VIN SPUMANT'.

All marks including images or names whose significance is transitory, either because they refer to persons or to public national or international institutions, or simple images of a verbal sign, figurative or combined, shall not be registered without permission or special authorization. They are included in the category of 'conceptual marks', which we have already analysed.

For example, following a special notification made in 1995 by the European Commission, the Romanian Office eliminated from the list of signs earlier protected as marks those including, without the permission of the European authorities, the specific sign of the EU, namely, the European stars. When the new law entered into force, this sign was refused protection without the application of a special authorization.

221. The list of signs which cannot be registered as marks, previously presented, is completed in the law by the provision which defines another category of signs which cannot be registered as marks either but have a different significance. These signs that might enter into conflict with previously obtained rights regarding marks constitute the so-called relative grounds of refusal. In this respect, Article 6 of the Law provides that, in addition to the absolute grounds, 'registration of a mark shall be refused or shall be susceptible of being cancelled, as the case may be, for the following 'relative grounds', as provided for in Article 6(1) of the law:

(a) if it is identical with an earlier trademark, and the goods and services for which registration is applied or the trademark has been registered are identical with the goods and services for which the earlier trademark is protected;
(b) if, because of its identity with or similarity to the earlier trademark and because of identity or similarity of the goods or services covered by the two trademarks, there exists a likelihood of confusion in the public perception, the likelihood of association with the earlier trademark included'.

Within the meaning of previous paragraph, earlier trademarks mean trademarks with a date of application for registration earlier than the date of application for registration of the trademark concerned or of the priority claimed in respect thereof, as the case may be, and contained in the following categories:

(a) EU trademarks.
(b) Trademarks registered in Romania.
(c) Trademarks registered under international agreements and having effects in Romania.
(d) EU trademarks for which seniority is duly claimed, in accordance with the provisions of EU trademark regulations, in respect of a trademark covered by letters (b) or (c), even where the latter has lapsed or surrendered.
(e) Application for registration of the trademarks covered by letters (a)–(d), under the condition of subsequent registration thereof.
(f) Trademarks which, on the date of the application for registration of the trademark or on the date of the claimed priority, as the case may be, are well known in Romania, within the meaning of Article 6*bis* of the Paris Convention.

The above-mentioned 'relative grounds refusal' are to be completed with provisions of Article 6(3) of the law providing that:

> Registration of a trademark shall also be refused or, if registered, shall be susceptible of being cancelled if:
>
> (a) it is identical with or similar to an earlier trademark registered in Romania or in the European Union, within the meaning of paragraph (2), irrespective of whether the goods and services for which it is applied or registered are identical with, similar to or not similar to those for which the earlier trademark is registered, where the earlier trademark has a reputation in Romania or, in case of the European Union trademark, in the European Union, and where, by the use of the later trademark without due cause, unfair advantage would be taken of the distinctive character or the reputation of the earlier trademark, or it would be detrimental thereto;
> (b) an application for registration of a designation of origin or a geographical indication had already been submitted in accordance with the national or the European Union legislation prior to the date of the application for the registration of the trademark or to the date of the priority claimed for the application, subject to its subsequent registration, and the designation of origin or the geographical indication confers on the person authorized to use it the right to prohibit the use of a subsequent trademark in Romania;
> (c) rights to a sign were acquired prior to the date of the application for the registration of the trademark or, where appropriate, to the date of the priority claimed for the application for the registration of the trademark and said sign confers on its owner the right to prohibit the use of a subsequent trademark in Romania;

(d) the agent or the representative of the trademark owner applies for the registration of the trademark in his own name and without the owner's authorization, unless the agent or the representative justifies his action.

Registration of a trademark shall not be refused or cancelled, as the case may be, where the owner of the earlier trademark or of the earlier right agrees with the registration of the subsequent trademark.

Registration of a trademark can be refused or is susceptible to be cancelled, as the case may be, under the conditions set forth by Article 6 *septies* of the Paris Convention.

The provision of Article 6 is quasi-identical to the provision contained and in the EU trademark regulation.

The provision of item (a) regarding identical mark for identical goods or services is the classical case and does not require supplementary commentaries on the identity of the previous mark, as well as on the goods or services this mark refers to.

The parameter of the risk of confusion for the public as an element of appreciation of the conflict of the mark for which protection is sought with an identical mark that refers to similar goods or services. For instance, the Office accepted for protection the mark 'GEROVITAL' registered by two different owners, one registering for cosmetics and another one for pharmaceuticals, by considering that the risk of confusion for the public is minimal, in spite of the identity of the marks.

The appreciation of the risk of confusion has a relevant role in situations where the similitude at the level of signs is linked to the identity or similarity, respectively, the risk of association between the products or services associated with the two marks.

Finally, a very sensitive problem is the reference to a well-known mark for goods or services identical or similar, or different goods or services, but along with two supplementary conditions. This results from the risk of confusion due to the establishment of a connection between these goods or services, as a consequence of the use of the mark and the existence of a risk of prejudice to the owner of the well-known mark.

With reference to the collective marks, according to Article 63 of the law:

> in addition to the grounds for refusal of an application for registration of an individual trademark, except provisions regarding signs or indications which may serve, in trade, to designate the geographical origin of the goods or services, an application for registration of a collective mark will be refused if:
>
> (a) the applicant does not have the capacity required by the law;
> (b) the requirements of the law regarding definition of the collective marks and of the regulations governing its use, are not satisfied;
> (c) the regulations governing the use of the mark are contrary to public order or to accepted principles of morality.
>
> The application for registration of a collective mark will also be refused if the public is liable to be misled as regards the character or the significance of

the mark, in particular if it is likely to be taken to be something other than a collective mark.

The law provides in Article 70, similar supplementary grounds of refusal for the certification marks: 'In addition to the grounds for refusal of an application for registration of an individual trademark, except for provision regarding signs or indications which may serve, in trade, to designate the geographical origin of the goods or services, an application for registration of a certification mark shall be refused if the requirements of the law regarding definition of the certification marks and of the regulations governing its use are not complied with. A certification mark consisting of signs or indications which may serve, in trade, to designate the geographical origin of the goods or services does not entitle the owner to prohibit a third party from using, in the course of trade, such signs or indications, provided that third party uses them in accordance with honest practices in industrial or commercial matters. Such a mark may not be invoked against a third party who is entitled to use a geographical name.'

A. *Notoriety of a Mark*

222. The well-known mark means, according to Article 3(d), 'a trademark that is widely known to the segment of the public concerned by the goods or services to which it applies, without being required either registration or use thereof in Romania for the trademark to be opposable'.

Rule 19 of the regulations, which specifies the mode in which the notoriety of a mark is determined and proved, should be added to the provision of the law. Thus, 'to estimate whether a mark is well-known, it is sufficient *that* this mark be well-known:

(a) in the territory of Romania; and
(b) to the segment of the public from Romania the goods and services represented by the mark are destined for'.

It is proved to be essentially the knowledge of the mark for which notoriety, in a segment of public is appreciated, which, according to rule 19(2), will be established:

- according to the following elements: the category of potential consumers aimed at for goods and services to which the mark refers; identification of the category of potential consumers is made on groups of consumers of certain goods or services in connection with which the mark is used and not on groups of consumers of a general series of goods and services;
- the distribution circuits of the goods or services to which the mark refers depending on the nature of goods and services; there must be taken into account various

means of distributing thereof, respectively of marketing by means of the shops, trade agents, directly from the company or to the client's residence.

The well-known mark is appreciated for being known in Romania by the respective mark's market share in Romania, in direct connection with its use for their goods or associated services.

The notoriety of a mark will be sustained by a multitude of means that have to bring as arguments the degree of penetration in the segment of the public previously mentioned. Therefore, there can be presented documents such as those referring to:

(a) marketing or offering for sale of goods or carrying out services under a well-known mark;
(b) importing or exporting goods to which the well-known mark applied;
(c) promoting or advertising the goods and services under the well-known mark in Romania, etc.

In appreciating the notoriety of a mark, other criteria are also taken into account, and they are derived from or complementary to the previous ones.

Thus, it is appreciated that it is necessary to mention, for determining the notoriety of a mark, also:

- the degree of inherent or gained distinctiveness of the mark in Romania;
- the duration and scope of the use in Romania of the mark in connection with the goods or services;
- the duration and scope of the publicity of the mark in Romania;
- the geographical area of use in Romania;
- the degree of knowledge of the mark in the Romanian market by the segment of the public to which it is addressed.

II. Geographical Indications

223. As directly derived from the definition of the geographical indications already mentioned, as well as from the similitude of its function with that of the mark, are the conditions provided by the law in Article 87 that exclude from protection the geographical indications which:

- do not comply with the provisions of Article 3 letter (g) regarding definition of a geographical indication;
- are the generic name of goods;
- are liable to mislead the public as to the nature, origin, manufacturing methods and quality of the goods;
- are contrary to public policy or to accepted principles of morality.

224. It should also be noted that the law provides that[41] 'geographical indications protected now or in the future under bilateral or multilateral agreements concluded by Romania shall not be subject to the registration procedure established by this law'.

The list of geographical indications recognized in Romania under the agreements referred to in the preceding paragraph shall be recorded by the Office in the National Register of Geographical Indications and shall be published in the BOPI.

§4. FORMALITIES

225. In Romania, the protection by trademark or by geographical indications is granted registration after a process of complex examination performed by the Office and as a result of an issuance of a registration certificate of the mark or of the geographical indication, if the legal conditions for protection are met.

Both the registration of the mark and the geographical indication, as well as the maintenance into force of the rights, are complex procedures which shall be analysed below.

I. Procedure for Obtaining Protection

A. Registration of the Application

226. The registration procedure of the mark has as a starting point the filing at the Office of an application for registration, drafted in the Romanian language. According to Article 9, 'the application for trademark registration filed with Office, drawn up in Romanian and containing the details provided for, shall constitute the regular filing of the trademark'. The application for trademark registration shall contain the following:

(a) an express request for the registration of a trademark;
(b) information identifying the applicant and, where appropriate, the representative;
(c) a representation of the trademark in accordance with the requirements of being so represented in the Trademark Register as to enable the competent authorities and the public to determine the clear and precise subject matter of protection granted to their owner;
(d) the list of goods/services in respect of which the trademark registration is applied for;
(e) proof of payment for the trademark registration application filing and publishing fee.

In addition to the requirements set out in paragraph above, the application shall include express mentions concerning:

41. Article 83(2) – Law No. 84/1996 as republished in 2020.

(a) the colour or colours claimed as a distinctive element of the trademark;
(b) the trademark type, if it is a three-dimensional trademark or a trademark of other types than the word or figurative ones;
(c) a transliteration or translation of the trademark or of elements thereof, when the trademark consists, fully or in part, of characters other than the Latin ones, or numerals other than the Arabic or Roman ones, or of one or several words in a language other than Romanian. The recently amended law in force brought significant additions regarding the designation of the products and services for which trademark protection is sought, that must be clear and precise and which finally shall contribute to the extent of protection.

Thus, according to Article 10 of the law:

> (1) The goods and services for which protection is sought shall be identified by the applicant with sufficient clarity and precision to enable the competent authorities and economic operators to determine the extent of the protection sought.
> (2) The goods and services in respect of which trademark registration is applied for shall be classified in conformity with the system of established by the Nice Classification. The goods and services shall be grouped by classes, each group being preceded by the number of the class to which it belongs, in the order of the classes.
> (3) The use of general terms or of the general indications comprised in the class headings of the Nice Classification, shall be interpreted as including all the goods or services covered by the literal meaning of the indication or term concerned.
> (4) Goods and services shall neither be regarded as being similar to each other on the ground that they appear in the same class nor be regarded as being dissimilar on the ground that they appear in different classes under the Nice Classification.

The use of general terms or general indications contained in the titles of classes in the Nice Classification shall be construed as including all products or services covered by the literal meaning of the indication or term.

In addition, it has been clarified that products and services cannot be considered similar because they belong to the same class, nor can they be considered different because they belong to different classes of the Nice Classification, aspects already established by the practice of the European Intellectual Property Office and OSIM, as well as the relevant case law.

The new Article 11 of the law brings further clarifications to the scope of trademark protection in connection with the list of goods and services by providing that:

> The owners of trademarks registered in respect of an entire class heading in the Nice Classification may declare that, on the date of filing the application for trademark registration, their intention was to claim protection for goods and services beyond those covered by the literal meaning of the heading of said class, provided that such goods and services are included in the alphabetical

list of that class in the edition of the Nice Classification in force on the date of filing the application for trademark registration. The declaration referred above had to be filed with OSIM up to the date of 30 September 2020 and it shall clearly and precisely state which are the goods and services, other than those covered by the literal meaning of the class heading, to which the owner intention initially referred and OSIM amending the Trademark Register accordingly. The declaration referred above does not affect application of the provisions of law regarding proof of effective use of an earlier trademark for five years, invoked during opposition procedure, revocation procedure of respectively invalidity procedure.

In case no declaration was filed within the time limit provided above, at the expiry of the said time limit, the trademarks are only deemed to refer to those goods and services covered by the literal meaning of the heading of the relevant class.

Where the Trademark Register is modified in accordance with the provisions presented above, the exclusive rights conferred by the trademark will not prevent third parties from the continued use of a trademark, provided that the use in respect of said goods or services:

(a) started before the amendment of the Register; and
(b) did not infringe the owner's rights in considering the literal meaning of goods and services entered in the Register at that time.

Amendment of the list of goods and services does not entitle the trademark owner to oppose a later trademark or to apply for invalidation of a later filed trademark if:

(a) the later filed trademark was already in use, or an application for trademark registration for goods and services was already filed before Register amendment; and
(b) trademark use in respect of the goods and services concerned did not infringe or would not have infringed the owner's rights considering the literal meaning of goods and services entered in the Register at that time.

The application shall relate to one trademark only and shall be presented under the prescribed conditions. As the requirement for the trademark to be represented graphically was removed by the provision of the law, the amended implementing regulations provide for new requirements and guidance for representation of figurative, tridimensional, movement, colour, sound, multimedia, etc. Essentially, the signs may be represented in any suitable form using generally available technology, provided that the representation is clear, precise, self-contained, easily accessible, intelligible, durable and objective.

The applications for registration filed under the Madrid Agreement or The Protocol thereof shall meet the conditions established by said treaties.

The trademark registration application may be filed with the Office Registry by mail or electronically.

The applicant for trademark registration must communicate, at the date of the application or within thirty days of the date of filing the application with OSIM, the proof of payment of the filing and examination fee in the amount prescribed by the law.

In case of failure to comply with the payment of the fees in due time, the applicant will be deemed to having renounced trademark registration and the application will be refused.

The date of the regular filing shall be that on which the application for registration of a trademark containing all elements referred to has been filed with the Office.

Where an application for registration of a trademark has been regularly filed for the first time in another Member State of the Paris Union or Member of the World Trade Organization (WTO), the applicant may claim the date of the first filing by means of an application for registration of the same trademark in Romania, on condition that the latter application should be filed with OSIM within six months of the date of the first filing.

227. The applicant may also request priority conferred by the presentation of the goods or of the services for which the protection is sought at official or officially recognized international exhibitions held on the Romanian territory or in another Member State of the Paris Convention, if an application for registration of the mark under which such goods or services were displayed is filed with the Office within six months of the date of the first display at the exhibition. The six-month period referred to shall not extend the priority period referred to in the previous paragraph.

The priority rights shall be claimed at the time of filing an application for registration of the mark, the priority documents shall be filed, and the prescribed fee shall be paid within thirty days following the date of the application for registration of the mark. Failure to comply with the time limit referred to shall entail refusal of the request for priority.

If the priority claim relies on a previous application, the application has to contain a declaration of claiming the priority right in which shall be indicated the State and the date of first filing, a document issued by the national administration from which should result in the date of the first filing, accompanied by a conform translation into Romanian of the document.

If the priority claim relies on temporary protection as a result of displaying the mark at an exhibition, the application shall be accompanied by a document that certifies that the mark has been applied to the goods or the services presented in the exhibition and which mentions the date of their introduction in the exhibition. For the particular case of a collective mark or a certification mark, the application must also include the regulation for their use, with all the elements mentioned in §3, Part II.

According to Article 14 of the Law:

> the registration of a mark may be applied for individually or collectively by any person, either directly or through a representative under the conditions provided by the Law. Applicants not having either their domicile, or their place of business or any real and effective industrial or commercial establishment on the

territory of the EU or the European Economic Area shall be compelled to be represented by a representative, except for the filing of the application for trademark registration.

228. The power of attorney shall contain the name and the signature of the applicant or the owner of the mark. The power of attorney may refer to one or more registration applications or registered marks or to all registration applications or registered marks, present or future, of the person who gave the mandate.

The general power of attorney given for the latter case and filed with the Office may be mentioned for every individual application.

For the special situations where the renunciation of an application for registration of a mark, for withdrawal of a mark, as well as any request related to a transfer of rights in connection with a mark is requested, this will be performed only according to a special mandate which shall mention the document of renunciation, withdrawal or transmission expressly.

229. In addition to the possibility already provided for in the previous legislation for the division of the trademark application, the division of an already admitted registration has been equally introduced. Thus, according to the Article 17 of the law:

> An applicant for registration of a trademark or owner of a registered trademark that relates to more than one good or service may request to OSIM to divide the initial application or the trademark registration into two or more applications or registrations, while indicating the goods or services in the divisional applications or registrations, upon payment of the prescribed fee.

Divisional applications or registrations shall maintain the filing date of the initial application and, where appropriate, shall enjoy the benefit of the priority right obtained in accordance with the provisions of law.

Where the application for trademark registration is already published, the division and the divisional application shall be published in the Official Industrial Property Bulletin. Publication shall not open a new period for filing oppositions or observations.

Division may be requested with OSIM at any moment during the procedure of trademark registration or after that.

Request for division shall not be admissible:

(a) if made before the filing date of the application for trademark registration has been accorded;
(b) if made within the legal period for filing an opposition;
(c) if it results in the division between the goods or services subject to opposition, up to such time as a decision to14;
(d) if it results in the division between the goods or services subject to an application for invalidation or revocation of rights, up to the final decision settling the same;

(e) after a levy of execution is entered in the Trademark Register, up to its cancellation.

The applicant for or the owner of the registered trademark shall be required to file the documents requested by OSIM in order to divide the initial application or registration and to pay the prescribed fee within thirty days as from the date of the request for division. Failing that, OSIM shall note that the applicant or owner has renounced division of the initial application or registration.

B. Registration of the Mark

230. The Office includes a specialized department and a body of examiners, who examine if the formal and substantive conditions for the registration of the mark are met.

Having in mind that Romania is a member of the Madrid Agreement as well as of the Protocol to that Agreement, the protection of the marks is made both in the 'national way' as well as 'in the international way'. More than that, EU trademarks valid in Romania in its quality of EU Member State and national trademarks are interacting. Below, we will present the registration procedure in more detail in each of the situations.

1. National Registration

231. Within seven days as from the date of receipt of the application for registration of a trademark, the Office examines whether the formal conditions set out have been complied with and, if so, shall grant a filing date to the application. If the application does not satisfy the conditions set out, the Office notifies the applicant of the irregularities in the application and affords him a period of thirty days to correct them. If the applicant corrects, within the prescribed time limit, the irregularities notified by OSIM, the filing date shall be the date on which the application for registration was corrected. If this is not the case, the application shall be refused.

232. As far as the examination of the relative grounds of refusal is concerned, the concept of a previously protected right has been previously analysed and in fact covers:

- an identical or similar mark registered in Romania for identical or similar goods or services, if the date of registration of this mark or the priority date (…) is prior to the date of the national regular filing of the mark for which the registration was applied;
- an identical or similar mark considered to be well known in Romania;
- a right of a personality with regard to his image or patronymic name;
- a protected geographical indication;
- a protected industrial design or model;
- a copyright;

– any industrial property right acquired prior to the date of the national regular filing of a mark.

The notion of similitude is as clear as it is difficult to appreciate with regard to both the sign which constitutes the mark for the goods and associated services and the registration of the mark. The notion of similitude has to be interpreted in relation to the risk of confusion or association that can be created as regards the public.

233. In the possible conflict with previous rights, particular attention should be given to the provision of Article 6(4) of the Law which might offer a good 'exit way' when providing that 'registration of a trademark shall not be refused or liable to be declared invalid, where the owner of the earlier trademark or of the earlier right agrees with the registration of the subsequent trademark'.

As a matter of fact, since there is no adverse provision in the law, the practice extends this acceptance of the registration of a mark that potentially infringes an intellectual property right, if one obtains the express agreement of the owner of that right.

Further, the law stipulates in Article 7 that 'the nature of the goods or services for which registration of a mark is requested in no way represents an obstacle to the registration of the mark. Where grounds for refusal of registration exist in respect of only some of the goods or services for which registration was sought, refusal of registration shall only cover those goods and services'.

234. Procedure of registration. The application for trademark registration which has been accorded a filing date shall be published electronically within seven days of the date of filing. Applications for registration of trademarks which are obviously contrary to public order or morality shall not be published.

235. If the application does not satisfy the formal conditions provided by the law, OSIM notifies the applicant of the irregularities in the application and affords him a period of thirty days to correct them. If the applicant corrects, within the prescribed time limit, the irregularities notified by OSIM, the application for trademark registration will be published. If such is not the case, the application will be refused.

236. The publication of the application for trademark registration will contain:

(a) the name or designation and address or headquarters of the applicant;
(b) the name or designation and address or headquarters of the representative;
(c) the representation of the trademark, accompanied by the elements and descriptions provided for in the law, if applicable; the representation provided in the form of an electronic file can be made available through a link to the respective file, as the case may be;
(d) the list of products and services, grouped by class according to the Nice classification, each group being preceded by the class number from the said classification which belongs to the group of products or services and presented in the order of the respective classification;

(e) the index of the Vienna classification;
(f) the date of filing and the filing number;
(g) indications regarding the priority invoked;
(h) the mention that the mark is individual, collective or of certification, as the case may be;
(i) date of publication of the request.

237. In application of the provisions of of the law, the applicant receives a decision which can be contested within the term and with the procedure provided for in the law. If the decision has not been annulled by a final decision, the publication fee is returned to the applicant.

238. When the publication of a registration application or a registered trademark involves, for reasons attributable to OSIM, an error or certain deficiencies, OSIM proceeds to ex officio rectification or at the request of the applicant.

239. The observation formulated according to the provisions of the law is made in writing, indicating the number of the registration application to which it refers and is not subject to any tax.

Within a time limit of two months as from the date of publication of the trademark registration application, any natural person or legal entity and any group or body representing manufacturers, producers, suppliers of services, traders or consumers may submit to the office written observations in respect of the application for trademark registration, based on the absolute grounds for refusal previously referred.

However, persons and groups or bodies, as referred to under above paragraph, shall not be parties to the trademark registration proceedings.

Observations shall be communicated to the applicant who may comment thereupon. Within a time limit of six months following publication, subject to payment of the prescribed filing and examination fees, the Office carries out a substantive examination of the application for trademark registration and decides to accept trademark registration, wholly or in part, or to refuse registration.

The Office examines:

(a) the capacity of the applicant;
(b) the conditions set out under provisions of the law for claiming priority, where priority is claimed in the application;
(c) the grounds for refusal set out under Article 5 paragraph (1) (absolute grounds) and submitted observations, where appropriate.

Where a non-essential element of the trademark is devoid of distinctive character and if the said element could give rise to doubts as to the scope of trademark protection, OSIM shall request that the applicant states, within thirty days of notification date, that he disclaims any exclusive right on said element. The statement shall be published together with the registered trademark.

In the absence of the statement provided for under paragraph (1), the application for trademark registration shall be admitted in part or refused, as the case may be.

In order to assess whether a trademark is well known or renowned, it is necessary that it be widely known:

(a) on the territory of Romania or in the European Union, as the case may be; and
(b) for the target audience segment for the products or services to which it applies.

The target audience segment should be established based on the following elements:

(a) the category of consumers targeted for the products or services to which the trademark refers; the identification of the category of consumers is done by groups of consumers of certain products or services in connection with which the mark is used;
(b) the distribution networks of the products or services to which the mark refers.

In the opposition procedure, when judging the reasons for refusal regarding well-known or renowned trademarks, the degree of knowledge of a brand by the public can be assessed according to its promotion, including advertising and promotion at fairs or exhibitions of the products or services to which the brand is applied.

The notoriety or reputation of a trademark can be proven by any means of evidence. In its support, can be used various types of documents such as those regarding:

(a) the marketing or sale of products or the provision of services under the well-known or renowned brand may be presented;
(b) the import or export of products on which the well-known brand is applied;
(c) advertising or advertising of products and services under the well-known brand.

In examining the grounds for refusal, in accordance with the criteria set out above, the Office may request public authorities, public institutions and private law legal entities for documents attesting to the notoriety of the trademark in Romania.

Where a relative ground for refusal is applicable only to certain goods and services for which trademark registration has been applied, registration shall be refused for said goods and services only.

If the examination of the application shows that the conditions prescribed by the law are satisfied, the Office shall decide to register the trademark. The trademark shall be published in the Official Industrial Property Bulletin, in electronic format, within two months as from the date of the registration decision and OSIM shall issue the trademark registration certificate only after payment of publication and issuance fee.

If the application does not satisfy the conditions prescribed for registration of a trademark, the Office shall notify the applicant thereof and shall afford him a period of thirty days for submitting his observations or withdrawing his application. Such period may be extended for another thirty days period upon request by the applicant, accompanied by payment of the prescribed fee.

On expiry of the period referred to above, OSIM shall decide, as appropriate, to register the trademark, refuse the application or note that the application has been withdrawn.

The application for registration of a trademark may be modified, at the request of the applicant, only in order to correct the name or address of the applicant or to make other corrections that do not substantially affect the trademark or that do not extend the list of goods or services.

Any modification requested by the applicant prior to registration and which substantially affects the trademark or the list of goods or services shall make the subject of a new application for trademark registration. During the registration procedure, OSIM may request the applicant to provide such explanations and documents as it deems necessary if there exists any doubt as to the exactness or the content of the elements of the application for trademark registration.

240. The application may, at any time, be withdrawn by the applicant. Also, the applicant may modify the list of goods or services, but only in the sense of its restriction. If the mark has been published already, withdrawal or restriction shall also be published in the Official Bulletin.

The law prohibits any modification which substantially affects the mark or which extends the list of the goods or services, in this case being necessarily the filing of a new application of the mark.

241. The application of trademark registration admitted in accordance with the provisions above, will be published in the Official Industrial Property Bulletin, in electronic format, in view of opposition. If the application for trademark registration is refused, the decision of refusal will be published when it is final.

242. As previously mentioned, by the recently amended provisions of the law, the opposition has been brought into a post-registration procedure and accordingly the opposition can be formulated within two months from the date of publication of the admission of the registration of the application. Another novelty is that the proof of use of the trademark should be made by reference to a period of five years preceding the date of filing or the priority date of the application for registration of the mark in connection with which the opposition was filed and not by reporting on the date of publication of the admission of the application for registration.

243. Thus, according to Articles 26 to 28 of the law:

> Within a time limit of two months as from the date of publication of registration of the trademark application, any interested person can oppose the registration of the trademark on the relative grounds for refusal. Oppositions shall be made in writing, comprising the legal basis and the reasons and shall be accompanied by payment of the legal fee.

244. Opposition may be based on one or more earlier rights, provided that all such rights belong to the same owner.

245. Upon request by the applicant, proof shall be made to OSIM by the earlier trademark owner who has made the opposition that:

(a) during a period of five years preceding the publication date or the priority date of the application for trademark registration, the earlier trademark has been effectively used on the territory of Romania in connection with the goods and services in respect of which it is registered;
(b) there are justified reasons for the non-use of said trademark.

246. The upper provisions are only applicable if the earlier trademark was registered at least five years prior to the date of filing or the date of priority of the application for registration of the trademark in respect of which opposition has been made.

247. The opponent shall prove the use referred to above within two months, at the most, of the date of receiving the notification from OSIM. In the absence of such proof of use, the opposition will be rejected.

248. Where the earlier trademark is a European Union trademark, the effective use of the EU trademark shall be determined in accordance with Article 18 of the European Union Trademark Regulation.

249. If the earlier trademark has been used in relation to only part of the goods or services for which it is registered, it shall, for the purpose of the examination of the opposition, be deemed to be registered in respect of that part of the goods or services only.

250. Where the prescribed conditions are not complied with, the opposition shall be deemed not to have been filed.

251. OSIM should inform the applicant for trademark registration on the opposition made, granting a period of two months in order to allow for the possibility of a friendly settlement. Upon common request by the parties, said period may be extended with another period, which shall be expressly indicated by the parties and cannot exceed three months.

252. If, within the granted period, the parties cannot come to an agreement, OSIM notifies the opponent, giving him a time limit of thirty days to submit his arguments and evidence in support of the opposition made.

253. OSIM communicates the documents filed in support of the opposition to the applicant for trademark registration and shall grant him a time limit of thirty days to submit his point of view regarding the opposition grounds.

254. In the absence of the applicant's point of view, the opposition will be settled based on the filed documents.

255. Legal proofs of use should be communicated to the applicant who, within thirty days of communication, may submit his point of view thereupon.

256. Opposition shall be settled based on all arguments and documents filed by the parties while observing the time limits granted by OSIM in this respect.

257. The documents filed within the opposition procedure shall be filed in as many copies as needed for communication to the parties plus one copy for OSIM.

258. The opposition made in respect of the registration of the trademark shall be settled by a Board within the Trademark and Geographical Indications Division of OSIM.

259. Within two months, at the most, of the expiry of the time limit provided by the law, the Board shall make a reasoned decision concerning the settlement of the opposition, which will be communicated to the parties within thirty days and which may be appealed against.

260. Opposition settlement may be suspended in the following cases:

(a) if it is based on an application for trademark registration prior to a final decision on the registration thereof;
(b) if there is evidence that the opposed trademark is subject to an invalidation or revocation action up to the final settlement of the case.

261. The reasoned decision of suspension shall be communicated to the parties and may be appealed against within thirty days of communication in accordance with the legal procedure.

262. During suspension, the applicant or the opponent may request the opposition settlement to be resumed, if the suspension reason has ceased to exist.

263. When, as a result of the examination procedure, a final decision to register the mark is reached, this shall be recorded in the National Trademark Register and the Office shall issue a registration certificate to the owner against payment of the prescribed fee

264. OSIM enters in the Trademark Register the trademarks admitted for registration, in respect of which the registration procedure is completed and shall issue the trademark registration certificate, subject to payment of the legal fee, within thirty days of the date of notifying the owner about completing the trademark registration procedure. The date of completing the trademark registration procedure will be entered into the register.

265. The trademark registration procedure shall be deemed to be completed on the date on which the trademark registration application admitted for registration may no longer be subject to opposition or, where an opposition has been made, on the date on which the decision concerning the opposition is final or the opposition is withdrawn. The same approach also applies to international trademark registration applications.

266. Failure to pay the legal fee within the time limit provided, the owner shall be deemed to have renounced registration of the trademark. Renunciation shall be entered in the Trademark.

267. Register and shall be published in the Official Industrial Property Bulletin.

268. The trademarks entered in the Trademark Register will be published in the Official Industrial Property Bulletin. The Trademark Register has a public character.

269. For the registration of collective trademarks, the upper provisions are applying '*mutatis mutandis*'. The application for registration of a collective mark will be accompanied by a trademark usage regulation. The usage regulation must contain at least the following elements: (a) the name and headquarters of the association or of the legal entity under public law; (b) the object of activity of the association or the entity legal entities under public law; (c) the persons authorized to represent the association or legal person under public law; (d) the conditions of affiliation, in the case of an association; (e) indications regarding the persons authorized to use the collective mark and, if applicable, the authorization as provided; (f) the conditions for using the collective mark; (g) the reasons why the owner may prohibit the use of the collective mark to a member of the association, as well as other sanctions that may be applied in case of non-compliance with the regulation; (h) indications regarding the necessity the agreement of all members of the association, in the situation where the owner of the collective mark transfers the rights regarding this mark.

270. In the case of a collective mark consisting of signs or indications that can be used to designate, in trade, the geographical origin of products or services, the regulation of use will indicate the persons whose products or services come from the respective area who are authorized to use the collective mark and the conditions that must be met in order to become a member of the association that owns the mark. If the deposit of a collective mark does not meet one of the conditions provided for in the law or if the regulation for the use of the collective mark does not contain all the elements provided, OSIM can grant the applicant a period of thirty days to fill in the gaps. If the deficiencies are not remedied within the given period, OSIM will decide to reject the trademark registration request or, as the case may be, not recognize the priority invoked. The owner of a collective trademark may claim in court, on behalf of the persons authorized to use the trademark, repairing the damage suffered by them as a result of the unauthorized use of the brand by third parties.

2. International Registration

271. Depending on the filing place of the application of the mark and on the country where the protection is requested, according to the Madrid Agreement and the Protocol to the Agreement, there are two situations which will be presented below shortly.

According to the first situation, OSIM acts as the origin Office and the international application where the States are designated, and protection is sought and transmitted to the International Bureau of the WIPO at Geneva by the intermediate of OSIM. The international fees due according to Article 8.2 of the Agreement or Article 8.2 of the Protocol are paid by the applicant directly to the International Bureau.

The mark may be the subject of an international registration if already registered in the origin country or where the international application is governed exclusively by the Protocol, if the application has been filed with OSIM.

We are reminding that in the case of an international application governed exclusively by the Agreement or by both the Agreement and the Protocol, OSIM may be an origin Office only if the applicant has a real and effective industrial undertaking in Romania; if not, it has to have its domicile in Romania and, if not, he has to be exclusively a Romanian citizen.

In the situation of an international application governed only by the Protocol, the applicant may have any origin Office of a contracting State, if the applicant meets one or more of the previous conditions.

272. In the second situation, the international application may be filed at another origin Office, and to obtain the protection in Romania, this country will be designated.

The application is examined according to the procedure previously presented and, when the protection is not refused, according to Article 3*ter* of the Agreement or to Article 3*ter* of the Protocol, the international registration of the mark whose protection is extended on the territory of Romania thereof produces the same effects as if the mark was filed directly with OSIM. The international registration of a mark with effects extended in Romania is registered in the National Trademark Register.

3. EU Trademark

273. Where an EU trademark application is filed with the Office in accordance with Article 25 paragraph (1) letter (b) of the EU trademark Regulation, the Office shall enter the date on which the application has been received and, without performing any examination, shall forward the application to the European Union Intellectual Property (EUIPO) within two weeks, subject to payment of the fee prescribed by the Law in case of filing of a national trademark application.

An EU trademark application or an EU trademark may be converted into a national trademark application in accordance with the provisions of Articles 139–141 of the EU trademark Regulation, subject to payment of the fee prescribed by the Law for the examination of a national application.

OSIM receives the requests for conversion/transformation of applications for trademarks/European Union trademarks and enters them into the national database with the date of deposit of the application for registration of the European Union trademark. OSIM notifies the need to pay the filing and publication fees, granting a period of two months from the date of notification. The publication of the trademark application following the conversion/transformation of an application or trademark of the European Union is done under the conditions provided for in the law, with the mention that the application results from the conversion of an application or trademark of the European Union, on the date of presentation by the applicant of proof of payment of the legal fee; otherwise, the application will be rejected. The applications for conversion/transformation are subject to substantive examination.

The owner of an earlier trademark registered in Romania or of an earlier trademark, subject to international registration with effects in Romania, which files an identical trademark meant to be registered as an EU trademark, in respect of goods and services identical with those in respect of which the earlier trademark has been registered or included in the list thereof, may claim for the EU trademark registration the seniority of the earlier trademark in respect of the trademark registration in Romania.

The owner of an EU trademark which also owns an earlier identical trademark registered in Romania or subject to an international registration with effects in Romania, in respect of goods and services identical with those in respect of which the earlier trademark has been registered or included in the list thereof, may claim the seniority of the earlier trademark in Romania.

II. Procedure of Registration of Geographical Indications

274. The whole procedure of the registration of geographical indications has a series of common elements with the registration of a mark and consequently this chapter will give only the specific elements with reference to the procedure for marks.

A. Application

275. According to Article 84(2), registration of a geographical indication may be applied for to OSIM, either directly or through a professional representative, and according to rule 43, the application of registration of a geographical indication shall contain the:

(a) express request with regard to the registration of a geographical indication and to the grant of the right of use thereof;
(b) denomination and registered Office of the association of producers who request the registration of the geographical indication;
(c) list of persons authorized to use the geographical indication;
(d) geographical indication which is the subject matter of the application;

(e) type of products which the geographical indication refers to, as well as the indication of the place of fabrication and of the limits of the production's geographical area;
(f) name or denomination and address or registered office of the authorized representative, if the association of producers appointed an authorized representative.

The application shall be accompanied by:

(a) an internal norm, which shall contain:
   - denomination of the goods to which the geographical indications refer;
   - description of the goods and of the main characteristics thereof;
   - delimitation of the geographical area of production;
   - elements proving that the goods have their origin in the geographical area of production;
   - description of the method of obtaining the goods;
   - elements which justify the connection of the goods with the zone or geographical area thereof;
   - reference concerning the procedures of goods quality control, as well as the body competent to carry out this control.
(b) a certificate of conformity of the products with the element provided for in the internal norm issued by the Ministry of Agriculture;
(c) proof of the payment of the fee for registration of the geographical indication;
(d) power of attorney for the representation of the applicant, if necessary.

If the applicant of the registration of the geographical indication is a foreign association of producers, the application shall be accompanied by a justifying document, on a certified copy, of the title of protection obtained in the country of origin.

B. Registration of the Geographical Indication

276. The application for registration of the geographical indication shall be examined within three months with regard to the fulfilment of the condition of protection.

If the Office finds that the application fulfils the legal provisions, it decides to register the geographical indication. It is significant that the association of producers receives a right to use the geographical indication, a right common to the members of the association.

Within two months of making this decision, the Office will publish the geographical indication and the list containing the persons authorized to use it in the Official Bulletin.

OSIM shall register geographical indications and afford to the applicant the right to use them after the central specialized public authority or, as appropriate, the competent authority of the applicant's country of origin has certified:

(a) the geographical indication for which registration is sought;
(b) the products that may be marketed under that indication;
(c) the geographical area of production;
(d) the characteristics that the products must possess and the manufacturing conditions they must comply with in order to be marketed under that indication.

277. Within two months from the publication, any interested person may apply for an opposition to the registration of the geographical indication for failure to observe the conditions of protection or if the interested person has a legitimate interest based on a previously protected industrial property right which the geographical indication would come into conflict with. The opposition to the registration of a geographical indication shall be settled in accordance with the provisions set out for trademarks.

The opposition is notified to the applicant, who is invited to present his observations in connection with the reasons for opposition. If the reasons for opposition are justified, the Office will reject the application for the registration of geographical indications and will publish the decision to reject in the Official Bulletin.

If, within the indicated time limit, no opposition is filed or the Office states that there are insufficient reasons for opposition, a decision to register the geographical indication in the National Register of Geographical Indications is taken. The Office issues the certificates of registration to the association of producers and grants the right of the use thereof.

The decision on the registration is published within two months from the date of the decision in the Official Bulletin.

The law provides that the registration of a geographical indication on behalf of an association of producers shall not prevent registration of the same indication by any other association having the required capacity to request it.

Persons authorized to use a geographical indication for certain goods shall be entitled to use it in the course of trade, but only for those goods in business papers, advertising or brochures and they may affix on such products the term registered geographical indication.

It shall be prohibited for non-authorized persons to use a geographical indication or an imitation thereof even if the true origin of the products is shown or if terms such as *kind, type, imitation,* and the like are added.

Persons authorized by OSIM to use a geographical indication for wines or spirits may prohibit the use of such indication by any other person for wines and spirits that do not come from the region suggested by the geographical indication concerned, even where the true origin of the product is expressly mentioned or the geographical indication is used in a translated form or accompanied by terms such as *kind, type* and the like.

The central specialized public authority may, ex officio or at the request of any concerned person, carry out verifications of the products marketed under a registered geographical indication.

§5. OWNERSHIP AND TRANSFER

278. As previously explained, in Romania, the right to the mark may be obtained through registration. This means that the right to a mark shall belong to the natural or legal person who was first to file an application for registration of the mark.

'Owner' means the natural or legal person in whose name a mark has been registered in the National Trademark Register. According to the law, ownership is a concept that may belong to a natural as well as to a legal person.

Rights to a mark may be transferred by assignment or licence, merger or succession, based on a court decision or in any other way provided for by the law in respect of transfers of property rights, at any time during the term of protection of the mark.

The rights to a mark may also be transferred under a levy of execution against the owner of the mark, carried out in accordance with the law. Recordal of the transfer of rights in respect of a trademark under dispute shall be suspended up to the date of a final court decision in respect thereof.

I. Assignment

279. Assignments are probably the most common form of change of ownership where the assignee receives the totality of the rights of the owner, who after the assignment becomes a third party with reference to the mark. Assignment shall be done in written form and signed by the parties to the contract, subject to condition of nullity unless it results from a court decision or contractual obligation.

An assignment contract shall be under the regulations of Common Law and, as far as the relationships between parties are concerned, shall be governed by the principle of autonomy of will of the contracting parties.

Rights to a mark may be assigned independently of the transfer of the business in which the mark is incorporated.

But, at the same time, the transfer of the whole of the estate of the owner of the mark shall include the transfer of the rights to the mark, unless there is agreement to the contrary or circumstances clearly dictate otherwise. The transfer of certain elements of the owner's patrimony does not affect his capacity as owner of the right in the trademark.

The transfer of certain elements of the owner's estate shall not affect his capacity as owner of the right to the mark.

Assignment of rights to a mark may be effected for all or a part of the goods or services for which the mark is registered; an assignment, even in part, may not limit the use of the mark for the goods or services applying to a given territory.

In the case of registered marks for more classes of products or services, the assignment may be done for a person for some classes of goods or services and for other persons for other classes of goods or services. Moreover, the owner may maintain its mark for at least one class. In this situation, every new owner will get the right to the mark only for the classes of goods or services to which the mark has been assigned.

Identical or similar marks belonging to the same owner, used for identical or similar goods or services, may be assigned only as a whole and only to one person, subject to the condition of nullity of the instrument of assignment. The beneficiary of the assignment contract, who obtained the right to the mark by assignment, has the obligation to ensure the maintenance of the quality of the goods or services the mark refers to.

The request for recordal of the assignment includes data on identification of the trademark, of the new owner, of the goods and/or services to which the assignment relates and it must be accompanied by the document attesting to the change of ownership of the trademark. Besides these, the request also includes, if appropriate, information on the identification data of the new trademark owner's representative.

OSIM refuses to enter the assignment in the Register if it is obvious that public is misled as to the nature, quality or geographic origin of the goods or services in respect of which the trademark is registered, unless the assignee accepts to restrict the trademark assignment to the goods and services in respect of which it is not likely to mislead.

Upon request of one party and subject to the payment of the prescribed fee, OSIM enters the assignment in the Trademark Register and publishes it in the Official Industrial Property Bulletin. Assignment may be invoked against third parties as from the date of its publication.

Where the conditions prescribed for the recordal of the assignment are not complied with, OSIM will communicate to the requesting party the irregularities ascertained within thirty days of filing the request referred to above. If said irregularities are not corrected within two months of the receipt of the communication from the Office, the request for recordal of the assignment will be refused.

In case of an assignment in part, any pending request made by the initial owner shall be effective for the trademark resulting from the partial assignment, as well. Where the request is subject to payment of fees and they have already been paid by the initial owner, additional fees is not to be due by the new owner in respect of the same request.

The assignment may be invoked against third parties as from the date of its entry in the National Trademark Register.

As from the date of the registration of the assignment, the assignee receives the right to exercise the action for infringement.

If the mark which was the object of an assignment is an international registered mark, then the assignee shall be, according to Article 9*bis* of the Madrid Agreement, a person who is entitled to file an international mark.

280. With regard to the certification mark, its owner, normally a legal person, may not assign the rights to the mark; the law provides in Article 75(2) that 'transfer of rights to a certification mark shall be decided by Government decision'.

281. Similarly, according to Article 95, 'the right to use a geographical indication may not be transferred'. This provision is a logical one, having in mind that, as already stated, the same geographical indication may be registered by more than one association of producers, the single criterion being that they should pursue production activity in the geographical area for products where qualities are essentially attributed to that geographical area.

II. Licensing

282. It is a common practice for the trademark owner to give third parties the right to use the registered mark.

The licence contract is the convention by which the owner-licensor transmits to another person-licensee the right to use that mark for a certain price.

The owner of a mark may, under a licensing contract, authorize other persons to make use of the mark on the whole or part of the Romanian territory for all or a part of the goods or services for which the mark was registered. A licence may be exclusive or non-exclusive.

As a principle, licensees are not allowed to assign the licence or to grant sub-licences.

In the case of an exclusive licence, the trademark owner is not allowed to licence the mark to any other person within the territory and for the list of goods or services for which the mark is registered.

In the licence contract, the owner of the mark retains the right to continue the exploitation of his mark and he alone may exercise the action for infringement. The licensing contract is concluded between the licensor, who has to have the capacity to conclude administration acts, and the licensee, who is any person having the capacity to contract. The licensing contract shall have the following effects:

(a) for the licensor:
   - to allow the use of the mark by the licensee, according to the contract;
   - to assure the licensee of eviction;
   - for exclusive licences, to conclude no other licensing contracts;
   - to maintain the mark into force.

(b) for the licensee:
   - to use only the mark which is the object of the contract, having nevertheless the possibility to affix on the goods signs which indicate that he is the manufacturer;
   - to put the mention ‘under licence’ on the mark affixed on the products that are the subject matter of the licence, in accordance with the contract;
   - to use the mark only for the goods and services under protection;
   - to maintain the aspect and the quality of the goods;
   - to use the mark within the territorial limits of its protection;
   - to use the mark effectively;
   - to pay the price for the licence agreement.

The doctrine distinguishes between more categories of licence contracts, as a function of the type of rights gained by the licensee, namely the:

- exploitation licence, which gives the right to the licensee to manufacture the goods and to affix the licensed mark, meaning that the same mark will be used for two or more products having a different origin but identical characteristics;
- use licence, which consists in giving the authorization to the licensee to use the mark of the licensor for goods originating from the latter;
- advertising licence, which authorizes the use of a denomination that is the object of a personal right of another party.

The law does not provide a written form of the contract as a condition of validity and it does not mention, as it does for the assignment contract, the consequence of nullity. In fact, it might be an implicit formulation when it is mentioned that a licence shall be recorded in the National Trademark Register on payment of the prescribed fee and shall be published in the BOPI. A licence may be invoked against others as from the date of its record in the register. Failure to register a licence with OSIM shall not affect:

(a) the validity of the trademark registration which is the subject matter of the licence or with regard to the trademark licence protection;
(b) the intervention in an infringement case instituted by the owner or the grant of damages within said proceedings as a consequence of the infringement of a trademark which is the subject matter of the licence.

Licence registration shall not be a condition for the trademark use by the licensee to be deemed to be equivalent to the trademark use by the owner within the proceedings relating to obtaining the trademark, maintaining the same in force or defending the rights therein.

The owner of a mark may invoke the rights conferred by that mark against a licensee who contravenes any provision in his licensing contract with regard to its duration, the form covered by the registration in which the trademark may be used and the nature of the goods or services for which the licence is granted, the territory where the mark may be used, or the quality of the goods manufactured or of the services provided by the licensee under the mark for which the licence has been granted.

Licenses are entered in the Trademark Register at the request of the trademark owner or of the licensee, accompanied by the attesting document upon payment of the prescribed fee and published in the Official Industrial Property Bulletin.

A license may be invoked against third parties as from the date of its publication.

Unless otherwise provided in the licensing contract, any of the licensees may not institute infringement proceedings without the consent of the owner of the mark.

The holder of an exclusive licence may institute infringement proceedings if, after having notified the owner of the mark of the infringing acts he has come to know about, the owner has not acted within the time limits prescribed by the licensee. Where infringement proceedings are instituted by the owner, any of the licensees may intervene in the proceedings in order to obtain compensation for damage caused by the infringement of the mark.

Throughout the term of the trademark licensing contract, the licensee shall be required:

(a) to use, for the goods on which the trademark is affixed, only the trademark that is the subject of the licensing contract, whilst remaining free to affix on such products signs which show that he is the manufacturer;
(b) to add the term 'under licence... ' to the mark affixed on the products that are the subject matter of the licence, in accordance with the contract.

283. As far as the certification mark is concerned, the law provides in Article 50 that 'the regulations governing the use of the collective mark may require that the collective mark may be transmitted by its owner only with the consent of all the members of the association'.

284. Article 75 stipulates that the rights to a certification mark may not be transferred by the legal person owning the mark because the Government is the only body allowed to decide on that.

285. Regarding the geographical indication, Article 95 stipulates that the right to use it may not be transferred.

A. *The Mark as Subject Matter of Mortgage*

286. The mortgage is the contract by which the debtor delivers to its creditor a good for the warranty of the execution of the obligation, with the possibility that, at the end of the term, in case of failing to observe the obligation, the creditor may be satisfied preferably by the value of the good.

Romanian authors, basing themselves on the existing case law,[42] admit that the fund of commerce may constitute subject matter of the commercial mortgage and that trademarks are part of the fund of commerce.

It results that a trademark which belongs to the fund of commerce may constitute, as part of the fund of commerce, subject matter of the commercial mortgage.

It is appreciated, although it is not explicitly provided in the law, that the trademark, due to its commercial value and independence from the fund of commerce, may be subject matter of the commercial mortgage.

B. *The Mark as Subject of Rights In Rem or of Levy of Execution*

287. The recently amended law introduced by the new provisions of Articles 51 to 53, the capability of a trademark to be also considered as subject of rights in rem or of levy of execution.

Thus, a trade mark may, independently of the undertaking, be the subject of rights in rem or of levy of execution.

---

42. Viorel Ros, *Intellectual Property Rights. Trademarks and Geographical Indications* 161 (Editura Sylvi 1999).

Rights in rem and levy of execution shall be entered in the Trademark Register at the concerned person's request, accompanied by the attesting document, on payment of the prescribed fee for recordal of transfers of rights.

Where the trademark owner is subject to insolvency proceedings, it will be mentioned by OSIM in the Trademark register, at the concerned person's request, accompanied by the attesting document.

These provisions shall apply *mutatis mutandis* to trademark applications, as well.

Recordals in the Trademark Register may be modified or cancelled, upon payment of the prescribed fee, at the concerned person's request, accompanied by suitable attesting documents.

§6. Scope of Exclusive Rights

288. First of all, there is a *territorial scope*, which means that where a mark has been protected, the effect of the protection covers the country where the mark has been protected through national or international routes or, if we are speaking about community mark, which covers the territory of each Member State of the EU, including Romania as from 1 January 2007.

289. There are nevertheless two main exceptions from the territorial scope. The first one is the protection of the mark 'as is' provided for in Article 6*quinquies* of the Paris Convention and which states that any mark which fulfils the required conditions must be accepted for filing and protected 'as is' in the other members countries, subject to certain conditions.

The list of the exceptions is given in the same article of the Paris Convention and, in summary, they are the following:

- where the mark infringes rights of the third parties acquired in the country where protection is claimed;
- when the mark is deprived of distinctive character or is purely descriptive;
- where the mark is contrary to the rules of morality or public order;
- if the registration of the mark would be an act of unfair competition;
- where the mark is used by the owner in a form which is essentially different from that in which it has been registered.

The second exception refers to the extraterritoriality of the well-known mark, which is provided for in Article 6*bis* of the Paris Convention. This states that the filing of a mark which might create confusion with a well-known mark is not attributive of the rights to the mark, if the use of the mark applied for registration would take unfair advantage of the distinctive character or the repute of the well-known mark or where such use could cause prejudice to the owner of the well-known mark.

290. Second, there is a temporal scope, namely where the protection is based on a legal prescription according to which the effect of registration is limited to ten years, but it may be renewed in principle indefinitely for further periods of ten years each. The law grants to the owner of the registered mark the following rights:

- exclusive right to use the mark;
- right to exclude others from using the mark;
- right to provisional protection.

I. Exclusive Right to Use the Mark

291. The exclusive right to use the mark is a patrimonial right, limited to the Romanian territory, but in principle unlimited in time.

According to Article 39, paragraph 1, 'the registration of a mark shall confer its owner an exclusive right in that mark. Without prejudice to the rights of owners acquired before the filing date or the priority date of the registered trademark, the owner of that registered trademark is entitled to request, by an infringement action, that the competent judicial body prohibits third parties from having his consent from using in the course of trade:

(a) any sign which is identical with the trademark, in respect of goods or services which are identical with those for which the trademark is registered;
(b) any sign in respect of which, because of its identity with or similarity to the trademark and because of the identity or similarity of the goods or services on which it is affixed, there is a likelihood of confusion on the part of the public, including the likelihood of association between the sign and the trademark;
(c) any sign which is identical with or similar to the trademark, in respect of goods or services which are identical with, similar or not similar to those for which the trademark is registered, where the latter has a reputation in Romania and where use of that sign without due cause takes unfair advantage of or is detrimental to, the distinctive character or the reputation of the trademark;
(d) any sign which is identical with or similar to the trademark and is used for other purposes than distinguishing the goods or services, where use of that sign without due cause takes unfair advantage of, or is detrimental to, the distinctive character or the reputation of the trademark. In application of that provision, the owner of the trademark may request that third parties should be prohibited from performing, in particular, the following acts:
    (i) affixing the sign to the goods or to the packaging thereof;
    (ii) offering the goods, putting them on the market or stocking them for such purposes under that sign, or offering or supplying services thereunder;
    (iii) importing or exporting goods under that sign;
    (iv) using the sign on business papers or in advertising;
    (v) using the sign as a trade or company name or part of a trade or company name;
    (vi) using the sign in comparative advertising in a manner that is contrary to Law No. 158/2008 on Deceiving Advertising and Comparative Advertising, as republished'.

Where the risk exists that the packaging, labels, tags, security or authenticity features or devices, or any other means to which the trademark is affixed, could be used in relation to goods or services and that use would constitute an infringement of the rights of the owner of a trade mark, the owner of that trademark has the right to prohibit the following acts if carried out in the course of trade:

(a) affixing a sign identical with, or similar to, the trademark on packaging, labels, tags, security or authenticity features or devices, or any other means to which the trademark may be affixed;
(b) offering or placing on the market, or stocking for those purposes, or importing or exporting packaging, labels, tags, security or authenticity features or devices, or any other means to which the mark is affixed.

Without prejudice to the rights of owners acquired before the filing date or the priority date of the registered trademark, the owner of that registered trademark will be also entitled to prevent all third parties from bringing goods to the territory of Romania, in the course of trade, without being released for free circulation in Romania, where such goods, including the packaging thereof, come from third countries and bear, without authorization, a trademark which is identical with the trademark registered in Romania in respect of such goods, or which cannot be distinguished in its essential aspects from that trademark.

'The entitlement of the trademark owner shall lapse if, during the proceedings to determine whether the registered trademark has been infringed, initiated in accordance with Regulation (EU) No. 608/2013 of the European Parliament and of the Council of 12 June 2013 concerning customs enforcement of intellectual property rights and repealing Council Regulation (EC) No. 1383/2003, evidence is provided by the declarant or the holder of the goods that the owner of the registered trademark is not entitled to prohibit the placing of the goods on the market in the country of final destination.'

In principle, this means that the owner may use exclusively the mark for those goods and services for which registration was made and, consequently, the use of the same mark by a third party, for other goods and services, is in principle not allowable, under the conditions that will be exposed further.

The right to use means first that the right of the owner of the mark to affix it on goods packaging, labels, etc., or to use it in any other way in relation to the goods under protection.

Second, it means the right to introduce the goods on the market under the mark. Third, it means the right of the owner to use his mark in advertising, on business papers, documents, etc.

II. Right to Exclude Others from Using the Mark

292. The negative aspect of the exclusive right, which according to some authors is even 'stronger' than the positive one, is the right to exclude others from using the mark without the consent of the owner.

The right to exclude others from using the mark comes from the basic function of a mark to distinguish the goods or services of the owner from those of others. In other words, the owner should be able to object to the use of confusingly similar marks in order to prevent the public from being misled.

Generally speaking, misleading shall refer on one hand to the distinctiveness of the mark and on the other to the identity or similarity of trademarks together with identity or similarity of marks.

In this respect, Article 39, paragraph 2 provides that:

> the owner of the mark may request the competent judicial body to prohibit any person not having his consent from using in the course of trade:
>
> - any sign which is identical with the mark in relation to goods or services which are identical with those for which the mark is registered;
> - any sign where, because of its identity with or similarity to the mark or the identity or similarity of the goods or services to which the sign is affixed with the goods or services for which the mark is registered, there exists a likelihood of confusion on the part of the public, including the likelihood of association between the sign and the mark;
> - any sign which is identical with or similar to the mark in relation to goods or services which are not similar to those for which the mark is registered, where the latter has a reputation in Romania and where use of that sign without due cause could take unfair advantage of the distinctive character or the repute of the mark or where such use would cause prejudice to the owner of the mark.

293. This provision is very similar to that of Article 5 of the European Directive. The owner of the mark may request that any other person be prohibited from performing, in particular, the following acts:

(a) attaching the sign to goods or to their packaging;
(b) offering the goods, putting them on the market or stocking them for such purposes under that sign, or offering or supplying services thereunder;
(c) importing or exporting the goods under that sign;
(d) using the sign on business papers and in advertising.

The owner of a registered mark may not request other persons to be prohibited from stocking, offering for sale or putting on the market goods under such mark if the goods have been put on the market by the owner himself or with his consent.

These provisions shall not apply if the owner submits legitimate reasons for opposing the commercialization of the goods, particularly where the condition of the goods is changed or impaired after they have been put on the market.

The owner of a mark may not request that other persons be prohibited from using it in the course of trade:

(a) the name/designation or address/headquarters of the owner;

(b) indications concerning the kind, quality, intended purpose, value, geographical origin, the time of production of the goods or the rendering of the service under that mark or other characteristics of the goods or service;
(c) the mark, where it is necessary to indicate the intended purpose of a product or service, in particular as accessories or spare parts.

The provisions of the preceding paragraph shall apply with the proviso that the elements referred to in items (a) to (c) are used in accordance with honest practices.

III. Right to Provisional Protection

294. The provisional protection is provided by Article 43, which stipulates that 'the applicant for registration may only request the prohibition referred to in Article 39 after publication of the mark'. The applicant may claim damages for acts subsequent to the publication of the mark under the general rules of law. A decision ordering payment of damages shall be enforceable only as from the date of registration of the mark. If the application for registration is refused, the applicant shall not be entitled to damages.

It is a normal provision, considering that a third party could know about a certain mark only after its publication, which is the only date which might be invoked by an owner to prohibit the use of the mark. After that date, the applicant is entitled to claim damages and, consequently, after the registration date of the mark, the owner is entitled to a decision order of the damage.

§7. Limitations of the Scope of Mark Protection

295. There are some main limitations of the scope of mark protection that arise from the function and the use of the mark.

I. Exhaustion of Mark Rights

296. The exhaustion of mark rights provides for in Article 44 that 'right in a trademark shall be exhausted, and the owner shall not be entitled to prohibit other persons the use thereof in respect of goods put on the market in the EU and the European Economic Area, under said trademark by the owner himself or with his consent. These provisions shall not apply if the owner submits legitimate reasons for opposing the commercialization of the goods, particularly where the condition of the goods is changed or impaired after they have been put on the market'. As appears obvious, the revised Law provides for the so-called community exhaustion due to the status of Member State of Romania as from 1 January 2007.

The consequence of the exhaustion of mark rights is that once the product covered by its mark is put on the market, the right to the mark cannot prevent the free circulation of the marked goods and may not be an obstacle to ulterior transactions.

The European Directive and French law provide the right of the trademark owner to oppose to its use by the intermediate, when legitimate reasons justify the opposition of the owner to the ulterior commercialization of the goods, determined by the modification or alteration intervened after they were put on the market.

II. Loyal Use of the Mark

297. The loyal use of the mark provides in Article 45 that:

> the owner of a mark may not request that other persons be prohibited from using in the course of trade:
>
> – the name or address of the third party, if it is a natural person;
> – signs or indications which are not distinctive or which concern the kind, quality, quantity, intended purpose, value, geographical origin, the time of production of the goods or of rendering of the service or other characteristics of the goods or services;
> – the trademark, for the purpose of identifying or referring to goods
> – or services as those of the owner of that trademark, particularly where the use of the trademark is necessary to indicate the intended purpose of a product or service, in particular as accessories or spare parts.

These provisions shall apply with the provision that the elements referred to above are used in accordance with honest practice in industrial or commercial matters.

Moreover, the owner of the mark may not stop third parties that are not competitors to mention the mark, for instance in books or other publications, in dictionaries or encyclopaedias.

III. Previous Use of the Mark

298. A special situation is when a mark has been used in spite of the existence of an earlier mark, but no opposition to its use has been seen from the owner's side. In this situation, the owner of the earlier mark who has acquiesced for a continuous period of five years in the use of the subsequently registered mark may not apply for cancellation nor oppose the use of the later mark for the goods and services in respect of which such later mark has been used, except if the registration of the later mark was sought in bad faith. In the case previously referred, the owner of the subsequently registered trademark may not oppose the use of the earlier trademark, even if the earlier trademark may no longer be invoked against the later trademark.

§8. USE REQUIREMENTS

299. The obligation to use the mark means that, in principle, the owner of a mark may be asked for its revocation if the mark has not been used within a certain period provided for in the law.

If the owner cannot prove that the non-use is justified, the revocation of the registration shall be ordered by the Court. In this respect, Article 55(1) provides that:

> any concerned person may apply to the Bucharest Court, at any time during the term of protection of the mark, for revocation of the owner of the rights conferred by the mark:
>
> – if, within a continuous period of five years as from the date of completing the registration procedure, the mark has not been put to genuine use on the territory of Romania in connection with the goods or services in respect of which it is registered or if such use has been suspended for a continuous period of five years and if there are no proper reasons for non-use;
> – if, after the date of registration, the trademark has become, in consequence of acts or inactivity of the owner, the common name in the trade for a product or service in respect of which it is registered;
> – if, after the date of registration and in consequence of the use made of it by the owner or with his consent, the trademark is liable to mislead the public, particularly as to the nature, quality or geographical origin of the goods or services in respect of which it is registered;
> – if the trademark has been registered by a person not having the capacity required by Article 3.

300. Furthermore, Article 55(2) stipulates that:

> – the following shall be considered genuine uses of a mark: use of the trademark in a form that differs in certain respects from that of the registered trademark but which does not impair its distinctive character, irrespective of its being registered on behalf of its owner or not; impossibility of using the trademark due to circumstances beyond the control of the trademark owner, for example, restrictions on import or other provisions by public authorities in respect of the goods or services to which the trademark applies;
> – affixing of the trademark on goods or their packaging exclusively for the purposes of export;
> – use of the trademark by a third party with the consent of the owner or by any person entitled to use a collective mark or a certification mark, where it is considered by the trademark owner himself to be a use of the trademark.

Revocation of the rights conferred by a mark shall take effect from the date of the final court decision.

If the owner proves the use or justifies the non-use only for some of the goods or services, the revocation shall be in part and extends itself either to all goods or services for which use cannot be proved or for all those non-similar to the goods or services that the owner has used.

The use of the mark can be proved by any means, including witnesses. The rights of the owner may not be revoked if, in the time between expiry of the period of five years referred to previously and the submission of the request for revocation, the trademark has been subject to effective use. However, if the beginning or resumption of use of the trademark takes place within the three months preceding submission to the courts of the request for revocation, use of the trademark shall not be taken into consideration if preparation for the beginning or resumption of use has been made only after the owner obtained knowledge of the intention to submit a request for revocation.

The burden of proof of use of the trademark shall rest with the trademark owner and proof may be furnished by any means. Revocation shall take effect as from the date of submission of the application for revocation to the competent court.

Before a revocation decision has been taken, the mark, although not used, is valid and the owner may introduce actions for counterfeiting or unfair competition. The revocation may be partial or total; if the revocation is partial, then reasons for revocation exist only for a part of the goods or services.

According to the territoriality of protection, the exploitation outside the country does not mean an act of use that may be opposed in a revocation application. A licence contract that has not been followed by an execution does not mean an effective and serious use of the mark.

It is irrelevant if the licence contract is valid or void, once the licensee uses the mark effectively and seriously. For the collective marks, the use shall correspond to the regulation adopted by the associates.

In all cases, the exploitation shall be made with the title of a mark and not with the title of a commercial name or emblem.

§9. Duration of Protection: Renewal: Termination

I. Duration

301. According to the law, the registration of a mark shall take effect on the date of the regular national filing of the mark and shall subsist for ten years.

During the term of protection of the mark, the owner may request the Office, upon payment of the prescribed fee, to make non-essential amendments to certain elements of the mark, on the condition that the modifications do not affect the general appearance of the mark. The Office shall record in the Trademark Register the amendments made without affecting the general appearance and shall publish the mark in its amended form.

All amendments made to the relevant data in relation to the mark: owner's name, address, designation, etc., may be asked at any time during the term of protection and shall be recorded in the National Trademark Register and shall be published in the BOPI.

II. Renewal

302. If the owner so wishes, the registration of a mark shall be renewed at the end of each ten-year period on payment of the prescribed fee, meaning that theoretically, the protection of the mark is unlimited in time. Practically, the mark will be renewed until the owner takes the managerial decision that the respective mark becomes either too customary for the public to be further considered a sign capable of distinguishing the goods or the services or too generic.

The request for renewal of a registration may be made by the owner of the trademark or by any other person authorized to do so by law or by contract, within a time limit of at least six months before expiry of registration. Renewal of a registration shall take effect as from the day immediately following the expiry of the current term of protection.

The fee for the request for renewal of a registration is due on the date of the registration; the fee may be paid within six months following the expiry date of the current term of protection on payment of the prescribed additional fee. Failure to pay the fee in the manner prescribed shall lead to the loss of the rights of the owner of the mark.

The renewal may be asked only for a part of the goods or services for which the mark has been previously registered. In that situation, the owner is required to state the name of the goods or services for which he requested renewal of the registration.

Where the Office ascertains that the conditions for renewal of the registration have not been satisfied, it shall communicate that fact to the owner who shall have a period of thirty days as from the date of receipt of the communication for making his reply. If the Office finds the reply unsatisfactory or the applicant fails to reply within the prescribed time limit, the request for renewal will be refused. The person requesting renewal may oppose the refusal decision within three months of notification.

Renewal of the registration shall be entered in the National Trademark Register and shall be published in the BOPI within six months as from the date of the request for renewal.

III. Termination

303. In the situation where a registration expires because of non-renewal of the registration of the mark, three other situations may be added where the registration terminates before the expiration of the normal duration of protection.

First, the registration may be surrendered by the owner of the mark. Second, the owner may lose the rights conferred by the mark if certain situations appeared.

Third, the registration may be invalidated by a decision of the Court. Below, we will present in a more detailed manner each of these situations.

A. *Surrender*

304. The owner may surrender his trademark in respect of some or all of the goods or services for which it is registered. The surrender of a mark shall be declared to the Office in writing and shall be signed by the owner of the mark or by a person authorized by him. The rights to the mark shall lapse, with respect to the goods and services to which the mark applies, as from the date on which the surrender is entered in the National Trademark Register.

Where the owner of the registered mark has granted a licence, he cannot surrender the registration without the consent of the licensee. If a licence has been registered, surrender of a mark shall be entered only if the owner of the mark proves that he has advised the licensee of his intention to surrender the mark.

Where security or levy of execution have been entered in the Trademark Register, surrender of a trademark shall only be entered if the security beneficiary consents thereto or after the recordal of the levy of execution is cancelled.

If the surrender was made only for a part of the goods or services for which the mark was registered, this situation is very similar to the limitation of the list of goods or services for which the mark has been registered.

B. *Revocation*

305. At any time during the term of protection of the mark, any person may apply for revocation of the owner of the rights conferred by the mark if one of the following situations occurs:

(a) if within a continuous period of five years, the mark has not been put to genuine use on the territory of Romania in connection with the goods or services for which it is registered, and there are no proper reasons for non-use;
(b) if, after the date of registration, the mark has become, due to acts or inactivity of the owner, the common name in the trade of a product or service for which it is registered;
(c) if, after the date of registration and due to its use by the owner or with his consent, the mark is liable to mislead the public, particularly as to the nature, quality or geographical origin of the goods or services in respect of which it is registered;
(d) if the mark has been registered by a person not having the requested capacity.

Revocation of trademark owner's rights may be applied for:

(i) by judicial way, to the Law Court of Bucharest; or
(ii) by administrative way, to OSIM.

Revocation of the rights conferred by the mark shall take effect from the date of submission of the application for revocation to the court. An earlier date on which one of the revocation reasons occurred may be established at the request of one of the parties.

The following shall be considered an effective use of a trademark:

(a) use of the trademark in a form that differs in certain respects from that of the registered trademark but which does not impair its distinctive character;
(b) impossibility of using the trademark due to circumstances beyond the control of the trademark owner, for example, restrictions on import or other provisions by public authorities in respect of the goods or services to which the trademark applies;
(c) affixing of the trademark on goods or their packaging exclusively for the purposes of export;
(d) use of the trademark by a third party with the consent of the owner or by any person entitled to use a collective mark or a certification mark, where it is considered by the trademark owner himself to be a use of the trademark.

The rights of the owner may not be revoked if, during the time between the expiry of the five-year period referred to earlier and the submission of the request for revocation, the mark has been subject to genuine use. However, if the beginning or resumption of use of the mark takes place within the three months preceding submission to the courts of the request for revocation, the use of the mark shall not be taken into consideration if preparation for the beginning or resumption of use has been made only after the owner obtained knowledge of the intention to submit a request for revocation. The burden of proof of use of the trademark rests with the trademark owner and proof may be furnished by any means.

According to Article 60, if one ground for revocation only applies to some of the goods or services for which the trademark is registered, the revocation shall have effect with respect to such goods or services only. Where seniority of a national trademark or a trademark registered under international agreements is invoked in respect of an EU trademark, revocation of the owner's rights in respect of the trademark providing the basis for the seniority claim may be established after the moment at which the trademark was surrendered or allowed to lapse, provided that the revocation could have been declared at the time the trademark was surrendered or allowed to lapse. In such a case, the seniority shall cease to produce its effects.

Revocation takes effect as from the date of submission of the application for revocation to the competent court. As a result of the revocation, the trademark in question shall be cancelled from the Trademark Register and notice thereof shall be published in the Official Industrial Property Bulletin.

306. As far as the revocation of the rights conferred by the collective mark is concerned, any interested person may apply to the Bucharest Municipal Court, at any time during the term of protection of the mark, a request for revocation if:

(a) within a continuous period of five years, the mark has not been put to genuine use in connection with the goods or services in respect of which it is registered, and there are no proper reasons for non-use;
(b) if the owner has used the mark in a manner other than that provided for by the regulations or has not taken steps to prevent such use;
(c) if the manner in which the mark has been used has caused it to become liable to mislead the public.

We have to underline that in this situation, the burden of proof of use of the mark rests with the owner of the mark and proof may be brought by any means.

C. Invalidity of the Registration

307. The invalidity of the registration of a mark may be asked by any concerned person on any of the following grounds:

(a) the mark was registered contrary to the provisions of the law regarding absolute grounds of refusal;
(b) the mark was registered contrary to the provisions of the law regarding relative grounds of refusal;
(c) the registration was applied for in bad faith.

Invalidity of a trademark registration may be applied for on the basis of one or more earlier rights, provided that they all belong to the same owner.

Invalidity applied for on the basis of an earlier trademark shall not be admitted if it would not have been admitted on the date of filing or of priority of the latter trademark application based on one of the following reasons:

(a) the earlier trademark, liable to be invalidated, had not yet acquired a distinctive character;
(b) invalidity is applied based on identity or similarity of signs and/or goods or services and the earlier trademark had not yet become sufficiently distinctive to support a finding of likelihood of confusion within the meaning thereof;
(c) invalidity is applied based on identity or similarity with an earlier trademark and the earlier trademark has not yet acquired a reputation within the meaning thereof.

Invalidation of trademark registration shall be effective as from the date of the regular filing of the trademark concerned.

Similar to the revocation procedure, invalidity of trademark registration may be applied for:

(a) by judicial way, to the Law Court of Bucharest; or
(b) by administrative way to OSIM.

Equally similar with the revocation procedure, within invalidity procedure the owner of an earlier trademark, or of a sign or earlier right, who has acquiesced for a continuous period of five years in the use, in Romania or in the European Union, as the case may be, of a subsequently registered trademark, while being aware of this use, shall no longer be entitled to apply for invalidity of the later trademark for the goods and services in respect of which such later trademark has been used, unless the registration of the later trademark was sought in bad faith.

Regarding the refusal of a registration of the mark based on absolute ground of refusal, it has been decided[43] that:

> on the other hand, the mere use of the mark has no relevance, but important is that after such use, the sign to have been acquired distinctiveness, this meaning that the public be able to distinguish the goods or services on which is applied from other products or services on the market regarding their origin from a particular commercial source, or the public to recognize its actual ability to identify the origin of that product or service. Consequently, the sign must have acquired secondary meaning through use (secondary meaning – from common law) that allows it to distinguish goods or services which it designates from those of competitors; therefore, therefore must be proved not only simple use but the acquiring distinctiveness of the sign itself.

Registration of a trademark in bad faith is another motive for cancellation, and in this respect, a court decision stated[44] that:

> bad faith, circumscribed to an objective and subjective attitude of the defendant, was analysed in terms of legal relations existing between the parties prior to the request for registration of the mark, as well as of obviously deliberate attitude that led to the decision-maker behaviour identified in the person of its administrator and which has contributed to the trademark registration, not for the purpose for which it was recorded but for a cause regarded as being outside this goal, unfair and thereby illicit. Bad faith, as an undefined concept in the Romanian legislation, should be analysed by antithesis with good faith what was necessary to indicate the relationship between parties according to their commercial nature and thus subject to accurate and fair practices on a commercial plane. The moral foundation of good faith is honesty, whose moral values are loyalty, prudence, temperance and order.

Cancellation of a registration may not be applied for on the grounds that the mark conflicts with an earlier mark if the former satisfies the conditions for revocation, including the assimilation with effective use.

The law provides that the owner of an earlier mark who has acquiesced for a continuous period of five years in the use, in Romania or in the European Union, as the

43. Court of Appeal, Division IX of the civil and intellectual property cases, civil decision No. 152R of 12 Mar. 2009.
44. Court of Appeal, Division IX for civil and intellectual property cases, civil decision No. 34A of 12 Feb. 2009.

case may be, of a subsequently registered trademark while being aware of this use, shall no longer be entitled to apply for invalidity nor oppose the use of the later trademark for the goods and services in respect of which such later trademark has been used, unless the registration of the later trademark was sought in bad faith.

In this case, the owner of the subsequently registered trademark may not oppose the use of the earlier trademark or sign, even if the earlier trademark may no longer be invoked against the later trademark.

In invalidity proceedings of a trademark registration invoking the existence of a registered trademark having an earlier filing date or priority date, upon request of the owner of the later trademark, the owner of the earlier trademark shall furnish proof that, during the five-year period preceding the date of applying for invalidity, the earlier trademark has been put to genuine use, for the goods or services in respect of which it is registered and which are cited as justification for invalidity, or that there are proper reasons for non-use of the trademark, provided that the registration procedure of the earlier trademark has, at the date of applying for invalidity, been completed for not less than five years.

Where, at the filing date or priority date of the later trademark, the five-year period in which the earlier trademark should have been put to genuine use had expired, the owner of the earlier trademark shall, in addition to the proof referred above, furnish proof that the earlier trademark has been put to genuine use during the five-year period preceding the filing date or priority date of the later trademark or that there are proper reasons for non-use.

Failure to furnish the proof referred above, the request for invalidity based on the existence of an earlier trademark shall be rejected.

Where the earlier trademark has only been used, for some of the goods or services for which the trademark is registered, the trademark shall be deemed, for the purpose of examination of the request for invalidity, to have been registered only for those goods or services.

These provisions apply when the earlier trademark is an EU trademark, in which case its genuine use shall be established pursuant to Article 18 of the European Union Trademark Regulation.

If the grounds for invalidity apply only to part of the goods or services for which the mark is registered, the invalidity shall have effect only with respect to such goods or services. Where seniority of a national trademark or of a trademark registered under international agreements is invoked in respect of an EU trademark, invalidity in respect of the trademark providing the basis for the seniority claim may be established after the moment at which the trademark was surrendered or allowed to lapse, provided that the invalidity could have been declared at the time the trademark was surrendered or allowed to lapse. In such a case, the seniority shall cease to produce its effects.

In the case referred to in the previous situation, the owner of the subsequently registered mark may not oppose the use of the earlier mark, even if the earlier mark may no longer be invoked against the later mark. A relevant court decision[45] provides for that:

45. Court of Appeal, Division IX of civil and intellectual property cases, decision No. 217 of 2 Oct. 2008.

to operate forfeiture of the trademark, effective use of the sign is related to the products/services for which the trademark is registered and not the products/services similar or complementary.

308. Any concerned person may apply for invalidity of the registration of a collective mark within a period of five years from the date of registration on any of the grounds referring to relative or absolute grounds of refusal, like the registration was applied in bad faith or the registration infringes a right of personal portrayal or a right to a name or the registration infringes earlier rights acquired in a protected geographical indication or a protected design, other industrial property rights or copyright.

If the registration of the mark has been applied for in bad faith, any concerned person may apply for cancellation of the registration at any time during the term of protection of the mark. The time limit for requesting cancellation of a registration on one of the other grounds shall be five years as from the registration date of the trademark.

309. Any concerned person may apply for invalidity of the registration of a certification mark within five years as from the date of registration:

(a) if any one of the following grounds, relative or absolute grounds of refusal, were valid at the date of registration or the registration infringed an earlier intellectual property right are applicable;
(b) if the mark has been registered with disrespect of the definition of the certification mark.

If the registration of the mark was applied for in bad faith or if the mark was registered by a person lacking the statutory powers to supervise the goods or services, or in the case when the regulations governing the use of the certification mark or the authorization attesting the legal exercise of certification activities were not valid, any concerned person may apply for invalidity of the registration, at any time during the term of protection of the mark.

If a certification mark ceases to be protected, it may not be the subject matter of an application for registration nor used prior to the expiry of ten years as from the date of the termination of protection.

§10. Infringement and Remedies

I. Appeals Against Decisions of the Office

310. OSIM decisions in respect of trademark registration applications as well as in respect of geographical indication registration applications may be appealed against with the Office by any concerned person within thirty days of communication on payment of the prescribed fee.

311. OSIM decisions concerning the entry of transfers of rights in the Trademark Register may be appealed against with the Office by any concerned person within thirty days of communication or, where appropriate, of publication.

Appeals shall be settled by a Board of Appeal within the Legal Directorate of OSIM.

312. The reasoned decision of the Appeals Board shall be communicated to the parties and may be appealed against at the Bucharest Court within fifteen days of its communication. The decision of the Bucharest Court may be appealed against at the Bucharest Court of Appeal within fifteen days of its communication. Decisions of the Bucharest Court given in the cases referred to in articles of the law may be appealed against the Bucharest Appeals Court within thirty days from their notification.

At the request of the judicial body, the OSIM may be required to communicate to such body all acts, documents and information required to settle the dispute submitted to it. Owners must be summoned in every dispute concerning trademarks.

Where a trademark registration, renewal or entry in the Trademark Register contains an obvious procedural error, within two months as from the date of registration or entry, as the case may be, the Office may revoke registration, renewal or entry in a reasoned manner; revocation shall be published in the Official Industrial Property Bulletin.

Invalidity of a trademark or revocation of the owner's rights in respect of the trademark applied for to OSIM, by administrative way, is settled within a specialized board of OSIM, the members of which shall only have competence in settling invalidity or revocation requests, without being involved in any other trademark procedure carried out in OSIM and without interfering with the activity of the Board of Appeal of OSIM, said board consisting of three members with legal expertise.

The reasoned decisions of the board referred to above shall be communicated to the parties within three months of pronouncement and may be appealed against to the Law Court of Bucharest within thirty days of communication.

The decision of the Law Court of Bucharest settling the appeal referred to above shall only be subject to appeal to the Court of Appeal of Bucharest.

II. Infringement

313. In accordance with Article 102 of the Law, it is an offence and shall be punished with imprisonment from three months to two years or with a corresponding fine, the commitment without having the right, of any of the following acts:

(a) infringement of a trademark;
(b) any act of putting into circulation a product bearing a mark identical with or similar to a registered trademark for identical or similar products;
(c) any act of putting into circulation products bearing geographical indications that indicate or suggest that the product concerned is originating from a geographical region other than at the place of origin.

The infringement of a trademark shall mean the pursuit or use without the consent of the proprietor of a third party, in the commercial activity, a sign:

(a) identical to mark for goods or services which are identical with those for which the trademark has been registered;
(b) which, in the light of his identity or his resemblance to a brand name or given identity or a likelihood of products or services which shall be subject to the sign in respect of the products or services for which the trademark has been registered, would result in public's perception a risk of confusion, including the likelihood of association of the mark with the mark;
(c) identical with or similar to mark for products or services other than those for which the trademark is registered, when it has acquired a reputation in Romania and if by use of that sign without a valid reason could take advantage of the distinctive character or brand reputation or use of that sign would cause an injury proprietor of the trademark.

By putting into circulation means providing products or marketing or holding them for this purpose or, as the case may be, offering or provision of the services under the sign, as well as import, export or transit of products under the sign.

The facts referred to in paragraph 1 above shall not constitute criminal offences if they have been committed before the date of publication of trademark.

In the case of an offence provided for in paragraph 1(a) above, reconciliation removes criminal liability.

In an infringement action, upon request of the defendant, the owner of an earlier trademark must furnish proof that, during the five-year period preceding the date of bringing the action, the trademark has been put to genuine use for the goods or services in respect of which it is registered and which are cited as justification for the action, or that there are proper reasons for non-use of the trademark, provided that the registration procedure of the earlier trademark has, at the date of bringing the action, been completed for not less than five years. If such is not the case, the action will be rejected.

If the earlier trademark has been used only for some of the goods or services in respect of which it is registered, it shall be deemed to be registered in respect of only those goods or services.

In infringement actions, the owner of a trademark is not entitled to prohibit the use of a later registered trademark where that later trademark would not be invalidated.

Equally, in infringement actions, the owner of a trademark is not entitled to prohibit the use of a later registered EU trademark where that later trademark would not be declared invalid pursuant to Article 60 of the European Union Trademark Regulation.

Where the owner of a trademark is not entitled to prohibit the use of a later registered trademark, the owner of that later registered trademark shall not be entitled to prohibit the use of the earlier trademark, even though that earlier right may no longer be invoked against the later trademark.

If the reproduction of a trademark in a dictionary, encyclopaedia or similar reference work, in print or electronic form, gives the impression that it constitutes the generic name of the goods or services for which the trademark is registered, the publisher of the work shall, at the request of the owner of the trademark, ensure that the reproduction of the trademark is, without delay, and, in the case of works in printed form, at the latest in the next edition of the work, accompanied by an indication that it is a registered trademark:

> For the purpose of law enforcement, marketing shall mean offering the goods, putting them on the market or stocking them for such purposes under that sign, or providing services thereunder, as well as importing, exporting or conveying them in transit thereunder.

Further on, the Law stipulates that 'the acts referred to previously, committed by an organized criminal group or likely to threaten consumers' safety or health shall be punished by imprisonment of between one and five years and deprivation of certain rights'.

The performance of any act of using the mark in the course of trade by a person not having the consent of the owner of the registered mark shall constitute an infringement. Carrying out or using a sign by third parties in their commercial activity without the consent of the owner of the registered trademark is deemed to constitute infringement of a trademark, if said sign:

(a) is identical with the trademark, in respect of goods or services identical with those for which the trademark is registered;
(b) given the identity with or similarity to the trademark or given the identity or similarity of the goods or services to which the sign is affixed with the goods or services for which the trademark is registered, would produce a likelihood of confusion on the part of the public, including the likelihood of association between the trademark and the sign;
(c) is identical with or similar to the trademark, in respect of goods or services differing from those for which the trademark is registered, where said trademark has a reputation in Romania and where use of that sign without due cause could take unfair advantage of the distinctive character or the reputation of the trademark and cause prejudice to the trademark owner.

Generally speaking, because the mark is associated with the list of goods or services for which it is registered, infringement acts are judged according to these goods or services. This means that, in accordance with the exclusive right to the mark, the use by a third party, in the commercial activity, of a sign that is identical or similar to the registered mark, for identical or similar goods or services, without the consent of the owner, constitutes an infringement.

At the same time, if the mark has been registered for more classes of goods or services and the third party uses an identical or similar sign but only for some of the registered goods or services, the act clearly means an infringement act.

314. In a special situation, are the marks registered in Romania for some classes of goods or services, having a reputation in this country and for which an infringement act means the use of an identical sign for other classes of goods or service, under the circumstances that the use of that sign without due cause could take unfair advantage of the distinctive character or the reputation of the trademark and cause prejudice to the trademark owners.

315. There are several conditions to be met by the act of infringement in order to be classified as such.

The first is that none of the acts referred to in the Law may constitute an infringement if carried out prior to the date of publication of the mark.

Another is that the owner of a mark may institute infringement proceedings only after the date on which the mark was recorded in the National Trademark Register. Proceedings shall be instituted upon a prior complaint by the injured party.

The third condition is that the infringement is a deliberate action done with the concrete goal of misleading the public or putting goods or services on the market with false marks or geographical indications.

Finally, infringement supposes the existence of a competitive environment determined by the principle of the speciality of the mark.

The owner of a mark or, as appropriate, the Ministry of Agriculture and Food, may apply to the competent judicial body to order confiscation or, as appropriate, destruction of products on which the marks or geographical indications have been attached. The provisions of the preceding paragraph shall apply to the material and equipment used directly to carry out the infringements referred to earlier.

Persons found guilty may be required to pay damages, in accordance with the general rules of law, for the prejudice caused by the performance of the acts of infringement.

Any use of marks or geographical indications contrary to honest practice in industrial or commercial activities, with an attempt to mislead consumers, shall constitute an act of unfair competition and shall be liable to imprisonment of between one month and two years or a corresponding fine. Criminal proceedings shall be instituted on a prior complaint by the injured party.

316. Referring to geographical indications, any person who proves a legitimate interest may ask the court to prevent any unauthorized person from using the geographical indication, even if indicated on the goods are the real origin thereof or mention such as kind, type, imitation or any other like.

The geographical indications for wines and spirits may benefit from additional protection. The person authorized to use these indications has the right to prevent the acts of using such indication by any other person for wines or spirits that do not originate from the region suggested by the geographical indication without it being necessary to prove that the consumers were misled or that unfair competition acts were carried out.

317. The owner of the mark or, where appropriate, the Ministry of Agriculture and Food may request the judicial body to order withholding measures if there is the likelihood of infringement by other persons of rights to the mark or protected geographical indication and if such an infringement is likely to cause an irreparable prejudice or leads to the destruction of evidence.

Such withholding measures may be ordered for the purpose of stopping the acts infringing the rights referred to in the preceding paragraph and of safeguarding evidence of the origin of the goods or services to which a mark or a protected geographical indication is unlawfully attached. Withholding measures may be ordered under the conditions set out by the Code of Criminal Procedure.

Provisions regarding withholding shall also apply to materials and equipment used directly for committing the offences referred to in Article 90.

The general rules of law on seizure shall apply to acts that infringe rights to a mark or a protected geographical indication.

The provisions of Articles 581 and 582 of the Code of Civil Procedure shall apply to the withholding measures ordered for the purpose of stopping the infringing acts and safeguarding.

Where the judicial body orders withholding measures, it may require the plaintiff to pay security to an amount that will be determined by the court.

The judicial body may require the plaintiff to provide any evidence at his disposal in order to prove that he is the holder of the right that has been infringed or whose infringement is unavoidable.

Where the evidence submitted in support of the plaintiff's claims is in the possession of the defendant, the judicial body may order the defendant to provide the evidence subject to a guarantee of confidentiality of information in accordance with the law.

The judicial body may order the plaintiff to refund the defendant for any damage caused as a result of an abusive institution of proceedings in relation to a mark or protected geographical indication.

The owner of a mark or, where appropriate, the concerned central specialized public authority may require the infringer to provide recent information on the origin and distribution channel of merchandise to which marks are unlawfully affixed and information on the identity of the manufacturer or merchant and on the quantity of merchandise manufactured, delivered, received or ordered.

In the cases referred to in Article 83, the customs authorities may order, ex officio or at the request of the right holder, the suspension of customs clearance on the import or export of goods to which marks or geographical indications are affixed.

The National Customs Authority shall be competent in enforcing the rights to marks and protected geographical indications at the borders, in accordance with the law.

In the last years, international legislation has imposed some efficient measures aimed at combating the mark and geographical indication infringements through administrative acts or decisions of the lower courts, especially against those third parties which diluted the power of the marks or geographical indications. With this purpose, measures have been taken to combat the users of the marks who, in bad faith, diminish the good name of the marks by using them, for instance, in the Internet domain names, or associate to the marks, goods or services of inferior quality or of a doubtful reputation.

III. Customs Enforcement

318. The very important problem of customs enforcement, which is directly derived from the TRIPS Agreement and European Directives, has been enacted by Law No. 344/2005 on 'Measures to Ensure Compliance with Intellectual Property Rights within Customs Operations.' The law provides a system of supervision, control and intervention of customs bodies within the framework of procedures of customs clearance of goods for the purpose of suspending the customs clearance procedures and retaining the goods liable to infringe intellectual property rights, namely the copyright, the neighbouring rights, the right to registered trademarks for goods or services, the rights to industrial designs or models, the rights to geographical indications, the rights of patents and deriving from supplementary protection certificates for pharmaceuticals and phytosanitarians and plant variety rights.

The goods infringing an intellectual property right are counterfeited goods, pirated goods, goods infringing a patent or a supplementary protection certificate and goods which infringe the right to a geographical indication (Article 1, item 13).

The counterfeited goods are:

(a) any goods including their packing, or which bear, without authorization, a trademark for a good or service which is identical with a lawfully registered trademark, or cannot be distinguished, with regard to its essential elements, from a registered product or service trademark, for same type of good and which, from these reasons infringes the rights of the owners of that mark;
(b) any symbol of a product or service trademark (including logo, label, self-adhesive, brochure, instructions for use or guarantee document bearing such a symbol), even if it is presented separately and which is in the same situation regarding the goods listed under letter (a).

The pirated goods are all copies made without the consent of the right's holder or of the person lawfully authorized by the right's holder in the manufacturing country, directly or indirectly, based upon a good holding the copyright or the neighbouring rights or a right to industrial models and designs if making such copies would constitute an infringement of the intellectual property in question (Article 3, item 12).

A good which infringes intellectual property rights is deemed any pattern or mould designed or adjusted for manufacturing a counterfeited trademark or goods bearing such trademark, for manufacturing pirated goods or goods which infringe a patent, a complementary certificate of protection or a geographical indication, provided that use of such patterns or moulds would prejudice the right holder (Article 3 paragraph 2).

The legal procedures for the intervention of the National Customs Authority are the following:

- If an application for intervention is not applied or during the period of its acceptance, the customs authority may suspend customs clearance and/or retain, for a period of up to three days, goods susceptible to infringe intellectual property rights, if it suspects that the goods are actually infringing an intellectual property right. The customs authority may require the right holder information on the protected right before its notification in relation to a possible violation of intellectual property rights.

- The customs authority notifies the right holder and the declarant/holder destination of the goods, if the latter are known. The period referred to previously runs from the date on which the holder has received the notification; if, within the time limit referred to, the right holder does not file a request for intervention, the customs authority shall raise the measure of detention of goods and/or releases the goods, if other legal requirements are met.
- For the intervention of the customs, the right holder submits a written request to the National Customs Authority. The written request shall contain all relevant information regarding the identity of the right holder, a detailed description of the original goods, specific information on the possible violation of rights, as well as any other information regarding quantities of goods, marketing places, means of transport, countries of fabrication, used routes, specific differences between original goods and counterfeited goods, etc.
- The application for intervention shall be accompanied by:
  - (a) declaration that the right holder assumes responsibility against all persons involved, if the civil action in court or criminal complaint does not follow its course because of an act or omission of the right holder or if the court establishes that the goods do infringe an intellectual property right; in the same statement, the right holder shall agree to bear all costs resulting from keeping the goods under customs supervision, including the costs of destruction of goods;
  - (b) proof that it is the right holder. National Customs Authority assesses application and communicates its decision in writing to the right holder within thirty working days of receipt of the request for intervention.
- The right holder may submit a complaint against the decision to refuse the intervention of the customs authority to the competent administrative court.
- Within fifteen days from the termination of the intellectual property rights in Romania, the right holder shall notify the National Customs Authority thereof.
- If the National Customs Authority accepts the request, it also sets the intervention period up to one year. Upon expiry of this period and subject to payment by the holder of the right of all legal costs by written request, the National Customs Authority may extend the period with another one-year intervention.
- Based on the accepted intervention application and when appropriate, after consultation with the right holder, the customs authority shall retain the goods suspected to infringe intellectual property and/or suspend customs clearance and shall notify in writing on this measure to the right holder and the declarant/holder/consignee of the good. In this case, the goods may be destroyed, if the following conditions are met:
  - (a) the right holder informs the customs authority in writing within ten working days of receipt of notification that the retained goods are infringing intellectual property in the case of perishable goods, the deadline is three working days;
  - (b) the owner submitted to the customs law, within the time limits indicated, the written consent of the declarant/holder/consignee of the goods to abandon the

goods for destruction; the condition is presumed to be satisfied if, within the time limit previously set, the declarant/holder/recipient does not preclude goods expressly in writing, withholds and/or suspends operation of customs or destruction of goods.

- The costs of destruction shall be borne by the right holder.
- If, within ten working days of receiving notification of the detention of the goods and/or suspension of customs operation, the right holder does not prove legal formulation of a civil action or criminal complaints, the customs authority shall release the goods, if other legal requirements are met.
- If the righty holder makes a civil action in court or a criminal complaint, the customs authority shall retain the goods until the court decision becomes final and irrevocable.
- If goods are likely to affect the rights of industrial designs, patents, supplementary protection certificates or plant variety patent, the declarant/holder/recipient of goods has the possibility to obtain the release of the goods and/or granting of the custom clearance release, with the constituting of a guarantee, if the following conditions are met:
  (a) the right holder has filed with the National Customs Authority proof of legal formulation of a civil action or criminal complaint;
  (b) has not been decided by the judicial, the measure of seizure or freezing of goods before the legal period;
  (c) all customs formalities have been fulfilled under the law – If a civil action in court or criminal complaint was formulated in a manner different than at the initiative of the right holder of industrial designs, patents, supplementary protection certificates or plant variety patents, the warranty will be made available if, within twenty working days of notification of the right holder, it makes no evidence of initiating a legal procedure for goods. The term may be extended with another ten working days.
- In order to determine whether an intellectual property right has been infringed, the right holder shall notify the customs authority, in his written request, information regarding the name and address of the declarant/recipient/holder of goods, origin and country of dispatch of goods likely to infringe an intellectual property right, if the customs authority has this information. The right holder who receives this information is not allowed to use it but is allowed to do so for the purposes of the customs proceedings.
- The customs authority will allow the right holder and the declarant/recipient/holder of goods to examine the goods suspected of infringing an intellectual property right, for which has been taken the action of retaining and/or of suspending the operation of customs clearance. Goods which have been proven to infringe an intellectual property right are not allowed to enter or leave the territory of Romania or in/from free zones or free warehouses and cannot be imported, exported, re-exported, or placed under a suspensive customs clearance regime. Such goods may have the following destinations:
  (a) destruction, according to law;
  (b) free of charge delivery, depending on the nature of the goods, to institutions in the field of social care, non-profit organizations or humanitarian associations, associations or clubs, educational institutions or individuals who have

suffered from disasters, whether there is written consent of the right holder and if goods are fit for consumption or use by individuals, under the prohibition not to be commercialized.

- Expenses related to storage, handling and storage of goods under customs supervision and the costs of destruction or other similar expenses are under the responsibility of right holder. Law No. 344/2005 defines the acts of contravention and sanctions, therefore:
  (a) the fact of the declarant/recipient/holder to introduce or remove goods from the territory of Romania goods established as infringing an intellectual property right;
  (b) failure of the right holder of the obligation to communicate to the customs authority about the termination of the right;
  (c) failure of the obligation to not sell the picked-up goods.

The offences are punishable by a fine.

§11. Overlap and Relationship with Other Intellectual Property Laws

319. The overlaps and relationship of the marks with other intellectual property laws are complex. This complexity comes from the role and function of the mark.

I. Overlap with Official Signs

320. The relationship with the official signs as presented in Article 6*ter* of the Paris Convention is provided in Article 5(k) and (l) of the Law, where it is mentioned that the following are excluded from protection and cannot be protected:

(a) marks which contain, without the permission of the competent authorities, reproductions or imitations of armorial bearings, flags, State emblems, signs, official hallmarks of control and warranty, coats of arms belonging to countries of the Union and which are governed by Article 6*ter* of the Paris Convention;
(b) marks which contain, without the permission of the competent authorities, reproductions or imitations of armorial bearings, flags, other emblems, abbreviations, initials or denominations which are governed by Article 6*ter* of the Paris Convention and which belong to international intergovernmental organizations to which one or more countries of the Union are party.

There are also signs that, in accordance with special conventions, are completely excluded from protection, such as the Red Cross or the five interlaced rings of the Olympic symbol.

II. Overlap with Industrial Designs

321. As already mentioned, there are also figurative elements, three-dimensional shapes and, particularly, the shape of goods or packaging thereof, combinations of colours, among the possible protected signs as marks. The condition is that they do not consist exclusively of the shape of the product, which results from the nature of the goods themselves.

The interferences with industrial designs start from the meaning of the expression 'consist exclusively'. In fact, very few shapes consist exclusively of the shape of the product, especially when the product is liquid, as is the case with perfumes, spirits, soda-drinks, etc. This is why, in many situations, the bottles presented in a stylized manner are protected as marks, but at the same time, they are also protected from the point of view of their appearance as industrial designs.

As already stated, the relationship between the mark and the protected rights relating to the image or patronymic name, geographical indications, industrial designs or copyright is legally regulated. As a general rule, it is provided that the owners of earlier rights may file opposition with the Office, with regard to a published mark, within three months from the date of the publication of the mark. The oppositions shall be filed in written form and with the payment of a legal fee.

The opposition is examined by a board of the Office, and if the reasons for applying the opposition are found, the board will decide to reject the registration of the mark.

III. Overlap with Trade Name

322. Because undertakings need to use marks to distinguish their goods and services from those of their competitors, but at the same time also need to distinguish themselves from other undertakings, there is a common function for these two intellectual property objects which sometimes produces confusion among the public.

There is however an important difference between them, residing in the fact that trade names distinguish one undertaking from another, quite independently of the goods or services which the undertaking markets or renders, unlike marks where the goods and services have the function of differentiating them.

If, for protection reasons and in accordance with Article 8 of the Paris Convention, there is no obligation to file or to register a trade name, irrespective of whether it is a part or not of a mark, it is obvious that a trade name may be protected as a mark. In this situation, the protected trade name becomes a mark as well, with all the functions and especially with all the attributes, including enforcement, of a registered sign.

In Romania, the marks and, respectively, the trade names are protected by different laws and institutions. The Registry of Commerce is in charge of the trade names.

Depending on the date of the registration of a trade name and of a mark carrying an identical or similar sign, there are some difficulties in the interpretation of the priority. We believe that, probably, the best solution is to have both industrial property objects protected by the same institution, as is the case in France, Finland, etc.

IV. Overlap with Internet Domain Names

323. Sometimes, the overlap of the trademark with domain names has a rather conflictual root and this is mainly due to the fact that the trademark and domain name are distinctive signs put on the market.[46] However, the domain name is not and cannot be considered synonymous with a trademark. Thus, while a trademark is a sign related to products or services made or performed by the owner which serves to distinguish them on the market in terms of manufacturer, the Internet domain name typically represents the Internet page of the website of a private entity. However, the domain name may still act as a trademark under certain conditions, but it is clear that in order to have the function of a trademark, the domain name *should not* be simply used as an address or location but in a manner similar to the trademark and should identify goods or services of persons or companies claiming that mark. This means that in order to be the subject of trademark registration, domain names should become part of the goods or services referred to their use. Although in the stated purpose, the connection with the domain name may exist in relation to any registered trademark protected on a certain territory, the overlap becomes critical for well-known trademarks for which usually the domain name holder cannot invoke bona fide in case of a dispute, in the sense that it was not aware of a trademark. In the case of well-known trademark marks, the sign constituting the mark is considered to be widely recognized by the relevant segment of public and therefore is predictable the desire of the domain name user, that is, similar or identical with a trademark, to get an undeserved profit from the notoriety of the trademark under discussion. Another difference is that, in general, in order to exercise the exclusive right given by the registered trademark which is a territorial and temporal right, the owner should register the trademark in the country or countries of interest (commercial) so that the sign constituting the mark may be available in some countries but not available in others. Unlike this situation, the domain name is either available anywhere in the world or completely unavailable, and the duration of maintaining the domain name in cyberspace remains basically up to the owner. Finally, another significant difference derives from the fact that in case of domain names, the concept of risk of confusion specific to interference or what often is called as domain name conflict with trademark, has revealed two basic types of casuistry:

(a) a third party deliberately chooses a domain name registration that is similar in nature to create confusion with a trademark whose owner is another person.
(b) we are facing the so-called CyberSquating and the situation has in view in particular the taking over of the domain name, a well-known trademark; the situation has generally as a starting point the desire of the domain name owner to undue profit of the reputation of well-known mark to promote their own interests;
(c) it is not clear whether and to what extent the holder of the domain name registered it in order to put under discussion the exclusive right granted to a trademark holder.

46. Alexandru Cristian Strenc, *Tehnologia informatiei. Protectia si respectarea drepturilor de proprietate intelectuala. Editura Universul Juridic; Colectia Busines* (2010).

In Romania, the registration of a domain name DN is done by the conclusion of a 'Convention for the registration of a domain name' which usually includes a clause for the selection of the applicable law, the competent judicial body and the Arbitration Board.

According to the Registration Rules ROLTD (rule 32), for registration of the domain names and under domain from zone '.ro', the disputes regarding the domain names are governed by the Romanian law, the Bucharest Court being the only one with authorization to solve them. Before going to Court, a dispute may follow a mediation or arbitration way based on the Uniform Dispute Resolution Policy (UDRP) regarding the domain name – UDRP, developed under the auspices of WIPO.

V. Relationship with Unfair Competition Law

324. The relationship with unfair competition law is directly provided in the Law which in Article 86 provides that 'any use of marks or geographical indications contrary to honest practice in industrial or commercial activities, with an attempt to mislead consumers, shall constitute an act of unfair competition and shall be liable to imprisonment of between one month and two years or a corresponding fine'. Criminal proceeding may be instituted upon a prior complaint by the injured party.

The following are considered acts of unfair competition and thus forbidden:

(a) any deed which can cause confusion with the company goods or with the industrial or commercial activity of the competition;
(b) any false statement in exercising the trade, which can discredit the company goods or the industrial or commercial activity of the competition;
(c) indications or statements whose use in exercising the trade can mislead the public with regard to the nature, manner of fabrication or characteristics of the goods.

An unauthorized use referring to the introducing into the circuit of goods bearing registered geographical indications is also an act of unfair competition, if this use can:

(a) affect the reputation of the persons authorized to use the geographical indication; or
(b) cause confusion for the consumers with regard to the real origin of the goods.

At the same time, according to Article 301 of the Criminal Code, the 'use or putting on the market of the goods which are carrying false appellations of origin or indications of provenance ...' represents unfair competition and is punishable with imprisonment of between one month and two years or with a corresponding fine. Having in view the similitude of concepts between appellations of origin and geographical indications, it results that the Criminal Code actually refers to the facts of unfair competition realized by means of geographical indications.

Also relevant for the relationship with unfair competition is Article 2 of the Law 11/1991 on unfair competition, which defines the *act of unfair competition* as being 'any act or fact against the honest practices, in the commercial or industrial activity' and Article 5 of the same law which states that it:

> is an act of unfair competition and shall be liable with imprisonment of between one month and two years or with a corresponding fine:
>
> – the use of a name of a firm, of an emblem, of special designations or of packaging of a nature to mislead regarding those legitimately used by another trader;
> – the production in any way, import, export, depositing, putting on the market or sale of goods carrying false mentions regarding the patents of inventions, the origin or the characteristics of the merchandises … .

It is obvious that the expression 'special denominations' includes marks and geographical indications which, as signs used in bad faith or against honest practices, represent clear acts of unfair competition.

Chapter 5. Trade Names

§1. Sources: Legislation

I. The Legal Framework

325. The trade name is regulated under several domestic laws, as follows: Law No. 26/1990 on the trade register, successively amended, last time modified through the Government Emergency Ordinance No. 52/2008; Law No. 31/1990 on commercial undertakings, as successively amended; Law No. 84/1998 on trademarks; Law No. 11/1990 on fighting against unfair competition; Article 301 of the Criminal Code, etc. The domestic provisions are rounded off by the provisions of the Paris Convention of 1883, which stipulate under Article 8 that the trade name must be protected in every Member State of the Union, even if not submitted to registration requirements.

Under Romanian legislation, the term trade name (of French origin) is equivalent to the term firm (of German origin); both are similarly used. According to Article 30 of Law No. 26/1990, the firm is the name used by an enterprise within the framework of its business and for its signature. Article 31 provides that the firm/trade name of the undertaking – natural person, consists of the name of the tradesman, while Article 31 states that the firm/trade name consists of a distinctive name. The firm must be mentioned in the merchant's application for registration; therefore, it is a *sine qua non* condition for the lawful performance of trade.

It is noted that the above definition of trade name complies with the definition stated by doctrine and other regulations. For example, in French doctrine, the trade name is deemed a sign that distinguishes a trade fund from other similar trade funds,[47] and in the doctrine of the Benelux, it is deemed a sign that brings in customers and is connected with the respective enterprise's business.[48]

As far as the firm of an undertaking is concerned, that of a natural person is called an individual firm and the firm of a company is called a legal firm.

The firm is not the same as the emblem, which is defined under Article 30, paragraph 2 of Law No. 26/1990 as 'the sign or name which distinguishes the merchants of the same class among each other'. The doctrine criticizes this definition, as it is rather similar to the definition of firm, and suggests the return to the definition of the Law of 1931, namely: 'the emblem is the sign or name which distinguishes the enterprises of the same class', with the observation of its specific characters: it consist of an image, alone or combined with a name, it is optional, the merchant can have only one firm, but several emblems and it can be transferred independently from the trade fund. However, it should be noted that both firm and emblem are distinctive signs and are used as identification attributes of an entrepreneur and his enterprise.

47. A. Chavanne & J.J. Burst, *Droit de la proprieté industrielle*, 5e edn (Dalloz, 1998), 805.
48. *Ibid.*

II. The Functions of the Trade Name

326.

(a) To identify a commercial undertaking within trade, financial, and administrative relationships and to distinguish it from other commercial undertakings.
(b) For the signature on legal deeds (Article 30, paragraph 1 of Law No. 26/1990). The legal signature consists of the firm sign and the signature of the persons entitled to represent the company.
(c) A competitive function for bringing in, keeping and increasing the number of customers, as the firm is a sign of recognition of an undertaking in relation to its competitors.[49]
(d) A credit function, as the fame of the firm induces the credit of the commercial undertaking.

III. The Elements of the Trade Name

327. Law No. 26/1990 on the trade register stipulates different rules for the structure of a trade name, depending on the class of the commercial undertaking:

(a) For the tradesman-natural person, the trade name consists of his surname entirely written or his surname and the first letter of his first name, as they are stated in the civil certificates, according to the real name principle (Article 31, paragraph 1). As a consequence, the doctrine states that a pseudonym or a diminutive can be used only as an emblem.[50]
(b) The trade name of an unlimited partnership consists of at least one partner's name and the 'unlimited partnership' name entirely written (Article 32).
(c) The trade name of a mixed liability partnership consists of the name of at least one of the partners who are unlimited liable, with the 'mixed liability partnership' name entirely written (Article 33).
(d) The trade name of a stock company consists of a distinctive name, freely chosen, which can be the name of a partner, a natural person, and the 'stock company' written in full or abbreviated (Article 35).
(e) The trade name of a limited partnership consists of a distinctive name, to which is added the name of one or more partners, and the 'limited partnership' name entirely or abbreviatedly written. Thus, the firm of this class of companies combines the characters of stock companies (legal name) and of the persons' companies (the addition of the name of one or more partners).
(f) The trade name of a Romanian branch of a foreign company consists of the trade name of that company and the headquarters abroad (Article 37).

49. O. Capatana, *The Law of Trade Competition. The Fair Competition* 158 (Lumina Lex 1992).
50. Ion Bacanu, *supra.*

The exposition of the legal provisions on the trade name reflects the limitations relating to its selection. Only the stock companies and the limited partnerships have the right to use a free name, a pseudonym, a first name, or a third party's name, provided that there is no risk of confusion.

IV. Conditions for a Lawful Trade Name

328. A trade name must fulfil four simultaneous requirements in order to be registered in the trade register:

(a) The availability of the trade name. This condition means that the indication chosen as the trade name must not belong to another merchant who previously registered it. According to Article 39, paragraph 2 of Law No. 26/1990 and Article 16 of Law No. 31/1990, the availability of trade name is examined by the trade register Office before drawing up the statutory documents or modifying the trade name, as the case may be. Paragraph 1 of Article 39 sets out the right of the Trade Register Office to reject the application for registration of a trade name which incurs the risk of confusion with other registered trade names. This examination called the research of 'precedent', is focused on the availability as well as the novelty of the trade name, compared with the identical or similar trade names previously registered, in order to ascertain if there is a risk of confusion or not.
The law prohibits registration of companies containing the words 'scientific', 'academic', 'university', 'school' or words derived therefrom and, for company names containing the words 'national', 'Romanian', 'institute' and words derived therefrom or collocations characteristic to public authorities and institutions, registration shall be subject to Government's agreement.
Moreover, no company name may include names used by traders in the public sector.

(b) The distinctiveness of the trade name (Article 38 of Law No. 26/1990), meaning that the chosen name must not be a necessary, generic, descriptive or usual name. The doctrine[51] states the following generic or usual names: 'Bakery', 'Butcher's', 'Greengrocer's', 'Pizza', 'Beer manufacture', if there is no particularizing term, such as names of places: 'Rahova', 'Bragadiru'.
The trade name must be new compared with already registered trade names. However, an absolute novelty is not required, as in the case of patents, but the trade name is only judged by comparison with the competing or potential competing trade names. The absolute novelty is not possible due to the limited vocabulary compared with the great number of commercial undertakings and the tendency of merchants to choose names suggesting their business' object. Likewise, the absolute novelty is also not rational, as the aim is to avoid the risk of confusion with competitors. Therefore, it is deemed that the coexistence of identical or similar trade names is possible if there is no risk of confusion due to the application of the particularity and territoriality principles, as in the case

51. *Ibid.*

of trademarks. For example, there are eleven hotels in Paris called 'Hotel d'Europe', but they are located in different sectors.

The principle of particularity applies to the object of the merchant's business: if there are different objects, there is no risk of confusion and the trade name may be granted. If the businesses' objects are not different, there is a risk of confusion and consequently the trade name cannot be granted.[52]

There are some cases of commercial undertakings with the same trade name in Romania. This provided under the statutory documents is an ample business object compared with the financially deficient means. For example, there are ninety-nine CONDOR and forty-five LION trade names registered at the Bucharest Trade Register, with some derivatives or prefixes, without any reference to the geographical area of use and with the same legal nature as the commercial undertakings. Therefore, the difference is analysed by means of examination of the effectively performed business, which is ascertained according to the classification of the national economy's commerce, approved by Government decision No. 656/1957. The tradesman is obliged to name a main object of business.

The principle of territoriality means the examination of the trade name in comparison with those of the respective registers or with those registered over the whole country. Article 43 stipulates the examination of the earlier trade names on the market within which the merchant performs his business, which can be a regional or national market. As the legislator does not establish the area of research, the merchant must name the territory depending on his predictable business. As a consequence of the above-mentioned issues, it was stipulated under Article 31, paragraph 2 of Law No. 26/1990 that, in case of the similitude of a new trade name with a previous one, a specification must be added, consisting of either a more accurate identification of a person or of his business, or any other particulars. Only well known or famous trade names are excepted and they cannot be used by other merchants, even if there is no risk of confusion due to the depreciation which may be caused to the trade name.

(c) The lawfulness of the trade name. Article 40 of Law No. 31/1990 states that:

> 'no trade name may include a name used by the enterprises of the public domain'. However, this provision is no longer applied, since the private domain is preponderant nowadays, compared with the contrary economic environment of 1990. The lawfulness principle also induces that a trade name cannot be registered if it infringes an imperative legal provision, the public order or the good morals, and the limits of fair competition, in general.

(d) The trade name must be written in the Romanian language (Article 30, paragraph 3) so that the Romanian customers could know it.

52. A. Chavanne & J.J. Burst, *supra*, 815.

V. Registration of the Trade Name

329. The methodological rule No. P.608/773/1990 on trade registers and registrations elaborated by the Romanian Chamber of Commerce and Industry and the Ministry of Justice stipulate under Article 27 the examination of the trade name's availability and under Article 28 the issuance of an evidence acknowledging that the trade name was reserved, by including a list of the previous trade names which are identical or similar to the reserved one. The statutory documents cannot be drawn up without this evidence.

According to Romanian law, the utilization of a trade name does not create a right to it, only if it is well known, in which case its holder can obtain profit from it. With regard to the exceptions, it is dismissed by the rule of the trade name's registration, even though the trade name is an intangible mobile good and, according to Article 1909 of the Civil Code, the person who has possession of the mobile good is presumed to be the owner.

VI. Transfer of the Trade Name

330. The transfer of a trade name is regulated under Articles 41 and 42 of the Law. As a general rule, the trade name can be transferred only together with the trade fund. The Romanian law states three cases:

(1) According to Article 41, paragraph 1, in case of transfer of a trade name consisting of the name of a merchant-natural person, the acquirer of the trade name is entitled to continue the business under the previous trade name, provided that the previous holder or his legal successors expressly agreed to it and that the status of successor is stated within the trade name.
(2) According to paragraph 2 of the same Article, in the case of a trade name consisting of a distinctive name, the previous trade name can be held without the requirement of stating the status of the successor within the trade name.
(3) If the trade name consists of a distinctive name and the name of a partner natural person, the provisions of paragraph 1 shall be applied (Article 41, paragraph 3). The transfer of the trade name is realized in common with the transfer of the trade fund by selling, share contribution, succession and legal liquidation.

A company cannot be alienated separately from the goodwill it is used for.

VII. Termination of the Protection of the Trade Name

331. The exclusive right to the trade name ceases by the cancellation or erasure of the trade name, by renunciation of the trade name or by termination of the trade fund.

§2. THE PROTECTION OF THE TRADE NAME

I. The Legal Nature and the Protection of the Right to the Trade Name

332. According to Article 30, last paragraph of Law No. 26/1990, 'the right of exclusive use to the trade name is acquired by registration in the trade register'. It results that the right to the trade name is deemed a utilization right, which fulfils the characters of an industrial property right.[53] This right can be exploited, rented, transferred or withdrawn by the owner of the trade fund, who may protest against the infringements of third parties. This right has an exclusive character, although it has material and temporal limitations, like all other distinctive signs. By registration of the trade name, exclusive use is granted to the merchant. As a consequence, the merchant who registers a trade name is protected by law against the merchant who previously created and used the same trade name but without registering it. It is noted that the granting system (priority of registration) prevails over the declaring system (priority of use).

The trade name belongs to the class of industrial property rights and is one of the main distinctive signs of a commercial undertaking, besides trademarks and origin indications.

Industrial and intellectual property rights are intangible goods included by a trade fund, as previously exposed.

Due to its importance, the trade name is protected under Civil Law as well as Criminal Law.

333. Civil means of protection. According to Article 25 of Law No. 26/1990, the injured party by registration or a note in the trade register is entitled to require the judge appointed by the tribunal to erase it.

Likewise, if the right on a trade name was infringed, the owner of the right could bring to court an infringement action, requiring the cancellation or the erasure of the unlawful trade name, as well as damages. The infringement may consist of an identical or similar reproduction of an earlier registered trade name or of a fraudulent imitation. The accused may defend himself by asserting that the trade name of the claimant is null.

If the conditions for laying an infringement action are not fulfilled, the interested party may use the unfair competition action as the common action in the field.

According to Article 998 of the Civil Code, the merchant may claim damages on the basis of extra-contractual responsibility.

Article 27 of Law No. 26/1990 establishes that the Chambers of Commerce and Industry are entitled to lay actions or to interfere in any trial on the registration of a trade name or on related mentions, if the legal provisions were infringed.

334. Criminal means of protection. According to Article 301 of the Criminal Code, the utilization of a trade name or of Chambers of Commerce and Industry's

53. Thierry Van Innis, *supra*, 31.

indications in order to mislead the consumers is deemed an act of unfair competition and shall be punished with imprisonment from one month to two years or with a fine.

The same offence is incriminated under Law No. 11/1991 on fighting against unfair competition, which provides in Article 5a that it shall be an offence of unfair competition to utilize a trade name which leads to a risk of confusion with the trade names lawfully used by other merchants, as well as the deeds set out in Article 5b, namely: the production, import, export, storing or selling of goods which bear false mentions with regard to the name of the producer or trader, in order to mislead the other traders and consumers.

The criminal action shall be set in motion at the preliminary complaint of the damaged person or at the request of the territorial Chambers of Commerce and Industry or other entitled bodies (Article 8).

Under Article 48 of Law 26/1990, it is stipulated that 'the person who, ill-intentioned, made inaccurate statements on whose basis an incorporation was made or mention was registered with the trade register will be sentenced to jail from three months to two years, or a fine will be imposed if, according to law, the fact does not represent a more severe infringement of the law'.[54]

Case law shows more and more frequent conflicts between the trade name and the trademark. Romanian law courts have adopted the decision made on 11 September 2007 by the ECJ in the case C-17/06 (Celine) under which the trademark prevailed against the trade name as a consequence of the risk of confusion between them. In case of identity with an earlier trademark, the owner of a trade name has no defence unless he can prove his good faith behaviour.

54. *See* the civil decision No. 1173/2010 of the High Court of Cassation and Justice, Civil and Intellectual Property Section, published in RRDPI No. 4/2010, 184 and ff.

Chapter 6. Designs

§1. Sources: Legislation

I. National Sources

335. Historically speaking, the protection of industrial or handmade designs began by granting some 'privileges' to the rulers, for a determinate period, forbidding the exploitation by third parties.[55] For example, we could mention that the ruler Alexandru Moruzi granted in 1800 a 'privilege' to Stanila for a 'work room of head clothes, bundles, quilts, pillows, blankets … up to fifteen years, starting this term from the contingent 28 May 1800'.

336. (a) The Industrial Designs Law No. 129 was promulgated by the President of Romania by the Decree No. 246 of 29 December 1992.

Adopted by the Senate at its session of 22 December 1992 and by the Chamber of Deputies at its session of 23 December 1992, the law was published in the Official Gazette of Romania, Part I, No. 1 of 8 January 1993, the date on which, according to the Constitution of Romania, it entered into force.

Republished within the meaning of Article IV of Law No. 280/2007 for amending and completing the Industrial Design Law No. 129/1992, published in the Official Gazette of Romania No. 729 of 26 October 2007, the texts are being given a new numbering. Law No. 129/1992 was also republished in the Official Gazette of Romania, part. I. No. 193 of 26 March 2003 and it has also been modified by the Emergency Government Ordinance No. 190/2005 for taking some measures necessary in the European integration process, published in the Official Gazette of Romania, part I, No. 1179 of 28 December 2005, approved with the corresponding amendments and completions by Law No. 332/2006, published in the Official Gazette of Romania, part. I, No. 629 of 20 July 2006.

The law has been recently amended and republished in the Official Gazette of Romania, part. I No. 242 of 4 April 2014, by incorporating the relevant provisions of Law No. 76/2012 on enforcing the amendments to the Code of Civil Procedure and consequently of Law No. 187/2012 on enforcing the amendments to the Criminal Code.

Law No. 129/1992, as republished, is structured in seven chapters, namely: Chapter 1 – General provisions; Chapter 2 – Requirements for the protection of industrial designs; Chapter 3 – Registration and grant of the title of protection; Chapter 4 – Rights and obligations; Chapter 5 – Community designs; Chapter 6 – Responsibilities of the OSIM in the field of industrial designs protection; Chapter 7 – Liabilities and sanctions.

337. (b) Implementing Regulations of the Design Law No. 129/1992 (as republished) was approved by the Government Decision No. 211 on 27 February 2008 and was published in the Official Gazette of Romania No. 181 on 10 March 2008.

55. Gheorghe Bucsa, L. Bulgar & T. Popescu, *Industrial Property Protection in Romania and Preventing Infringement* (OSIM Publishing House 1994).

The Regulations are structured in six chapters, as follows: Chapter 1 – Requirements for protection; Chapter 2 – The right to registration certificate; Chapter 3 – The registration proceeding; Chapter 4 – Rights and obligations; Chapter 5 – Appeal against OSIM decisions; Chapter 6 – Transitional and final provisions.

338. (c) The Governmental Ordinance on fees in the industrial property protection field and the conditions for using the same, No. 41 of 30 January 1998, published in the Official Gazette No. 43 of 30 January 1998 and entered into force on 2 March 1998.

Republished within the meaning of Article IV of Law No. 381/2005 for amending and completing the Government Ordinance No. 41/1998 on the fees in the industrial property protection field and the conditions for using the same, published in the Official Gazette of Romania, part I, No. 6 of 4 January 2006, with a new renumbering of the texts.

Government Ordinance No. 41/1998 on the fees in the industrial property protection field and the conditions of using the same was published in the Official Gazette of Romania, part I, No. 43 of 30 January 1998, was rectified in the Official Gazette of Romania, part I, No. 90 of 26 February 1998 and was amended by:

- Law No. 383/2002 for the approval of the Government Ordinance No. 41/1998 on the fees in the industrial property protection field and the conditions for using the same, published in the Official Gazette of Romania, part I, No. 471 of 2 July 2002 and corrected in the Official Gazette of Romania, part I, No. 691 of 20 September 2002.
- Law No. 381/2005 for amending and completing the Government Ordinance No. 41/1998 on the fees in the industrial property protection field and the conditions for using the same, published in the Official Gazette of Romania, part I, No. 6 of 4 January 2006.

II. International Sources

339. As international sources, we mention:

(a) The Paris Convention for the protection of industrial property of 20 March 1883, to which Romania acceded by Decree No. 1176/1968.
(b) The Berne Convention for the protection of literary and artistic works, of 9 September 1886, to which Romania first acceded in 1926, and in 1998 to the Paris Act by Law No. 77 of 8 April 1998.

Among the provisions of this Convention, we mention those that especially relate to industrial designs: Article 2.7 provides:

> as regards works protected solely as industrial designs in the country of origin, only the special protection granted to industrial designs in this country may be

claimed in another country of the Berne Union; nevertheless, if such special protection is not granted in these States, the works shall be protected as artistic works.

The first part of this provision represents a derogation from the principle of national treatment in favour of the principle of reciprocity and the second part of Article 2.7 represents a sanction for the States that do not protect the industrial designs:

- The Hague Agreement concerning the International Registration of industrial designs, of 6 November 1925, to which Romania acceded by Law No. 44 of 28 April 1992.
- The Locarno Agreement establishing an international classification for industrial designs, of 8 October 1968, to which Romania acceded by Law No. 3/1998.
- The Agreement on Trade-Related Aspects of Intellectual Property Rights, known as the TRIPS Agreement (Annex 1C of the Marrakech Agreement on the establishment of the WTO), to which Romania acceded by Law No. 133/1994.

§2. Subject Matter of Protection

I. Categories of Designs That May Be Registered

340. Law No. 129/1992 gives the definitions for design and product as follows:

- a design is the appearance of a product or of a part thereof in two or three dimensions, resulting from the combination of the main features, particularly lines, outlines, colours, shape, texture and/or materials of the product itself and/or its ornamentation;
- a product is any article produced through an industrial or handicraft process containing, *inter alia,* elements designed to be assembled in a complex product, packages, forms of presentation, arrangements, graphic symbols, or typographic symbols; the computer programs shall not be deemed as a product.

Taking into consideration these definitions established by Law and the fact that Romania acceded to the Locarno Agreement by Law No. 3/1998, we can mention the following categories of designs:

- foodstuffs, articles of clothing, footwear and accessories, personal belongings;
- textile piece goods, furnishing and accessories, household goods and hardware, packages and containers;
- measuring, checking and signalling instruments, industrial machines and equipment;
- articles of adornment, optical apparatus, musical instruments;
- artist's, teaching and office materials and equipment;
- sales, advertising and indicator signs, equipment and materials;
- games, toys and sports goods;

- medical and laboratory equipment, pharmaceutical products, cosmetics and toilet articles;
- constructions, building units elements, lightning apparatus;
- articles for the care and handling of animals.

II. Designs Excluded from Protection

341. The Designs Law does not allow the protection of designs in two situations:

(1) If the appearance of the designs is determined by a technical function.
(2) If the purpose or appearance of these designs is contrary to morality or public policy.

342. We mention that these categories of designs excluded from protection are also provided for in the TRIPS Agreement (Article 25) as well as in Directive No. 98/71/EC.

§3. CONDITIONS OF PROTECTION

I. Formal Conditions

A. Constitution of the Regular National Filing

343. A first condition to ensure the protection is to file with the OSIM an application for registration of the design, comprising the established necessary particulars, accompanied by annexes. Filing of the application and the constitution of the regular national filing is, actually, an attributive act of rights, as the sole modality to obtain the exclusive right of exploitation on the territory of Romania, as the law establishes a provisional protection, starting on the date on which the regular filing was constituted, and the rights deriving from the application for registration of the design may be transferable wholly or in part.

344. The regular national filing ensures a right of priority to the applicant, starting on the date on which it was constituted, related to any other later filing regarding the same design.

The regular national filing constitutes:

(a) request for the registration of design;
(b) applicant's identification data;
(c) number of designs for which protection is claimed;
(d) indication of the products which incorporate the design, if appropriate;
(e) description of the novel characteristic elements of the design for which protection is claimed, as they appear in the filed graphical representations;

(f) the authors' names or a statement on the applicant's responsibility that the authors have waived their right of being mentioned in the application and/or in the design publications;
(g) graphical representations of the design in three copies.

The application for registration may further contain, if appropriate, other elements which do not represent a condition for the regular deposit date:

(a) identification data of the professional representative, if designated in the application for registration;
(b) priority documents, if one of the priorities provided for in Articles 16 and 17 is claimed;
(c) request for deferment of publication;
(d) power of attorney for representation before OSIM;
(e) statement indicating the information which, according to the applicant's knowledge, allows to prove the fulfilment of the conditions to grant the protection for the design whose registration is claimed.

The application for registration of the design shall be written in Romanian and typed in two copies on a printed standard form, compulsorily comprising the following: the personal particulars of the applicant, of the creator, the express request for the issue of a certificate of registration, the denomination of the product in which the design is intended to be incorporated, the denomination of the industrial design, the brief description of the new characteristic elements regarding exclusively the external aesthetic appearance.

The application may also comprise other particulars, such as: the name of the authorized agent, the claimed priorities according to the Paris Convention, the request for postponing the publication of the industrial design.

345. The application may comprise up to a hundred industrial designs intended to be incorporated in the same category of products and belonging to the same class and sub-class of the International Classification, thus constituting a multiple filing.

346. Implementing Regulations of Law No. 129/1992 specify that the brief description of the design shall be made directly on the application or on signed and stamped annexes and shall exclusively comprise the new characteristic elements of the external aesthetic appearance that appear in the reproductions enclosed with the application (a hundred words maximum). The description shall not comprise: technical or functional details, technical characteristics, dimensions, reference points. At the same time, its field of use shall be specified, especially for industrial designs that cannot be identified according to the denomination of the product.

347. The graphical reproductions that are filed at the same time as the application may be:

(a) black-and-white or colour photographs, meeting professional quality standards with an adequate contrast in order to be reproduced by printing methods;

(b) black-and-white or colour graphic reproductions, meeting professional quality standards, performed with drawing instruments, in China ink on tracing paper or on high quality white paper;
The design shall be preferably represented in perspective, without any other accessories (persons, animals, etc.). The minimum size of the graphic reproductions shall be 60 mm × 60 mm or a multiple thereof of 180 mm × 240 mm maximum, and the original copies shall be signed and, as the case may be, stamped by the applicant of the application for registration. If the same product is represented in several positions or different angles, the numbering shall comprise two figures separated by a period (e.g., 1.1, 1.2, 1.3, etc. for the first product and 2.1, 2.2, 2.3, etc. for the second product). This numbering shall be mentioned on the original copy.
Other documents enclosed the application that do not condition the date of national filing, provided for in the Implementing Regulations to Law No. 129/1992.

(c) the power of attorney. If the application for registration of the industrial design is filed by an authorized agent, under his signature, it is necessary to file an original power of attorney, under the private signature of the applicant, at the same time as the application or, within fifteen days at the latest, on the date on which the application was filed. The applicant may designate an authorized agent after the filing of the application. The power of attorney shall mention the subject matter of the application (denomination of design) and shall specify the name, first name and address of the signatory of the power of attorney. For foreign persons, the representation by an authorized agent is compulsory, according to Article 3 of the OSIM's Instructions, the power of attorney being written in Romanian or in an international language;

(d) priority documents: certificate of priority, certificate of guarantee. If one or several priorities have been claimed in the application for registration of the industrial design, according to Articles 16, 17 and 18 of the Law, it is necessary to file one or several original priority documents, within three months at the latest, from the date on which the application was filed. Failure to file the priority documents shall determine the non-recognition of claimed priority. The conditions to recognize the claimed priority are identical to those provided for in the Paris Convention for the protection of industrial property:
   - the application shall be filed within six months at the latest from the date of the claimed priority;
   - the claim shall be made at the same time as the filing of the application;
   - it shall be confirmed by priority documents within three months and the fees of priority shall be paid;
   - the design for which the priority is claimed, represented in the priority documents, shall be identical to the design for which the protection is required. All these conditions are cumulative. The certificate of priority, necessary to recognize the priority of first filing, according to the Paris Convention, is a document issued by an Industrial Property Office, by which the constitution of the regular filing is confirmed in one of the countries of the Paris Union, attesting the date of registration and the authenticity of the enclosed regular filing.

The certificate of guarantee is a document necessary to claim the priority of exhibition, issued by the institution that organized the exhibition, by which it is confirmed that the article for which protection has been requested was really and statutorily exhibited. The certificate of guarantee shall comprise: the denomination of the issuing institution, respectively of the organizer of the exhibition, the denomination of the exhibition; the place and duration of the exhibition; the personal particulars of the natural or legal person who put the industrial design on display at the exhibition; the certificate that the article was really and statutorily exhibited and the duration of display; the number and date of the issue of the certificate; the signature of the organizer of the exhibition. The certificate of guarantee shall include, as enclosed, the graphical representation of the displayed design as well as a brief description thereof.

(e) authorization to invoke priority is the necessary document in case the applicant of the application for registration of the design invokes a right of priority which belongs to another person. The authorization shall certify that the applicant is entitled to invoke the priority of first filing, after the owner has transmitted the right of priority;

(f) the solemn declaration of the creators is the declaration given by them, on their own responsibility, that they are the creators of the designs that constitute the subject matter of the application;

(g) the contract of assignment or the declaration of assignment represents the legal basis upon which the registration of the design may be made by another natural or legal person and not by the creator.

We would like to underline that, in accordance with Article 15 of Law No. 129/1992, the filing has an 'attributive' character, ensuring a right of priority to the applicant related to any other later filing. The filing is also attributive in the legislation of other States, for example, in the Italian, Polish, Hungarian legislation as well as in the uniform legislation of Benelux.

348. Another important element that has to be underlined is the fact that the proceeding to constitute the national filing allows for keeping the confidential character of the design by postponing the publication of the application for registration for a period of thirty months at the most, at the applicant's request:

- The duration of the period to keep the confidential character of the industrial design is an issue much debated upon in the doctrine[56] and we mention that.
- The London Act of 2 June 1934 of the Hague Agreement concerning the international deposit of industrial designs stipulates, in Article 8, that it is accepted that, during the first period of protection of five years, the filing shall be secret, respectively, in a closed envelope (Soleau system).
- The Hague Act of 28 November 1960 of the Hague Agreement stipulates, in Article 6.4a, that the publication of graphic reproductions of the filing may be postponed during a period of twelve months at the most, at the applicant's

56. Gheorghe Bucsa, *Protection of Design: Case Law* (OSIM, Publishing House, 2008).

request. Consequently, the period to keep the secret character of the industrial design has been reduced from five years to one year.
- The Geneva Act of the Hague Agreement stipulates, in Article 10.4 that the International Bureau shall keep in a secret regime any international application and any international registration, up to the publication. At the applicant's request, the publication of the filing may be postponed for a period of thirty months.

The duration of the period to keep the secret character of the design, respectively, by postponing the publication, is differently regulated from country to country, some States having a larger period and other States having a shorter period.

At a worldwide level,[57] the formal conditions vary depending on the legislation of the respective States, being, generally, similar to those of Romania. In a study realized by the WIPO,[58] it is mentioned that: some States allow specimens at the filing of application; some States do not compulsorily request the disclosure of creators, and some other States do not allow that an application comprises several designs.

B. Regime of Fees

349. According to the regulations into force (Government Ordinance No. 41/1998), all proceedings regarding the applications for registration of the design, as well as the maintenance into force of the certificate for registration, are subject to the payment of fees. The fees shall be paid into the OSIM's account in full amounts and within the provided legal time limits.

The registration of as many versions of designs as possible in one application is supported, and for the fees of registration and examination from the second industrial design onwards a reduction of fees to about 50% is perceived.

The reduction of fees provided for in Romanian legislation shall apply if the applicant is a natural person who has not taken over or transmitted his right up to the date of the payment of fees and has had a gross monthly average income during the last twelve months, less than five times the overall gross income. In this case, the applicant may benefit from a reduction and shall pay only 50% of the following fees: registration of the application in the National Register of Applications, publication of the industrial design, examination of the application for registration, issue and maintenance into force of the certificate of registration during the first five years.

The legal entities shall pay only 50% of each due amount if the rate of their turnover for the preceding financial year is less than the equivalent in RON of EUR 2 million.

---

57. Anne Marie Greene & Elizabeth Hanellin, *Designs and Utility Models Throughout the World* (Clark Boardam Callaghan Publishing House, 1996).
58. WIPO, *Manual Regarding the Information and Search in the Industrial Property Field* (WIPO 1995). Study on the proceedings and exigencies in the filing field, methods of examination and proceedings of publication in the industrial designs field.

II. Substantive Conditions

350. Analyzing Article 6 of the Industrial Designs Law provides that the object of the application may be registered to the extent in which it constitutes a design, within the meaning of Article 2, is new and has individual character; one may come to the conclusion that there are three substantive conditions to grant the protection: the definition of a design, the novelty and the individual character. These conditions are cumulative.

The first condition, defining the notion of design emphasizes the fact that the subject matter of protection shall be the appearance of a product or of a part thereof, in two or three dimensions, resulting from the combination of the main features, particularly lines, outlines, colours, shape, texture and/or materials of the product itself and/or its ornamentation. In other words, the subject matter of protection shall be the appearance of the product.

The second condition, 'the novelty', provides that a design shall be regarded as new if it was not made available to the public, at home or abroad, in respect of the same category of products, prior to the date of the regular filing or of the recognized priority.

This condition may be considered absolute in time and space, as the law does not stipulate a limit on time or for a specific geographical area – the only exception provided for in the law being the disclosure deriving from the creator or his successor in title, made within twelve months from the date on which the application was registered.

We may consider this condition as also relative, as the novelty of a design cannot be, practically, absolute, totally separated from other known forms. It can be taken into consideration, almost in the totality of cases, that the novelty of a design derives from the particular, original, unique character of the combination of some known elements.

In Article 4 of Directive 98/71/EC, it is mentioned that a design is regarded as new if, at the date of submission of the application for registration or of the claimed priority, no other identical design had been made available to the public. The designs are regarded as identical if their characteristics are different only by insignificant details.

French Law dedicates in Article L511–6 of the Intellectual Property Code that the publicity of a design, prior to the filing date, by its putting up for sale or any other method, shall entail the non-granting of protection.

In Italy, the protection is not granted if the design is made available to the public by use, by written publicity or verbal description as well as by any other methods.

In the doctrine,[59] it is mentioned that the novelty may be the result of an original combination of some known elements and it is not necessary that each part of the design be new.

In some States, for example, England, the novelty is not limited in time, but to the exclusive territory of Great Britain. Therefore, the novelty cannot be destroyed by foreign publications or by use in other States.

---

59. Yolanda Eminescu, *Protection of Industrial Designs* (Lumina Lex Publ. House 1993). Christine Fellner, *Industrial Design Law* (Sweet & Maxell 1995).

The third condition, 'the individual character' must be analysed as follows:

- a design shall be deemed to have individual character if the overall impression it produces on the informed user differs from the one produced by such user by any design rendered available to the public before the date of filing the application for registration or before the priority date, if the priority was claimed; but;
- in assessing the individual character, the degree of freedom of the author in developing the design shall be taken into account.

At the same time, substantive conditions may be considered those provided for in Articles 8 and 9 of the Law, respectively that:

- Designs determined exclusively by a technical function cannot be registered.
- Designs contrary to public order and morality shall be excluded from the protection.

§4. Formalities: Procedure for Grant and Obtaining Protection

351. In Romania, the protection of industrial designs is ensured according to the attributive system of rights, respectively, as the result of a substantive examination of the application for registration. The main steps in the proceeding for registration are the following: preliminary examination, publication of the application, opposition by third parties, substantive examination of the applications filed nationally and of the international applications for which Romania has been designated, analysis of the application by a board and the taking of a decision by the commission, issue of the certificate of protection.

I. Preliminary Examination

352. This proceeding is accomplished according to Article 18 of the Implementing Regulations and supposes a complex analysis of the application, from which it shall result:

- the fulfilment of formal conditions of the application provided for in Article 10 of Law No. 129/1992, respectively, if the application comprises the personal particulars of the applicant and of the creator, the title of the industrial design, including the indication of the product in which the industrial design is intended to be incorporated; if there is a brief description of the characteristic elements of the industrial design and graphical representations have been filed;
- the fulfilment of the conditions provided for by graphical representations, especially their professional quality;
- the right of the applicant to the issue of the certificate according to Article 3 of Law No. 129/1992;
- that the authorized agent is entitled to represent the applicant before the OSIM;
- the payment of fees to the full amounts and within the provided legal time limits;

– that all necessary deeds and documents provided for by the legislation into force have been enclosed with the application.

If irregularities regarding the fulfilment of conditions provided for by the Law and the OSIM's Implementing Regulations are found in the preliminary examination, they shall be notified to the applicant, allowing him a time limit for remedies.

If all the above-mentioned conditions provided for by the legislation in force are fulfilled, the Regular National Filing shall be constituted which shall be registered in the National Register of Applications.

II. Publication of Applications

353. The application for registration of the design and the graphic reproductions thereof, for which the regular national filing was constituted, shall be published in the BOPI – Industrial Designs section not later than four months from the date on which the application was filed at the OSIM. For each application for registration, the bibliographic data, harmonized at national level with the relevant data published in the International Designs Bulletin, issued regularly by WIPO from Geneva, shall be published.

The bibliographic data published together with the registration application of the design, indexed by the INID codes as standardized under the auspices of WIPO, are the following:

(1) The number of the national filing. (22) The date of the national filing.
(2) The date of publication.
(3) The name and address of the applicant. (74) The name and address of the authorized agent. (72) The name of the creator.
(4) The denomination of the industrial design. (28) The number of industrial designs. (51) LOC(9) Cl.
(5) Description of the design.[60]
(6) The number of the international filing. The date of the international registration.
(7) The date of the international publication.
(8) The claimed priority. (33) The country. (32) The date. (31) The number of the certificate.

The graphical representations shall be published, in the dimensions requested by the applicants, in black-and-white or, upon request, in colour.

60. The description of the characteristic elements of the industrial design shall be published at the applicant's request.

III. Opposition by Third Parties

354. Any interested person may file objections (oppositions) regarding the registration of the design within two months from the date of its publication in the BOPI – Industrial Designs section, according to Article 21 of Law No. 129/1992.

The opposition shall be made in writing and shall be grounded on enclosed official documents (booklets, books, magazines, prospectus, etc.), published prior to the date of the regular national filing of the design (the date that shall be registered on the official documents), indicating exactly the design having as subject matter the opposition, according to the OSIM's Implementing Regulations.

The oppositions shall be filed directly at the OSIM's General Registry, by mail or telefax, together with the proof of the payment of the provided legal fee. As a rule, the applicants to whose applications for registration of industrial designs oppositions have been filed, shall be notified in writing, asking their opinion within a term of a maximum of thirty days for the applicants residing in the country and for the applicants residing abroad.

IV. Substantive Examination

355. The substantive examination of the application for registration of the design is an elaborate analysis having as a purpose of emphasizing whether the conditions provided for by the law to grant the protection are fulfilled, especially if the subject matter of the application refers to the appearance of an industrial product, the industrial design satisfies the condition of absolute novelty and has an individual character. At the same time, it shall be verified if the subject matter of the application complies with the provisions of Articles 8 and 9, respectively: the design does not have an appearance determined exclusively by a technical function and it is not contrary to morality or public policy.

Implementing Regulations mention that, during the examination of the application, the Examination Board shall establish that the designs are not new, if they do not significantly differ from the known designs. The destruction of the elements of novelty shall be grounded on published documents (booklets, books, magazines, prospectus, etc.) prior to the date of the regular national filing of the design, provided that the design be totally visible.

In the doctrine,[61] it is mentioned that the association type 'mosaic' from two or three documents is not allowed for the destruction of the novelty.

In order to evaluate the characteristic elements of novelty, the industrial design shall be examined as a whole, in its totality, as presented in the published graphical representations.

In a study published by WIPO,[62] the following aspects are mentioned regarding the examination of novelty of the applications of designs:

61. Christine Fellner, *Industrial Design Law* (Sweet & Maxwell 1995).
62. WIPO, *Intellectual Property Reading Manual* 229 (WIPO Publication 1998).

- some States perform this examination systematically for all applications (Australia, England, Bulgaria, Canada, Chile, Czech Republic, Denmark, Finland, Hungary, Japan, Republic of Korea, Portugal, Russia, Romania, Sweden, USA, etc.);
- other States examine the novelty in the case of an opposition, taking into consideration the material provided by the opponent (Spain, Sweden, Romania, etc.).

V. Taking the Decisions

356. The decision to accept the application for registration – thus, to grant the protection or to reject the application, shall be taken by a Board of Specialty within the 'Industrial Designs' Division of the OSIM within twelve months at the most from the date on which the application was published. All decisions shall be substantiated.

If we take into consideration the fact that the publication of the application shall be made within a time limit of four months maximum from the date on which the regular filing was constituted, and the decision shall be taken within a time limit of twelve months at the most from the date on which the application was published, it results that the decision of acceptance or rejection of the application shall be taken within sixteen months at the most from the date of the regular filing.

The registration of accepted designs shall be made in the National Register of Designs and shall be published in the BOPI – Designs section.

As a rule, the OSIM shall notify the decision of the commission to the applicants of the applications for registration of the industrial designs within a maximum of thirty days from the date on which it was taken.

For failure to comply with the conditions provided for in the law regarding the conditions to grant the protection, the OSIM may revoke its decisions ex officio, according to Article 23 of the Law.

VI. Issuance of Certificates of Protection

357. According to Article 27 of the Law, the issuance of certificates of protection, respectively, of certificates of registration of designs shall be made by the OSIM within a maximum of thirty days from the date on which the acceptance decision became final.

§5. Right to the Industrial Design: Ownership and Transfer of Right

358. A. The right to the design is stipulated in Romanian Law as belonging to the creator of the design or to his successor in title (Article 3) for a design created in an independent way.

When more than one person has created the same design independently of each other, the right to the issue of the certificate shall belong to the one who first filed the application for registration at the OSIM or to the person whose application has the earliest priority date.

Where the creators of the designs are employees, the law provides that the right to the issue of the title of protection – the certificate of registration of the design – may belong both to the employees and to the employer, depending on the contractual provisions. In absence of more favourable contractual provisions for the creator, the right to the issue of the certificate of registration shall belong to the employer, when the designs are made during the execution of a contract of employment that provides for a creative activity that corresponds to his actual duties.

For this situation, the law provides that, in absence of an agreement between the parties on the contract price, the latter shall be established by the judicial courts according to the common law.

359. B. The transfer of rights regarding the designs is expressly provided for in Law No. 129/1992 (in Article 38) which also emphasizes the rights liable to be transferable, either wholly or in part:

(1) the rights deriving from the application for registration of the design;
(2) the right to the issue of the certificate of registration of the design;
(3) the rights deriving from the issued certificate of registration.

Law No. 129/1992 specifies the legal means by which the transfer of rights may be effected, namely: assignment, exclusive or non-exclusive licence, legal or testamentary succession.

In order to produce effects for third parties, Article 38 of the Law mentions the obligation that the transfer of rights be registered at the OSIM. In this case, the transfer shall produce effects for third parties from the date of its registration at the OSIM in the National Register of Applications or, as the case may be, in the National Register of Designs. The registration at the OSIM of the transfer of rights regarding the designs shall have as effect also the right of assigner (from the date of registration) to take an action against third parties in actions of infringement, unfair competition or damages.

Taking into consideration the provisions of the legislation in the designs field, we can conclude that the moment of the transfer of rights to designs may be:

(a) prior to the filing of the application for registration at the OSIM:
  - prior to the creation of the design;
  - after the creation of the design.
(b) at the same time as the filing of the application for registration at the OSIM;
(c) after the filing of the application for registration at the OSIM:
  - prior to the examination of the application;
  - after the examination of the application but before the issue of the certificate of registration.
(d) after the issue of the certificate of registration.

I. Assignment

360. The assignment is a means of transfer of rights regarding the designs, provided for by Law No. 129/1992 (Article 38), effected, as a rule, by a written contract (especially because of the obligation to be registered at the OSIM), where is mentioned the intention agreement of the contracting parties (assignor and assignee) regarding the obligations they freely decide to assume.

The assignment of rights to designs may be wholly or in part when the assignor wishes to keep a part of his rights and transfer to the assignee only some rights (e.g., the exclusive right of exploitation on a certain territory).

The assignment of rights to industrial designs may be effected prior to the filing of the application for registration at the OSIM, at the same time as its filing, as well as after the filing of the application or after the issue of the certificate of registration.

II. Licence

361. The licence is the authorization given by the right's owner to the design (licensor) to a natural or legal person (licensee) to exploit the design in some conditions established, as a rule, on a written contract (the written form is imposed by the legal obligation to be registered at the OSIM in order to produce effects for third parties). The right of exploitation by licence may be transferred in exchange for financial advantages granted to the licensor (payment or due), and in such a case, it is an onerous licence or without payment, thus a free licence.

Law No. 129/1992 stipulated that the transfer may be done by exclusive licence by which the licensor shall be obliged to grant no more licences to other persons or by non-exclusive licence by which the licensor is entitled to grant licences to other persons.

Taking into consideration the provisions of Article 38 of Law No. 129/1992 which stipulates that the rights are transferable wholly or in part, the licensor may grant:

- a total licence (right of total exploitation, without any limitation);
- a partial licence (right of partial exploitation, limited in time, space, number of designs, number of products or other limitations).

III. Legal or Testamentary Succession

362. Law No. 129/1992 stipulates that the transfer of rights to designs shall be effected also by legal or testamentary succession.

The legal succession appears in case of the decease of the right's owner, natural person, and, in absence of a Will, the rights to designs shall be transferred to the legal successors.

The testamentary succession appears in case of the death of the right's owner, natural person, and the persons who will benefit from all rights regarding the industrial designs mentioned in the Will.

§6. Scope of Exclusive Rights, Content and Rights

363. The Designs Law confers to the owner of the certificate of registration of the industrial design the following rights: the exclusive right of exploitation, the right to the issue of the certificate of registration, the priority right, the right to forbid third parties from performing, without his consent, acts that infringe his right of exploitation, the right to apply the 'D' sign on the product, the right to transfer, wholly or in part, the rights deriving from the certificate of registration, the right to damages for the caused prejudices.

364. The exclusive right of exploitation of the design is an economic right, exclusive and absolute, but limited in time and space.

It is an exclusive and absolute right, since only the owner may benefit from the right to use the industrial design, exclusively and absolutely. Nevertheless, this exclusive right is transferable to some third parties.

365. A. Subject matter of the right. The subject matter of the exclusive right of exploitation is the design as presented in the graphic reproductions.

The new appearance of a product having an individual character utilitarian function may be registered, respectively protected as a design, thus the protection shall be granted for the appearance of the product and not for the respective product.

We should emphasize the fact that an aesthetic or ornamental creation per se, not applied to a certain product, shall not be protected according to Law No. 129/1992, this requirement being determined by the specification that the application for registration of the design shall expressly comprise the 'statement of article or articles in which the design is intended to be incorporated' (Article 12).

At the same time, the law provides that the design whose appearance is determined by a technical function shall not be registered, thus the protection shall not be granted for technical or technological effects determined by the appearance of the respective product.

The legislation also provides that the brief description of the characteristic elements of the design and the graphic reproductions thereof shall be enclosed within the application in order to constitute the regular national filing.

As a synthesis, we may conclude that the scope of the protection is determined by the external appearance of the product, as presented in the graphical representations and explained in the brief description of the characteristic elements, and not by the technical structure of the product, by its title or by the ensemble in which the product is incorporated.

The protection is granted for the appearance of the product and not for the constructive, technical and functional characteristics of the product.

Directive 98/71/EC provides that the scope of protection conferred by a right regarding the design shall include any design that does not produce a different overall impression on an informed user. To establish the scope of protection, the degree of freedom of the designer to create his design shall be taken into account.

The USA right assigns the right to the creator to claim the industrial design as 'it is presented in the graphical representations'. The design may not be abstract, having to be attached to a product or an article that can be industrially manufactured.

The design shall be considered a visual impact created by the appearance of a product in the onlooker's mind.

The doctrine[63] generally considers the design as a creative activity aimed at realizing an ornamental form for industrial production, with limited prices, in order to satisfy both the functional needs and the visual requirements of consumers. At the same time, it is mentioned[64] that the design is considered a materialized, concrete creation and not an idea or a concept that may not be protectable.

366. B. The source of the exclusive right of exploitation of the design, according to the specific legislation of industrial property protection, is complex. In order for this right to emerge, the creator's act of creation, the constitution of the regular filing at the OSIM and the issue of the certificate of registration of the industrial design are necessary.

367. C. Provisional protection. As regards the published applications for registration, the natural or legal persons entitled to the issue of the certificate of registration shall provisionally benefit from the same rights conferred to the owner, according to Articles 30 and 34 of Law No. 129/1992, starting from the date on which the regular filing of the application was constituted until the issue of the certificate of registration.

The infringement of the above-mentioned provisions shall entail, for the guilty persons, the obligation of damages according to the Common Law (Article 998 of the Code of Civil Law); the title for the payment of damages may be executed only after the issue of the certificate of registration of the design.

368. The right to the issue of certificate of registration of the design is established by Romanian Law in Article 3.

As a rule, the right to issue the certificate of registration shall belong to the design's creator or his successor in title.

In the event that more persons have created the same design independently of each other, the right to the issue of the certificate shall belong to the first who filed the application for registration at the OSIM or to the one whose application has the earliest priority date. The law provides, in Article 3, the situations in which the right to the issue of the certificate shall belong to the employee or to the employer where he is carrying on his activity, namely:

63. WIPO, *Intellectual Property Reading Manual* (WIPO Publication 1995).

64. Denis Cohen, *La protection internat. des dessins et modeles* (Editura Economica, 1999).

– where the right was created as a consequence of a contract with a creative mission or by employees in the execution of their employment duties, the right to be granted the certificate of registration shall vest in the person who commissioned the carrying out of the design.

369. Right of priority:

(a) Right of priority of first filing.
(b) Right of conventional priority.
(c) Right of provisional priority.
(d) The right of priority of first filing is recognized by Romanian law, according to Article 15 as the owner's right to oppose his creation to other later creations that, thus lacking novelty, may not be registered and protected.

Thus, the law supports the creator who hastens to register his creation at the OSIM and, by publication, to make it available to the public:

– The right of conventional priority is (according to the Paris Convention) the special, privileged situation, recognized to the natural or legal persons who made a regular filing in one of the Member States of the Paris Union and thus acquire a right of priority, in order to file an application for the same creation, within an established time limit, in the other Member States of the Union.

A Romanian specialist[65] demonstrated that 'the right of priority appears as a legal fiction, having as effect the fact that the later filed applications invoking the priority are to be considered as filed on the same date as the first application'. This right of conventional priority may be considered a favour or an exception established by the Paris Convention to the owner's advantage in order not to take into consideration any acts of disclosure performed during this period.

The legal effect to claim this right of priority is that, during this period, the later filing of the owner, filed within the six months period of time established by the Paris Convention, may not be invalidated by legal documents of third party acts, as, for example, filings from third parties, publication or marketing of designs.

Right of provisional priority. According to Article 17 of the Law, priority may be invoked as a consequence of the design's display at an international exhibition, if the application is filed within six months from the date on which the product was put on display at the exhibition.

Where certain goods and services have been exhibited by the applicant within an official or officially recognized international exhibition, within the meaning of the Convention on international exhibitions signed in Paris on 22 November 1928 and ratified by Romania through Law No. 246/1930, with the subsequent amendments and completions, the exhibition being organized on the territory of Romania or in a Member State of Paris Convention, for the protection of industrial property, in the form revised in Stockholm on 14 July 1967, the applicant shall enjoy a priority right

65. Ion Camenita, *Protection of Inventions by Patents* (Romanian Academy 1977).

as from the date of presenting the said good within the exhibition, provided that an application for design registration in respect of said products has been filed with OSIM within six months from the date of presenting the good in the exhibition.

This period shall not extend the conventional priority term to six months.

370. Right to forbid third parties from performing, without consent, acts that infringe his exclusive right of exploitation is stipulated in Article 30 and expressly mentions the following acts: reproducing, manufacturing, marketing or offering for sale, using, importing or storing for the purpose of marketing, offering for sale or use, the industrial design of the product in which it is incorporated.

This right is, actually, a component of the exclusive right of exploitation.

371. Right to apply the 'D' sign to the products, accompanied by the owner's name or the certificate's number (provided for in Article 37), certifies that the industrial design is protected according to Law No. 129/1992. Failure to mention this sign shall not infringe on the exclusive right of the owner.

372. Right to transfer, wholly or in part, the rights deriving from the certificate of registration is stipulated in Article 38, namely:

- the transfer may be effected by assignment or by exclusive or non-exclusive licence as well as by legal or testamentary succession;
- the transfer shall produce effects for third parties, starting from the date of registration at the OSIM, in the National Register of Applications or, as the case may be, in the National Register of Industrial Designs.

373. Right to damages for caused prejudices is provided for in Article 52 and refers to the owner's right to be entitled to damages where his creation has been unlawfully exploited.

Any unlawful reproduction of the design belonging to the owner shall constitute an offence of infringement and shall be punishable by imprisonment or a fine. For the caused prejudices, the owner shall be entitled to damages, if the legal conditions are met, respectively, if infringement acts determining such prejudices are committed with guilt.

§7. Limitation of the Scope of Protection

I. Limitation of Rights Conferred by the Certificate of Registration

374. The rights conferred by the certificate of registration of the design shall be limited in time for a period of ten years from the date on which the regular national filing was constituted, but they can be prolonged by three more successive periods of five years.

At the same time, these rights are limited in space, being conferred to the owner only on the territory of Romania.

II. Limitation of Exclusive Rights

375. The Designs Law does not provide for the grant of compulsory licences for limitations of the exclusive right of exploitation.

Although they can be considered limitations of owner's rights, the following facts are provided for in Article 32:

> The rights conferred by Article 30 shall not apply to:
>
> (a) acts performed exclusively for personal, non-commercial, experimental, research or educational purposes, on the condition that these acts are not detrimental to the normal exploitation of the designs and that they mention the source;
> (b) activities of reproducing in the field of research or education, for making citations or teaching, provided that such activities are compatible with fair trade practice and do not unduly prejudice the normal exploitation of the design and that mention is made of the source;
> (c) equipment existing on the sea or air transportation vehicles registered in another country, when these vehicles temporarily enter the territory of Romania or importing accessories and spare parts for the purpose of repairing such vehicles or executing repairs in such vehicles;
> (d) using or taking effective and serious measures for the use of the designs by third parties within the period from the forfeiture of the holder's rights to the certificate revalidation;
> (e) use of the designs in good faith within the period from the date of publication of the forfeiture of the holder's rights to the date of publication of the reinstated right.

§8. Duration of Protection, Renewal and Termination

I. Duration of Protection

376. The term of protection of the design, registered according to the Industrial Designs Law, shall be ten years from the date on which the regular national filing was constituted, but they can be prolonged by three more successive periods of five years.

II. Renewal

377. The Law provides that the term of validity of a certificate of registration of the industrial design may be renewed during three successive periods of five years. Thus, the total period of protection is twenty-five years, provided that the owner pays fees during the entire period of validity of the certificate.

In the doctrine,[66] it is mentioned that the term of protection for designs varies from country to country, usually being between ten and twenty-five years.

The Directive EC 98/71 provides for a period of protection of a maximum of twenty-five years from the date of the registration of the application and the TRIPS Agreement provides for a period of a minimum of ten years.

III. Termination

378. The ceasing of the exclusive right of exploitation is possible in the following situations:

- at the expiration of the period of validity of the certificates of registration;
- by the forfeiture of the owner's rights for the non-payment of fees;
- by the cancellation of the certificate of registration;
- by the owner's renunciation of the rights conferred by the certificate of registration.

§9. Defence of Industrial Designs Rights, Infringement

379. In Romania, the rights regarding designs may be defended by:

(1) Administrative means:
  - the opposition;
  - the contestation.

(2) Legal means:
  - the action by which the decisions of the Re-examination Board of the OSIM are appealed against;
  - the cancellation action of the certificate of registration;
  - the unfair competition action;
  - the civil action;
  - the infringement action.

I. Administrative Means of Defence of Rights

A. Opposition

380. According to the statutory provisions, any interested person may submit written oppositions at the OSIM regarding the registration of designs within two months from the date of their publication (Article 21 of Law No. 129/1992).

66. WIPO, *Intellectual Property Reading Manual* (WIPO 1995).

We mention that it is compulsory that the opposition shall be presented in writing and shall depend on enclosed official documents (booklets, books, magazines, prospectus, etc.), published prior to the date of the regular national filing of the design (the date shall be mentioned on the official documents), indicating exactly the designs that are the subject matter of the opposition. The oppositions may be deposited directly at the General Registry of the OSIM, by ordinary mail or telefax.

Regarding the opposition, we emphasize some issues:

– the legislation provides that 'interested persons' may submit oppositions; thus, it is compulsory that this issue results from the content of the opposition filed at the OSIM;
– the opposition shall be submitted within two months from the date of the publication of the design in the BOPI – Designs section; otherwise, it shall not be taken into consideration;
– the opposition shall depend on the enclosed official documents, published prior to the date of the regular national filing of the design that is the subject matter of opposition;
– a legal fee shall be paid for the examination of the opposition.

B. Contestation

381. Law No. 129/1992 provides, in Article 24, that the decisions regarding the applications for registration of the designs may be contested administratively at the OSIM. We may briefly emphasize the following:

– the term within which the decision may be contested is thirty days from its notification;
– the contestation shall be made at the OSIM, in writing and on valid grounds; otherwise, it shall not be taken into consideration;
– the person entitled to contest the decision regarding the application for registration of the design is the one to whom the decision has been notified, namely the applicant;
– a legal fee shall be paid for the examination of the contestation.

The contestation shall be examined within three months from its registration by the Board of Appeal of the OSIM whose composition is different from that of the Examination Board.

The Board of Appeal may decide on the acceptance or the rejection of the contestation. According to Article 35 of the Law, 'the decision of the Board of Appeal shall be communicated to the parties within thirty days from its ordering and may be appealed against the Bucharest Court, within thirty days of the day on which they were notified. The judgment may be subject to appeal.

Judgments of final opposition shall be published in the BOPI of O. S. I. M., within sixty days after the delivery of a judgment'.

II. Defence of Rights in a Legal Way

A. *Action by Which the Decisions of the Re-examination Board of the OSIM Are Appealed Against*

382. According to Romanian legislation, the Court of Bucharest has the material and territorial jurisdiction to judge the actions by which the decisions of the Appeals Board of the OSIM are appealed against. The decision of the Appeals Board may be appealed against before the Court of Bucharest within three months from the notification.

The person who is entitled to appeal against the decision of the Re-examination Board is the one who was notified of the decision, namely the person who filed the request for re-examination.

B. *Unfair Competition Action*

383. The unfair competition action is stipulated by Law No. 11/1991 as: 'Any act or fact contrary to fair practices in the commercial or industrial activity'. In order to resort to an unfair competition action, some conditions[67] have to be met: the prejudice, the unlawful fact, the existence of a relation of causality between the prejudice and the unlawful fact, and the author's fault.

The acts of unfair competition specific to the designs, provided for also by Law No. 11/1991 (republished in 1996, 2001 and 2005), are the following:

– It constitutes a criminal act and it is punished by imprisonment from six months to two years or by payment of a fine from RON 2,500 (ca. EUR 600) to RON 5,000 (ca. EUR 1,200):
  (1) The use of a company, of a patent, a trademark, a geographical indication, a design or a model, topographies from integrated circuits, of an emblem or a package with those legitimately used by another trader, in order to create confusion.
  (2) Manufacturing, in any manner, importation, exportation, storage, offering for sale or selling some goods/services bearing false mentions regarding patents, trademarks, geographical indications, designs or models, integrated circuits topographies, other type of intellectual property such as the external appearance of a company, the design of a display or the design of the personnel clothes, the way to make advertising and so on.
  (3) Other acts: use of appearance similitude of products or packages, producing confusion between products, packages, etc.

384. Jurisprudence. We shall present *infra* two examples of Romanian jurisprudence:

67. Gheorghe Bucsa, *Protection of Design-Case Law* (OSIM Publishing House 2008).

- *The first example* relates to an unfair competition action (file No. 385/1998), submitted by the plaintiff S.C. SHAMS PRODIMPEX S.R.L., that proceeded against the defendant S.C. MIM PROD S.R.L., asking to ascertain the fact that:

> the defendant performs an act of unfair competition by using the industrial design similar to that registered on the plaintiff's name in eight graphical representations (strawberries, oranges, raspberries, coconut, sweet cherries, lemons, teacup and coffee beans, bananas) and protected by certificate No. 001452/ 20.02.1996' and, thus, to oblige the defendant to cease any commercial act involving the use of an industrial design identical or similar to that protected as well as to pay some damages and compensations.

The Municipal Court of Bucharest – Commercial Section, by civil sentence No. 2730, in the public session of 16 June 1998, decides:

> It rejects the main action and the additional request submitted by the plaintiff S.C. SHAMS PRODIMPEX S.R.L., with its premises in Bucharest, against the defendant S.C. MIM PROD S.R.L., with its premises in Bucharest, on the following grounds:
>
> - After analysing the acts and documents of the file, it has been ascertained that the packages used by the defendant comprise industrial designs having a new appearance, different from those of the plaintiff's and taking into consideration that the industrial designs used by the defendant are new and different in the sense of Articles 8 and 9 of Law No. 129/1992, it rejects the action and the additional request by the plaintiff as ungrounded. With the right to appeal against.

In this case, one may come to the conclusion that the court considered that the legal conditions for competition were not met, respectively an unlawful fact and implicitly an author's fault, that created confusion with the products and packages used by another trader, as provided for by Law No. 11/1991:

- *The second example* relates to the civil action No. 2537/1998, where the plaintiff S.C. ION ART GLASS S.R.L., with its premises in Avrig, proceeded against the defendants S.C. FABRY S.R.L. Avrig and S.C. DANEX S.R.L. Avrig, for unfair competition.

The Municipal Court of Sibiu County, by the civil sentence No. 762/C/1999, in the public session of 24 September 1999, decides:

> It admits the action submitted by the plaintiff S.C. ION ART GLASS, Avrig against the defendants S.C. FABRY S.R.L., Avrig and S.C. DANEX S.R.L., Avrig.

It obliges the defendants to cease the manufacturing of the glass products that imitate the products manufactured by the plaintiff; in the event of refusal, it obliges the defendants to pay the sum of RON 300,000 (amount expressed in old money) per day as comminatory damages to the plaintiff, starting with 19 May 1998 until the execution of the obligation.

It obliges the defendants to withdraw from the market all glass products manufactured by imitating the plaintiff's products; in case of refusal, it authorizes the plaintiff to withdraw the products at the defendants' expenses.

It obliges the defendant S.C. FABRY S.R.L. to publish the judgment in two widely read newspapers and in a local newspaper, at their own expense. With the right to appeal against.

In this case, the instance took into consideration both Law No. 129/1992 as only a part of the glass products were registered at the OSIM and Law No. 8/1996 on copyright and related rights.

Sanctions of the unfair competition, provided for by Law No. 11/1991 are of a civil, contravention and criminal character.

The contravention is ascertained at the intimation of the injured party, by the employees specially entitled by the territorial Chambers of Commerce and Industry or by the Commercial State Inspection. The agents ascertaining contravention shall impose fines at the same time as they ascertain the contravention.

The offences of unfair competition are punished by imprisonment from six months to two years or by a fine, Law No. 11/1991.

The actions deriving from an act of unfair competition shall belong to the jurisdiction of the local court where the fact has been performed or under whose territorial jurisdiction the defendant's premises are; in the absence of premises, the jurisdiction shall belong to the Court under whose jurisdiction the defendant's domicile is.

The criminal proceeding shall be initiated by the preliminary filing of a complaint by the injured party or at the intimation of the territorial Chamber of Commerce and Industry or of another professional organization.

The right to action provided for by the law shall be prescribed within one year from the date on which the injured party knew or should have known the damage and the person who caused it, but not later than three years from the date on which the act was performed.

C. Civil Action

385. According to Law No. 129/1992, Article 43, 'any litigation concerning the status of creator of the industrial design, the status of owner of the certificate of registration, concerning the economic rights arising from the assignment or licensing contracts, shall be within the jurisdiction of the courts'.

Article 52(4) of Law No. 129/1992 provides that 'the owner shall be entitled, for prejudices caused to him, to damages according to the law'.

The courts have the competence to judge:

- the actions on the economic rights arising from the assignment or licensing contracts;
- the actions regarding the disputes for establishing the contract price between the creator-employee and the employer. Litigations concerning the status of author of the design, the status of holder of the certificate of registration, those concerning the patrimonial rights deriving from the assignment or licence contracts are the competence of the judicial instances, according to the Civil Law;
- the actions regarding the disputes for granting damages to the owner of the certificate for registration of an industrial design, during its term of validity, according to Article 52 of Law No. 129/1992;
- the actions regarding the disputes for granting damages to natural or legal persons entitled to the issue of the certificate of registration who benefit from provisional protection, according to Article 34 of Law No. 129/1992.

In this latter case, the entitlement to the payment of damages shall be enforceable only after the issue of the certificate of registration.

According to Article 53:

(1) if the holder of a registered designs or any other person exercising the right of industrial property with the consent of the proprietor, furnished credible proof that the industrial property rights to the designs is the subject of an illicit actions, actual or imminent and that this action is likely to cause an injury difficult to be repaired, may request court provisional measures.

(2) Court may dispose in particular:

  (a) a prohibition of circumvention, or its provisional termination;

  (b) take the necessary steps in order to ensure the conservation of samples. Provisions applicable to the Executive Emergency Ordinance No. 100/ 2005 on ensuring compliance with industrial property rights.

(3) procedural provisions applicable shall be covered by the provisions of the Code of civil procedure concerning the provisional measures in the matter of intellectual property rights.

(4) provisional measures may be ordered and against an intermediary whose services are used by a third party to infringe a right protected by this law.

The Court of Bucharest has the jurisdiction to judge:

- the actions regarding the request for cancellation of the certificate of registration of the industrial design, according to Article 42 of Law No. 129/1992.

According to the Law, the certificate of registration of the industrial design, issued by the OSIM, may be cancelled, wholly or in part, where it is ascertained that the conditions for protection were not met on the date of registration of the application.

The cancellation may be requested throughout the term of validity of the certificate.

Jurisprudence. We are presenting hereunder an example of a cancellation action. By the application filed on 22 March 1996, File No. 2501, the plaintiff S.C. SOMET S.R.L. requested contradictorily with S.C. ROMET S.R.L. and the OSIM to cancel the patent No. 109280 and the Certificate of Registration of the Industrial Design with filing No. 1284/6 April 1994 with the title 'Mechanical draining filter'. For the valid grounds of the application, the plaintiff asserts that the technical solution was not new on the date of the national filings.

We mention that the instance noticed the fact that the cancellation of the certificate of registration of the industrial design had been requested on the grounds that the technical solution was not new, thus, contradictory to Article 8 of Law No. 129/1992, which provides that the new appearance of a product having a utilitarian function may be registered. The instance emphasized the fact that 'the appearance of the product, and not the technical solution is protected by an industrial design, no criticism regarding the appearance of the product being mentioned in the plaintiff's request'.

'Taking into consideration the presented grounds, the Court, under the provisions of Law No. 64/1991 and Law No. 129/1992, ascertains that the plaintiff's request is not grounded and decides: it rejects the action submitted by S.C. SOMET, Buzau as ungrounded, by the Civil Sentence No. 169, in its public session of 14 March 1997. With the right to appeal against.'

D. Criminal Action

386. According to Romanian legislation, the infringement of industrial property rights shall be judged by the judicial courts for the following situations that are considered offences:

- the unlawful reproduction of the industrial design for the purpose of manufacturing products of an identical appearance, the manufacture, offering for sale, importation, using or storing of such products for the purpose of putting into circulation or using, without the consent of the owner of the certificate of registration of the industrial design, during the term of validity thereof; the provided sanction shall be imprisonment from six months to two years or a fine (Article 52 of Law No. 129/1992). The criminal proceeding shall be initiated by the preliminary filing of a complaint by the injured party.

Also the law stipulates that the unlawful performance of any act provided for in Article 30 after design registration shall constitute the offence of counterfeiting and shall be punishable by imprisonment for six months to five years.

Where the acts referred to in paragraph (1) are liable to represent a danger to public safety or health, they shall be punishable by imprisonment for two to ten years and interdiction of rights.

Criminal investigation authorities may initiate ex officio, during preliminary acts, the required measures for seizing the products incorporating counterfeited designs and for preserving the evidences according to the civil law and the special provisions in the field.

E. Infringement Action

387. The infringement action is stipulated by Article 52 of Law No. 129 as 'the unlawful reproduction of an industrial design for the purpose of manufacturing products of an identical appearance, the manufacture, offering for sale, importation, using or storing of such products for the purpose of putting into circulation or using, without the consent of the owner of the certificate of registration of the industrial design, during the term of validity thereof'.

Conditions of infringement. The conditions provided for by the law for the offence of infringement are met if:

- there is a title of protection, respectively, a certificate of registration of the industrial design during its term of validity;
- an infringement has been made to the rights of the owner of the certificate of registration of the industrial design by the unlawful reproduction of the industrial design for the purpose of manufacturing products of an identical appearance, the manufacture, offering for sale, importation, using or storing of such products for the purpose of putting into circulation or using;
- existence of a deliberate element.

Acts of infringement. According to Romanian legislation, the acts of infringement are the following:

- Manufacturing products of an identical appearance by the unlawful reproduction of the industrial design.
- The reduced quantity of products or the restricted geographical area (village, commune) shall not be taken into consideration as significant, but only the acts of infringement of a protected industrial design.
- Offering for sale, importation, using or storing of such products for the purpose of putting into circulation or using.
- The provision of Law No. 129/1992 is very important: not only the persons who manufacture products but also the person who offers for sale, imports, uses, or stores such products for the purpose of putting into circulation or using performs acts of infringement and shall tolerate the legal consequences. The use shall have a commercial character and a profit:
- Unlawful reproduction of the industrial design for the purpose of manufacturing products of an identical appearance.

Sanction of infringement. Damages. The sanction of infringement, provided for by Law No. 129/1992 is the imprisonment from six months to five years or a fine.

Damages:

- Article 52 of Law No. 129/1992 provides that 'the owner shall be entitled, for prejudice caused to him, to damages according to the law'.
- Article 34 of Law No. 129/1992 provides for 'the obligation to the payment of damages under civil law' for the infringers. The payment of damages shall be made by civil action, according to Article 998 of the Code of Civil Law.

Infringement action. Law provides that the criminal proceeding shall be initiated by the preliminary filing of a complaint by the injured party.

The right to exercise the infringement action shall legally belong to the owner of the certificate of registration of the industrial design or to his successor in title, respectively to the assignee.

The owner of a licence shall not be entitled to exercise the infringement action. In this respect, only the owner of the certificate of registration of the industrial design shall be entitled to file a criminal complaint to the body of criminal pursuit under whose territorial jurisdiction the infringement was performed.

§10. Overlapping and Relation to Other Intellectual Property Laws

I. Plurality of Protection for Creations of Applied Art

388. The creations of applied art in industry, found in the specialized literature under the denomination of designs, are situated at the crossing of the artistic and industrial fields, their dual character being also emphasized by the fact that these creations are the subject matter of protection of two legal systems, respectively the industrial property and the copyright.

In order to present the situation of designs protection in Romania, we consider that the basis is the Designs Law No. 129/1992 and Law No. 8/1996 on the copyright and related rights.

Analyzing the two laws, we ascertain that a system of protection of the design by plurality has been adopted in Romania. Therefore, Law No. 129/1992 provides, in Article 5(2), that 'the protection secured through this Law shall not exclude the benefit of protection conferred through copyright', and Law No. 8/1996 provides that 'the acknowledgment of rights provided for by this Law shall not be prejudicial and shall not exclude the protection granted by other legal provisions'.

By plurality of protection granted to the creations of applied art in industry, respectively to designs, the theory of the art unity shall be implicitly acknowledged.

It is extremely difficult to emphasize the advantages or disadvantages of ensuring the protection of design creations according to the specific legislation through registration or copyright, but we can mention the following:

- the protection through copyright, according to Law No. 8/1996, shall not require the constitution of a national filing and the payment of registration fees, according to the principle of automatic protection, but the starting date of protection is uncertain in most cases and often, difficult to prove;
- the protection through registration at the OSIM, according to Law No. 129/1992, shall ensure a certain date of priority, conferring to its owner an exclusive right of exploitation;
- the term of protection is twenty-five years according to the copyright and is identical to the one given by the Designs Law No. 129/1992.

In the doctrine,[68] it is mentioned that there are differences between the protection through copyright and the protection through special designs laws as regards the disclosure, the period of protection and the granted rights, respectively:

- according to the designs legislation, the protection shall not be granted if the industrial design is made available to the public prior to the registration of application, while the copyright legislation provides for automatic protection without any formal proceeding;
- the right conferred by the designs legislation shall be an absolute right in the sense that any act may be considered an infringement, whether or not the infringement's author had any knowledge of the registration of the respective design.

According to the copyright, it shall be considered infringement or piracy 'only in the reproduction of the work in which copyright subsists'.

II. Interferences Designs: Trademarks

389. The present Law on Trademarks and Geographical Indications (Law No. 84/1996) provides that the trademarks may be constituted of: words, including personal names, designs, letters, numerals, figurative elements, three-dimensional shapes and, particularly, the shape of goods or of packaging thereof, colours, combinations of colours, holograms, acoustic signals, as well as any combination thereof.

We ascertain that the appearance of the product or its package may be registered as a trademark and may produce confusion to the applicants, especially regarding the option for the protection of products of wide consumption or of their packages.

Many specialists[69] are actually debating the possibility that the appearance itself of the product or of its package shall constitute a trademark. In this respect, the existence of normative acts in some States is brought as pro arguments, that allow that the appearance of the product or of its package shall constitute a trademark. Therefore, series of bottles of spirits or perfumes are registered as trademarks. The temptation to use as a trademark the appearance of the product or its package is enormous, as the term of protection, in case of protection as an industrial design, shall be between ten and fifty years, and in the case of protection as a trademark, it shall be unlimited.

In Romania, Law No. 84/1998 on Trademarks and Geographical Indications provides (Article 5e) that 'trademarks constituted exclusively of the appearance of the product that is imposed by the nature of the product or is necessary to obtain a technical result or confers a substantial value to the product' are excluded from protection and shall not be registered. At the same time, Law No. 84/1998 provides

68. WIPO, *Intellectual Property Reading Material* (WIPO 1995).

69. AIPPI, *Reports. Q 148*, Executive Committee Meeting in Sorrento (2000).

(Article 19) that the owner of a prior right (regarding a protected industrial property) may oppose at the OSIM regarding the published trademark, within three months from the date of the publication of the trademark.

We mention that the European Community Directive and the Regulation on the EU trademark provide that the designs are excluded from protection as a trademark where:

- the appearance is imposed by the nature of the product itself;
- the appearance of the product is determined to obtain a technical result;
- the appearance confers a substantial value to the product.

Practically speaking, at the European level, it is ascertained that many companies protect the appearance of the products or of their packages both by a certificate of industrial design and by a trademark.

III. Designs and Inventions

390. Although both inventions and industrial designs are the result of an intellectual creation activity, it is necessary to make a precise delimitation.

In the doctrine[70] it is mentioned that, if the appearance of the article is determined by its function, the Patent Law shall first be applied. In this respect, the right of patent is prevalent to the right regarding the designs in many legislations (e.g., France).

Practically speaking, the following situations may frequently appear:

(a) The appearance and the function are strongly linked – in practice, we have several situations where the appearance of an article is uniquely determined by its utilitarian function and, if the appearance is modified, the functional result of the article shall also modify, demonstrating that the respective appearance may not be protected as a design, but only through a patent.
(b) The appearance is separable by the function – if the appearance of the article is purely aesthetic, ornamental, fantastic and the function of the article shall therefore be maintained even if the appearance is modified, these appearances shall therefore be protected as designs. For instance, the design of a Persian carpet may be modified without determining the modification of the function of the carpet, the appearance of glasses may vary without changing their function.
(c) Coexistence of the aesthetic appearance and the technical creation – if the new aesthetic appearance is separable by the function, but is also generator of technical results, it may be protected both as a design and invention.

This appearance shall be protected through a patent for the new and functional appearance, generator of technical effects, and as design for the original appearance that confers a new, personal aspect to the article.

70. Claude Rodhain, Made in France, *Comment protéger nos innovations et créations* (Edition Technique & Documentation, 1982).

For example, we mention the case of a car coachwork, studied in the wind tunnel, with a view to increasing the rigidity, earth stability, approach to an ideal aerodynamic appearance or saving of energy, where it is possible that this coach work presents special technical performances that allow the protection by a patent.

At the same time, this coachwork has an original configuration, conferring a particular, proper appearance to the car, that allows its protection as an industrial design. Concretely speaking, the 'Renault' company has protected the coachwork of the car R12 similar to the car Dacia 1300, by the patent France No. 2049639 and the patent Romania No. 56026. At the same time, this coachwork was also protected as an industrial design in the USA.

IV. Protection of User Interfaces

391. An extremely interesting case is that of a user interface (graphical representations used in computer software) known under the generic denomination of Graphic User Interface (GUI).

As the user interface belongs to computer software, this one shall be protected according to Law No. 8/1998 on copyright and related rights that provides that protection of computer software includes any expression of software, the application software and the operating systems, expressed in any language, either in code source or object code, the preparatory conception material as well as the manuals.

Although their protection is ensured by the Law on Copyright, these user interfaces have begun to be registered, both in Romania and in other European States, according to the Industrial Designs Law as well.

Chapter 7. Plant Variety Protection

§1. Sources: Legislation

I. National Sources

392. The law of the protection of new plant varieties – was adopted by the Senate at its session of 24 September 1998 and by the Chamber of Deputies at its session of 25 November 1998. The law was promulgated by the President of Romania by Decree No. 480 of 26 December 1998 and was published in the Official Gazette of Romania No. 525 on 31 December 1998. It entered into force ninety days later, namely on 31 March 1999.

On the entry into force of this Law No. 255, the provisions on the protection of plant varieties and hybrids laid down in Articles 7(3) and 11 of Patent Law No. 64/1991, the provisions on plant varieties and hybrids in Chapter 4 of Government Decision No. 152/1992 and any other contrary provisions shall be repealed. Also, the applications for variety patents filed with the office under Patent Law No. 64/1991 and Government Decision No. 152/1992 approving the Regulations implementing Patent Law No. 64/1991, for which no decisions have been taken to grant or refuse grant, shall be settled in accordance with the provisions of this Law.

In the last years, Law No. 255 has been several times revised, mainly because the granting protection authority in this matter has been totally switched from the Romanian Patent Office – OSIM – to the State Institute for Testing and Registration of Varieties – ISTIS. This major change caused important legal and procedural amendments which will be subsequently presented and analysed.

The last consolidated version of this law dates from 01/02/2014 as republished in the Official Gazette No. 230 – 01/04/2014. The revised law has also incorporated the relevant provisions of Law No. 76/2012 on enforcing the amendments to the Code of Civil Procedure and consequently of Law No. 187/2012 on enforcing the amendments to Criminal Code.

393. The Regulation for implementing Law No. 255/1998 regarding the protection of new plant varieties was approved by Government Decision No. 200/17 March 2000 and was published in the Official Gazette of Romania No. 134 of 30 March 2000.

In order to reflect previously amendments of the law, its Implementing Regulation was accordingly revised as republished in the Official Gazette, part I, No. 637 from 7 September 2012.

II. International Sources

394. They include: The Paris Convention for the Protection of Industrial Property of 20 March 1883 and The International Union for the Protection of New Varieties of Plants (UPOV convention) from 1991.

The Agreement on Trade-Related Aspects of Intellectual Property Rights, known as the TRIPS Agreement (Annex 1C of the Marrakech Agreement on the establishment of the WTO).

Council Regulation (EC) No. 2100/94 of 27 July 1994 on Community plant variety rights.

§2. The Subject of Protection

I. Varieties That Can Be Protected

395. The law regarding the protection of new plant varieties recognizes the breeders' rights to new varieties of all genera and species of plants. In the meaning of this law, 'variety' means a plant grouping within a single botanical taxon of the lowest known rank, which grouping may be:

(a) defined by the expression of the characteristics resulting from a given genotype or combination of genotypes;
(b) distinguished from any other plant grouping by the expression of at least one of the characteristics under (a);
(c) considered a unit with respect to its suitability for propagation unchanged; the hybrid with the parental forms is also considered to be a variety.

§3. Conditions for Protection

I. Formal Requirements

396. According to the law, the application for the grant of a variety patent shall be filed with the ISTIS, named for the purpose of this chapter as the Office, by any natural or legal person entitled to such grant, or by the authorized representative of such person as provided by law.

The application for the grant of a variety patent shall relate to one variety only and shall contain:

(a) name of the applicant (natural person or legal entity) and identification data;
(b) authorized representative (power of attorney), whether this is the case;
(c) denomination of species;
(d) proposed denomination of species;
(e) provisional denomination of species (denomination awarded by the breeder);
(f) must mention if the variety has been genetically modified;
(g) breeder/breeders (name and address);
(h) if the breeders are not the same as the applicant, the type of applicant's variety assignation;
(i) information on any applications submitted in any European Union Member State or UPOV;
(j) the right of priority;

(k) commercial exploitation of the variety;
(l) official technical examination. The official filing date of the variety patent application shall be the date on which it is filed with the Office, provided that at least the requirements specified have been met and that the application filing fee has been paid.

The official filing date may also be the filing date of the application under the paragraph *supra* where, for valid reasons, foreign applicants, whether natural or legal persons, have submitted documentation in a foreign language, provided that a Romanian translation of the application is produced within three months of the date of receipt of the documentation.

The application for the grant of a variety patent shall be accompanied by the following documents:

(a) technical questionnaire issued by the Community Plant Variety Office (CPVO), by the International Union for the Protection of New Varieties of Plants (UPOV) or by a national guide filled out by the breeder;
(b) technical questionnaire – the confidential part, only for parent lines of hybrid varieties;
(c) proof of payment of the filing fee;
(d) power of attorney for the representation of the applicant or holder, drawn up in Romanian or accompanied by a certified translation in Romanian, if necessary;
(e) the form for assigning the legal representative (power of attorney)completed by the applicant, whether this is the case;
(f) name/denomination of the breeder and a declaration from the applicant, according to which, to the best of his knowledge, no other persons have been involved in breeding, discovery and development of the new variety;
(g) the contract for assigning the patent variety rights, if the applicant is different from the breeder;
(h) documents confirming the priority in another state;
(i) other documents and information regarding the provenience and variety breeding conditions.

The patent variety application can be filed together with the technical examination report and variety registration certificate, if they were issued prior to the application date.

Variety's denomination proposal is filed by the applicant using a separate form.

The variety patent application can be accompanied by any other documents providing information about a first application filed in another country.

The application can be submitted:

(a) directly at ISTIS Office;
(b) by mail with an acknowledgement receipt card;
(c) by email, if an electronic signature exists.

The application shall relate to one variety only.

The fees are established by the Article 43, as follows: Romanian applicants or holders, whether natural or legal persons, shall pay the forms in RON.

Foreign natural and legal persons who are applicants or holders or to whom industrial property rights have been transferred, shall pay the fees in currency. Where there are two or more applicants or holders, the fees owed jointly shall be paid in currency:

– Applicants for or holders of variety patents whose rights have not been transferred to them or who have not transferred their rights as provided by law before the time of payment shall pay the fees specified in the Appendix, reduced by 50% for each fee, if they are natural or legal persons or domestic research or education institutes.

II. Substantive Requirements

397. According to the law, the substantive requirements are established in Article 5 which says that the Office grants protection for a new plant variety and issues a variety patent if the variety is: new, distinct, uniform, stable, designated by a denomination conforming to the provisions of Article 15.

There are five essentials requirements in order to obtain the protection: novelty, distinctiveness, uniformity, stability and denomination.

NOVELTY – according to the law, the variety is new if, on the filing date of the application for the grant of protection or on the priority date, propagating material or harvested material of the variety has not been sold or otherwise disposed of to others, either by or with the consent of the breeder, for the purpose of exploitation of the new variety:

(a) on the territory of Romania, earlier than one year before the filing date of the application for a variety patent;
(b) on the territory of other States, earlier than six years before the filing of the application for a variety patent for fruit trees, vines and ornamental trees, and earlier than four years for another species.

Novelty shall also likewise not be lost where the variety:

(a) forms part of an agreement on the transfer of rights and the commercial exploitation of the variety did not take place prior to the filing of the application;
(b) forms part of an agreement between the breeder and another person by virtue of which the breeder authorizes the multiplication of the propagating material under his control;
(c) forms part of an agreement between the breeder and a third party concerning the conduct of a study, a field test, laboratory trials, or small-scale processing trials for the evaluation of the variety;
(d) has been disposed of to others as propagating or harvested material of the variety used for the purposes specified in Article 27(1) and not used for subsequent

propagation, those acts not being deemed commercial exploitation of the new variety within the meaning of Article 27(1);

(e) has been disposed of as a result of the breeder having displayed the new variety at an officially recognized exhibition;

(f) has been disposed of to an official body, for statutory purposes or under a contract, with a view to production, reproduction, multiplication, processing or storage, provided that the breeder retains the exclusive right of exploitation of the variety and no other previous disposal for commercial purposes has taken place; if the variety has been thus disposed of for the production of a hybrid which has been marketed, the provisions of paragraph (1) shall be applied;

(g) has been disposed of by a company or firm to another company or firm to which it is subordinate or which is wholly owned by a third such company or firm, provided that no other such disposal has taken place.

DISTINCTIVENESS – according to the Law, a variety is distinct if it is clearly distinguishable by the expression of one or more relevant characteristics that result from a particular genotype or combination of genotypes, from any other variety whose existence is a matter of common knowledge on the filing date of the application with the Office or, where applicable, on the date of the priority claimed.

The distinctiveness of a variety is defined by its morphological and physiological characteristics, provided that those characteristics are capable of precise recognition and description.

It is established under Article 7 that where a plant variety has been granted protection or has been the subject of a variety patent application for such protection or has been entered in the official register of plant varieties of any country, which application would result in the grant of breeder's rights to that particular variety, the said variety shall be deemed a matter of common knowledge on the filing date of the patent application.

UNIFORMITY – according to Article 8, a variety is uniform if, subject to the variation that might be expected of it owing to the particular features of its propagation, it is sufficiently uniform in the expression of those characteristics that are included in the examination for distinctiveness, as well as any other characteristics used for variety description.

STABILITY – according to Article 9, a variety is stable if the expression of the characteristics that are included in the examination for distinctiveness and any other characteristics used for variety description remain unchanged after repeated propagation or in special cases at the end of each propagation cycle.

§4. Procedure for Grant and Obtaining Protection

I. Formal Examination of the Application

398. According to the Law, within two months from the filing date of an application for the protection of a new variety, the Office shall ascertain whether the documentation filed by the applicant satisfies the formal requirements for the application set forth in Articles 10(1) to (4) and 12.

If the application meets the requirements referred to in the paragraph *supra*, the Office shall enter the application in the National Register of Variety Patent Applications and notify the applicant accordingly.

Applications for the protection of new varieties filed with the Office shall be published within three months from the date of filing, in the BOPI.

Where the application for the grant of a variety patent does not meet one of the provisions of Articles 10 and 12, the Office shall decide, within an examination board, to reject the application.

II. Substantive Examination of the Application

399. The substantive examination requirements are established by the Law in Article 17.

The Office shall within nine months carry out a substantive examination of the variety patent application with respect to its novelty and the variety denomination as provided in Articles 6 and 15.

The Office shall notify the applicant or his successor in title of the result of the substantive examination of the application; where the result is negative, a period not exceeding three months shall be accorded for reply.

The applicant may for legitimate reasons ask the Office for a two-month extension of the period for reply.

If, after the substantive examination, the Office decides that the application meets the requirements laid down in Articles 6, 12 and 16, the variety shall undergo technical examination by a competent national authority to which the Office shall send the documentation within one month from the decision.

Where the application has not met the requirements of Articles 6, 10, 12 and 16 and the applicant neither responds to the notification within the prescribed period nor applies for an extension, the Office shall reject the application.

III. Technical Examination of the New Variety

400. Law No. 255/1998 says that the variety shall undergo a technical examination in order:

(a) to verify that the variety belongs to the botanical taxon stated;
(b) to establish that the variety is distinct, uniform and stable within the meaning of Articles 7 to 9;
(c) to establish the official description of the variety.

According to Article 18, the technical examination shall be performed by a competent national authority if the applicant fails, on filing the application with the Office, to submit the findings of growing tests carried out by another internationally recognized authority.

Where growing tests on a new variety have not been performed by the national authority or by an internationally recognized authority, the Office may take into account a technical report drawn up by another competent authority and purchased with the applicant's consent, provided that the prescribed fee is paid.

The Office shall reject the application for a variety patent if the validity of the tests is disputed by the national authority.

IV. The Decisions of the Office

401. The Office shall decide, on the basis of the technical report of the national authority or of an internationally recognized authority, whether the new variety meets the requirements laid down in Articles 7 to 9 and 16 and shall grant the variety patent or reject the application as appropriate.

Decisions to grant variety patents, each with the description of the variety attached, shall be published in the BOPI within three months from the decision.

According to the Law, the time limit for the examination of the application for a variety patent and for verifying the growing test findings may be extended by one year on payment of the fees provided for in items 3 and 4 of the Appendix.

Also, the application for a variety patent may, on a request submitted to the Office by the applicant, at any time be withdrawn until the decision on the grant of the variety patent has been taken.

V. Revocation of the Decision to Grant the Variety Patent

402. Within three months from publication, any person may apply to the Office for revocation of the decision to grant a variety patent where at least one of the conditions set forth in Articles 6 to 10 and 15 has not been met; the request shall be made in writing and substantiated.

The request for revocation shall be examined by the Board of Appeal within three months from the filing thereof with the Office. The Board of Appeal may, if it sees fit, ask the national authority to repeat the growing tests on the variety or to use the services of an expert who shall take part in the re-examination of the new variety.

The decision of the Board of Appeal shall be communicated to the parties within fifteen days of being pronounced and may be appealed against as provided in Article 38. Final decisions shall be published in the BOPI within thirty days.

VI. Issue of the Variety Patent and Registration of the Variety Denomination

403. According to the Law, the variety patent shall be issued by the Director General of the Office in pursuance of the decision to grant the variety patent. Where the application is filed by two or more applicants, the variety patent shall be issued to the first applicant mentioned in the application, and the others shall be issued duplicates thereof.

Where the breeder is not the holder of the patent, he shall be entitled to receive a duplicate of the granted variety patent on request. The variety patent and the variety denomination shall be entered in the National Register of Protected Varieties, which is open to the public and may be consulted by third parties on payment of the inspection fee prescribed by the Law.

§5. Ownership and Transfer of the Rights

I. The Right to a Variety Patent

404. According to the Law, the right to a variety patent shall belong to the breeder. Where that right has been assigned under Article 35, it shall belong to the person to whom it has been assigned.

If two or more breeders have bred or discovered and developed a new variety jointly, the right to protection shall belong to them jointly. The right to the grant of a variety patent shall also belong jointly to the breeder and to any other person if the breeder and the other person have declared in writing that they agree to such joint entitlement.

A breeder who has created a new variety in an employment relationship is entitled, unless otherwise provided in his employment contract, to the breeder's rights and equitable remuneration.

II. Transfer of the Rights

405. According to Law No. 255/1998, the right to apply for a variety patent, the rights to the variety patent, the rights deriving from the filing of the application for the variety patent with the Office and the rights derived from the variety patent, may be transferred to other natural or legal persons.

The transfer of rights is performed by assignment, by an exclusive or non-exclusive licence contract or by legal or testamentary provision. The rights to a new variety shall likewise be transferred in the case of prosecution of the holder in accordance with the Law.

The transfer of rights shall not affect rights acquired by third parties before the date of transfer.

The assignment or exclusive licence shall be entered in the National Register of Variety Patent Applications or the National Register of Protected Varieties, as the case may be, and shall become enforceable against third parties on the date of registration.

The variety for which a patent application has been filed or for which a patent has been granted may be the subject of an assignment contract.

According to Article 36, a variety for which a patent has been granted may be the subject of a licence contract. Where an exclusive licence is granted, the licensee shall enjoy the exclusive right of exploitation of the new variety within the limits specified in the licence contract.

Whenever a non-exclusive licence is granted, the holder shall retain the right to grant licences to third parties. The licensee does not have the right to transfer the right of exploitation of the variety to third parties. The holder may publish his offer to grant the licence in the BOPI.

The Office shall enter the exclusive licence contract in the National Register of Protected Varieties and publish it in the BOPI. Other licence contracts may also be entered in the Register at the request of the interested party.

§6. Scope of the Exclusive Rights: The Contents of the Rights

406. The Law regarding the protection of new plant varieties grants to the owner the following rights: the exclusive right of exploitation of the new variety, the priority right, and the provisional protection right.

I. The Exclusive Right of the Holder of the Variety Patent

407. According to Article 27, the holder of rights shall enjoy the exclusive right of exploitation of the new variety and the right to prevent any person, without his authority, from performing the following acts in relation to the propagating material and harvested material of the protected variety: production or reproduction, processing for the purpose of propagation, offering for sale, selling or other marketing, importing, exporting, stocking for one of the purposes mentioned *supra*.

The above-mentioned provisions shall also apply to varieties:

- that are essentially derived from the protected variety, where the protected variety is not itself an essentially derived variety;
- that are not clearly distinguishable from the protected variety within the meaning of Article 7;
- the production of which requires repeated use of the protected variety.

A variety shall be deemed 'essentially derived' from another variety when:

- it is predominantly derived from the initial variety or from a variety that is itself predominantly derived from the initial variety;
- it is distinguishable in terms of Article 7 from the initial variety from which it is derived;
- it conforms to the initial variety in the expression of the essential characteristics resulting from a genotype or combination of genotypes thereof, except for the differences resulting from the derivation.

II. Rights of Priority

408. The filing of an application for a variety patent confers a right of priority, starting on the filing date, for any subsequent application for a variety that is not clearly distinguishable from it as provided in Article 7.

Any person who has previously filed a first application in a State party to an international convention in the field of new plant variety protection to which Romania is party, shall enjoy a right of priority of twelve months from the filing date of the first application if, within that period, he applies to the Office for the grant of a patent for the same variety, provided that the first application was properly filed on the priority date claimed.

In order to prove the claim of priority from another State, the applicant shall submit to the Office, within three months from the filing of the application, certified copies of the documents of the first application, as well as the propagating material or other evidence proving that the varieties referred to in both applications are identical.

Priority claimed under the paragraph *supra* shall be recognized in so far as the priority fee prescribed by law has been paid. Failure to observe the time limit provided for in the paragraph *supra* or failure to pay the priority fee shall result in non-recognition of the priority claimed. Acts performed within the period provided for in the paragraph *supra*, such as the filing of another application or publication or use of the variety to which the first application relates, do not constitute grounds for refusal of a subsequent application and do not give rise to any third party right.

III. Provisional Protection

409. Law No. 255/1998 established that during the period between the publication of the variety patent application under Article 16(3) and the grant of the variety patent, the applicant shall provisionally enjoy all rights conferred on the patent holder under Article 27. The infringement by third parties of the rights provided for in the paragraph *supra* shall make the infringers liable for damages under civil law, payment of the damages being enforceable once the right has been granted.

IV. Forfeiture of Rights

410. According to the Law, the Office shall declare the holder's rights forfeit where one of the following situations occur:

(a) the holder does not fulfil his obligation to maintain the protected variety as provided in Article 33(1);
(b) the holder does not act on a request by the Office or the national authority that he supply information or material for the purpose of verifying the protected variety during the term of the patent;

(c) the holder does not, within the time allowed, propose a suitable denomination for the plant variety where the Office has asked for a change in the denomination because it no longer fulfils the conditions set forth in Article 15;
(d) the holder fails to pay the fees for keeping the variety patent in force.

The Office shall not declare the holder's rights forfeit before having notified him of his failure to comply with one of the obligations under paragraphs (a) to (e). Forfeiture of rights shall be published in the BOPI and shall be effective as from the date of entry in the National Register of Protected Varieties.

The holder may, within six months from the date of publication of the forfeiture, request the Office for a restoration of the variety patent on just grounds.

V. Invalidation of the Variety Patent

411. Any person having a legitimate interest may file a request for invalidation with the Office at any time during the period of protection. The Board of Appeal shall invalidate the variety patent when it is established:

(a) that the variety was not new in terms of Article 6 or distinct in terms of Article 7 on the filing date of the application, or on the date of any priority claimed;
(b) that, where the grant of the variety patent was essentially based on trials carried out or on information and documents submitted by the applicant, the variety was not uniform in terms of Article 8 or stable in terms of Article 9 on the date of grant;
(c) that the person who has been granted the variety patent is not entitled to it, except where the rights have been transferred to the entitled person.

Decisions shall be communicated to the parties within fifteen days of pronouncement, and may be challenged under Article 38. The decision to invalidate the variety patent shall be entered in the National Register of Protected varieties and published in the BOPI. The decision to invalidate the variety patent shall come into effect on the date on which the application was filed with the Office.

VI. Renunciation to the Variety Patent

412. The holder may renounce the variety patent at any time during the protection period on the basis of a written declaration submitted to the Office. According to the Law, the holder is obliged to inform the breeder of his intention to renounce the variety patent. At the breeder's request, the holder is obliged to transfer his rights to the patent to him before filing the written declaration of renunciation.

Renunciation shall be effective as from the date of its submission to the Office. Renunciation shall be recorded in the National Register of Protected Varieties and published in the BOPI. Where the variety patent has been the subject of a licence contract, renunciation is possible only with the consent of the licensee.

§7. Limitations of the Scope of Protection: Compulsory Licences

I. Exceptions to the Exclusive Rights of the Holder

413. The rights conferred by a variety patent under Article 27 shall not extend to:

- acts done privately and for non-commercial purposes;
- acts done for experimental purposes, including those done in the process of breeding other varieties from initial material.

The persons who use the protected variety in the manner provided for in the paragraph *supra* are obliged to inform the holder accordingly.

II. Exhaustion of the Holder's Rights

414. According to Article 28, the holder's rights shall not extend to acts in relation to any propagating or harvested material of the protected variety or of a variety covered by the provisions of Article 27(2) or to those in relation to parts of the plant of the protected variety or to any material derived from that variety that have been sold or marketed by the holder or with his consent unless such acts involve:

- propagation of the protected variety;
- exporting the material of the protected variety to a third country that does not protect varieties of the genus or species to which the new variety belongs, except where the exported material is used for consumption.

III. Compulsory Licences

415. The compulsory licence is mentioned by Romanian Law, regarding the protection of the new plant varieties, in order to avoid the non-exploitation of the patent by the owner.

The articles of Law No. 255/1998 meet the requirements of the Paris Convention for Industrial Property which says that the compulsory licence cannot be granted until after three years from the date of grant of the variety patent and the compulsory licence is non-exclusive.

According to the law, the Office may grant a compulsory licence at the request of any interested party after the expiry of a period of five years from the date of the grant of the variety patent when:

(a) the holder does not exploit the protected variety and cannot justify his inaction;
(b) the protected variety is a matter of public interest.

A compulsory licence shall not be exclusive and shall be granted on specific conditions regarding duration, the exploitation of the variety and the amount of compensation payable to the holder.

The compulsory licence confers on the licensee the right to receive original propagating material from the holder. Compulsory licences shall be granted by the Office, acting through the Board of Appeal, and by the Ministry of Agriculture and Food Industry, acting through its representatives.

Where it is ascertained that the licensee has failed to fulfil his obligation to exploit the variety in the manner specified, the compulsory licence may, at the holder's request, be revoked by the Office, acting through the Board of Appeal referred to in the paragraph *supra*.

The Office shall register the compulsory licence in the National Register of Protected Varieties and publish it in the BOPI.

§8. Duration of Protection

416. The term of protection of the variety shall be twenty-five years as from the date of the grant of the variety patent. For species of fruit trees, vines and ornamental trees the term of protection shall be thirty years as from the date of the grant of protection.

§9. Infringement of the Rights Regarding the New Plant Varieties

I. Appeals Against Decisions of the Office

417. According to the Law, the decisions of the Office may be appealed against by interested parties before the Office within three months from communication.

The appeal or the request for revocation or cancellation of the variety patent, as the case may be, shall be considered by the Board of Appeal within three months of being filed. The composition of the Board shall be different from the composition of the Examination Board, being composed of representatives of the Ministry of Agriculture and Food Industry and the Office.

The finding of the Board of Appeal shall be communicated to the parties within fifteen days of being pronounced and may be challenged in the Court of Bucharest within thirty days of being communicated.

II. Competence of the Courts

418. Litigation seeking to deprive of his status the breeder, patent holder or holder of other rights derived from the variety patent, including economic rights under an assignment or licence contract, or litigation relating to failure to comply with the provisions of Articles 33(1) and 34, shall be within the competence of the courts of law.

III. Infringement and Disclosure

419. According to Law No. 255/1998, any of the acts mentioned in Article 27 and any of the acts mentioned *infra* performed without the variety patent holder's authorization shall be deemed infringement:

(a) using a denomination other than the registered denomination of the new variety for propagating material produced and sold;
(b) using the registered denomination of a new variety for propagating material produced and sold that does not belong to that variety;
(c) giving a denomination to propagating material produced and sold that is so close to the denomination of the protected variety that it may cause confusion;
(d) selling propagating material with a false indication that it belongs to a variety for which a variety patent has been granted, thereby misleading purchasers;
(e) falsehood in the registration of a variety in the National Register of Protected Varieties;
(f) drawing up false reports and falsification of documentation required by this Law;
(g) submitting documents containing false information.

The acts specified in the paragraph *supra* shall constitute an offence punishable by imprisonment for a term of three months to three years or with a fine of RON 3 million to 15 million, which amount shall be updated by Government decision according to the rate of inflation. The attempted act shall likewise be punished.

Disclosure of data and information constituting a trade secret concerning a new variety for which a variety patent has been applied or granted shall be punished under criminal law.

Where any of the offences provided for in the paragraphs *supra* is committed by a public official in the course of his duties, it shall be punished with imprisonment for a term of six months to five years. Criminal proceedings shall be initiated on a complaint by the injured party.

The holder is entitled to claim damages under the provisions of ordinary legislation for prejudice caused to him and the infringing goods shall be seized under the provisions of criminal law.

IV. Actions for Infringement

420. A legal action for infringement may only be initiated by the holder after publication of the grant of the variety patent. Where a licence has been granted and where not otherwise provided in the contract, the licensee may not sue for infringement without the consent of the holder.

The holder of an exclusive licence may initiate a legal action for infringement if the variety patent holder has been informed of the alleged infringement and has not taken any action within a time limit requested by the licensee.

Where a legal action for infringement has been brought by the variety patent holder, any of the licensees may intervene to demand that the prejudice caused by the infringement be made good.

Chapter 8. Chip Protection

§1. Sources: Legislation

421. The topographies of integrated circuits, or chips, are protected in Romania by Law No. 16/1995 on the Protection of Topographies of Semiconductor Products, as republished in the *Monitorul Oficial part I, No. 824* of 6 October 2006 and Order No. 6/2006 on Regulations on the Registration of Topographies of Semiconductor Products, published in the *Monitorul Oficial No. 90* of 6 November 2006.

The fees regime in the process of registration and maintenance in force of the protection of the topographies of integrated circuits is regulated by Government Ordinance No. 41/1998 regarding the Fees in the Field of Industrial Property, as republished in the *Monitorul Oficial part I, 959/*29 November 2006.

The law has been recently amended by incorporating the relevant provisions of Law No. 76/2012 on enforcing the amendments to the Code of Civil Procedure and consequently of Law No. 187/2012 on enforcing the amendments to Criminal Code. The law regulates the principles of obtaining protection for the topographies of integrated circuits by registration at the OSIM, under specified conditions. It is a modern law, harmonized by main international treaties and conventions, as well as the legislation of the main industrialized countries.

Romanian legislation has two main sources, namely the Washington Treaty on Intellectual Property with Respect to Integrated Circuits (1989) and the European Directive 87/54 of 16 December 1986. The provisions contained in Articles 35 to 38 from the TRIPS Agreement, section 6, dedicated to topographies of integrated circuits, are also followed.

Everywhere within Chapter 8, when not otherwise mentioned, the following abbreviations of terms will be used:

- Law – Law No. 16/1995 as republished in 2006 and amended in 2014 on the Protection of the Topographies of Semiconductor Products.
- Regulation – Regulation for Implementing the Law, given by Order No. 6/2006 – Office – OSIM.

§2. Subject Matter of Protection

422. According to Article 3 of the Law, 'original topographies' shall be protected, namely 'topographies which are the result of an intellectual effort made by their creators and if they are not commonplace among the creators of topographies and manufacturers of integrated circuits, at the time of their creation'.

The concept of originality may also refer to only a part of the topography which is claimed and for which one can obtain protection, or to a combination of elements and interconnections which, taken as a whole, should be original. The originality of a combination of elements shall be understood according to the Romanian practice, in its broadest sense, so to be built up, including by usual interconnections and elements, associated with original elements and interconnections. The assembly of elements should be original.

The law defines, in a European harmonized manner, the topography of a semiconductor product as being a series of related images, however, fixed or encoded, which represents the three-dimensional configuration of the layers which form a semiconductor product, and in which each image reproduces the pattern or a part of the pattern of a surface of the semiconductor product, in any manufacturing stage.

In the understanding of the law, 'semiconductor product means the final or intermediate form of any product which:

- comprises a substrate having a layer of semiconducting material;
- consists of one or several layers of conducting, insulating or semiconducting materials, said layers being arranged according to a predetermined three-dimensional configuration; and
- is intended to perform, exclusively or not, an electronic function'.

The law is permissive in the sense of protecting any expression of a three-dimensional disposition and does not ask for any condition for the granting of the rights to the owner depending on incorporation or non-incorporation of the integrated circuit in a product.

Article 5 provides for that 'the protection granted according to Article 3 shall be applied only to the actual topography, any concept, process, system, technique or encoded information embedded in said topography being excluded'.

§3. Conditions of Protection

423. The obtaining of the protection of the topographies is done by the issuance of a certificate of registration of topographies, as a result of the examination and the fulfilment of the legal conditions needed for the protection to be granted by the Office.

An application for registration of a topography shall be deemed as having been regularly filed, if the following documents are filed:

(a) a written request for the registration of the topography, specifying at least:
  - creator's (creators') full name and address;
  - applicant's full name or designation and address, where the applicant is not the creator of the topography;
  - indications with respect to the applicant's right to register the topography;
  - designation and destination of the semiconductor product to be manufactured by using the topography;
  - date of fixation or of first encoding of the topography;
  - date of the first commercial exploitation of the topography, where appropriate;
  - full name or designation and address of the professional representative, where appropriate;
  - signature of the applicant or of the professional representative, as the case may be.

(b) technical documentation comprising graphical material and texts providing sufficient information for allowing the identification of the topography and for pointing out the electronic function of the semiconductor product incorporating the topography;
(c) two copies of the semiconductor product, if it was manufactured and commercially exploited;
(d) power of attorney for the professional representative, where appropriate;
(e) proof of payment of legal fees.

All documents mentioned above shall be typed in Romanian and filed as such.

424. The application shall be signed by the applicant or his professional representative; in this latter situation, the power of attorney shall be filed with the Office together with the application or within two months of the filing date; failure to comply with this requirement results in the refusal of the application.

425. The technical documentation for the identification of the topography represents the most important part of the application form. It is built up by graphical representations and explanatory text and it has the role of clearly evidencing the originality of the topography.

The following forms of graphical materials are allowed:

- the drawing or photograph representing the configuration of the set of layers of the integrated circuit;
- drawings or photographs of the individual layers of the integrated circuit;
- drawings or photographs of the masks employed for the manufacturing of the integrated circuit.

Consequently, if from the assembly of the topography, only a part of the topography is made evident and claimed as such, the exposed graphical materials shall be pointed out distinctly.

If the applicant invokes the protection of the trade secret of a certain area of the topography, then in the copy of the graphical part of the application which will be the basis for publication, the mentioned area shall be covered.

The explanatory text shall comprise the presentation of the minimum information necessary for the identification of the topography. The original part of the topography, the electronic function of the integrated circuit and the specification of the destination of this circuit have to be pointed out.

Where the topography is defined under a coded form or in any other form, it is recommended that the applicant should file the relevant data carriers.

426. The Office, within the specialized Bureau, shall examine whether the applications for the registration of topographies meet the legal requirements for regular filing. Where the requirements are met, the Office shall register the topography in the National Register of Topographies and shall publish the topography. The Office shall also issue a certificate of registration within three months from the official date of regular filing.

The official date of regular filing shall be the date when the application is filed.

427. In the process of examination of the application, the analysis of the unity of the topography is provided. Thus, if starting from the legal provision that a topography application shall have as a subject matter a single topography, where from examination of the application results that this refers to two or more applications, the Office notifies the applicant on the non-unitary character of the application and gives him a two-month term limit to pronounce himself on the topography which will be the subject matter of the unity application. Consequently, it is considered that if no answer is received, the subject matter of the application will be the first one of the mentioned topographies.

Also, if the applicant files within three months from the date of the notification of the Office regarding the lack of unity of the application, subsequent applications having as subject matter the other topographies of the non-unitary application, these shall be considered divisional applications and shall receive as filing date the filing date of the original application.

The failure to observe the three-month time limit has as a legal consequence the non-recognition of the character of divisional applications and, implicitly, their processing as usual applications, having as filing date, the registration date at the office.

The lack of unity of an application may not be a reason for refusal of registration. The law regulates that, along with the filing of the application or at the latest within two months from the notification regarding the payment of the fees, the fees should be paid. These include the filing fee, the examination fee, the registration fee, the publication of the registration fee and the fee for the issuance of the certificate.

428. Where, upon examining the application, deficiencies are found in relation to the specified documents, the applicant shall be notified in writing within fifteen days from the date of filing and shall be given two months for necessary remedies. Where all the remedies have been made within the prescribed time limit, the OSIM shall follow the procedure provided by law. Then, the official date of regular filing shall be the date when all the necessary rectifications and completions have been received. Where the necessary rectifications and completions have not been submitted within the given time limit, the application shall be refused and the ground of refusal shall be made known to the applicant in writing.

The decision to register the topography is taken if the following conditions are met cumulatively:

- the subject matter of the application is deemed to be a topography, in the sense defined in the Law;
- the applicant is entitled to the protection of the topography;
- the topography was not previously registered with the Office;
- the application was filed after the expiry of the period of two years from the date of the first commercial exploitation of the topography or if the topography was not exploited commercially, within fifteen years from the date of the creation or first coding.

If one or more conditions are not met, the Office notifies to the applicant that the legal requirements for the registration of the topography are not met and gives him a period of two months to reply. The application is rejected if the presented arguments are not relevant for proving that the legal requirements for the registration of the topography are met.

The decision of registration shall be written in the National Register of the Topographies, together with all relevant data regarding the legal status of the registered topography as well as with all modifications during the period of protection. Within three months from the date of national regular filing, the certificate of registration of the topography is issued to the owner.

429. Within two months from the date of the issuing of the certificate, the Office publishes the registration of the topography in the BOPI. The publication shall contain:

- the registration number of the topography;
- the official date of the regular filing;
- the name of the integrated circuit that can be manufactured using the registered topography;
- the name/designation of the owner;
- the full name of the creator(s) of the topography;
- the date of creation of the first coding of the topography;
- the term of protection.

The Office publishes all changes in the legal status of the topography. After the publication of the registration of the topography, all documents regarding the regular filing, with the exception of those documents which have been declared by the applicant as being trade secrets, may be available to the public.

The decisions referring to applications for the registration of topographies may be appealed against by administrative means, in writing and on valid grounds, with the Office within three months of communication. The appeal shall be examined within three months from the lodging thereof by the Board of Appeal in the Appeals Department of the Office. The substantiated decision of the Board of Appeal shall be communicated to the parties within fifteen days from the pronouncement thereof and may be appealed against with contestation to the Bucharest Court within thirty days of the day on which they were notified.

Judgment of the Court in Bucharest can be challenged only with an appeal to the Court of Appeal. The final and irrevocable decisions of the Board of Appeal shall be published in BOPI within sixty days.

§4. Ownership and Transfer

430. According to Article 6 of the Law:

> the following entities shall benefit by the protection granted by law: natural persons who are nationals of a Member State of the EU or of the WTO, or

which have their place of residence on the territory of such State; companies or other legal persons having a real and effective industrial or commercial establishment on the territory of Romania or of a Member State of the EU or of the WTO.

In case of negotiating international agreements with third States or in case of adopting internal provisions for the extension of protection granted by Law to other persons than those already provided, the European Commission shall be notified accordingly thirty days in advance.

The conclusion of the agreements or adoption of the provisions under previous paragraph cannot take place in less than two months from the notification to the European Commission, if, within the time limit provided by the previous paragraph, it communicates to Romania its intention to submit to the European Council a proposal as to the extension of protection to said persons or third States by all Member States. If, during said period of two months, the European Commission submits such a proposal to the European Council, the conclusion of the agreements or adoption of the provisions cannot take place in less than four months from the date of submission of the proposal. In the absence of such a communication from the part of the European Commission within the time limit provided under paragraph (3) or the submission of the proposal or the adoption of a decision by the European Council within the legal time limits provided, Romania can conclude the agreements or can adopt the provisions previously provided.

431. The Law establishes the fundamental principle that the right to the protection of the topography of an integrated circuit shall belong to the creator of the topography or to his successor in title and, where there are several creators, as joint authors, the rights shall belong to them jointly. According to Article 8, the right to protection shall also be granted to the persons mentioned, which:

- first commercially exploit in Romania or in the EU a topography which has not yet been exploited commercially anywhere in the world; and
- have been exclusively authorized to exploit commercially the topography on the territory of Romania or of the EU by a person entitled to dispose of it.

It is obvious that the laboratory of creation of the integrated circuits is, as a rule, that of big companies that support research, designs and eventually produce integrated circuits. Consequently, the Law has a special provision regarding 'service creations'.

432. According to Article 9 of the Law:

- Where the topography has been created by an employee in the course of his duties, the right to the protection of the topography shall belong to the enterprise where the creator of the topography is employed.
- Where the topography has been created as a result of an order placed by a natural or legal person, the right to the protection of that topography shall belong to the person who ordered it.

- Where there are contract provisions contrary to the provisions in the above-mentioned paragraphs, the contract provisions shall prevail.
- The right to protection as well as the rights deriving from the registration of a topography shall be transferred in whole or in part by assignment or by legal or testamentary succession.
- The rights conferred by the registration of a topography shall be transferred by grant of exclusive or non-exclusive licences.

433. The transfer of rights shall have effects for third parties starting with the date when it has been registered with the Office. Also, the transfers are published in the BOPI within three months from the registration.

The contractual aspects regarding the transfer by licence or assignment are similar to those analysed at other objects of industrial property.

§5. Scope of Exclusive Rights

434. According to Article 21 of the Law, 'the owner of a registered topography shall have, over the whole period of protection, the exclusive right to commercially exploit the topography as well as the exclusive right to authorize or prohibit the following acts:

- reproduction of the topography;
- commercial exploitation or the importation for that purpose of topography or of a semiconductor product manufactured by using the topography'.

The exclusive right to authorize or prohibit the acts of commercialization exploitation or importation for that purpose does apply to the acts committed after the topography or the semiconductor product has been put on the market in Romania or in the EU by the owner or with his consent. The exclusive rights provided for under Article 21 shall come into existence on the date when the registration application is regularly filed or on the date when the topography is first commercially exploited anywhere in the world, if this date is earlier than the previous date.

The specificity of the technical character of a topography underlines the intrinsic character of the three-dimensional disposal of the elements of circuits, which in their turn are elements of an electronic circuit, that may be generically called a product. The exploitation of the topography is a complex concept that refers to all these characteristics of the exploitation.

435. Correspondingly, the Law defines the commercial exploitation as being the sale, rental, leasing or any other method of commercial distribution or offer made for these purposes. However, the commercial exploitation does not include the exploitation under conditions of confidentiality; it shall be applied on condition that no further distribution to third parties takes place, except where the exploitation of the topography takes place under conditions of confidentiality required by the necessary measures for the protection of the main national security interests.

As previously mentioned, the incorporation or non-incorporation of the integrated circuit in a product does not condition the rights of the owner of a registered topography to the integrated circuit.

Where the topography has been incorporated in an integrated circuit, the owner shall have the right to mark the integrated circuits manufactured on the basis of the protected topography, by using a capital 'T'.

The rights of the creators of topographies have a material and a moral component. The moral component refers to the right of the creators of the topographies to have their names and role as creators of the topographies mentioned both in the issued title of protection as well as in all publications of the Office regarding the registered topography.

The material component concerns the legal right of the creators who are not owners, to receive a remuneration established on a contractual basis, concluded with the authors of the topographies.

§6. Limitation of the Scope of Protection

436. Following the international legislation in the field, Romanian law provides four important situations where the exploitation of a topography without the consent of the owner is not considered an infringement of the exclusive right.

The first one refers to the granting of compulsory licence and the law provides that the Court of Bucharest may grant compulsory licence of exploitation to those persons who, despite their efforts, have not been able to get the owners' authorization to exploit a protected topography if:

(a) the grant of the licence is necessary in emergency cases referring to national defence and security, prevention or elimination of the effects of natural disasters, infringement of the Competition Law No. 21/1996, as republished, or non-observance of national standards concerning environmental pollution;
(b) at least four years have elapsed since the start of the protection period and the topography has not been commercially exploited on the territory of Romania.

The extent and duration of compulsory licences shall be limited to the purposes for which they have been authorized. The Government or third parties authorized by the Government may also be beneficiaries of compulsory licences.

At the justified request presented by the interested person, the Court of Bucharest may withdraw the compulsory licence, when the circumstances leading to the grant thereof ceased to exist, provided that the legitimate interests of the licensee should be protected adequately.

The licence shall not be withdrawn, if the circumstances which determined the grant thereof are likely to occur again.

The decisions of the Court of Bucharest concerning the grant of a compulsory licence, as well as those concerning the withdrawal thereof may be appealed against with the Court of Appeal of Bucharest within fifteen days since communication. The final and irrevocable decisions concerning the grant of a compulsory licence or the withdrawal of the compulsory licence, as the case may be, shall be communicated by the interested person to the Office which shall enter them into the National Register of Topographies and publish the mention of said decisions in BOPI within thirty days from the communication.

The owner of a compulsory licence shall pay a reasonable compensation to the right holder.

437. Second, it refers to the reproduction of the topography privately, for non-commercial purposes.

438. Third, it has in view what is generically called 'reverse engineering', in other words: the reproduction of the topography by a third party with the purpose of evaluation, analysis, research or teaching of the concepts, systems, processes or technologies of design or achievement of the topographies. Even more, the law provides a situation where a person who created a topography that meets the requirement of originality as a result of 'reverse engineering' has the right to perform acts in relation to a protected topography created on the basis of an analysis and evaluation of another topography, carried out according to reverse engineering.

439. Fourth, is the so-called exhaustion of rights, meaning that according to the Law, the exclusive right to authorize or prohibit the acts of commercial exploitation or the importation for that purpose of topography or of a semiconductor product manufactured by using the topography does not apply to the acts committed after the topography or the semiconductor product has been put on the market in Romania or in the EU by the owner or with his consent.

440. Finally, the situation which regards the continuation of exploitation of a topography by a person who has purchased the integrated circuit in good faith without possibly knowing that the integrated circuit incorporated a protected topography which was reproduced illegally. Starting from the date when that person has learned that the topography was protected, the mentioned person shall no longer have the right to purchase similar integrated circuits without the proprietor's authorization, but will be permitted to further exploit commercially the integrated circuits that were purchased or contracted before that date, against payment of fair compensation to the proprietor. These provisions also apply to the successors in title of the owner of the protected topography.

§7. Duration of Protection

441. The duration of protection is limited in time and it is considered an important element of the date of the first commercial exploitation of the topography, if this took place before the date of the national regular filing made with the purpose of protection.

According to Article 20, for a topography of an integrated circuit registered at the Office, 'the exclusive rights shall become extinct ten years from the earlier of the following dates:

(a) the end of the calendar year in which the topography is first commercially exploited anywhere in the world;
(b) the end of the calendar year in which the application for registration is regularly filed'.

The law provides two important restrictions regarding the request and granting of the protection, with reference to the date of the first commercial exploitation. If a topography has been commercially exploited, both in Romania or outside, the topography may benefit from protection only if the application has been filed with the Office within two years from the date of the first commercial exploitation.

The second restriction provides that if the topography of the integrated circuit has not been commercially exploited for a period of fifteen years from the date of its creation or of its first codification, then, if the topography has not been registered yet, it may not be registered.

The rights of the owner will exhaust before the expiry of the legal period of protection in one of the following situations:

(a) fifteen years have passed from the date when the topography was created or coded for the first time;
(b) the owner renounces the protection of the registered topography; the renunciation results in the exhaustion of the owner's right, starting with the date of registration at the Office or the date of the declaration of renunciation;
(c) the cancellation of the registration, in whole or in part, by a decision of the Court of Bucharest, at the request of an interested person, when the legal conditions for granting the protection were not fulfilled at the date of the registration of the application. The cancellation request may be filed during the whole period of protection of the topography. The effect of the cancellation is retroactive, in the sense of the cancellation *ab initio* of the rights to the topography or, as the case may be, the part of the topography which was the subject matter of the cancellation.

§8. Infringement and Remedies

442. According to Article 38 of the Law, 'commercial exploitation or production without the right of a topography or protected of a product semiconductor on which is built in a topography protected or a circuit element which incorporates such a product semiconductor, in so far as this item continues to contain a topography, if offence was committed after the date of publication of the registration topography on the national register of topographies, constitutes an infringement of infringement and can be punished with imprisonment from three months to two years, or corresponding fine. Reconciliation removes criminal liability'. The criminal action shall be initiated ex officio.

In case of prejudice caused to him, the proprietor is entitled to damages, as regulated by Civil Law, and may require the competent jurisdiction to order the seizing or destroying of the counterfeited products, as the case may be; said provisions shall also apply to the equipment used directly for committing the infringement offence.

For the period prior to the coming into existence of the exclusive rights, namely on the date when the registration application is regularly filed or on the date when the topography is first commercially exploited anywhere in the world, if this date is earlier than the previous date, the person having the right to protection under this law, who can prove that a third party has fraudulently reproduced, commercially exploited or imported the topography for such purposes may claim damages according to the common law.

Disputes concerning authorship or ownership, or the rights deriving from the registration of topographies – creators' patrimonial rights included – or from assignment or licence contracts shall be settled by the courts.

Where the final and irrevocable decision of the court states that a person other than the owner of a certificate for registration is entitled to the protection of the topography, the Office shall issue the certificate of registration to the entitled person, shall write the change concerning the owner in the National Register of Topographies and shall publish it in its official bulletin.

If the rights to a registered topography have ceased to exist over a certain period of time as a result of the renunciation of the protection, the forfeiture or the cancellation of the registration, the compensations and the other patrimonial rights of the owner corresponding to the above-mentioned period, shall be returned by him to the persons from whom he got them.

At the request of the law court, the Office shall be obliged to submit the papers, documents and information necessary for judging the cause entrusted to the law court, papers and documents to be returned at the end of the trial. Summoning to the court shall be made only for this purpose.

§9. Overlap and Relationship to Other Intellectual Property Laws

443. The protection of the topography of semiconductor products according to other laws of intellectual property may not be directly excluded, although this is not expressly provided for in the law.

A first foreseeable overlapping is that with the patent protection having as a subject matter a semiconductor product, an electronic circuit which incorporates a semiconductor product or a process of obtaining a semiconductor product, namely when a technical solution of achieving the semiconductor product may be illustrated in the description by examples of carrying out the topography.

It is obvious that the scope of the protection of invention shall refer to the technical solution of carrying out a technical problem and not to the three-dimensional disposal of the elements of the circuit. But if the disposal is a result of a particular technological solution, this disposal may be illustrated by examples.

In addition, under the fundamental condition of definition of the protectable industrial designs, which is not to be dictated by a technical function, solutions of industrial designs are possible in the field of the three-dimensional disposal.

Although this is not the general sense of the development of the technologies in the field of topographies, there are still possible solutions to three-dimensional disposal, which should satisfy some aesthetic criteria.

Of course, the most significant overlapping is, in principle, that with copyright law, having in view that topography may also be seen as a production in the scientific field.

Otherwise, while in Romania the protection of the topographies is granted by the Office, as an industrial property office, it is very significant to note that in a top technological country such as the USA, the protection of the topographies is managed within the copyright office.

Chapter 9. Trade Secrets

§1. Sources: Legislation

I. National Sources

444. Romania enacted in 2019 the 'Emergency Ordinance No. 25/2019 on the protection of know-how and undisclosed business information that constitute trade secrets against the illegal acquisition, use and disclosure, as well as for the modification and completion of normative acts' which put an end to a previous unsatisfactory legal situation where trade secrets were protected only by indirect provisions of several non-specific laws on industrial property. For the purposes of this chapter, Emergency Ordinance No. 25/2019 will be called Ordinance. Its content is fully in line with the provisions of the 'Directive (EU) 2016/943 of the European Parliament and of the Council of 8 June 2016 on the protection of know-how and undisclosed business information (trade secrets) against illegal acquisition, use and disclosure', and thus, Romania complied with the obligation to transpose into national law the said *acquis communautaire*. Its coverage, scope and approach are indeed objective factors that should be considered as the main and direct national source for trade secrets protection.

Unlawful use of a trade secret by an unauthorized person should be considered one of the possible acts of unfair competition and Law No. 11/1991 on the Fight against Unfair Competition, as republished in 2019, stipulates some relevant provisions.

445. Thus, the provisions of Article 1(1) let. d, introduces the definition of the trade secret, which will be further presented on the next Point I: Definition of the Trade Secret. Letter d) of the same article defines the holder of the trade secret as 'any natural or legal person who has the legal control over a trade secret'. Article 2(1) defines unfair competition, as 'the business practices of the company which contravene the honest practices and the general principle of good faith and which cause or may cause harm to any market participants'.

Direct reference to trade secrets is provided in paragraph (2) let. b) of the same article, which provides among prohibited unfair competition practices 'the hijacking of the clients of a company by a former or current employee/ his representative or by any other person using of trade secrets, for which the respective company has taken reasonable measures to ensure their protection and whose disclosure may harm the interests of that company'.

446. According to Article 5:

> It is a criminal offence and punishable by imprisonment from 3 months to 2 years or with a fine:
>
> a) …
> b) the commercial use of the results of experiments or other confidential information relating thereto, transmitted to the competent authorities for

the purpose of obtaining marketing authorizations for pharmaceuticals or agricultural chemicals, containing new chemical compounds;

c) disclosure, purchase or use of the trade secret by third parties, as a result of a commercial or industrial espionage action, if by this the interests or activity of a legal person are affected;
d) disclosure or use of trade secrets by persons empowered by the legitimate holders of these secrets to represent them in front of public authorities or public institutions, if by this the interests or activity of a legal person are affected;
e) the use by one of the persons provided for in art. 175 paragraph (1) of the Criminal Code of the commercial secrets of which he became aware in the exercise of the duties of service, if by this the interests or activity of a legal person are affected.

447. Finally, Article 7 deals with proceedings before competent courts in cases of unfair competition and provides that:

(1) Any person who has a legitimate interest may address directly to the competent courts for the termination and prohibition of unfair competition practices, to cover the patrimonial and moral damages suffered as a result of an unfair competition practice, without having to go through any formalities before the Competition Council.
(2) The actions arising from a practice of unfair competition are within the competence of the court of the place where the deed was committed or in whose territorial area the defendant's office is located; in the absence of a seat, the court of domicile of the defendant is competent.
(3) In order to prevent imminent damage, the competent courts may order, in an emergency procedure, if they find, at a first assessment, the existence of unfair commercial practices, their termination or their prohibition until the case is resolved.
(4) If the court ordered the termination, respectively the prohibition of unfair competition practices, and the court decision ordering the measure remained final, the national competition authority will provide, at the request of the person who made the request for a trial, publication on a web page of a communiqué, which must include the headquarters and other identification data of the company, the practice of unfair competition, as well as the measures ordered by the court.
(5) At the expense of the guilty person, the court may order the publication of the court decision, in whole or in part, in a wide circulation newspaper.
(6) At the request of the legitimate owner of the trade secret, the court may order measures to prohibit the industrial and/ or commercial exploitation of the products resulting from the illicit acquisition of the trade secret or the destruction of these products. The ban ceases when the protected information has been made public.

Protection of confidential information is also indirectly provided by the other domestic laws on industrial property rights, as follows.

A. *Law No. 64/1991 on Patents*

448. Article 63(1) of the Patent Law provides that the claims in relation to the rights entailed by a patent and by transfer and license agreements shall be settled by courts.

Another relevant provision is to be found in Article 62 (1) of the Patent Law which stipulates that 'Disclosure, by the staff of Romanian Patent Office, as well as by persons doing work in connection with inventions, of the information contained in patent applications, prior to the publication thereof, shall constitute an offence and shall be punished with imprisonment from three months to three years or fine.'

B. *Law No. 83/2014 on Employees' Inventions*

449. Substantial provisions on trade secrets contained in an employees' invention are stipulated in Article 10 of Law 83.2014 which provides that:

(1) The inventions referred to under Art. 3(1) (e.g., employees' inventions) may be subject to a trade secret.
(2) The employee-inventor is bound not to disclose or publish the invention referred to under Art. 3(1) without the employer's written agreement. The same interdiction of disclosure or publishing applies to the employer, as well as to the persons other than the inventor, who, by the nature of their service duties, have knowledge of the existence of the invention.
(3) In case of disclosure of the employee's invention by the persons referred to under paragraph (2), they can be liable for it by virtue of the individual employment contract concluded between the employee and the employer, where a confidentiality clause is provided therein.
(4) Where the individual employment contract does not contain a confidentiality clause and a prejudice results from the disclosure of the employee's invention by the persons referred to under paragraph (2), it may entail civil liability, as provided by Art. 1349(1) and (2) corroborated with Art. 1357 of the Civil Law Code.

C. *Law No. 350/2007 on Utility Models*

450. By making in Article 28 a direct reference to a series of provisions of the Patent law, consequently, the considerations exposed in point A above on the Patent Law are *mutatis mutandis* valid here.

Moreover, according the Article 19(6) 'the invention which is the subject matter of the utility model application has the character imparted by the special law and may not be disclosed without the applicant's consent, up to publication. OSIM shall maintain the secrecy level established by the competent authorities to the filed documents. Where the secrecy of documents is not lifted prior to the publication of utility model registration, OSIM shall publish the registration within a time limit of one month from the communication of information secrecy lifting'.

D. Law No. 129/1992 on Industrial Designs and Models as Republished in 2014

451. According to Article 52, paragraph 4 of the Law, 'For damages caused the holder has the right to compensation, according to the common law, and can request the competent court to order the measure of confiscation or, as the case may be, the destruction of the counterfeit products; these provisions also apply to materials and equipment that have served directly in the commission of the infringement offense.'

E. Law No. 16/1995 on the Protection of the Layout Design of Semiconductor Circuits as Republished in 2014

452. Article 38 of the Law provides that the right owner is entitled to compensation for the damages incurred by him as a result of the infringement of the exclusive rights.

F. The Romanian Criminal Code, as Republished in 2020

453. According to Article 304:

> The disclosure, without right, of secret service information or which is not intended for publicity, by the person who knows them due to the service duties, if by this way the interests or activity of a person are affected, it is punished with imprisonment from three months to three years or with a fine.

The disclosure, without right, of secret service information or which is not intended for publicity, by the person who is aware of them, shall be punished by imprisonment from one month to one year or by a fine.

II. International Sources

454. As previously mentioned, deriving from its EU membership, Romania transposed in its national legislation the 'Directive (EU) 2016/943 of the European Parliament and of the Council of 8 June 2016 on the protection of know-how and undisclosed business information (trade secrets) against illegal acquisition, use and disclosure.' Under these circumstances, said Directive constitutes indeed main international source. It is however fair to mention that due to a delay of transposition, the European Commission notified the Romanian authorities on 20 July 2018, the

Letter regarding the delay in non-communication of the national measures for transposition of Directive (EU) 2016/943, a procedure that was the subject of Case 2018/0224. At the request of the Romanian term for communication of the measures transposing the said Directive, it has been extended by two months, ending on 20 November 2018. At the same time, the European Commission has drawn attention to the financial sanctions that the Court of Justice of the European Union may impose, pursuant to Article 260 paragraph (3) of the TFEU, if it will be notified in connection with the failure by Romania of the obligation to communicate the national measures for transposing the directive adopted under a legislative procedure. As these circumstances constituted extraordinary elements that required legislative intervention, this transposition was made by an Emergency Ordinance, as mentioned in paragraph 1.

455. Other main international sources derived from the international conventions, treaties and agreements on industrial property and trade, to which Romania is a party and which regulate the confidential information, as follows.

A. *Paris Convention of 1883 on Industrial Property Protection*

456. Where relevant is Article 10*bis* which provides for that:

(1) the countries of the Union are bound to assure nationals of such countries effective protection against unfair competition;
(2) any acts contrary to honest practices in industrial or commercial matters constitutes an act of unfair competition.

B. *The Agreement on TRIPs, Ratified by Romania, Law No. 133/1994*

457. Article 39 of section VII 'Protection of non-disclosed information' stipulates the protection right of trade secrets, as follows:

> The natural and legal persons shall have the right to prevent the disclosure, acquire or use by third parties, without their consent and contrary to the fair commercial practices, of the information lawfully owned by the first, on the condition that the relevant information:
>
> – is confidential, namely that it is not widely known and that it cannot be easily known to third parties acting in the field;
> – has commercial value, which results from their confidential nature;
> – it is subject matter of reasonable measures to preserve the secrecy taken by the persons who lawfully own it.

C. The US-Romania Agreement on Trade Relationships

458. Signed at Bucharest on 2 April 1993 by the Government of the USA and the Romanian Government, ratified by Romania by Law No. 50/1992 and entered into force on 8 September 1993.

Article VIII provides that 'each party shall take measures for an adequate and effective application of the agreement and for the protection of the patents, trademarks, copyrights, trade secrets, topographies of integrated circuits, as it is stated by the enclosed letter on intellectual property'. The letter sets forth under item 2e that:

> each party shall establish by the domestic legislation and practice the legal means to be used by individuals and companies in order to prevent the disclosure, acquire or use of trade secrets by third parties, in a manner contrary to the fair commercial practices, on the condition that:
>
> – the entire information or its accurate ensemble of elements is not widely known and it cannot be easily known to third parties;
> – the information has an actual or potential commercial value, which results from its confidential nature;
> – the information is the subject of reasonable measures under the circumstances to protect its secrecy.

None of the parties to the agreement shall have the right to limit the duration of the trade secrets' protection as long as the conditions provided under item 2e of this letter are fulfilled.

§2. Protection of Trade Secrets/Confidential Information

459. Besides the rights of industrial property protected by law, there is a system of information and data that are not protected by registration and which is kept confidential and it is generically named *trade secrets*. As mentioned, effective protection of trade secrets by a dedicated law, previously called a direct legislative source, started quite soon, in 2019, by enacting and enforcing the 'Emergency Ordinance No. 25/2019 on the protection of know-how and undisclosed business information that constitute trade secrets against the illegal acquisition, use and disclosure, as well as for the modification and completion of normative acts.'

460. Consequently, its provisions constitute the basis of our subsequent presentation. However, it makes reference to the definition of trade secrets which is to be found in *Law No. 11/1991 on the Fight against Unfair Competition,* as amended by the said legislative act,

I. Definition of the Trade Secret

461. The content of the concept of *trade secret* has the same extent under the domestic regulations.

For example, the Uniform Trade Secrets Act adopted in 1979 in the USA defines a trade secret as:

> information including a formula, pattern, compilation, programme, device, method, technique or process that:
>
> – derives independent economic value, actual or potential, from not being generally known to, and not being readily ascertainable by proper means by, other persons who can obtain economic value from its disclosure or use; and
> – is the subject of efforts that are reasonable under the circumstances to maintain secrecy.[71]

462. In France, the concept of trade secret includes the secrets of manufacturing (such as a formula, a method or an invention, an improvement of a known or patented process, a specific use of a device), confidential business information (such as the information relating to the commercial organization of a company and of the distribution networks, the wording of the sale agreements, the strategy of sales, the prices' discounts, commissions, market studies on sales and lucrative character of business, customer lists, investments, bank relationships, legal disputes, research and marketing methods) and know-how (*savoir-faire*), defined by jurisprudence as an ensemble of transferable technical knowledge, which is not readily ascertainable to the public and is not patented.[72]

463. In Romania, the concept of trade secret is fully in line with that stipulated in the 'Directive (EU) 2016/943 of the European Parliament and of the Council of 8 June 2016 on the protection of know-how and undisclosed business information (trade secrets) against illegal acquisition, use and disclosure.'

464. Naturally it has same characteristics with the view of TRIPS, to which Romania has adhered. The obligations provided under Article 39 with regard to the protection of non-disclosed information are entirely assumed by Romania.[73]

Thus, according to the provisions of Article 1(1) let. d of *Law No. 11/1991 on the Fight against Unfair Competition*, 'trade secret' means information that cumulatively meets the following requirements:

---

71. C. Lee Lewis & J. Scott Davidson, *Managing Intellectual Property Rights* (J. Willey 1993).
72. A. Chavanne & J.J. Burst, *supra*, 346.
73. Tiberiu Popescu, 'Protection of Trade Secrets', *Romanian Revue for Industrial Property*, nos 3–4 (State Office for Inventions and Trademarks-1996).

- it is secret in the sense that it is not, as a body or in the precise configuration and assembly of its components, generally known among or readily accessible to persons within the circles that normally deal with the kind of information in question;
- it has commercial value because it is secret;
- it has been subject to reasonable steps under the circumstances, by the person lawfully in control of the information, to keep it secret.

Same legislative source defines the holder of the trade secret as 'any natural or legal person who has the legal control over a trade secret'.

465. The doctrine defines the trade secret as the technical, commercial, financial or administrative information, which is not disclosed to third parties and is owned by an entrepreneur as documents or knowledge, being related to the object of the respective enterprise and having or at least might have economic value, which induced the entrepreneur to take reasonable measures of protection.[74]

II. Conditions to Qualify Information as a Trade Secret

466. The commercial information promotes best results and includes the following: formula of combination, manufacturing methods and conditions, best temperatures, etc., the errors of a technical operation which must be avoided, inclusive, and even not patented inventions.

In order to qualify as a trade secret, a certain information must fulfil the following conditions:

(a) Have a technical, commercial or administrative character. The technical or technological information can be: formula, methods, processes, techniques, designs, projects, programmes, etc.
(b) Have an economic value from not being generally known by others.
 and
(c) Reasonable efforts have been taken to protect the said information.

The information that is widely known by the experts of the respective field and was made publicly known is not a trade secret, nor the information that is gained by licences or transfers from third parties, if a confidential/secret character is not assigned to it.

With regard to the technical information created by an employee within the framework of the employment agreement, the information is a trade secret only if it is the property of the employer and measures were taken for its protection. The commercial information is related to the conception of offers, negotiations with different partners, the content of contracts, the volume of production and offer, the

74. Mioara Radulescu, *Guide for the Protection of Technical* (1995), technological and commercial information, *Romanian Revue for Industrial Property*, nos 3–4; Rzvan Dinc, *Protecţia secretului commercial în dreptul privat* [*Protection of Trade Secret in the Private Law*] (2009).

prices, the financial indicator, the strategy of advertisement and market evaluation, the strategy of protection against unfair competition, etc.

467. The administrative information includes statements by the administration board, the registers of correspondence, and the notebook containing the names, addresses and contact numbers of company and business partners:

- To be proper for transfer to third parties. This condition refers to the information construed as an economic value, which consequently can be transferred.
- To have a confidential nature, that is, the information is not ascertainable to the public.

The trade secrets do not require novelty, but only the keeping of secrecy. The merchant selects information and takes measures for preserving its secrecy through the agency of experts.

468. In order to benefit from protection, the information must fulfil the following conditions:

- it shall be known to a narrow circle of experts in the respective field, and therefore it shall not be widely known or readily ascertainable to an average expert in the field. Consequently, if an expert discovers information with observance of fair competition rules, for example, by reverse engineering or experiment, such information cannot be a trade secret;
- it shall have actual or potential economic value;
- it has ascertainable competitive advantages;
- it was acquired at the entrepreneur's expense;
- the entrepreneur wants to keep its secrecy.

III. Acquisition, Use and Disclosure of Trade Secrets

A. *Lawful Acquisition, Use and Disclosure*

469. According to Article 3:

> The acquisition of a trade secret shall be considered lawful if the trade secret is obtained by any of the following means:
>
> (a) independent discovery or creation;
> (b) the analysis, study, disassembly or testing of a product or object that has been made public or is lawfully in the possession of the person who acquired the information and to who is free from any legally valid obligation to limit the acquisition of trade secret;
> (c) exercise of the right of employees and workers or representatives of employees or workers to information and consultation in accordance with European Union law, national law and national practice;

(d) any other practice which, under the given conditions, is in accordance with fair commercial practices, does not contravene honest practices or the general principle of good faith and does not produce or is not likely to cause harm to market participants.

470. The acquisition, use or disclosure of a trade secret shall be considered lawful insofar as such acquisition, use or disclosure is imposed or permitted under European Union law or national law. Usually, trade secrets are obtained by an entrepreneur from his own business (production techniques, the activity of functional sections) or by acquisition.

Trade secrets can be acquired from the public domain, namely the specialized literature already published or other means at public disposal, the recipient of trade secrets having no obligation, provided that the information was disclosed and the publication has a certain date. Likewise, the trade secret can be obtained from cooperation with business partners on a given subject or from the association of more entrepreneurs.

Finally, the acquisition can be made through contracts that are either agreements on transfer of technology or agreements on licence or transfer of industrial property rights.

471. In case of cooperation, associations, as well as agreements, parties can provide special clauses with regard to the confidentiality of trade secrets, having the following content:

- commitments, taken by managers and employees who have access to the trade secrets, on keeping the secrecy pending certain time periods;
- the basis of the trade secrets' evaluation during the negotiations and the performance of contracts;
- the entitled persons to communicate, receive or exchange confidential information;
- the selection and approval procedure for publishing the results obtained from the cooperation and association agreements;
- the exploitation of trade secrets after the termination of contracts;
- the liability for not observing the obligations undertaken with regard to the secrecy of information.

B. Unlawful Acquisition, Use and Disclosure

472. Specific situations of unlawful acquisition, use and disclosure are provided in Article 4 of the Ordinance.

Thus, the acquisition of a trade secret without the consent of the holder of the trade secret should be considered unlawful whenever it is carried out by:

(a) unauthorized access, acquisition or copying of any electronic documents, objects, materials, substances or files that are legally under the control of the holder of the trade secret and which contain the trade secret or from which it can be deduced;
(b) any other behaviour which, in the given circumstances, contravenes fair commercial practices.

473. The use or disclosure of a trade secret should be considered unlawful whenever it is committed, without the consent of the holder of the trade secret, by a person who fulfils any of the following conditions:

(a) the acquired trade secrets illegally;
(b) violates a confidentiality agreement or other obligation to not disclose trade secrets;
(c) breaches a contractual or other obligation that limits the use of trade secret.

In its turn, the acquisition, use or disclosure of a trade secret should be considered unlawful when a person, at the time of acquisition, use or disclosure, was aware of or should have been aware, in the given circumstances, that the trade secret was obtained, directly or indirectly, from another person who has used or disclosed the illegal trade secret according to the previous provisions.

474. The production, offering or placing on the market of goods which contravene the rules or the import, export or storage of such goods for these purposes should be also considered as an unlawful use of a trade secret when the person carrying on such activities was aware or should have been aware, in the given circumstances, that the trade secret was used unlawfully for the purposes exposed, the provisions exposed on lawful acquisition being applied consequently.

475. At the request of the holders of trade secrets, the competent court may apply the measures, procedures and remedial actions provided for by law to prevent the illegal acquisition, use or disclosure of their trade secrets or to obtain reparations as a result of such acts.

The above-mentioned provisions should be corroborated with relevant dispositions of the Romanian Criminal Code as republished in 2020, which in Article 304 provides that:

> The disclosure, without right, of secret service information or which is not intended for publicity, by the person who knows them due to the service duties, if by this way the interests or activity of a person are affected, it is punished with imprisonment from three months to three years or with a fine.

The disclosure, without right, of secret service information or which is not intended for publicity, by the person who is aware of them, shall be punished by imprisonment from one month to one year or by a fine.

IV. Rights to Trade Secrets

476. The exclusive use of a trade secret is ensured by not disclosing it to the experts of the related field. However, there is no official protection offered by registration to a competent authority, as it is in the case of the patent granted for an invention by the competent State office.

The exclusive use of a trade secret involves economic exploitation of the secret by the entrepreneur, personally or through agents, or agreements in secret in order to get profit.

The holder of a trade secret may protect his right of exclusive use by civil, contraventional or criminal claims.

V. Duration of Trade Secrets' Protection

477. The holder of a trade secret protects it by preserving its secrecy. Therefore, he may use it without any time limits. If the secret becomes common knowledge by proper means, including due to the technical and informational development in the related field, the information ceases to be a trade secret.

VI. Enforcement of Trade Secrets

A. Actions in the Court

478. According to Romanian regulations, the infringement of trade secrets shall involve criminal, contravention and civil responsibility. Right to action belongs to the owner of the trade secret who, for the protection of the commercial secret against illegal acquisition, use and disclosure, can address the court.

1. Principles of the Measures Taken in the Court

479. According to Article 7 of the Ordinance, the measures ordered by the courts should follow the following principles:

- proportionality in relation to the objective pursued;
- avoiding the creation of obstacles to the legitimate trade in the internal market;
- establishing appropriate safeguards against their abusive use.

480. In applying the measures, procedures and remedial actions, the court should ensure that they:

- are fair and just;
- do not imply unnecessary complexity or costs, unreasonable deadlines or unjustified delays;
- are effective and have a deterrent effect.

2. Limitation Period

481. The right to action regarding the protection of trade secrets against illegal acquisition, use and disclosure shall be prescribed within six years (Article 8 of the Ordinance). Term begins from the date on which the applicant knew or should have known the illegal acquisition, use or disclosure of the trade secret by the perpetrator of the infringement. The suspension and interruption of the limitation period shall be subject to the provisions contained in the Civil Code.

3. Confidentiality of Trade Secrets During Judicial Proceedings

482. If the court, ex officio or at the motivated request of a party, considers that the conduct of the trial in the presence of the public may affect or compromise the commercial or presumed commercial secret, taking into account the circumstances provided for on conditions of application and guarantees, it may order that the process be carried out without the presence of the public, the relevant provisions in Civil Procedure Code being applicable accordingly. The court may classify as confidential the trade secrets or the alleged trade secrets that are the subject of a duly motivated request of an interested party participating in the judicial proceedings related to the illegal acquisition, use or disclosure of such trade secret or alleged trade secret, which has access to documents that are an integral part of these court proceedings or that have also become aware of trade secrets as a result of this participation or access (Article 9 of the Ordinance).

483. At the justified request of a party or ex officio, the court may take the appropriate measures to maintain the confidentiality of any trade secrets or alleged trade secrets used or mentioned during the judicial procedure.

484. In applying the above provisions, the court may order:

– restriction, in whole or in part, to a limited number of persons of access to any document containing trade secrets or alleged trade secrets and which has been presented by parties or third parties;
– restriction to a limited number of persons of access to the court hearings, when trade secrets or alleged trade secrets may be disclosed, as well as to the records or transcripts related to the respective court hearings;
– making available to any person other than those who are part of the decided limited number of persons a non-confidential version of any court decision, from which passages containing trade secrets were removed or concealed;
– any other measures provided by the law to ensure the confidentiality of trade secrets or alleged trade secrets.

485. The court ensures that the total number of persons does not go beyond what is necessary to ensure the parties' right to legal proceedings, to an effective remedy and to a fair trial, including at least one natural person from each party and lawyers or other representatives thereof parties to court proceedings. When deciding on the measures provided and when assessing their proportionality, the court shall consider the need to guarantee the right to an effective remedy and to a fair trial, the legitimate interests of the parties and, where appropriate, third parties, as well as any possible harm caused to anyone between the parties and, where appropriate, third parties, resulting from the approval or rejection of such measures. Any processing of personal data under this Article shall be carried out in accordance with the provisions of Regulation (EU) 2016/679 of the European Parliament and of the Council of 27 April 2016 on the protection of natural persons with regard to the processing of personal data and on the free movement of such data and repealing Directive 95/46/EC (General Data Protection Regulation), published in the Official Journal of the European Union, series L, No. 119 of 4 May 2016, and of the national legislation in this matter.

4. Provisional and Insurance Measures

486. At the request of the holder of the trade secret, the court may order (Article 10 of the Ordinance) any of the following provisional and insuring measures against the alleged perpetrator of the infringement:

- cessation or, as the case may be, the provisional prohibition of the use or disclosure of the trade secret;
- prohibition to produce, offer, place on the market or use goods that contravene the rules or to import, export or store such goods for the aforementioned purposes;
- unavailability of goods suspected of violating the rules, including imported goods, so as to prevent their entry or circulation on the market.

Alternatively to the mentioned measures, the court may order that any continuation of the alleged unlawful use of a trade secret shall be the subject of the establishment of a bail established by the court designed to insure the compensation of the holder of the trade secret. Disclosure of a trade secret in exchange for establishing guarantees should be strictly forbidden.

5. Conditions of Application and Guarantees

487. Article 11 of the Ordinance lists a series of relevant conditions of applicability and guarantees in court decisions ordering provisional and insuring measures. Thus, the court may request the applicant to provide evidence that can be reasonably considered available to be convinced with a sufficient degree of certainty that:

- trade secret exists;
- the applicant is the holder of the trade secret;
- the trade secret is acquired, used or disclosed illegally or that an illegal acquisition, use or disclosure of the trade secret is imminent.

488. When assessing the proportionality of the approval or rejection of the request, the court should take into account a series of specific circumstances of the case, such as:

- value and other specific features of the trade secret;
- measures taken to protect the trade secret;
- defendant's behaviour in acquiring, using or disclosing the trade secret;
- impact of the illegal use or disclosure of the commercial secret;
- legitimate interests of the parties and the impact that the approval or rejection of the measures could have on the parties;
- legitimate interests of third parties;
- public interest;
- protection of fundamental rights.

489. At the request of the defendant, the court orders the cessation of the provisional and insuring measures provided by the law, if:

- the applicant did not initiate judicial proceedings leading to the court ruling on the settlement of the merits of the case within thirty calendar days after taking them;
- the information in question no longer meets the requirements of a trade secret for reasons that cannot be imputed to the defendant.

490. In order to approve the provisional and insurance measures provided by the law, the court may order the plaintiff to compose an appropriate security or equivalent guarantee to cover any damage suffered by the defendant and, where appropriate, by any other person affected by the measures in question.

491. The court may order at the request of the defendant or of the injured third party the award of an adequate compensation for the damage caused by the measures taken in the following situations:

- the measures ceased due to the fact that the applicant did not initiate judicial proceedings leading to the court ruling on the settlement of the merits of the case within thirty calendar days after taking them;
- the measures ceased as a result of any action or omission of the applicant;
- when it is subsequently ascertained that there has been no illegal acquisition, use or disclosure of the trade secret or threat of producing such behaviours.

492. The solutions that the court can pronounce with the settlement of the merits of the case are stipulated in Article 12 of the Ordinance. When, after the trial of the merits of the case, the court, at the request of the applicant, makes a decision finding that was an unlawful acquisition, use or disclosure of a trade secret. It may order against the defendant, perpetrator of the infringement, one or more of the following measures:

- cessation or, as the case may be, prohibition of the use or disclosure of the trade secret;
- prohibition to manufacture, offer, place on the market or use goods that contravene the rules or to import, export or store such goods for these purposes;
- adoption of corrective measure to eliminate the illicit characteristics of the goods that contravene the norms.

493. In the case of the corrective measure to eliminate the illicit characteristics of the goods that contravene the norms, the court orders it to be implemented at the expense of the infringer, unless there are good reasons not to have it.

The measures on cessation or prohibition of the use or disclosure of the trade secret or on prohibition to manufacture, offer, place on the market or use goods that contravene the rules or to import, export or store such goods for these purposes, do not prejudice the right to damages that could be due to the holder of the trade secret as a result of the illegal acquisition, use or disclosure of the trade secret.

6. Conditions of Applicability

494. Conditions of application, guarantees and alternative measures are provided in Article 13 of the Ordinance. When analyzing the applicant's request to take the legally provided measures, as well as for assessing their proportionality, the court should take into account the specific circumstances of the case, including as appropriate:

- value or other specific features of the trade secret;
- measures taken to protect the trade secret;
- behaviour of the offender in acquiring, using or disclosing the trade secret;
- impact of the illegal use or disclosure of the commercial secret;
- legitimate interests of the parties and the impact that the approval or rejection of the measures could have on the parties;
- legitimate interests of third parties;
- public interest;
- protection of fundamental rights.

495. When determining the duration of the measures, the court should consider that it is sufficient to eliminate any commercial or economic advantage that the perpetrator of the infringement could have obtained as a result of the illegal acquisition, use or disclosure of the trade secret.

496. If the information under decision no longer fulfils the requirements of being considered as a trade secret for reasons that cannot be directly or indirectly imputed to the defendant, the court, at its request, may order the cessation of the measures legally provided.

As an alternative, at the request of the defendant, the perpetrator of the violation, the court may order the payment of pecuniary damages to the injured party, if the following conditions are cumulatively fulfilled:

- at the time of use or disclosure, the person was not aware and would not have had reason, in the given circumstances, to be aware that the trade secret was obtained from another person who used or disclosed the trade secret in an illegal manner;
- the execution of the measures in question would cause disproportionate damage to the person concerned;
- the measure of granting pecuniary damages to the injured party is considered by the court to be more appropriate in relation to the concrete circumstances of the case, being sufficient to cover, fairly, the damage suffered by it.

The amount of the damages, considered as an alternative, should not exceed the amount of the royalties or rights that would have been due if the person concerned had requested the authorization to use the trade secret for the period in which the use of trade secret could have been prohibited.

7. Damages of Interest

497. In Article 14 of the Ordinance are stipulated regulations on damages the author of the infringement of a trade secret should be paid by order from a court.

Thus, at the request of the injured party, the court may order the author of the infringement, who knew or should have known to be involved in the illegal acquisition, use or disclosure of a trade secret, to pay damages in proportion to the actual damage suffered as a result of the illegal acquisition, use or disclosure of the trade secret. However, if the court finds that the employees have illegally acquired, used or disclosed a trade secret of the employer without intent, it may order the reduction of the amount of damages.

When determining the amount of the damages court should take into account the negative economic consequences on the injured party, including its loss of profit, the undue benefits realized by the perpetrator of the infringement and, if applicable, any other element besides the economic factors, such as the moral damage caused to the owner of the secret trade through the illegal acquisition, use or disclosure of trade secrets.

As an alternative to the way of establishing the damages, where the circumstances of the case allow, the court may order the offender to pay damages in the amount of a lump sum established on the basis of elements such as, at least, the amount of the royalties or rights that would have been due if the author of the infringement would have required authorization to use the trade secret in question.

8. Publication of Court Decisions

498. At the request of the applicant and at the expense of the perpetrator of the infringement, the court may order publication, in whole or in part, of the court decision (Article 15). The measure of publication should ensure the confidentiality of trade secrets. When disposing and evaluating the proportionality of the measure of publication, the court should consider the following elements, as the case may be:

- value of the trade secret;
- behaviour of the offender in acquiring, using or disclosing the trade secret;
- impact of the illegal use or disclosure of the commercial secret;
- probability of a new illegal use or disclosure of the trade secret by the offender.

499. When disposing the measure of publication, the court should check whether the information on the perpetrator allows the identification of a natural person and, in this case, whether the publication of such information would be justified in particular in relation to any possible harm that such a measure could bring to private life and its reputation.

9. Sanctions for Failure to Comply with Court Decisions

500. Failure to comply with the provisional and insurance measures legally provided is sanctioned (Article 16) with a civil fine between RON 500 and 5,000 for natural persons, respectively between 0.1% and 1% of the turnover realized the previous year for legal persons, but not less than RON 10,000. When individualizing the amount of the fine, the court will ensure that it is efficient, proportionate and dissuasive in relation to the specific circumstances of the case. The civil fine, as provided above, is established according to the gravity of the deed by the court invested with the judgment of the litigation, by executor conclusion, given in the council chamber, which can be appealed within fifteen days from the communication to the superior court. The case is judged urgently in the council chamber. The decision of the Court of Appeal is subject to no appeal.

The court may order the payment of damages between RON 100 and 5,000 per day for delay in non-observance of the measures decided.

501. The Law permits however a limited number of exceptions, namely:

- if, in the financial year prior to the sanction, the legal person did not register a turnover, the turnover for the financial year in which it was recorded the turnover will be taken into account immediately prior to the reference year for calculating the turnover business with a view to applying the sanction;
- in the case of the newly established legal person who did not register the turnover in the year before the sanction, it will be sanctioned with a fine from RON 5,000 to 50,000;
- in the case of the turnover in the previous financial year, sanction cannot be determined; the legal entity shall be fined from RON 10,000 to 100,000.

502. Failure to comply with the measures ordered by the court (Article 17) by the person to whom they were ordered constitutes a crime and is punished with imprisonment from three months to two years or with a fine. Criminal action shall be initiated upon the prior complaint of the injured person.

10. Exceptions from the Enforcement Measures

503. The Ordinance provides in Article 5 a number of exceptions from the enforcement measures as previously exposed. Accordingly, requests for enforcement measures, procedures and remedial actions under this emergency ordinance are rejected if the alleged acquisition, use or disclosure of trade secrets held in any of the following cases:

- for the exercise of the right to freedom of expression and information, as provided for in the European and national law, including respect for the freedom and pluralism of the mass media;
- for the disclosure of an offence, of a reprehensible factor of an illegal activity, provided that the defendant has acted in order to protect the general public interest;
- disclosure by their employees to their representatives as part of the legitimate exercise by their respective representatives of their functions in accordance with European Union law or national law, provided that disclosure was necessary for this legitimate exercise;
- in order to protect a legitimate interest recognized in the law of the European Union or in the internal law.

Selected Bibliography

AIPPI. *Reports Q 148* (2000). Executive Committee Meeting in Sorrento.

Benckard, Georg. *Patentgesetz Gebrauchmustergesetz* (1993). C.H. Beck'sche Verlagsbuchhandlung.

Bertrand, André. *Le droit d'auteur et les droits voisins*. 3rd edn. Dalloz, 1999.

Bucsa, Gheorghe and others. *Industrial Property Protection in Romania and Preventing Infringement*. Editura OSIM, 1994.

Bucsa, Gheorghe. *Protection of Industrial Designs*. Tribuna Economica, 2000.

Camenita, Ion. *Protection of Inventions by Patents*. Romanian Academy Publishing House, 1984.

Capatina, Octavian. *The Law of Commercial Competition: Fair Competition (I), Pathological Competition*. The Monopoly (II), Unfair Competition on Domestic and International Market (III), Lumina Lex, 1992, 1993, 1994.

Chavanne, Albert & Jean-Jacques Burst. *Droit de la propriete industrielle*. 5th edn. Dalloz, 1998.

Cohen, Denis. *La protection internationale des dessins et modelles*. Editura Economica, 1999.

Cornish, William. *Expansion von Schutzrechten*. Symposium in Max Planck Institute, 12–13 October 1999.

Dietz, Adolph. 'The Copyright in Romania and Harmonization thereof According to the European Norms. Evolution and Current Situation Following Romaniaîs Accession to the European Union'. RRDPI, no. 4 (2009): 13–14.

Dinca, Razvan & Corneliu Barsan. *Trade Secrets*. Universul Juridic, 2009.

Eminescu, Yolanda. *Treaty of Industrial Property: New Creations* (I), *Distinctive Signs* (II), *Unfair Competition* (III). Bucharest: Romanian Academy Publishing House, 1982, 1983, 1984.

Eminescu, Yolanda. *Patents Law. Commentary*. Lumina Lex, 1993.

Eminescu, Yolanda. *Legal Framework of Trademarks*. Lumina Lex, 1996.

Eminescu, Yolanda. *The Protection of Designs and Industrial Models. Romanian Law and Comparative Law*. Lumina Lex, 1993.

Eminescu, Yolanda. *Unfair Competition. Romanian Law and Comparative Law*. Lumina Lex, 1994.

Eminescu, Yolanda. *The Copyright: Commentary on Law No. 8/14.03.1996*. Lumina Lex, 1997.

Erhan, Valeriu. *The Grant of Patents in Romania*. Editura Economica, 1998.

Erhan, Valeriu. *The Patent of Invention. Obtaining and Granting*. Editura Lex, 1995.

Selected Bibliography

European Patent Office. *Guidelines for Examinations in the European Patent Office*. Published by the European Patent Office, 1999.

Fellner, Christine. *Industrial Design Law*. London: Sweet & Maxwell, 1995.

Gheorghiu, Gheorghe. *Audiovisual Works*. Lumina Lex, 2004.

Gheorghiu Gheorghe, Strenc Alexandru Cristian Commentary on the Law on Employees' Inventions Romanian Revue of Intellectual Property, November 2015.

Greene, Anne Marie & Elizabeth Hanellin. *Designs and Utility Models Throughout the World*. New York: Clark Boardam Callaghan Publishing House, 1996.

Van Innis, Thierry. *Les signs distinctifs*. Editure De Boeck & Larcier, 1997.

Macovei, Ioan. *Treaty on Intellectual Property Right*. C.H. Beck, 2010.

Mathely, Paul. *Le nouveau droit fracais des brevets des inventions*. JNA, 1991.

Osterrieth, Christian. *Patentrecht. Einfuhrung für Studium und Praxis*. C.H. Beck'sche Verlagenbuch, 2000.

Passa, Jerome. *Contrefacon et concurrence deloyale*. Litec, 1997.

Perot Morel, Marie-Angele. *Les principes de la protection des dessins et modelles dans les pays du marche commun*. Editure Mouton, 1998.

Pollaud-Dulian, Frederic. *La brevetabilité des inventions-Etude comparative de jurisprudance France-OEB*. Imprimerie France-Quercy, Litec, 1997.

Rodhain, Claude. *Comment proteger nos innovations et creations*. Edition Technique & Documentation, 1982.

Romitan, Ciprian. *Protectia penala a proprietatii intelectuale* (2006).

Ros, Viorel. *The Law of Intellectual Property. Trademarks and Geographical Indications*. Sylvi, 1999.

ROS, Viorel, D. Bogdan & Octavia Spineanu-Matei. *Copyright and Related Rights. Treaty*. C.H. Beck, 2005.

Schulte, Rainer. *Patentgesetz* 9. neubearbeitete und erwiterte Auflage Carl Heymans Verlag KG, 2007.

Stauder, Dieter & Margarete Singer. *Europaisches Patentubereinkommen Kommentar*. Carl Heymans Verlag KG, 2000.

Strenc, Alexandru Cristian, Bucura Ionescu & Gheorghe Gheorghiu. *Treaty on Patent Law*. Editura Lumina Lex, 2005, 2007.

Strenc, Alexandru Cristian. European Software Directives and European Software Patents. Wolters Kluwer 2017.

Strenc, Alexandru Cristian. European Patent Convention. Wolters Kluwer 2018.

Strenc, Alexandru Cristian. *Information Technology. Protection and Enforcement of Intellectual Property Rights*. Editura Universul Juridic, Colectia Business.

Strenc, Alexandru Cristian. *State of Play and Outlook in the Central and Eastern European Countries. The Romanian Experience*. Proceedings of the International Conference on Industrial Property in the European Integration, Cracaw, 15–17 September 1996.

Strenc, Alexandru Cristian. *The Legal and Financial Conditions influencing the Diffusion of technical Innovation and R & D in Central and Eastern Europe. Legal Protection of IP in Romania*. Inco-Copernicus Project, Res. Report, 1998.

Strenc, Alexandru Cristian. 'On the Criteria of Patentability of Inventions-a comparative Study between the Praxis of OSIM and EPO'. *Romanian Review of Industrial Property* nos 2–5 (1999).

Takenaka, Toshiko. *Interpreting Patent Claims: The United States, Germany and Japan*. IIC Studies in Industrial Property and Copyright Law.

UEFISCDI (team of authors, including Strenc Alexandru Cristian and Gheorghiu Gheorghe), Guidelines of good practices on law enforcement regarding employees' inventions, UEFISCDI, June 2015.

WIPO. *Background Reading Material on Intellectual Property*. WIPO Publication, 1988.

WIPO. *Introduction au droit et a la pratique en matière de marques. Notions fondamentales*. Manuel de formation de l'OMPI, 1994.

WIPO. *Manual regarding the Information and Search in the Industrial Property Field*. Study on the Proceedings and Exigencies in the Field, Methods of Examination and Proceedings of Publication in the Industrial Designs Field, 1995.

WIPO. *Intellectual Property Reading Material*. WIPO Publication, 1998.

Selected Bibliography

Index

The numbers here refer to paragraph numbers.

Index

www.ingramcontent.com/pod-product-compliance
Lightning Source LLC
LaVergne TN
LVHW011109300926
849160LV00008B/318